LOBSTERS

Florida • Bahamas • the Caribbean

Martin A. Moe, Jr.

To Dominico Madonia —
With Best Wishes
Martin A. Moe, J.

Green Turtle Publications
P.O. Box 17925
Plantation, FL 33318

Green Turtle Publications
P.O. Box 17925
Plantation, FL 33318

Library of Congress Cataloging-in-Publication Data

Moe, Martin A.
LOBSTERS : Florida • Bahamas • the Caribbean / by
Martin A. Moe, Jr.
p. cm.
Includes bibliographical references (p.   ) and index.
ISBN 0-939960-06-0 : $22.95
    1. Caribbean spiny lobster. 2. Lobster fisheries—Caribbean Area. 3. Lobster fisheries—Florida. 4. Lobster fisheries—Bahamas. 5. Lobster—North Atlantic Ocean—Identification. 6. Lobster culture. I. Title.
    SH380 .2.C27M64 1991
    639' .541—dc20   91-23948
                                     CIP

Printed in the United States of America
10 9 8 7 6 5 4 3 2

To Bob

With many thanks

This dedication is extended to more than one Bob, but all are equally important in shaping the events of my life that have led up to the reality of this book. Were it not for the encouragement and support of all three, this book would not exist.

To Bob Ingle, who gave me a chance to be a marine biologist.

To Bob Moore, who supported and worked with me during the early years of Aqualife Research Corporation in the Florida Keys.

To Bob Abplanalp, who supported and encouraged me during my last years with Aqualife Research Corporation.

Acknowledgments

Many people: commercial fishermen, fish house operators, recreational divers, scientists, aquaculturists, and fishery managers have directly or indirectly helped me to create this book by giving of their time and expertise. Over the years, I gained insight into the biology and fishery of spiny lobster from sources as diverse as an underwater chance encounter with a Bahamian commercial spear fisherman and long talks with lobster biologists. All were helpful, friendly, and straightforward, and I greatly appreciate their contributions. I am especially indebted to the following individuals: William (Bill) Lyons who provided a wealth of published and unpublished information from his years of research experience with spiny lobster; David Camp, for reading and commenting on Chapters One through Five; Austin Williams, for reading and commenting on Chapter Three; Roy Williams for his invaluable guidance through the legal perplexities in Chapters Five and Six; Drs. Joe and Sally Bauer, for reading and commenting on all the chapters; John Hunt for reading and commenting on Chapter One; Billy and Laurie Causey, for reading and commenting on Chapter Five; Greg Waugh, for reading and commenting on Chapter Six; and Ross Witham, for reading and commenting on Chapter Four.

Green Turtle Publications is a very small publishing company and the production of this book would not have been possible without the intense effort of my wife and companion, Barbara Battjes Moe. She read and edited the entire manuscript many times, worked on the layout and design, and also helped with the culinary section. My daughter, Andrea Moe, contributed her editorial talents to the book as well, screening the manuscript for typographical and syntactical errors. If there are errors, however, and there may still be a few, they are my responsibility, for I committed them, and I will strive to correct them in future printings.

Contents

List of Figures

Chapter 5

Chapter 6

Introduction

Wherever people touch the sea in the western central Atlantic, the Caribbean spiny lobster is an important part of daily life. Many livelihoods and many passions revolve around this lobster in every country throughout its range. Commercial divers, trappers, and wholesale lobster processors run their lives on its season; millions of sport divers plan their vacations on the time and place of best lobstering; dive shops and hotels staff up for the beginning of the lobster season; and coastal residents either fight for their share of this succulent crustacean when the season opens or retreat from the frenzied invasion of their calm, coastal hamlets. Even the casual, landlubber tourist encounters this spiny denizen of the deep in every restaurant and every tee shirt shop from Palm Beach to Rio.

I have long been interested in spiny lobster. During our ten years in the Florida Keys we caught them, ate them, kept them in aquariums, tried to breed them, built offshore shelters for them, observed them on the reefs, followed the many lobster research programs, and observed the trials of the commercial fishery. The original concept of this book was simply a guide for recreational lobster divers with the inclusion of an accurate description of the life history of the Caribbean spiny lobster. The Caribbean spiny lobster has a long and complex life history. Its fisheries are many, some complex and some simple, all interdependent, and all stressed and facing an uncertain future. It quickly became obvious that there was a need for a book that interprets the rigid format, precise language, and biological jargon of the scientific literature, brings together what is now known of spiny lobster biology and fishery management, and makes it available to everyone. I have tried to do this.

When every fishery within its range is counted, this species, the Caribbean spiny lobster, *Panulirus argus*, supports the world's third greatest lobster fishery. Only landings of the clawed American and Norway lobster exceed those of the Caribbean spiny lobster, and landings of the Caribbean spiny lobster are about three times greater than any other spiny lobster in any other part of the world. The western red lobster from western Australia is second in spiny lobster landings with an average of 22.05 million pounds per year.

The average annual landings for Caribbean spiny lobster throughout its range for the five year period of 1975 through 1982 were 64.2 million pounds (Williams, 1986). This catch comes from the Bahamas, the Florida Keys, Cuba, Mexico, Jamaica, Puerto Rico, dozens of Caribbean countries, Venezuela, Brazil and other Central and South American countries—many fisheries based on a common resource. This single species accounts for about 16 percent of the 401.92 million pounds landed of **all** species of lobster throughout the world.

The 64.2 million pounds of Caribbean lobster landed in the total reported annual commercial catch does not include lobsters not reported in the commercial catch, spiny lobsters taken by recreational divers, or the illegal, undersize lobsters taken throughout these fisheries. In communities with large coastal populations or an active tourist industry, the entire lobster catch is utilized locally, and additional lobster may even be imported. Spiny lobster production in remote areas or in centers of high production are exported to foreign markets, and usually represent one of the most important sources of revenue to the community. The dockside price of a spiny lobster to the fisherman varies with the fishery, the season, local supply and demand during the season, the export and import market, and usually, the marketing skills of the fisherman or fish house manager.

So what is the total value of the Caribbean spiny lobster resource? Well, we could assume that the average dockside price of a pound of spiny lobster in the early 1990's is $3.50 (probably a bit low), and based on the total average commercial production of 64.2 million pounds, the total value of the Caribbean spiny lobster resource is about 225 million dollars. Not bad, but obviously a low figure. Let's assume that the combined unreported commercial and recreational catch amounts to about 20 percent of the catch, bringing the total annual catch up to about 77 million pounds, not an unreasonable estimate, especially when all the fisheries of the Caribbean and South and Central America are included. Also, there is a considerable multiplication of value as the lobsters move from dockside, through the wholesaler, and into the local and export retail and restaurant markets. The lobsters probably at least double in value to $7.00 a pound, which brings the total annual value of the Caribbean spiny lobster catch to at least 539 million dollars. We could also fold in a figure that represents what is spent by recreational divers on travel, food, equipment, and lodging, but we're already pulling figures out of thin air, and the order of magnitude of the value of the resource is now established.

Is this then the value of the Caribbean spiny lobster resource? A half billion 1990 dollars annually? We always measure things in terms of money and time. Those are our common dominators. There are many things, however, that can't be accurately measured by how much and how long: things such as exceptional sunset, a visit with old friends, and the health of a natural resource. These are things that have a value far beyond just the expense of a visit or receipt of a days pay; a value that can't be expressed in mere dollars. The spiny lobster resource throughout the Atlantic and Caribbean is one of these things. Its value to the people of these areas is beyond dollars and cents. It is their history and it is their future. Its value is the same as the value of their environment and the value of their children's children.

However one looks at the Caribbean spiny lobster resource, in dollars or in intrinsic value, it is so important to the present and future of so many people, that it must be protected and preserved—and it is the people that use the resource that are ultimately responsible for its protection and preservation. We can not take on this responsibility without knowledge. We must have access to the essential information on the resource and be able to understand it. We must know of the life history of the spiny lobster and the effects of the fishery on the future of the resource. With this knowledge, we can appreciate and cooperate with fishery regulations, and this brings me to the book you now hold in your hand.

In his introduction to *The Log from the Sea of Cortez* (New York, Viking, 1951), John Steinbeck makes the statement, "The design of a book is the pattern of a reality controlled and shaped by the mind of the writer." This is true of all writing. A scientist, however, works and writes to accurately record reality with as little human bias as possible. Analysis, interpretation, and judgement are essential, of course, but putting down the facts accurately and completely is most important. A writer of popular science writes to interpret scientific reality as accurately as possible, yet must still create meaning and form beyond mere recitation of fact.

The reality of the Caribbean spiny lobster that makes up this book is drawn from my interpretation of the scientific literature and my own experience. It contains a great deal of information, and it is not designed to be read from cover to cover. The first chapter on spiny lobster natural history is easy to read and will provide the background for understanding most of the other chapters. I recommend that you read the narrative in Chapter One first and then skip to the areas that interest you most.

The addendum that follows Chapter One provides scientific and technical explanation and expansion on the basic information presented in the narrative. Other chapters address basic subject areas in detail. Use the index to find specific topics. I have written this book as accurately and as without bias as possible within my limitations. I have enjoyed writing it. I hope you enjoy reading it and that you learn something new about spiny lobsters.

Chapter One

NATURAL HISTORY
The Life Cycle

There are about 35 species of lobster in six families that occur in the Caribbean Sea and nearby tropical waters. Of all of these species, however, the Caribbean (or Florida) spiny lobster, *Panulirus argus*, is the most common, most researched, and most important to the recreational and commercial lobster fisheries from Florida to Brazil. The ecology and natural history of each species is different although similar species have similar life histories.

I have chosen to present the life history of the Caribbean spiny lobster, *Panulirus argus*, in a narrative style, and to follow the thread of life of a single individual. The story is fictional, of course, but it is based on information from published scientific papers and personal observations.

There is an Addendum to the narrative, because additional information and/or explanation is often needed to provide a better understanding of the animal or the fishery. The subject areas included in the addendum are referenced in the text of the narrative (for example[1]), and additional information on that topic is included in the addendum. Note that scientific terms and structures are defined and explained in Chapter Two. Also, one may wish to refer to the diagrams illustrating spiny lobster body structure on pages

145, 146, and 147 and the glossary on page 150 to define any unknown terms.

Our knowledge of spiny lobster biology and ecology has greatly expanded in the last decade, but there is still very much to learn about these complex and fascinating animals. Although the story is based on available scientific knowledge, the following account of the life history of one individual is speculative. To the best of my knowledge, however, every event in our fictional lobster friend's life could actually have happened.

Lola's Story

On the western edge of the Caribbean Sea, a few miles offshore of the Central American country of Belize near the Turneffe Islands, lies the longest barrier coral reef in the Atlantic Ocean. The coral colonies are large and well formed and most species of Atlantic reef life flourish in the clear, tropical waters that flow over the reefs. Spiny lobsters grow large on these reefs; the deep waters are not heavily fished, and few of the lobsters that dwell here have ever seen a trap or a diver. This is where the story of our particular lobster begins, under a small coral head in 60 feet of water on the offshore edge of a Central American, Caribbean coral reef.

The Beginning of Life

It was early in September. For three weeks the huge female lobster had remained under or near the refuge offered by her small, deep-water coral head. The three million eggs she carefully carried were slowly developing into a new generation of spiny lobsters.[1] They were attached to long, thin hairs (ovigerous setae) that grew along the edges of the inner leaves of the paired swimmerettes attached to each segment of her curled, muscular, tail-like abdomen. These clumps of eggs that she held and protected looked very much like a handful of tiny berries carefully cupped under her abdomen, and so female lobsters bearing eggs are considered to be "in berry". The eggs were bright orange when she first attached them to herself. Now, 25 days later, they were a brownish orange, about a millimeter in diameter, and the eyes of the fully developed embryos were visible as dark specks within the thin membranes around the eggs.

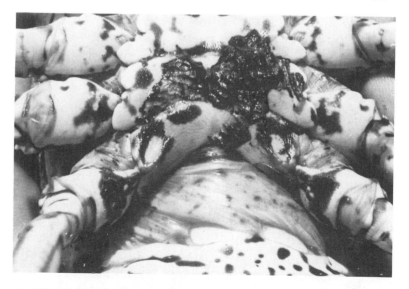

Figure 1. A spermatophore (tar spot) attached to the underside of a female spiny lobster (*Panulirus argus*). The spermatophore was already used in a spawn and shows erosion. A sharp eye can also discern the tiny gonopores at the base of each of the third legs.

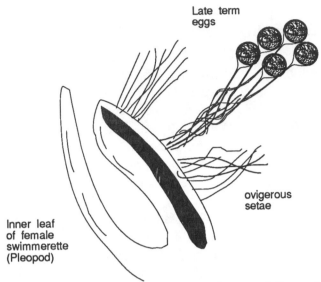

Figure 2. Late stage eggs entwined around the ovigerous setae on the edge of the inner leaf of the female's swimmerette (biramous pleopod).

Spawning. This process was not new to the old lobster; she had produced a spawn two or three times a year for the last five years. Her first spawns, when she was three and four years old, were small, only a few hundred thousand eggs. As she grows older, the frequency of spawns and the quality of her eggs may decline, but now at eight years of age she was at her reproductive peak and able to make her greatest contribution to the future of her species. Her carapace length (CL) was 5 ½ inches (140 mm), and she weighed almost 5 pounds. The large ovaries just under the back of her carapace had gradually enlarged and changed from white to orange during the warm, late summer months.

She had spawned three weeks before. During the first week of August, she passed the ripe, orange eggs from the ovaries under her carapace, through the oviducts at the base of her third pair of walking legs, and attached them to the ventral surface of her abdomen. Spawning was an extended process. Each day for three days she spent hours spawning her eggs before the process was complete. She had mated several weeks before spawning, and the male had left her with his black, tar-like spermatophore cemented to the hard sternal plate on the underside of her carapace between her last pair of walking legs. The presence of his spermatophore on her body eliminated the need for him to be present at the precise moment the eggs were ready for fertilization.[2]

When the eggs within her were mature, and her physiological rhythms told her that the time to spawn was at hand, she curled her tail-like abdomen up underneath her and rested her weight upon the back surface of her curled tail. Her antennae extended backward and braced her up off the bottom at an angle of about 60°, which freed her legs to

Figure 3. Recently spawned eggs attached under the abdomen along the edges of the inner paddle (endopods) of a female spiny lobster (*Panulirus argus*). The eggs are a bright orange at this stage.

control the spawn. Her tail was cupped so that her broad tail fan extended forward over the tiny gonopores at the base of her third pair of legs. The swimmerettes along each side of her tail completely enclosed the spawn chamber formed by the curled abdomen and extended tail fan. The eggs emerged from the gonopores and flowed downward over the active spermatophore toward their sites of attachment on her swimmerettes.

She scratched the spermatophore with the sharp spines and false pincers on the tip of her fifth pair of legs. The hard black surface of the spermatophore was broken and the soft, grey, sperm-carrying interior was exposed. An enzyme released along with the eggs attacked the gel of the spermatophore and helped release the sperm. Sperm and egg met in the enclosed spawn chamber, and the eggs were quickly fertilized. The outer membrane of each egg was extended into a long, sticky tendril 5 to 8 mm long. The filaments of groups of 6 to 12 eggs were entangled into a common trunk, and this trunk was then tightly woven about clumps of 4 to 8 of the long, hair-like ovigerous setae that lined the edges of the inner leaf of each pair of the double swimmerettes. These hair-like setae develop as the ovaries mature, and they appear on the swimmerettes at the molt before spawning.

Each of the inner paddles of the swimmerettes (the endopods) then had a thick, inch-long fringe of dense clumps of bright orange eggs. All but about five percent were successfully fertilized. There they remained, protected and cared for during their helpless time of embryonic development. Rhythmic movements of her tail and swimmerettes and grooming with the false pincers on her rear pair of walking legs kept the eggs well oxygenated during the three to four weeks that she carried them. The old female gradually increased the frequency of her egg grooming activity as the time of hatching approached.

Hatching. Now embryonic development was complete and the period of development and protection under their mother's tail was at an end. The young lobsters were about to begin their life in the vast and uncaring sea. The old female waited patiently until darkness settled in over the reef. A couple of hours later she crawled out from under the coral head and found an open area on the reef. Her tail-like abdomen relaxed and extended behind her, and she began to move the fan shaped telson and lateral uropods of her broad tail fan in a slow pumping action. The swimmeretts also beat strongly back and forth, and the mass of eggs beneath her was flushed repeatedly. At a millimeter in diameter, the eggs are very small, not much bigger than a pinhead. The long legs of the larval lobster are tightly curled around the tiny body within the egg. Each individual egg that is ready to hatch takes up water and expands until hydrostatic pressure breaks the egg membranes, and then the new lobster larva is released.

The natural world has many competing evolutionary pressures, and reproduction in the harsh environment of the sea presents great conflicts. Each egg represents only one chance in many millions to produce an individual that will live to become a reproductive adult. The greater the number of eggs, the greater the possibility that enough individuals will survive to carry on the species. Therefore, the available reproductive energy of the female must be broken up into the largest possible number of individual eggs, and the smaller the eggs, the greater their number. The hatched larvae, however, must also have the best possible chance for survival, and large eggs can produce large larvae with complete development of feeding and defensive capabilities at hatch. Although relatively few in number, large larvae have the best chance of avoiding predators and beginning rapid growth. Thus there are simultaneous conflicting evolutionary pressures toward production of large numbers of small eggs that hatch small, undeveloped larvae—and toward production of relatively few large eggs that produce large, well-developed larvae.

Spiny lobster play the game of larval survival very well. The tiny egg is protected and cared for by the female for several weeks, which gives the larvae time for complete development within the egg. Before hatching, the long legs are wrapped closely around the compressed body, and the larvae are tightly compacted within the egg membranes. After hatching, the larvae expand into a form that is thin and flattened with long, well developed appendages. Like a thin sheet of paper, their mass is small, but their surface area and apparent size is relatively large. Because of the long development time within the egg, the larvae hatch with senses and swimming ability fully developed; yet the female is still able to produce and care for a very large number of eggs. Lobster phyllosoma larvae are ready to swim and feed on the day of hatch, and they begin larval life well adapted to the harsh, planktonic world where they must survive for many months.

The transparent spider-like larvae do not look at all like the juvenile or adult spiny lobster. In fact, they were first described in 1816 as a separate group of animals, the *Phyllosoma* (leaf-like) and were thought to live their entire lives as a small planktonic animal. For almost 100 years scientists thought that spiny lobsters and their larvae were two completely separate species. It was not until the early 1900's that the phyllosomes were found to be the larval stages of spiny, slipper, and coral lobsters.

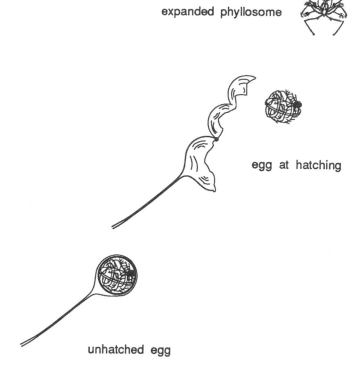

expanded phyllosome

egg at hatching

unhatched egg

Figure 4. The spiny lobster egg at hatching.

The old female stood high on the darkened reef, and as she flexed her tail back and forth, and sent currents of water through the egg mass, clouds of newly hatched larvae surrounded her. Some time before hatching, the larval lobsters began to take in water through the semipermeable egg membranes that tightly encased them. The egg membranes allowed free passage of oxygen, carbon dioxide, and water molecules to and from the developing larvae while barring passage of other large molecules and bacteria.

Now, as the larvae swelled with retained water, great pressure was exerted on the containing egg membranes. During hatching, when the outer egg membrane ruptured, the flushing action of the old female's tail fan and swimmeretts washed the tiny larvae free of the egg. The outer egg capsule splits open from the base of the holding filament to the very top of the egg. The tightly rolled larvae, still encased in the delicate inner membrane, were easily washed from the outer egg capsule. The thin, inner membrane is firmly attached to the thick, outer membrane at only one point—the top of the egg capsule. When the balled larvae roll out of the outer capsule, the thin inner membrane tears at this point of attachment, and the larvae are flushed free of both membranes. The outer egg capsule and the inner membrane remain attached to each other and to the hair-like ovigerous setae on the female's swimmeretts, and it is this firm attachment that allows the larvae to be flushed free of the egg and its membranes. The larvae can not work themselves free of the egg membranes without the washing action provided by the female.[3]

As the egg membranes ruptured, the larvae were flushed from the egg mass under their mother and ejected into the surrounding water. Their long, jointed legs unfolded from the constriction of the tiny egg, and their small flattened bodies continued to take up water and expand to their full size of almost 1/16 of an inch (1.5 mm) in length. Including the now fully extended three pairs of legs, the distance across the newly hatched larval lobster is only about 1/8 of an inch (3 mm).

The body of the larva is divided into two parts, the anterior pear-shaped forebody (cephalic shield) and a posterior elliptical hindbody (thorax). The gills and digestive gland are located in the anterior section, and the legs and maxilla join to the hind-body. What will become the tail-like abdomen in the late stage larval and adult forms is represented by only a small projection on the hindbody of the first stage larva. The body of the larva is mostly transparent. At hatching, the legs are marked with bright bands of red pigment at the joints, and the remnants of the yolk are bright yellow. The brightness of the red bands on the legs fades within hours of hatching, and the remnant yellow yolk

Figure 5. Ventral view of the second stage of a phyllosome larva of the spiny lobster (*Panulirus argus*).

quickly turns to white. By the middle of the first day, only the two large, dark eyes and a dense white spot in the center of the thorax are easily seen. The white spot is the remains of the yolk, and its energy will quickly be used by the young larva.[4]

All but a few hundred thousand of the old female's eggs hatched on this night. She did not recognize the clouds of larvae that swept out from under her as her offspring, and after they hatched she could do nothing more to protect the life she had so carefully nurtured under her tail. After about an hour of flushing the egg mass and hatching most of the larvae, she retired back under her coral head to groom and clean the remaining eggs. Within another night or two, all the fertile eggs will hatch. She will then clean off the remains of this spawn and once again begin the reproductive cycle of mating, fertilization, incubation, and hatching.

Larval Life in the Plankton

Of the two and a half million larvae the old female hatched that night only one survived to become an adult lobster. Her name is Lola and we will follow her through the trials of her existence.[5] There was nothing to distinguish Lola from the millions of lobster larvae hatched on the reef this gentle September night. She survived not because of any special qualities—all the larvae, with perhaps a very few exceptions, had the same genetic potential for survival. She survived because chance, or fate, or luck always placed her in a favorable circumstance. Just as there is always one jellybean that is the last to be eaten, one card that is the last to be drawn, so Lola was the one lobster from that spawn to survive. Lola expanded her tightly constricted body as soon as she was free of the egg and began to beat the feathery swimmeretts attached to her long legs near her flattened body.

Newly hatched lobster have very well developed eyes and instinctively swim toward low intensity light. This draws them away from bottom dwelling plankton feeders such as stony corals and sea fans. They move toward surface waters where they find food and some measure of safety.

Swept by the currents, the mass of larvae began to disperse and move across the reef toward open water. If the old female had hatched her spawn in daylight, swarms of wrasses, damselfish, and other plankton predators would quickly consume the larval lobsters before they could disperse into the waters off the reef. In darkness, however, most of the creatures of the reef were still. Except for the few larvae that brushed against night feeding corals, anemones, and basket starfish, they rose above the plankton feeders on the coral reef, swam upward toward the dim surface light, and into the currents that carried them away from the dangers of the reef.

The old female was not the only lobster releasing her spawn on the reef that night. Several other females in her immediate vicinity were also hatching eggs, and this activity was common over the entire reef tract. A few night-feeding fishes—yellowtail snapper, blackbar soldierfish, and dusky squirrelfish—attacked the moving mass of larvae as they rose toward the surface and snapped up many of them. The larvae were very small, however, and as soon as the mass dispersed, the larvae were too tiny to be seen and taken individually by any but the smallest yellowtail. Lola escaped the predators and made her way toward the surface waters.

Dawn found Lola many miles seaward from the reef of her birth. The currents had totally dispersed the spawn, and except for a few chance encounters, she would not interact with another lobster until she became a juvenile nine to eleven months in the future. As the sun rose and the intense tropical sunlight began to penetrate the water, Lola drifted downward to a depth of about 40 feet. This was a pattern she would follow for most of her larval life, living near the surface at night and dropping down to depths of 40 to 60 feet during the day.[6] She did not feed the first day, although she may have if she had been successful in attempts at capturing food. She subsisted on the remains of her yolk as her organ systems, musculature, and exoskeleton became conditioned for the task of survival in a harsh environment. The second day of her existence dawned, and she must feed this day or lose the battle for survival that had just begun.

Larval feeding. Phyllosomes have tiny mouth parts and a delicate body with long thin appendages. It is easy to think of them as gentle creatures that feed on the most infinitesimal of the planktonic plants and animals that cohabit the vast surface waters of tropical seas. However, this is not the case. They are in fact rapacious predators that feed on animals that equal and even exceed their own bulk. The feathery swimmeretts that extended from the second joint of Lola's long legs gave her great power of movement within the restricted world of tiny planktonic creatures.

Although she was at the mercy of the oceanic currents for long-range movement, especially during the early period of her larval life, she could move distances of several inches quite rapidly and was also capable of a sustained directional movement of many yards. She also possessed very formidable weapons, ones that enabled her to capture, hold, and feed upon most of the soft bodied creatures that shared the plankton with her. The microscopic sword-like spines on the tip of her first and second legs rested in pincer fashion against a second, fixed, smaller spine and were very capable of piercing and then securely holding soft bodied prey during their final struggles.

The tip of the third leg carried three major spines. The center spine was strong and curved and moved back and forth between two thin, fixed, fork-like spines that extended straight out from the tip of the leg. This arrangement of

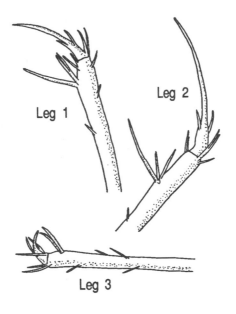

Figure 6. Detail of the leg tips of the phyllosome larva of the Caribbean spiny lobster, *Panulirus argus*. Drawn from a photomicrograph. Also see Figure 63.

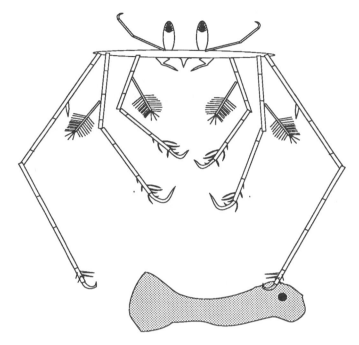

Figure 7. Feeding mode of a phyllosome larva.A fish larva is held securely in the grasping spines at the end of the third leg.

spines could securely grip the dead prey and carry it trailing along behind her until it could gradually be consumed by her tiny mouth and small-capacity digestive system. Thus she was equipped to capture animals with a body mass as great or greater than her own and to hold and consume them over a long period of time.

As sunlight penetrated the surface waters and her second day of life began, Lola drifted downward toward her daytime level. A nearby larval yellowtail snapper made a quick movement, and Lola moved toward it. The larval fish had just begun feeding on tiny copepod larvae and was unaware of Lola's approach. Her well-developed eyes and nervous system enabled her to coordinate the rapid movement of her swimmeretts and feeding spines, and she quickly pierced the larval fish with the long, curved spine on the tip of her second leg, and then wedged it firmly against the shorter second spine. Death came quickly to the tiny yellowtail. Lola brought it up to her mouth where her mandibles and maxillae tore it apart and pushed the microscopic pieces into her gut. When her digestive gland was full, she gripped the remains of the larval fish with the spines on the tip of her left third leg and carried it along for a future meal. She continued her restless search for food and soon had a second larval fish pierced, killed, and carried on her right third leg. The capacity of her digestive gland was not great, and she depended on her legs to carry the food until she was able to consume it.[7]

For seven days Lola rode the currents and fed on fish and crustacean larvae, tiny meduse, and other planktonic creatures that were spawned in the reefs and coastal waters and were swept seaward in the same eddy that carried Lola. Because of the abundance of plankton, Lola fed well and had ample energy for hunting and growth. Lola's hard exoskeleton did not allow for a gradual expansive growth like mollusks and mammals. Even in the larval stage she could grow and change only by forming a new exoskeleton beneath the old one. Then, after molting her old hard shell, hydrostatic pressure expands her new, soft exoskeleton before it hardens.

Her first molt occurred on the night of her seventh day, and she entered her second intermolt period. All of the many molts she would experience during her life would take place at night, usually only a few hours after first dark. Her greatest vulnerability to predators occurred during and immediately after molting, when her exoskeleton was soft and she was defenseless. Accomplishing her molt in the hours after first dark provided the maximum protection from detection and attack that nature could offer. She would remain transparent except for her dark eyes during her entire larval life. Transparency is the most effective form of cryptic coloration for concealment of tiny organisms in clear oceanic waters. Sight, however, depends on focusing light rays on a light sensitive surface of dark pigmented cells, thus the eyes of a sighted predator must be dark.

After her first molt, she was suddenly larger by about 25%, her eyes were now on short stalks, and her fore-body had become a little more elongate. The tiny abdomen was slightly larger, and the buds of new swimmeretts appeared on her long third pair of legs. She would molt ten more times during her nine to eleven months as a phyllosome larva, increasing in size each time until she was about an inch in length and ready to become a juvenile lobster. Her second intermolt period would last 15 days, the third about 24, and successive periods between molts may be as long as 30 or 40 days.

Lola was fortunate. The coastal water mass she was riding moved offshore in a huge eddy just as the Caribbean Current (the arm of the North Equatorial current that moves through the Caribbean Sea) was pushed close to the coast by a mild tropical wave. The eddy, and its planktonic life, was captured by the oceanic currents and swept northward toward the Yucatan Straits. Most of the phyllosomes spawned with her were also captured by the north running current, but those that were in the coastal arm of the eddy and those that were entrained earlier by southerly inshore currents were carried toward the coast of Honduras. Some of these larvae would be washed into shallow coastal areas and perish. Others would enter current systems that would allow them to survive in the Caribbean Sea or be carried into the Gulf Stream months later than Lola.

Lola became a voracious predator. As she grew and molted, the sword-like spines on the tips of her legs became larger and stronger, and she was capable of capturing, holding, and consuming a wide variety of planktonic animals. Her favorite foods were fish larvae, with their soft bodies and high caloric value, and small, easily caught medusa. She also fed on mollusk and crustacean larvae and, as she became larger, she did not disdain to feed upon phyllosomes smaller than herself when she chanced across them.

Because of her large, flattened shape and spiny legs, there were few planktonic predators that could successfully attack Lola. Once, however, she was almost a victim of a larger phyllosome herself. Toward the end of her second intermolt period she was suddenly attacked by a phyllosome in his fifth intermolt. The larger phyllosome grabbed her by her body from above, just missing her left eye. His sharp spine glanced off her hard exoskeleton, and his long spiny legs became entangled with the plumose setae of her swimmerettes. She pumped water hard and fast with her swimmerettes and pushed away from the larger phyllosome with her legs. He tried to hold onto her and impale her on his feeding spines, but she was able to elude him and swim away from the encounter.

A day later she molted and entered her third intermolt period. She would not have survived the attack had it occurred shortly after her molt, for her exoskeleton was soft then, and could be easily pierced by the feeding spines of the attacker. Within a day, however, her new exoskeleton hardened into a strong, protective shield. Later on, she captured and consumed several smaller phyllosomes that had the misfortune to be attacked right after a molt. Lola was fortunate and was not attacked again during her larval life.[8]

Travels in the oceanic currents. During the first week of November, when Lola was in her third intermolt, she passed through the Yucatan Straits and into the Gulf of Mexico. The western tip of the island of Cuba and the Mexican Yucatan peninsula bend gracefully toward each other at the 21st parallel and form a narrow strait at the northern tip of the Caribbean Sea. The Yucatan Channel at the center of the strait is deep, over 1000 fathoms. The South Equatorial Current that flows across the Atlantic and branches into the southern Caribbean pushes vast quantities of warm water through the Straits northward into the southern and central Gulf of Mexico. Water on the western side of the Yucatan Straits tends to flow over the Campeche Banks and into the western Gulf. Much of the immense flow through the Straits, however, joins with flows from the eastern Gulf and forms the Florida Current, which then moves eastward

around the tip of the Florida peninsula between Florida,
Cuba, and the Bahamas. The Gulf Stream begins where massive flows from the Florida Current and the Antilles Current
northeast of the Bahamas join and move northward up the
eastern coast of the United States.

Again, Lola was fortunate. The eddies and counter currents she encountered positioned her west of the middle of
the Straits, and she was carried northward toward the center
of the Gulf of Mexico. The phyllosomes east of her were
swept rapidly around the tip of Florida and entered the Gulf
Stream. Many of them rode the Stream into the North Atlantic and perished in cold, temperate waters. Others were
more fortunate, and through eddies and surface currents,
they remained in central western Atlantic waters and eventually settled in the Bahamas or Bermuda. Those phyllosome larvae in the water masses near the western shore of
the Yucatan Straits entered the current circulation patterns
of the western Gulf, and many eventually became adult
spiny lobsters on the reefs of the Campeche Banks.[9]

The surface waters of the Gulf of Mexico were warm and
heavy with plankton this November. Lola was transported
gradually northward by the wind driven currents near the
surface and entered the rapid northward flow of the Loop
Current system in the central Gulf of Mexico. Many of the
larger phyllosome larvae in the Gulf currents were taken by
small oceanic tunas and bonito. Lola was not among these.

The weeks passed as she traveled northward, and Lola
molted and grew in size and complexity. With each molt her
eye stalks became longer, the buds at the rear of her hindbody gradually became another pair of legs, and her tiny
abdomen enlarged and gained segments. As she grew, she
retained the transparency and broad, flattened form that
adapted her so well to life in the surface plankton. The
currents transported her in many directions. Often she
would travel northward in the surface currents during the
day and southward in subsurface currents at night. Although she was a creature of the restless surface waters of

the sea and never ventured near the bottom, she did occasionally cling to floating debris and ride the smooth, rounded backs of huge moon jellyfish.[10]

Occasionally, when different water masses meet, great circular flows called gyres form—and phyllosomes, other planktonic creatures, and floating objects tend to concentrate at the centers of these massive, gentle whirlpools. Here the danger from predators and the opportunity to feed were both increased. The gyres lasted from days to weeks but eventually broke down, and she resumed her travels with the mainstream currents. The Loop Current circled her around the eastern Gulf in January. She was now in her eighth intermolt and could swim with ease over relatively large areas of surface waters. The Loop Current travels southward far offshore of the Florida west coast during early spring, and vast quantities of water move from the central eastern Gulf toward a rendezvous with the Florida Current west of the Florida Keys.

Lola moved southward in the Loop Current during February and March. Her movement was slow, and at times winds and storms drove the surface waters northward or westward, but the sum of movement was always to the south. She progressed through her tenth intermolt during this time and entered her final larval stage, the eleventh intermolt, in mid March about 150 miles due west of Sanibel Island offshore of Florida's southwest coast.[11] She fed voraciously during this stage, for she would need all the energy she could store for the difficult time ahead. At a total length of about an inch (25 mm), she was still superbly adapted for life in the plankton. She had feeding spines on all her long legs, large plumed swimmeretts for rapid and sustained swimming, and a broad flat shape for maximum flotation. Only the small, but now well-developed, tail-like abdomen that protruded from her hindbody, gave an indication that her juvenile lobster form was not too far in the future.

Mid-April found Lola near the edge of the continental shelf over 100 fathoms of water off the Dry Tortugas at the

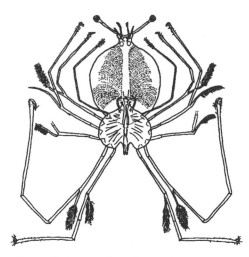

Figure 8. Ventral view of the eleventh stage of the phyllosome larva of the Caribbean spiny lobster, *Panulirus argus*. (The extensions of the third legs are not illustrated.)

western edge of the Florida Keys. She was about to molt for the eleventh time, and great changes were occurring in her diminutive body.   Although the body form that emerged from each molt up to this time was always a little larger than the previous stage and incorporated some development of new structures, the new body was always recognizable as a phyllosome larva. The body that would occupy her twelfth intermolt period, however, was vastly different from her old form. The phyllosome skeletal form had done its job, and was now no longer functional.

The phyllosome form was superbly adapted for an oceanic, planktonic existence, but it could not survive in the nearshore habitat required by the juvenile lobster. In fact, the phyllosome form could not even bring the young lobster into the shallow, shoreline waters where food and shelter for the juvenile stage were available. A transitional form was necessary to link the transparent, oceanic phyllosome with the tiny, cryptically colored, bottom-living juvenile lobster.

Metamorphosis—
The Long Journey to the Shallows

Figure 9.
The Puerulus.

The form that emerged from Lola's last phyllosome stage looked very much like a small lobster. The radical changes in form and function that occur in this molt are the most dramatic and profound of any crustacean transformation. Although Lola now had the general appearance of a spiny lobster, there were significant differences. She was still transparent, and her carapace, although now rounded, was still a bit flattened and quite smooth. The characteristic spines that adorn the carapace of the juvenile and adult were not yet present. This transitional, postlarval stage was greatly unlike the phyllosome that preceded it, and yet it was obviously not quite a lobster. It was given the genus name *Puerulus* (meaning child) when it was first described because it was so different from the adult form.

The antennae, already elongate in the last phyllosome stage, were now as long as the body and quite straight and tapered. A thin line of plumose setae ran along the length of the underside of each antenna. These thin sensory hairs provide the new postlarva with information on surface currents and water conditions that help direct its movement toward inshore waters. The flattened forebody (the cephalic shield) and the thorax (hindbody) of the phyllosome were now fused to form the cephalothorax (carapace) of the typical lobster body. The long eye stalks were gone, and the eyes were nestled into the protective carapace. The long legs that gathered food and provided locomotion for the phyllosome became small walking legs with no trace of the plumose appendages that had provided swimming power for the larval form. The new legs were short, more adapted for walking than predation and swimming, and had little apparent use in the planktonic environment. The tail-like abdomen that had begun as only a tiny bud on the rear of the thorax was now the major propulsive structure for the tiny postlarval lobster. The new abdomen was half the length of the body, and its broad tail fan and powerful abdominal muscles gave the puerulus the ability to swim rapidly backwards for several feet to avoid predators. The main swimming structures, however, were the swimmerettes (pleopods) on the underside of the abdomen. These swimmerettes now had large plumose setae that turned them into efficient paddles capable of propelling the postlarvae at constant speeds of about 10 cm per second, roughly a quarter mile per hour, in any desired direction.

The new moon was a tiny silver crescent on the mid-April night when Lola became a puerulus. Darkness is a friend of the spiny lobster, especially during a difficult molt. The changes that had taken place in her physical form made this final larval molt difficult and dangerous. Her ability to protect herself with her hard exoskeleton and rapid swimming capability were severely compromised this night. After a short struggle, she worked free of the old form that had served her so well for many months, and her final phyllosome exoskeleton drifted slowly into the depths. Behavioral changes that were awakening as the puerulus formed within the phyllosome during her last days of larval life now directed her movement. As a puerulus, she had but one goal—to deliver the potential lobster that lived within her to the tropical shallows where it could survive. As a puerulus, she would not feed, and she would feel the sea bottom for the first time.[12]

As soon as her new exoskeleton hardened, she began her long, perilous journey toward the edge of the sea. She began to swim in the manner suited to her new body: antennae pointed straight ahead, walking legs tucked in for maximum streamlining effect, abdomen fully extended, her

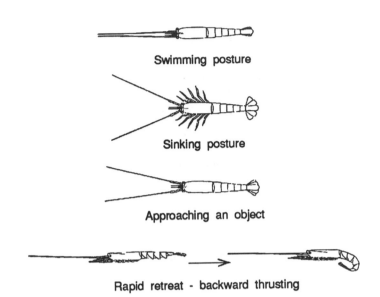

Swimming posture

Sinking posture

Approaching an object

Rapid retreat - backward thrusting

Figure 10. Swimming and protective behavior of the puerulus of *Panulirus argus* in Caribbean waters—from Calinski and Lyons (1983).

broad tail fan folded—but ready for instant action if a rapid escape maneuver were necessary—and her new swimmerettes, pumping indefatigably, propelling her toward her destination. She always swam near the surface of the sea; so close to surface, in fact, that her tiny antennae created two small wakes when she swam through calm surface waters. She could detect the swirls created by fish and other objects and distinguish them from the surface turbulence of waves and currents. When alarmed by a nearby object, her antennae extended upward and apart, her legs and tail fan extended, and she stopped swimming and began to sink. If she perceived a threat, she swam backward rapidly by flexing her abdomen and using her tail fan to propel herself backwards in two or three rapid thrusts.

As a phyllosome, she always remained in the upper strata of the sea, never venturing below the thermocline that separated the warm, surface waters from the cool, benthos below. As a puerulus, she also remained in the surface waters and followed the same migration from the upper surface at night to the deeper waters during the day. The sweep of the Florida Current brought her around the islands of the Dry Tortugas and carried her toward the Florida Keys. Lola had been a puerulus for over a week now, and her constant swimming had brought her closer and closer to the shallow water of the Florida coast. How she knew which currents to ride and which direction to swim remain her secret. Recent studies, however, suggest that the tiny spines and feathered setae that line the puerulus antennae function as receptors for chemical and vibrational signals that indicate the direction of the coast. Vibrational clues seem most important, and wave structure and the noise associated with surf and shallow reefs may keep the puerulus oriented toward the coast during its long swim.

Thousands of other pueruli were also moving toward shore in the same currents, and many added to the stomach contents of small pelagic fish such as juvenile tunas and bonitos. Lola's transparency and quick backward avoidance reaction to any turbulence or objects she encountered saved her several times during her migration. She entered shallow water toward the end of her second week as a puerulus. She had caught a strong incoming tidal current the night before that carried her over the reef, and when she swam downward at the first hint of dawn, she encountered the sand bottom of a grass flat in 20 feet of water offshore of the central Florida Keys. Obeying ancient instincts, she buried in the sand with only her transparent antennae uncovered and awaited the coming of the next darkness.

The full moon was at its peak a few days before Lola made her first bottom fall, and the dark phase of the moon was now beginning. The moon did not rise these days until several hours after sunset, and Lola did her traveling only during those dark hours. Each night she moved toward the shore swimming steadily near the surface during the dark of night. She dropped back to the security of the bottom sediments as the waning moon flooded the sea with its ghostly light. The time of darkness increased as the moon rose later on subsequent nights, and Lola traveled closer to her goal. She rode the incoming tides, and one dark night just after the last quarter of the moon in early May, she passed under one of the many bridges that linked the Keys together for the purposes of humans.[13]

The time to settle, or to die, was now upon her. She must find a settlement site within 7 to 10 days. Her eyes had darkened from golden yellow to brown and then to black, and the base of her antennae began to develop a pinkish tinge. She swam very near the surface as she entered shallow water near the shore. Surface turbulence and ripple action could provide much information about bottom structures and shorelines that lay ahead of her. Two days later, precisely on the new moon in May, the currents steered her

Figure 11. A Caribbean spiny lobster puerulus just before molting into the juvenile stage. The coloration of the first juvenile stage can be seen beneath the transparent exoskeleton of the puerulus.

in a favorable direction, and she found a large clump of red alga, *Laurencia*, growing near the surface in a shallow bay on the Gulf of Mexico side of Grassy Key in the central Florida Keys.

This shallow area would be her home for the next few months. Other pueruli settled out in algal masses that hung from the drooping, submerged prop roots of red mangrove, in the growths that fouled the bottoms of untended boats, in the thick tangle of washed-out grass beds, and even on clumps of algae that grew on the seawalls of new housing developments. Enormous numbers of newly settled lobsters appeared each month, with most arriving in winter and early spring. Relatively few of the millions of tiny lobsters that settle in the Florida Keys make it though the biological funnel of the first year. Most are taken by octopi, crabs, grey snappers, small groupers, grunts, and other fish. Only those that find a microhabitat that provides ample shelter and food survive.

Two days after Lola arrived at her clump of red alga, she developed light brown stripes along the length of her body on each side of the mid-dorsal line, her antennae became brown wands tipped with pink, and her legs developed bands of yellow and brown pigment. This pattern of coloration provided excellent camouflage in her new environment, and when she remained hidden and still, the sharpest eye could not discern her position. She molted four days after she settled, and the old, transparent shell of the puerulus was discarded. The coloration she displayed in the final days of her puerulus stage was due to pigment deposited in her new exoskeleton that was developing under the old shell of the transitional puerulus. It had done its job. The puerulus form had taken her from the vast expanse of oceanic waters to a shallow, hard-bottom area of algae and sponges close to where the sea meets the land. Now after almost nine months of survival and growth in the most predatory environment on Earth, she was at last a juvenile lobster.[14]

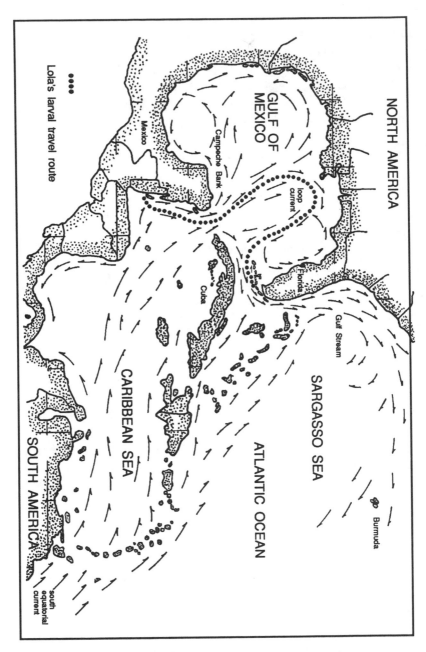

Figure 12. Lola's travel route as a phyllosome larva.

A Juvenile Spiny Lobster's First Year

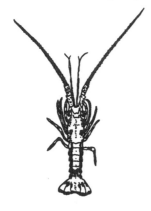

Lola's new exoskeleton was harder than the shell of the old transparent puerulus. She could now include calcium salts in the chitinous matrix of her shell, and this gave her additional weight and hardness that helped her to survive the rigors of life on the sea bottom. Her carapace length (CL) was about ¼ inch (6 mm) and her total length, excluding the long antennae, was almost 1 inch (25 mm).

She remained hidden deep within the algal mass while her new exoskeleton hardened and did not feed until two days after her first molt. On the third night she left her refuge well after darkness settled over the quiet bay, and she explored her immediate surroundings for food. Her mandibles were now strong crushers, capable of breaking and tearing the chitinous shields of small crustacea and the hard calcareous shells of small mollusks. Throughout her life—as a larva, juvenile, and adult lobster—Lola was an opportunistic carnivore. Bits of algae and sea grass occasionally found their way into her diet, but usually only as incidental attachments on the animals she captured and consumed.

Foods and Feeding. The first organism she chanced across on her first feeding excursion was a small snail, *Batillaria*. Her legs were no longer tipped with the sharp feeding spines of her larval days, but they served a similar purpose by grasping and manipulating food organisms into the best position for an attack by her crushing and tearing mouth parts. The small snail resisted her naive attempt at feeding, however, and she soon dropped the well protected creature and continued the search for her first food as a juvenile lobster. The night before, a small nudibranch (a green sea hare) laid a patch of green eggs on the underside of a broad blade of a calcareous green alga. When Lola's antennae brushed the eggs, the sensory receptors located in her antennae and on her legs "tasted" the eggs and told her that food was present. She fed well for most of the night on her first meal and retired deep into the algal masses long before the first light of the next day. This pattern of nocturnal foraging and hiding or "denning" during the day would be the primary behavior pattern for the rest of her life.

This small area—a few square yards of little corals, dense algae, small sea fans, and sponges in water only two feet deep—would be her home for several months. It was a productive area: small snails, shrimp-like amphipods, and other small crustaceans were abundant in the algal masses, and tiny clams and marine worms filled the sandy bottoms between the rocks. Only in areas such as this where small sea life flourished was there enough food and shelter to support a population of juvenile lobsters. She required a lot of space for such a small creature. She was the only small

Figure 13. A recently settled, juvenile spiny lobster (*Panulirus argus*).

lobster in an area of almost 400 square feet (36 sq. m). Her nearest neighbor was 20 feet (6 m) away. Lola became more adept at feeding as the days went by. She could soon crush small snails and clams with ease and capture the faster moving small shrimps and tiny crabs that shared her shallow habitat. Her diet consisted primarily of tiny snails (gastopods) and bivalve mollusks although small crustaceans were also a large part of the diet. Other small animals such as echinoderms, hydroids, and bryozoans and some algae were also included.

She was not gregarious in this early portion of her juvenile life. Like wind-borne seeds, pueruli seldom settle in exactly the same spot. Although Lola's solitary residency in the early juvenile stage was not by choice, it greatly reduced the danger of predation. Although she occasionally encountered other small lobsters, she did not seek them out and usually ignored them when chance brought them together. Cannibalism is rare in the juvenile stage. Only if food is scarce and a newly molted small juvenile happens underfoot, do the tiny lobsters prey upon each other. In this early life stage, she depended on cryptic coloration and a hidden, solitary life for survival. She would not seek out the security of communal lobster dens until the end of her first year.

Predators. Life on the shallow algal patch was not tranquil for Lola. There were many predators to avoid. The swift octopus that lived in a hole on the offshore edge of her little algae patch was the most dangerous. The entrance to his den was littered with the empty shells of cowries, tulip snails, and clams. The many small lobsters and crabs he also consumed left no lasting remains as evidence of his varied appetite. All her life Lola would have to remain alert to the danger from octopus. The largest species, the common reef octopus, could capture a mature spiny lobster and often fed on small juveniles. Joubin's octopus, a small species, could quickly end the existence of any postlarval lobster that was unlucky enough to catch the eye of this efficient predator. The octopus hunted at night—a blue blur of soft tissue with a sharp poisonous beak and long grasping arms that wrapped its prey in quick death. Large crabs were also quick to avenge their tiny cousins when they found a small lobster; and snappers, grunts, and porgies were more than happy to consume every small lobster they could find.

Lola kept hidden during the day and fed at night. She did not fall prey to any of the many predators that shared her habitat, and she fed on the abundance of small animals that surrounded her. Because of the hard exoskeleton that contained her, Lola could not grow and change unless she exchanged the old, hard shell for a new one that could expand for a brief period before it also hardened into a protective shield. Her next molt took place 10 days after she shed the puerulus shell. Since the water temperature was warm and food was abundant, she grew very well. Lobsters that settle in winter when the water is cool or in areas where food is not abundant do not grow as rapidly. Her carapace length (CL) was 6 mm (about ¼ inch) when she first became a juvenile, and after her first juvenile molt, her CL increased to 8 mm. When she reached a CL of about 18 mm, she left the small clumps of red *Laurencia* alga and frequented rocky holes, small ledges, and the undercut edges of grass beds. Her total length, not including the long antennae, was now 28 mm or about 1¼ inchs.

She averaged about one molt per month during her juvenile year. The early molts were 10 to 20 days apart, and her intermolt period gradually expanded to 35 to 40 days by the end of the first year. Her CL increased by 2 to 4 mm after each molt, and at the end of seven months (about the end of November), she had molted 10 times, and her CL was 38 mm (about 1½ inches). Her total body length, excluding the antennae, was about 110 mm or 4⅜ inches.[15]

Her behavior and habits began to change as Lola gained in size and passed her first six months as a juvenile. Her coloration, the cryptic blend of bands and lines that merged her small form so well with the algal growths, began to turn to the reddish brown and yellow spotted coloration of the adult spiny lobster. Now a little larger, she occupied a small hole in the rocky bottom during the day, and she often shared her den with lobsters her size or slightly larger. The area she covered during her nightly feeding forays gradually expanded until she was moving 15 to 20 yards (75 to 100 meters) from her den each night. She was also able to defend herself with her spiny antennae from many of the small fish that would have made a quick meal of her a few months ago. Her days as an early juvenile were coming to an end. After her next molt, she would leave the shallow area that gave her protection and food and move out to deeper waters as a sub-adult or "short" lobster.

Molting. Fully half of Lola's life was spent preparing for a molt or recovering from one. Molting, or ecdysis (the technical term for molting), was not just a simple matter of stepping out of an old exoskeleton with a shiny new exterior. The exoskeleton of a lobster is much more than a hard supporting structure like the shell of a clam or a snail. The bones of mammals, their "endoskeleton", provide the rigid supports and leverage for the action of muscles, and the exoskeletons of lobsters and other crustaceans perform the same function. The exoskeleton also contains cell projections on the antennae and legs that function as chemoreceptors (taste and smell), and it forms the outer covering of the eyes, the hard crushing mandibles of the mouth, and the structures of locomotion and defense. These functions can not be "turned off" while a new exoskeleton forms beneath the old. The lobster must function normally through the old exoskeleton as the new one forms beneath it, yet be able to shed the old one in only a few minutes when the proper time arrives. Every sensory hair, the tip of every leg, swimmerette, and antennae, the delicate structure of the gills, and every tiny structure of the mouth (including the lining of the gut) is newly formed at every molt.[16]

Lola passed through four stages with each molt: the premolt, the actual molt, the postmolt, and the intermolt period. The molt cycle is controlled by at least two hormones, the molting hormone (MH) and the molt-inhibiting hormone (MIH). The eyestalks release MIH, and MH is released by a tissue deep inside the lobster. Removal of the eye stalks also removes MIH from the lobster's system and causes the molt cycle to begin immediately. The interaction of these two hormones, along with other factors such as nutrition, water temperature, light, and injuries, determines the length of the molt cycle. Even though cool water temperatures in winter inhibit molting, winter is a time of active molting because short days block the release of MIH, and this stimulates molting. The average increase in CL per molt for lobsters over a year old is about ¼ inch, roughly an inch every year assuming four molts per year and no injuries or lost appendages to repair.

Lola prepared for her next molt by gradually reducing her activity. By the time the molt was only a few days off she had stopped feeding and was spending most of her time quietly within her den. Although she did not feed, she was quick to defend herself with the sharp spines on her antennae or to escape danger by swimming rapidly across the bottom with quick snaps of her tail fan. Lobsters usually move by simply walking forward or backward, rapidly or slowly, over the bottom. A provocation of some type is usually required before a lobster engages in rapid backward swimming behavior. This is sort of a last resort in a lobster's bag of tricks for escaping a predator. The powerful tail muscles pump the cupped tail fan, the antennae trail behind, the legs are tucked up, and the streamlined lobster looks almost like a squid as it shoots over the bottom a distance of 10 to 50 feet (3 to 15 meters). Even though the large tail muscle that makes up the abdomen is very powerful, it tires quickly, and a lobster's swimming capability is limited.

Lola's new exoskeleton was now fully formed under the old, and she was making final preparations for the molt during her quiet days. Some of the calcium from the old shell was reabsorbed into her system, especially from a thin line along the bottom of the carapace just above the legs.

Figure 14. A molted exoskeleton. The lobster exited the molt through the break between the dorsal surface of the carapace and the abdomen.

On the day of the molt, Lola began to take water into her tissues. She held the water against an osmotic gradient and exerted hydrostatic pressure against her old rigid shell. She was approaching the point of no return. Now, however, if she was disturbed, she could still stop the molt activity and make an escape. Soon the pressure became too great for the weakened break point on the old carapace, and it split in a thin line above the legs on each side. The pressure between the new and old exoskeleton increased, and the thoracoabdominal membrane bulged outward. This membrane stretches between the rigid cephalothorax (carapace or "head") and the jointed, flexible tail-like abdomen. It allows the "tail" to move independently of the hard, rigid carapace. The membrane finally burst, and it was then molt or die.

Lola's forebody began to emerge from the opening created in the middle of her back when the connecting membrane ruptured, and the carapace lifted upward. Lubricated by fluid secreted between the new and old exoskeleton, Lola's forebody, including the long antennae, withdrew from the shell of the old carapace. It took her about four minutes to extract all her new legs and other body parts, and as soon as her forebody was free, she flexed her abdomen and quickly freed it from the old shell. The actual extraction process, the time when she was most vulnerable to attack, took only seven minutes. Sometimes it takes only three and seldom more then ten minutes. Rarely, a leg or antenna is not withdrawn quickly enough from the old exoskeleton and is trapped in the old shell when the new shell expands. When this occurs, the lobster breaks off the appendage and leaves it with the old shell.

The internal water pressure she maintained expanded her new exoskeleton, and the growth potential she developed during the intermolt period was now expressed. The post-molt period extended for four weeks. Her new exoskeleton firmed up within a few hours and would be hard within a week, but it would take a few more weeks to deposit enough calcium to completely harden the new shell. Occasionally she ate parts of her old exoskeleton and regained some of the inorganic matter she lost in the molt, but usually the old exoskeleton was gone before she began to feed a day or so later.

Lola stayed in her old area for only a week after her eleventh molt. It was now the first of December, and she was now 42 mm in carapace length (1⅝ inches), and almost 5 inches in total length. Late one night she found a large loggerhead sponge with a small hollow at its base, just right for a small lobster. She did not return to the shallow, rocky algal patch that had been home for the last seven months.

She stayed with the sponge for a week or so and then moved further offshore and took up a residence in a rocky hole with three other sub-adult lobsters of similar size. Now she would always associate with other lobsters in dens during the day if at all possible. When her first year as a juvenile lobster passed in May she measured 2 3/16 inches CL (55 mm). Her growth increment was now about 1/4 inch (about 6 mm) at each molt.

By the end of her second summer, after 15 months as a juvenile lobster, Lola measured 2½ inches CL (63 mm) and was just over 7 inches in total length. She lived in rocky holes on hard rock bottoms overgrown with algal masses, sponges, and sea whips several miles offshore of Grassy Key in the Gulf of Mexico. Six to ten lobster, many larger than she, occupied the same dens during the day. At night, however, when many of the predators that feed on lobsters were least active, the lobsters forged over a wide expanse of bottom area. They fed on any small animals they could catch— snails, clams, sea hares, small crabs, shrimps, an occasional dead fish, a live one if they could catch it, and marine worms. They usually returned to the same den before each morning but gradually moved about to new dens as new feeding areas were needed. Lola always sought dens where lobsters were already in residence, for there was safety in numbers. One lobster alone was ready prey for nurse sharks, octopus, groupers, large rays, and even triggerfish; but in numbers, with a dozen or two spiny antennae barring entry to their den, they were safe. It was the end of July, however, and the ultimate predator, man, was about to enter Lola's life.

Survival as a Juvenile in Florida Bay

The sound of boat motors was not new to Lola, especially since she had moved to deeper waters. Now, however, in the heat of late July, if she could notice such things she would have observed that the boats were running more slowly and frequently stopping and idling their motors. After a couple of weeks, the boats were active every day, and the number of lobsters that shared dens with Lola was rapidly decreasing. One night, on the dark of the moon, as Lola was foraging for small clams on the edge of a turtle grass flat, she came upon a rectangular wooden box about three feet long by two feet wide and a foot and half high. It was made of wooden slats spaced an inch and half apart and had two concrete slabs in its bottom to weight it down. There were several lobsters inside along with a fresh piece of cowhide that attracted Lola with the promise of food. She searched the perimeter of this strange structure trying to find an entrance. Soon she climbed up on the top of the box and found a large hole in the center with short wooden slats funneling inward and extending about a third of the way down toward the bottom. Entry was easy and she was now in the company of four other lobsters, two larger than herself and two about her size.

Trapped. She was content to spend the next day inside the trap despite the roaming movement of the other lobsters. When night fell, however, she became restless and attempted to begin her nightly foraging. She wandered aimlessly about the trap seeking an opening. It was easy for her to grip the slats and move upside down over the top of the trap, and she could climb downward along the wooden funnel of slats that guarded the opening, but she was too heavy to climb around these slats into the opening. Each time she tried, she fell back to the bottom of the trap. Only by swimming backwards up from the bottom directly into the opening could she escape, and seldom was any large trapped lobster lucky enough to perform this maneuver. If a bait container had been located near the entrance funnel where it could provide an additional foothold, it would have been easier for her to find her way out of the trap.

Actually, about 15% of all trapped lobsters manage to escape over a 5-day period. The escape rate for small lobsters, CL less than 2.56 inches (66 mm), is much higher, 53% over a 5-day period. Larger lobsters, CL greater than 2.93 inches (75 mm), are less mobile than small lobsters and have an escape rate of only 11.6% over a 5-day period. The typical

Figure 15. A typical lobster trap set on a shallow grass bed bottom in Florida Bay. The lead weight on the line beneath the bouy prevents the polypropylene trap line from floating across the water's surface.

wooden lobster trap is very efficient at holding legal and just sublegal sized lobsters. Lola stayed in the trap for four days. She roamed the trap at night and usually stayed in a corner during the day. The inside of the trap was clean of any marine growths. The lobsters searched every slat and corner and consumed every mollusk and every growth that dared settle in the trap.[17]

Bob Johnson had named his lobster boat MYSTERY TWO. He named it that, he said, because the first mystery was why he stayed in the lobster business and the second was why he had gone into debt to buy a new boat. Actually, he did make good money in a good year and had managed to come out a little ahead in the few bad years. He also liked the freedom of being a fisherman and loved his life on the sea. Despite his complaints, he had no intention of going back to selling insurance. Bob and his mate Joe worked two lines of 50 traps each this morning. They were baiting the inshore traps with cowhide and the offshore traps with sublegal size (CL less than 3 inches) lobsters. These short lobster

Figure 16. A trap pulling platform on the back of a small commercial lobster boat. The traps have heavy algal growth at the end of the season.

were good bait, not because large lobsters entered the trap to eat them, but because lobsters searching for a daytime den enter the trap just because other lobsters are already there. Besides effectively attracting large lobsters, shorts are free to the fishermen and are easy to handle. The low cost of the shorts is actually an illusion, however, for every time a short lobster dies in a trap, the lobster industry loses a potential legal size lobster a year or two in the future.

Lola was fortunate. The trap she had entered was the last trap in the last line to be pulled. As Bob idled the boat up to the trap buoy, Joe expertly hooked the trap line under the buoy and wrapped it around the drum on the trap puller. The electric motor hummed, and the trap jumped from the bottom and effortlessly sped toward the boat. Joe guided it onto the stainless steel platform that hung over the side of the boat, and when the trap rode up on the platform, the entire apparatus flipped up onto the boat. The puller motor shut off, and Lola was high and dry for the first time in her life.

Joe reached into the trap and with gloved hand pulled out the two largest lobster and dropped them into the fish box behind him. He measured one lobster a little larger than Lola, and since the CL was a just a hair over three inches, it followed the other two into the fish box. Lola and the last lobster were obviously under legal size, and Joe placed them in a separate box along with 50 other shorts destined as "attractants" for the offshore traps. Joe put the top back on the trap and dropped it over the side, making sure that the line did not foul the boat's propeller. He placed a canvas cover over the box of shorts, wet it down with a bucket of sea water, and went into the cabin for a beer and a sandwich while Bob set course for the next trap line six miles further offshore.

Lola was in shock. Water no longer supported her body, and she could not move effectively against gravity without that support. All she could do was to move her legs weakly and ineffectively snap her tail. Water drained from her gills, and she could not efficiently exchange oxygen and carbon dioxide. Ammonia and other waste products began to accumulate in her body, and heat built up under the canvas. Slowly her life was ebbing away. After a half hour the canvas was pulled back, and Joe reached in and picked up four shorts, including Lola since she was on the top. He placed them in a trap that was waiting on the table, secured the top, and pushed it over the side. Cool, salty water flooded over Lola and washed out the froth that had accumulated in her gill chambers. The descent of the trap through the water pushed her up against the top until it thudded into the bottom. She was alive, but still trapped, and her chances for survival were not good.

Lola had been out of the water for only 30 minutes, and the box had been in the shade. She could survive. However, many of the short lobsters that had shared the holding box with her were not so fortunate. Those that were taken in the first traps pulled that morning were on the bottom, and had the misfortune to be "first in and last out". Some of them would be out of the water for 2 to 4 hours, and 30 to 50 percent of these lobsters would die within a month. Even those held out of water for only a half hour would suffer a mortality rate of up to 25% within four weeks.[18]

August was not a good month for Bob Johnson. A small hurricane formed in the Caribbean and moved over Cuba and into the Gulf of Mexico. Even though it missed the Keys, the rough water and hurricane preparations prevented him from pulling his traps for two weeks, and then, when he did get out, the engine of the MYSTERY TWO broke down, and they had to be towed in before they finished the first trap line. A blown head gasket and a valve job, another five days lost. Joe needed work and shipped out with a snapper boat for a couple of weeks. Bob was hurting, he hadn't pulled traps for three weeks, and money was tight. Help couldn't be found since all the boats were working hard to make up for the time lost to bad weather.

Billy Johnson was eleven years old, a little young to mate on a lobster boat, but his dad had no choice this time. Bob could pull the traps by himself, and he did the inshore lines this way, but it was hard to keep the boat on the trap line and work the traps at the same time. So when Saturday came, father and son ran the MYSTERY TWO out to the offshore trap lines.

Lola was in bad shape. She had been in the trap for almost a month now, and she was slowly starving. You couldn't tell it by looking at her, however; her hard exoskeleton did not shrink or bend, and she did not look wasted as a fish or other animal might appear after a month of not feeding. To the casual eye, she still looked the same as she did on the day Joe put her in the trap. There were three other lobsters in the trap with her. Two had entered a week ago, and one was another short that had been put in at the same time as Lola. One of the original shorts had died after the first week. He had been in the first trap for two weeks before being transferred to the offshore lines. He had also been infected with a microsporidian parasite that gave his flesh a cotton-like appearance. His weakened condition allowed this parasite to overrun his natural defense against it.

A few nights later a large octopus took the other short lobster. It searched all around the trap before finding and entering the funnel at the top. All three remaining lobsters darted wildly about the trap in fear. The octopus had no difficulty capturing one of the trapped lobsters and consumed most of it right in the trap. He also had no problem finding the exit when he had eaten his fill. Lola and the other remaining short consumed what was left when the octopus was gone. Although spiny lobsters are not the cannibals that Maine lobsters are, they will consume a dead or grossly injured fellow, especially if other food is not available. Lola lost weight during her period of starvation in the trap. Her muscular tail lost condition and thinned out within her shell as she broke down her muscle tissue for energy to stay alive. Another two weeks without food and she would be starved beyond the point of recovery. If this did happen, the strong musculature within her abdomen would diminish to a fraction of its normal size.

Billy and his dad soon worked out a regular routine. Billy would grab the buoyed line with his hook when Bob eased the boat up to the buoy and then hold it until his dad ran back to the stern from the wheel house. Bob grabbed the line from his son, and as Billy stepped back out of the way, Bob pulled the trap up to the boat and onto the tubular steel platform. As soon as the trap was safely on the boat, Bob ran back to keep the boat on course while Billy took the legals from the trap, sealed the shorts back up, and then pushed the trap over the side. Billy wore thick cotton gloves and a straw hat. He was proud to help out, but he wasn't experienced in handling live spiny lobsters and worked slowly.

Once again Lola was pulled from the water and lay draining on the bottom of the trap on the pulling platform. Billy opened the trap and reached in to grab the one large lobster for the fish box. He was about to close the trap and push it back with the two shorts when he thought Lola might be a legal. He reached for her with one hand and for the measuring gauge with the other. Lola had grabbed the bottom corner of the trap with her legs and resisted Billy's attempt to pull her from the trap. Billy adjusted his grip and in doing so applied a shearing pressure to the legs on her left side. Three of these legs broke off as he pulled her from the trap. When he turned her in his hand to put the measuring gauge across the top of her carapace, Lola's right first leg found the edge of Billy's glove. The strong, hair-like bristles raked across Billy's sensitive wrist, and with a squeal, Billy threw the lobster from his hand. Bob turned just in time to see Lola hit the rail and drop overboard into the sea.

"Hey Billy," he hollered, "We won't make any money tossing them back. Hold onto those critters, you hear?"

Life in the Bay. Lola did not understand or care about the affairs of men. She drifted to the bottom, and she was free. Food was available to her for the first time in weeks.

She immediately picked up the long blades of turtle grass that surrounded her and began to feed on the small organisms that grew on each blade. She held the grass blade with her legs and drew it quickly through her mouth parts combing off all attached organisms for her gastric mill.[19] The boat moved overhead, the trap entered the water fifty feet away from her, and man moved out of her life, at least for the immediate future.

In her weakened and injured condition, starved and missing three legs, Lola was easy game for any predator that might be cruising about. Lola's lucky star was still shining, however, and she managed to find a rocky hole near a bed of small clams. Her needs for food and shelter were filled, and she began to repair the damage caused by her encounter with man. Like most Crustacea, Lola was capable of autotomy. She could break off or assist in breaking off (autotomy), some of her appendages (legs and antennae) if they were caught by some outside force such as the jaws of a fish, the claw of crab, or the hand of a human. This was a valuable mechanism for it enabled her to leave the captured appendage behind to keep the predator busy while she escaped, and by making the break herself she could do it at a special joint (the fracture plane) that sealed quickly with a membrane across the break point and prevented undue loss of body fluids.

This capability was also useful during a difficult molt. If an appendage did not pull free during the molt, she could break it off and quickly escape a helpless attachment to the old shell. Punctures and breaks in the hard shell of the carapace were a different matter, however. If a spear point or tooth broke the hard shell where she could not erect a protective membrane and prevent loss of body fluids, she could bleed to death from a relatively small injury.

Lost appendages are easy to regenerate, especially for young lobsters, but regeneration of lost parts consumes energy that otherwise would go into normal growth. The regenerated appendage forms completely but compactly

Figure 17. The fracture plane that seals the end of a lost leg.

within the last joint of the lost appendage. After a molt, the regenerated appendage expands and hardens into a smaller but fully functional replacement.

Lola's growth rate over the next six months would be reduced by 40 percent because of these injuries. If she had lost more than three appendages, she probably could not have survived despite her favorable circumstances. Lola molted about ten weeks after her experience in the trap. Her CL and total length did not increase at all after the molt, in fact she even lost a fraction of an inch in these measurements.

Growth in the cold winter water of Florida Bay was not rapid. The average intermolt period was 15 weeks compared to the 8 week average intermolt period of summer. She did gain back the weight she had lost, and she had three new legs to replace the ones lost to Billy's rough grasp. The new legs were obviously smaller than her other legs. They would not completely regain their normal proportion for yet another two molts.

Injuries among the lobsters that shared Lola's habitat in Florida Bay were common. In April, at the end of the lobster season, 25% of the short lobsters were injured, most because of encounters with recreational divers or commercial fishermen. The average during the season was close to 15%, and this did not include the lobsters that were injured so badly that they could not survive. A lobster in the wild could seldom survive the loss of both antennae and several legs.[20]

It was May again. Lola had been a juvenile lobster for two full years and had survived against great odds. She measured only a little over 2⅝ inches (67 mm) CL, close to her size of last fall. Had she not been injured and starved, she would have been near the legal size of 3 inches CL (76 mm). Divers and fishermen did not frequent the area she inhabited since it was fairly far offshore and did not have the reputation of being a good lobster ground. Thus, she did not encounter man while she was recovering from her experience in the trap. She was now one of the largest lobsters in the area, and usually had her choice of the most protected spots in the few available rocky dens.

She came across a few traps during the winter of her recovery. One had four starved and dying lobsters that would never grace a shoreside dinner table. The trap was a cut-off. A fast outboard had threaded its way through the maze of buoys a month before. The boater had not seen the buoy on this particular trap because it was hidden in the surface glare of the late afternoon sun. The propeller had wrapped the buoy line tightly around the shaft and then parted the rope, leaving the trap with no buoy to mark its location. The boater struggled to free the tightly wound line from his propeller shaft and swore, "These damn traps! You can't run a boat out here. There's nothing but wall-to-wall buoys." There was little hope for the lobsters, for it was a new trap. The wooden slats would not decay for ten months or more and these lobsters, and perhaps a few more that might enter the trap and not be able to escape, would not survive until the wood rotted and the trap could no longer hold a lobster against its will. Within a few years only the two concrete slabs that had weighted the trap would remain, and small lobsters would den up in the hollows under them.

Lola became quite active after her recovery from the trials of the trap. She seldom stayed in the same den more than a few days at any one time. Most of her daytime activity consisted of grooming herself. Her hard exoskeleton was an attractive substrate for fouling organisms such as algal growths and barnacles, but these are seldom found on lobsters. Lola used the bottle brush tips of her long, articulated legs to scrub her body and keep herself clean and free of attached growths. Several times each day she brushed herself down with each leg moving over every area it could reach. Large, old lobsters that molt infrequently, however, may harbor a barnacle or two that did not succumb to the daily brushing. Her nightly movements took her over extensive grass flats, hard bottoms with growths of sponges and sea whips, and soft muddy areas. Travels of a mile or two in one night were not uncommon. She met many other nomadic lobsters, most just under legal size, that were also wandering without a fixed daytime den. There was no strong directional pattern to her movement, but the general trend was southwesterly—toward the coral reefs on the edge of the Gulf Stream.[21]

The summer and early fall passed well for Lola. The water was warm, food was plentiful, traps were scarce, divers did not find her rocky dens hidden among the grass flats—and Lola grew well in her next three molts. Her activity slowed before each molt; she stopped feeding, and her random, nomadic movement gradually ceased as the time of the actual molt approached. She remained in and near her den for several days before and after each molt.

She had only one close call during that summer. A couple of lobster divers, despicable poachers that cared only for a few extra dollars, visited the area. They took every lobster they could catch without regard to size, sex, or condition, and they took only the tails. They wrung the tail from the body as they caught the lobster, stuffed the tail into their bags, and left the head on the bottom. Unfortunately, there were buyers for their illegal catch. There were always a few contemptible individuals and restaurant managers, usually in other areas of the country, that would knowingly buy shorts and out-of-season lobster.

The poachers discovered a large lobster den about 50 yards from Lola's den one afternoon in late June. They became so busy rounding up the small lobsters that they failed to notice the Florida Marine Patrol airplane fly overhead. A quick call was made to the patrol boat in that area, and when the poachers surfaced with their bags of tails, they were met by two determined Marine Patrol officers. The poachers dropped their bags to the bottom when they saw the Marine Patrol and protested that they were only spear fishing. Wise to the ways of the poachers, a Marine Patrol officer dove down and recovered the bags of tails as evidence of the illegal activity. The poachers were arrested, punitively fined, and disgraced—their catch and their boat confiscated, and they were out of business before they had the chance to find one small lobster named Lola.

Life and Travels as an Adult Spiny Lobster

November arrived, and Lola had now achieved man's magic number, the legal size of 3 inches (76 mm) in carapace length. The greater freedom from natural predators that accompanied her larger size was more than overshadowed by her greater attractiveness to man. She was now located about five miles on the Gulf of Mexico side of the great Seven Mile Bridge that connects the middle and lower Florida Keys. The first fall cold front had already moved through the Keys and had taken a few degrees off the lukewarm summer temperatures of Florida Bay. Most important, however, the strong winds induced regular water movements and a wave surge on the bottom that triggered queuing behavior. There was now more direction in Lola's night time wanderings. Often, she and several other lobsters, sometimes five to ten individuals, joined together in a nightly march. This behavior is called "queuing" (pronounced cueing) because the lobsters move single-file in long lines termed queues.

Once or twice each night, Lola formed queues with a few other lobsters and marched for an hour or so before breaking up to forage individually. After a week, her travels brought her to the concrete pilings of the Seven Mile Bridge. There were many other lobsters moving with her now; they denned wherever they could each day, for cover was scarce with so many lobsters on the move. Several times a night Lola encountered a trap, most with many lobsters within. She never entered one of these traps, perhaps because of some vague memory of her past experience, or more likely, because her share of good fortune was not yet exhausted.

One day in mid November, the bay was a mass of wind whipped whitecaps. Even on the bottom, Lola could feel the surge of the waves and watch the silt particles lift and cloud the waters. She could sense the wave surge through tiny hairs (mechanoreceptors) scattered over the surface of her body and along her antennae. The angle and depth of the waves told her a great deal about where she was and where she had yet to go. She could not see the heavy, dark clouds of the first fall cold front sweep out of the northwest that afternoon, but she could feel the change in her environment. The wind shifted to the north after the passage of the front, and the breath of winter blew through the Keys. Water temperatures dropped quickly that night in response to the cold north winds that churned the shallow bay waters.

The Migration

Lola and the other lobsters were agitated the next day. They did not remain in the dens as usual, but frequently left the shelter to form short queues and march short distances to other dens where other lobsters were also restless in the cool and silty water. The offshore migration began the next night. When conditions are just right—enough lobsters of the right size are gathered together, water temperatures cool, and wind and weather change after passage of a strong cold front—then a great lobster march might begin. Marches may occur during the day or night. Great marches occur only once in a while, more rarely now in the Florida Keys since populations of large lobsters are uncommon. Some marching usually occurs each year, although it is barely noticeable in some years when cold fronts blow gently.[22]

Queuing. A queue of lobsters may be composed of 2 to 65 individuals, although more than 40 lobsters in one queue is unusual. Lola's queue began with the seven lobsters that shared her daytime shelter the last night before the march. She was third in line, not by design but just by chance.

No one lobster was ever designated the leader. The lead changed often as the queues broke up into smaller lines and then occasionally joined into long lines of 30 to 40 lobsters. Lola walked closely behind the lobster directly in front of her. Her short, flexible antennules and first pair of legs were constantly touching the extended abdomen of the large male lobster in front of her. This kept her head only about 6 inches behind the trailing edge of his carapace. Her constantly waving antennae spread outward at about an angle of 90°. This angle increased as the forward speed of the lobsters slowed and narrowed to a minimum of 30° when the lobsters were traveling at maximum speed. Newly formed queues traveled at speeds of about a third of a mile per hour (0.34 mph or 15 cm/sec), and well formed queues moving over large expanses of smooth bottom traveled at speeds up to 0.78 mph (35 cm/sec).

The queues moved southward over the shallow inshore bottom toward the deeper waters of Hawk Channel. They continued marching until early afternoon the next day and then rested for the afternoon hours wherever some shelter could be found. The queuing of the lobsters seemed to serve several purposes. It made possible the relatively rapid movement of large numbers of lobsters from the inshore nursery grounds to the offshore reefs where breeding would take place the next spring, and it provided a measure of safety and energy conservation as well during the journey.

Water is thick and heavy compared to air, and each lobster has to push through this medium as it moves; and as it pushes through the water, a drag against the movement of the lobster is created. By queuing, lobsters are able to take advantage of water turbulence created by the lobsters ahead and reduce the drag on their own forward movement. At speeds of 0.78 mph (35 cm/sec.), a queue of 19 lobsters reduces drag by 65% over the drag that each lobster would experience if it moved by itself, and at 15 cm/sec. drag reduction was only 10%. The faster the lobsters move, and the more individuals in the queue, the greater the overall savings in energy expenditure.

Lola was part of a queue of 25 lobsters as they moved into the deeper waters of Hawk Channel the next day. They were moving over open sandy bottom when the nurse shark found them. He was a good size nurse shark, about seven feet long. He didn't usually move about much during the day, and he would have stayed nestled up under a giant coral head a mile up the channel if some divers hadn't disturbed him. He circled over the file of marching lobsters, and the lead lobster immediately turned in a tight circle and pointed its spiny antennae at the interested nurse shark. The line of lobsters marched into a tight central coil at this threat (typical behavior for lobsters caught out in the open), and the 50 pointed, waving antennae presented a formidable barrier to the capture of any single lobster. If the shark had been very hungry, or less disturbed by the prodding of the divers, he may have attempted to break up the mass of lobsters and crush one or two with the tiny teeth in his powerful jaws, but the massed lobsters deterred him, and he moved on in search of a quiet daytime refuge.

The queues were constantly forming and reforming, and the energy consuming lead position frequently fell to different lobsters. A large grey triggerfish, attracted to the disturbance created by the passage of the nurse shark, arrived at the area just as the queue was reforming. A single lobster had wandered off a few feet from the group and was quickly attacked by the triggerfish. The lobster file began to coil again and despite their rasping stridulation, the triggerfish was able to prevent his prey from joining the safety of the mass. Although the triggerfish could seldom successfully attack a group of exposed lobsters, or a single lobster in a den, a lone lobster in the open was no match for the sharp teeth and powerful jaws of the triggerfish.

The triggerfish first concentrated its attack on the lobster's eye stalks. It dove in between the waving defense of the antennae and bit fiercely at the eye stalks and their protecting rostral horns. The leather tough skin and thick scales of the triggerfish gave it some protection against the sharp antennal spines. As soon as the hapless lobster was blinded, the triggerfish attacked the legs and soon turned the lobster over to expose the vulnerable abdomen. Then, bit by bit and piece by piece, the triggerfish, and other smaller fish attracted by the activity and the presence of lobster blood in the water, consumed the remains.[23]

Lola and the rest of the lobsters moved rapidly away from the area and reformed into queues to continue their march to the offshore reefs. The queue made it to a large patch reef on the offshore side of Hawk Channel and broke up into the maze of coral growths and limestone rock reefs. Although some of the lobsters continued on to reefs further offshore, Lola remained at this reef for the winter months. Her behavior changed from the summer pattern of activity from sunset to sunrise, to the winter pattern of feeding and active movement from sunset to about midnight, and then denning with other lobsters under coral heads and rocky caves until the next sunset. She fed mostly on mollusks that she found on and near the reefs, particularly the turkey wing clam, *Arca zebra*. She also consumed many other animals such as polychaete worms, other crustaceans, and even fish. At night, when many small fish rested quietly in the reef, she was occasionally able to capture one by encircling it with her first three pairs of walking legs and then killing it with her sharp and crushing mouth parts. Sponges, algae, and reef detritus were also consumed, perhaps along with other food organisms.

Lobster sounds. She coordinated her activity with other lobsters by creating rasping noises with her stridulation apparatus. Each rostral horn sweeps downward around the

Figure 18. A close up of the file and plectrum that create the sounds of spiny lobsters.The rostral bar (file) is the long ridge that curves down under the eye. The antennal pad (plectrum) is attatched to the base of the antenna (the triangular pad in the center of the photograph) and is drawn over the file.

eye stalk and forms into a ridge that extends forward along the base of the antenna. This ridge is surfaced with microscopic scales and is termed the "file". A special pad (the "plectrum") on the base of the antenna contains hard, microscopic ribs. As the base of the antenna is moved up and down, the plectrum is drawn over the file to create harsh sounds in the range of 85 Hz to about 12 kHz. The sounds are classified as "popping", "fluttering", and "rasping" and are correlated with low, moderate, and high levels of arousal. The rasping sound is always emitted when predators disturb the denned or massed lobsters; and the lighter sounds may serve as a "sonic beacon" aiding the return of lobsters to their dens after a night of foraging.[24]

Lola's carapace length (CL) increased by ¼ inch over the winter months. By early March she measured 3¼ inches (83 mm) CL and weighed about 1¼ pounds. Had she not been injured the previous winter, she might have made the journey to the outer reefs the year before and possibly spawned for the first time the previous summer. Now, however, she was fully mature, ready to reproduce—and an ideal recruit for the large commercial and recreational lobster fishery of the Keys.

She remained under a large head of brain coral during the day and at night roamed the reef and nearby grass flats for small mollusks and crustaceans. Only one trap was placed near her patch reef that winter. A half dozen lobster were lost to this trap the first two weeks it was in place. Lola had explored it twice and almost entered it the second time. Fortunately for Lola, a large sport fishing boat caught the trap line in rough seas and dragged the trap a half mile before the buoy line parted. Her next brush with man occurred in mid March.

Escape from the divers. The lobster season was nearly over and Mike and Don had trailered their boat down from Jacksonville to do some diving and get a few lobsters. They had been out all morning on the reefs off Bahia Honda with little luck. The few lobsters they had seen were buried so far into the reef structures that they could not reach them. They were not practiced in the art of tapping or tickling lobsters out of the reef, and the few lobsters that remained on the shallow offshore reefs were so wary of divers that they remained hidden deep in the limestone crevices during the day.

Mike and Don were good divers and it hurt to head back to the campsite with an empty catch box. On impulse, Mike turned the boat eastward when the water deepened over Hawk Channel, and he watched the depth recorder for reef formations. They each had one tank of air left, and Mike thought that they might try a patch reef if they found a promising area. They ran across a good trace on the recorder, a relief of 3 to 8 feet, about two miles down the channel. Don dropped the anchor just off the reef in 35 feet of water and both of them looked at the murky water below with some trepidation.

The current pulled the boat around on the anchor, and Don watched the dark green water flow rapidly past the boat.

"You really want to dive here?" he asked Mike.

"Sure," said Mike, with a little more confidence than he actually felt. "The visibility will be better on the bottom and the current isn't as fast as it looks."

They gathered up their gear, donned the SCUBA tanks, and slipped over the side in search of the succulent Florida spiny lobster. They could see the reef on the bottom after a descent of about 10 feet, and Don suddenly felt much better about the dive.

Lola and the other lobsters knew that something was on their reef. They could feel the movement of the divers in the water, and their chemoreceptors picked up the odor of wet suits and rubber dive gear. Their den was a high head of brain coral with a large cavity hollowed out underneath it. Don chanced across this particular head, grabbed the lower edge, and pulled himself down to peer under it. Lola and the other lobsters suddenly saw an upside-down human face encased in dive mask looking into their den. The intrusion caused them to rasp loudly and back far up under the coral head. The largest male, the dominant lobster, stepped forward and aimed his antennae at the intruder.

Don was excited. He had never seen so many large lobsters in one place before, and within reach, too. He reached up under the coral head and grabbed the large male lobster next to Lola by the antennae and began to pull him out from the under the coral head. The lobster slapped its tail strongly just before it was pulled free of the coral head, snapped off one of its antennae, and shot free of Don's grasp. It crawled out from under the coral head and began to walk away over the reef. Don dropped the antenna and didn't know whether to chase the lobster he missed or go back under for a different lobster. He decided to chase the escapee, figuring that the others would stay put until he returned. It took him awhile, and the male lobster lost its other antenna, but he finally caught it and put it in his bag.

When he returned to the lobster den, he found most of the lobsters out in the open moving away from the den in many directions. He caught only three of the eight that had been under the coral head. Two of the five that got away did so only at the expense of an antenna or a leg or two. Lola moved out quickly and made good her escape while Don was chasing down the large male lobster.

Mike saw her walking over the reef and tried to grab her. She did not hole up, as did some of the other lobsters, but swam off the reef onto the grass flat with several strong snaps of her tail. Mike followed her onto the grass flat and tried several times to catch her. Every time, just as his arms swept forward, Lola would snap her tail and sail away from him, and his fingers only brushed the tips of her antennae.

Mike suddenly realized that he was moving further and further away from the reef. He was in danger of getting lost on the featureless grassy plain, so he reluctantly watched Lola disappear into the watery mist and turned back toward the reef. Mike and Don collected a total of seven lobsters, all legal size, which was lucky for them, because a Marine Patrol Officer stopped them as they were returning and helped them measure the carapace length on each lobster.

Don was quite a bit more fortunate than he realized. In his excitement at discovering the lobster's den under the coral head, he did not take the time to carefully examine the den and make sure that a large, green moray eel was not sharing space with the lobsters. He had immediately reached in and grabbed for a lobster; and if the five foot moray that had been in the den that morning had still been there, he might have suffered a very nasty bite on his hand or arm. The green moray had chased an octopus away from the den that morning and had not returned. Octopus is a favorite food of moray eels, and octopi are attracted to lobster dens. Moray eels and lobsters frequently inhabit the same dens, and there is apparently a mutual advantage gained by this loose association. The moray gives the lobster a measure of protection from a major predator and may catch an extra octopus or two by hanging around lobster dens.[25]

Lola returned to the reef as Mike and Don were leaving and spent the day among the torn legs, lost antennae, and injured lobsters that had escaped the unpracticed hands of the lobster divers. That night she left the reef that had sheltered her for several months and moved further offshore. She continued her gradual offshore movement each night for several weeks and soon found another reef area in 50 feet of water that was home to a population of mature lobsters.

Reproduction —
Closing the Circle of Life

Lobster season was over at the end of March. Fishermen picked up their traps, and divers ignored the occasional lobster they happened to see. As the water warmed and the April days lengthened, the paired ovaries under Lola's nearly three-year-old carapace developed more rapidly. Yolk was deposited in the developing eggs, and the ovaries changed from whitish in color to a bright orange. She molted in mid April and was ready to mate for the first time. Her carapace length was now 3⅜ inches (86 mm), slightly larger than average for a first mating female in the Florida Keys. As her ovaries enlarged with developing eggs, males were attracted to her. The largest two or three males on the reef mated with most of the females. The large males drove smaller males from the females that were ready to mate and initiated the courtship behavior themselves. The males often fought each other this time of year for dominance of a particular reef area. Fighting consisted of a frontal attack on each other with the anterior walking legs and the weight and strength of the forebody. The larger and stronger of the two males soon overpowered the smaller and sent it scurrying off to the protection of the reef.

Mating. Lola emerged from under her coral head late one afternoon a few days after her new exoskeleton had hardened, and walked about the reef rather than beginning to forage. She attracted the attention of the dominant male on the reef, and he began to follow her closely. He was a relatively small male; few male lobsters in the Keys ever gain normal adult size. His second pair of walking legs were just beginning to gain the extra length and the long dense hairs on their tips characteristic of the adult male spiny lobster. Unless they have suffered injuries, adult males are usually larger than females of the same age.

Lola turned to face him, and her long spiny antennae kept him from getting too near. For several minutes the two lobsters faced each other with their antennae pointed on guard. Gradually, the lobsters moved toward each other and swung their long antennae to the side so that they were eventually standing head to head with their antennae pointing straight out to the side. Their flexible antennules were touching and vibrating rapidly against each other. They held this position and maintained this activity for about five minutes. The male would occasionally close in on Lola, but she pointed her antennae toward him and forced him back.

Gradually she allowed him to close the few remaining inches, and as he approached, they both stood as high as possible on their legs. The male was a little higher than Lola, and as they closed he attempted to grab her with the first two pairs of his long walking legs. Lola resisted, and their positions returned to the head-to-head stance. Things happened very quickly on the next approach. The two lobsters moved toward each other and raised their bodies high, and as before, the male grabbed Lola with his legs. Then, just as a small child swings under a railing, the male swung his abdomen under Lola between her extended legs and thrust the swollen gonopores on the base of his last pair of legs hard against the posterior underside of Lola's cephalothorax. He pushed hard against her several times in rapid succession, and sperm mixed in a gelatinous matrix extruded from the paired gonopores at the base of his fifth walking legs and adhered to the sternal plates between Lola's last walking legs. She flipped away from him when he relaxed his grip from around her body. The light grey spermatophore he left behind gradually hardened on Lola's body and turned a dark grey-black in color.[26]

Lola did not mate again before she ovulated and fertilized her eggs. Females seldom carry more than one spermatophore. She was ready in the first week of May, and like uncounted generations before her, she passed the ovulated and fertilized eggs onto the overigious setae of the paired swimmeretts on her strong tail. For three weeks and four days she cupped her tail carefully around her eggs and kept them well flushed and protected. Although she had never incubated eggs before and was never taught by any other female lobster how to care for her eggs, she knew exactly what to do and when to do it. The eggs hatched one dark night at the end of May. The new larvae swept out over the reef and into the currents that would carry them northward into the Gulf Stream. Some might survive, and find their way to the shallows of Bermuda or the eastern Bahamas, or perhaps even circle down into the eastern Caribbean. Depending on current patterns at the time, a few, or many, might even be washed back through the island chain of the Keys and develop in the Gulf of Mexico. Their chances for survival, however, were probably considerably less than larvae hatching in the Caribbean Sea.

By mid-June, Lola was carrying a second spermatophore. She had not molted, but since fertilization in spiny lobsters is external, she did not need to molt before mating. She ovulated and fertilized her second spawn of eggs at the end of June. This time she remained backed into a hole in the reef while a larger male courted her in the open area before her lair. When they were ready, the male grasped her with his extended second legs and pulled her gently from her refuge. He rolled on his back pulling Lola onto him and supporting them both on the tripod fashioned from his backward directed antennae and extended tail.

Lola flipped back into the reefs after mating was completed. She was an old hand at reproduction now, and she cared for her developing offspring very well. The second spawn hatched in the last week of July, and Lola molted not long after the hatch. Lola gained only 2 mm in carapace length at this molt. Were it not for the energy drain of two spawns, she would have gained another 3 or 4 mm CL at this molt. She was now 3½ inches CL (89 mm) and weighed about 1½ pounds. Her enemies were large grouper, nurse sharks, an occasional loggerhead turtle, a rare triggerfish, and, of course, man. She could effectively deal with her natural enemies. Through eons of interactive evolution her species had developed ways of coping with natural predators, and the abundance of spiny lobsters on the reef was eloquent testimony to their success at survival. But mankind, with intelligence and tools, is an unnatural predator, and an effective defense against human technology cannot be developed through the slow process of biological evolution.

A Lobster's Fate

By coincidence, Bob Johnson on the MYSTERY TWO had decided to set out some deep-water traps at the beginning of the season this year. It was harder to fish the deep water and the running time was longer from his Gulf side dock, but the lobsters were larger and there were fewer shorts. He set out only 150 deep traps the first week in August to see how they did and what his trap losses would be off the reef in 40 to 60 feet of water. He knew his traps would produce better and he would lose fewer traps if he set them near, but not on top of, the reef formations. He also knew that many lobsters left the offshore reefs after spawning and moved to shallower waters in late summer and early fall. He thought he might be able to pick up a number of these larger lobsters as they moved in toward shore.

One of his traps was dropped a few feet from the reef that Lola now called home, and her lucky star suddenly lost its shine. Two nights after the trap had thudded to the bottom near her reef, Lola picked up an interesting scent in the water. She was now in the phase of her intermolt period when she fed most actively, and all indications of food were investigated. She followed the scent up-current to one of those slat-sided wooden boxes that were so familiar and that she had frequently avoided in the past couple of years. Any avoidance reaction to traps that she might have had in the past was now overshadowed by her desire to find the source of the protein molecules that stimulated her chemoreceptors. A small can punctured by a few random stabs of an ice pick was tied inside the trap and was gradually leaking the aroma of inexpensive cat food to the surrounding waters. Lobster fishermen know that cat food is a good bait for lobster. Few fishermen, however, know that this is because cats can't make their own taurine. Taurine is a chemical that is present in high concentration in the flesh of sea urchins, clams, oysters, the brains of humans, and in other animal tissues. Many cat food manufacturers add taurine to cat food since cats can't make it for themselves. Oddly enough, the only animal found so far that has a sense receptor specific for taurine is the spiny lobster.

Lola was not the only lobster interested in this apparent food source. Three lobsters were crawling about the trap seeking entrance, and two others had already found the funnel and were inside the trap. Lola climbed on the top and found the funnel of sloping wood slats that led down into the trap. She soon joined the other lobsters that were trying in vain to get to the oils and proteins inside the silvery little can.

Lola was not imprisoned very long this time. The MYSTERY TWO was back in three days to pull the traps and reap the bounty of the sea. Billy was more experienced now; he often worked for his father on weekends, and lobsters no longer eluded his grasp. Lola's trap went sailing upward one afternoon, and once again she lay draining on the bottom of a trap resting on a gently rolling boat. This time, at 3½ inches CL and 1½ pounds, Billy unquestioningly dropped her into the fish box with the legals and not the holding box for shorts. Lola had survived to reproduce against the great odds presented by nature and an intensive fishery, but now her time had ended, and she would contribute to the economy and gastronomic delight of humanity.

The last trap was pulled at four o'clock, and the boat headed back to the dock. The catch was unloaded at the fish house, and Lola was dumped, still barely alive, onto the scales with dozens of other lobsters. The boil pot followed after weighing, and Lola quickly gave up the thread of life that had carried her so far from her birth on a dark Caribbean coral reef four long years ago.[27] After boiling, her antennae were taken off at the base, the sharp rostral horns were clipped, and her legs were removed. She was then carefully placed between layers of shaved ice and held in the cooler for marketing.

Lola was sold to a restaurant that specialized in native seafood and catered to the tourist trade. It was Saturday night and Lola was split, stuffed with a delicious crabmeat stuffing, and broiled to perfection. She was nested in a bed of lettuce, surrounded with French fries and hush puppies, and served with melted butter to a family from Michigan that had never tasted Florida lobster before. Thirteen-year-old Anne, a most curious little girl with a bubbly personality, enjoyed the meal tremendously. She wondered where spiny lobster live and what they eat and how long they live and how many babies they have and how they grow up. She asked her dad all this, but her dad didn't know.

This narrative should really have two endings. The first, which you have just read, is the ending that is almost sure to happen in the Florida Keys where lobster are so severely fished that relatively few live to become reproductive adults. However, such a fate should not befall Lola, who fought the battle for survival for so long and so well.

It is possible, of course, that when Billy removed her from the trap and turned his wrist a little to toss her into the catch box, she violently flapped her tail at exactly the right moment, broke his grasp and fell back into the sea. If this did occur, then she might move further offshore in the next few weeks to depths of over 80 feet, as do many large females. (Some large males, however, move back into shallow water after the spawning season.)

Fewer traps are set in deep water for it is more difficult to pull deep traps, and trap losses due to boat traffic and strong currents are greater. Traps lost in these depths are seldom recovered. Lobster divers also seldom work at these depths, so the few lobsters that live deep have a much better chance for survival. Lola could then live for many years if she stayed in deep water and might even move along the reef tract southwestward to the Dry Tortugas. She would continue to grow and become a mature old lobster at 6 to 8 years of age. With continued good luck she may even reach an age of 20 to 25 years and a total weight of 15 pounds or more. Lola's story could have either ending.

Month	Age from Settlement		Carapace		Total L		Major Events	Life Stage	Environment
	month	year	mm	inch	mm	inch			
September	-8						Hatch and first feeding	phyllosome larvae	surface currents of the open ocean
October	-7								
November	-6								
December	-5								
January	-4								
February	-3								
March	-2						last larval molt		
April	-1						journey to shore and settlement	puerulus	open ocean to shallow water
May	0	0	6	1/4	25	1			
June	1							sedentary early juvenile	shallow algal flats in Florida Bay
July	2								
August	3								
September	4								
October	5								
November	6								
December	7		42	1 5/8	127	5			
January	8							nomadic juvenile	grass flats and shallow reefs in Florida Bay
February	9								
March	10								
April	11								
May	12								
June	13	1	55	2 3/16	156	6			
July	14								
August	15								
September	16		63	2 1/2	178	7	first capture		
October	17								
November	18						escape with loss of legs		
December	19								
January	20								
February	21								
March	22								
April	23								
May	24		67	2 5/8	192	7 1/2			
June	25	2							
July	26								
August	27								
September	28								
October	29						attained legal size		
November	30		76	3	217	8 1/2			
December	31						migration to offshore reefs	adult	offshore shallows and deep reefs on the Atlantic side of the Florida Keys
January	32								
February	33		83	3 1/4	237	9 1/3			
March	34						escape from divers		
April	35								
May	36		86	3 3/8	245	9 2/3	first spawn		
June	37	3							
July	38						second spawn		
August	39		89	3 1/2	253	10			
September	40						final capture		

Figure 19. Summary of Lola's life history.

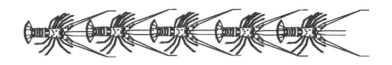

Addendum to Chapter One: The Science

Spiny lobsters have a long and complex life history. Although the imaginary life of one individual can provide a basic knowledge of their natural history, it is a simplistic approach, and one should be aware that the story of a single individual is not a description of an entire population. The reader is advised to seek out the references provided at the end of the book to fuel any serious interest in these fascinating creatures. The following comments and discussions on particular sections of the narrative are drawn from personal observations as well as from much of the scientific work that has contributed to our current understanding of the biology of the Caribbean spiny lobster, *Panulirus argus*. **The number of each of the following comments refers to the number in Chapter One placed at the appropriate point in the narrative.**

1. How many eggs? The number of eggs a female spiny lobster carries is directly proportional to her size. Young females with a CL in the 3 to 3.5 inch range produce from 250,000 to 500,000 eggs (Crawford and de Smidt, 1922; Dawson, 1949; Smith, 1958; and Kanciruk and Herrnkind, 1976). Larger, older females produce many more eggs per spawn. Creaser (1950) studied spiny lobsters in Bermuda and recorded 669,196 eggs from a 3.5 inch CL female; 1,118,656 eggs from a 4.2 inch CL female; and 2,566,916 eggs from a 5.3 inch CL female. Munro (1974) calculated that a female Caribbean spiny lobster produces an average of 830 eggs per gram of body weight. (Incidently, the way one finds out how many eggs a lobster carries is to weigh a small sample of the egg mass, and then count the number of eggs in the sample. Then by weighing the whole egg mass, the total number of eggs can be calculated.) Of course, the number of eggs an individual female lobster can produce depends on many variables other than size, such as water temperature, genetic potential, availability of food, and effects of injuries and disease. The first spawn of the season by a well-fed, uninjured lobster in warm water will contain more eggs than the first spawn of a lobster in a less ideal environment.

In the Florida Keys, reproductive activity begins for female lobster at a size of about 2.75 inches CL (70 mm) (Lyons et al., 1981). Very few smaller females have been reported carrying eggs. According to a comprehensive study by the Florida Department of Natural Resources Marine Research Laboratory (Lyons et al., 1981), female lobsters in the size range of 3.0 to 3.3 inches CL (76 to 85 mm) are by far the most reproductively active size group. Two recent studies on spiny lobster populations in the Florida Keys (Warner et al., 1977; Lyons et al., 1981) agreed that the most reasonable size for initial sexual maturity in females was 2.75 inches CL (70 mm). This does not mean, however, that all female spiny lobsters begin to spawn at 2.75 inches CL. Only 13.9% of the 395 egg-carrying female lobsters taken in the F.D.N.R. study were in the size range of 71 to 75 mm CL, just under the legal size of 3 inches CL. A total of 10,447 female lobsters were examined in that research project, and only 2.5% of the 2,216 females in the above size range were carrying eggs. In a study of Bermuda spiny lobsters, Sutcliffe (1952, 1953) found that sexual maturity was attained at 3.5 to 3.75 inches CL (90 to 95 mm).

According to Lyons et al. (1981), it is possible that female lobsters in heavily fished populations may mature at a smaller size than females of unexploited populations. This may be due to an absence of breeding inhibitions in small females that might be caused by the presence of large, reproductively active females; or because some females may have sustained injuries that slowed their growth but did not inhibit reproductive maturity at a smaller size. A commercial fisherman in the Florida Keys, the late Val Matvejs, kept live lobsters in a small pool for various scientific research projects, and he reported having seen a female lobster, CL 2 inches (50 mm), with a spermatophore attached, and a female lobster, CL 2.5 inches (63 mm), carrying eggs but with no evident spermatophore. Aiken (1977) reports an egg carrying female in Jamaican waters with a CL of 73 mm, and Munro (1974) mentions that reports of egg carrying females as small as 45 mm CL are found in the literature. Both papers however, report first maturity of female spiny lobsters in Jamaican waters at 83 to 90 mm CL. Even though reproductive activity may begin at a CL of 2.75 inches, it is very important to note that 70.6% of all the female lobsters carrying eggs that were examined in the study by Lyons et al. (1981) were in the size range of 3 to 3.5 inches CL—just above the legal size limit!

Although a large lobster produces more eggs than a small lobster, there are far fewer large lobsters, especially in heavily fished populations, and so the greatest reproductive effort comes from the smaller size ranges of mature females. In other words, small female lobsters produce more larvae, overall, because they are far more abundant than large females. A female spiny lobster that spawns actively for many years, however, makes a greater individual genetic contribution to the species than an individual that spawns only a few times at a small size or not at all.

2. Spawning. Once a female spiny lobster develops eggs in her ovaries, she will spawn and attach them to herself whether or not she is carrying a spermatophore. Unfertilized eggs are carried only a few days before they die and are shed from the female. The behavior of a female spiny lobster while she spawns, fertilizes, and attaches her eggs to her

abdomen was described by Sutcliffe (1952, 1953) from observations of captive Bermuda lobster. He makes the statement
in his paper that according to observations recorded by
Crawford and de Smidt (1922), Florida lobster do not take
the upside down position supported by the dorsal surface of
the abdomen and the two antennae while spawning their
eggs. However, Don Sweat, a marine biologist who did extensive work with spiny lobsters in Key West in the mid
1960's, described to me the behavior and positions of female
lobsters that spawned in his laboratory, and they were just
as Sutcliffe recorded them. The lobsters observed by Crawford and de Smidt (1922) may have been missing antennae
or perhaps were in water too shallow to allow assumption
of the natural spawning position.

3. **Egg development and rearing experimentation.** In
the course of research on artificial propagation of spiny
lobsters, I maintained several reproductively active adult
spiny lobsters in our laboratory in the middle keys. I observed mating behavior and closely monitored egg development, care of the egg mass, physical structure of the egg and
its attachment, and the hatching process. The description of
the egg and hatching process in the text is drawn from my
own observations. Experimentation on rearing and culturing spiny and slipper lobsters is detailed in Chapter 4.

4. **Larval development.** The basic paper on the physical
description of the 11 stages of development of the phyllosome larvae of *Panulirus argus* was done by Lewis (1951) at
the University of Miami. He obtained his material by hatching the first stage larvae from captive females and then
searching through the catch from plankton tows for subsequent stages. Except for papers by the Cuban biologists
Baisre and De Quevedo (1962, 1964), little more has been
done on the description of the wild larval stages of *Panulirus
argus*. It is very difficult to rear phyllosome larvae and probably impossible to observe them under natural conditions.

Thus, our knowledge of the larval stage must come from captured wild specimens, laboratory attempts at rearing them, and through qualified observations on related species. The Japanese spiny lobster, *Panulirus japonicus*, has recently been reared through the larval and puerulus stage under laboratory conditions (Yamakawa et al., 1989). One individual metamorphosed into a puerulus after 28 molts 307 days after hatching. The puerulus molted into a juvenile 13 days later. Kittaka and Kimura (1989) also reared *Panulirus japonicus* through the phyllosome stage in 340 to 391 days. Descriptions of the first few larval stages of *Panulirus argus* were developed from my personal observations of living and preserved larvae and from the published descriptions by Lewis (1951).

5. Lola? LOLA LOBSTER? Good grief, Moe. Shades of Mickey Mouse! Next thing you know you'll have her wearing a skirt and earrings.

OK, OK, so it is anthropomorphic and unscientific to give a lobster a name and describe her "adventures", but, after all, this isn't a scientific paper. Giving her a name is just a device to help describe the natural history of the spiny lobster in a readable and entertaining manner. My apologies to all who don't like their lobsters with skirts, earrings, or names.

6. Larval distribution. The only way we know where lobster larvae are, both vertically in the water column and horizontally across the expanse of the sea, is to catch them and record where and when they were caught. This is done with a large plankton net towed behind a slowly moving boat. A plankton net is a conical, fine meshed net with a circular mouth of ½ to 1 meter (1½ to 3 feet). It tapers down over a length of 6 to 15 feet to a diameter of 2 to 4 inches and ends in collecting jar of up to a quart capacity. The catch from a tow over a specific period of time, usually 15, 30, or even 60 minutes, is preserved and labeled with the time,

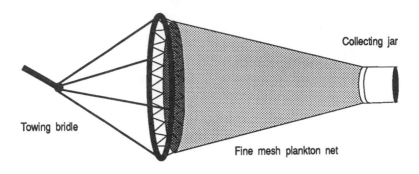

Towing bridle

Collecting jar

Fine mesh plankton net

Figure 20. A typical plankton net rig.

date, location, depth of tow, and other pertinent data. Some plankton nets, termed closing nets, can be rigged to sink to a specified depth, open at the beginning of the tow and close at the end of the tow before they are brought to the surface. This way, only organisms at a specific depth are taken and the vertical distribution of planktonic life can be determined. Studies by Sims and Ingle (1967), Buesa Mas (1970), Austin (1972), Richards and Potthoff (1980), Farmer (1983), and Farmer et al. (1989) using these and other methods, such as drift bottles to determine direction and speed of surface currents, generated basic information on distribution of phyllosome larvae in the Atlantic Ocean, Caribbean Sea, Yucatan Channel, Gulf of Mexico, and Florida Straits.

7. Larval rearing. Most attempts at laboratory rearing of phyllosome larvae are conducted in small jars or shallow compartmented trays, and the food is usually newly hatched brine shrimp or small pieces of dead food such as fish, jellyfish, shrimp, clams, and marine worms. Such methods allow careful observation of growth and development, but provide little information on natural feeding and swimming behavior. In 1976 and in 1980-81 we reared laboratory hatched phyllosome larvae of *Panulirus argus* in 60, 75, 250, and 1000 gallon tanks. They were observed swimming and feeding in concentrations of natural plankton and laboratory spawned fish larvae. They were also reared under conditions of high density and artificial foods and were maintained for 81 days into the seventh intermolt period. Descriptions of phyllosome feeding activity are based on these laboratory observations. Additional information on care and culture of spiny lobster can be found in Chapter 4 .

Laboratory rearing of the Japanese spiny lobster (*Panulirus japonicus*) phyllosomas through the phyllosome larval stage, the puerulus stage, and into the juvenile stage has been reported by Yamakawa et al. (1989) and Kittaka and Kimura (1989). The few individuals that survived to become juveniles in these laboratory rearings spent 306 to 406 days in the phyllosome and puerulus stages. The puerulus stage extended 12 to 15 days, and the puerulus did not feed until after metamorphosis into the juvenile stage.

8. Larval cannibalism. No one knows for certain whether or not phyllosome larvae prey upon each other in nature, although encounters such as the one described in the text were not uncommon in mass rearing tanks. Densities of phyllosomes were far greater in the tank than any that would occur in nature. There are times, however, when many phyllosomes are taken in a small plankton net over a short period of time, and this indicates that high densities of phyllosomes do occur in some areas. Since such predation does occur under artificial conditions, it is probable that it also occurs in natural populations, although it may be a relatively rare event.

9. Where do our spiny lobsters come from? This is an important question, not only for Florida but also for Bermuda, the Bahamas, Cuba, Mexico, and all Caribbean nations. If spiny lobsters, because of the wide distribution of their long-lived larval stage, are a common resource to all the Caribbean and western, central Atlantic nations, then great cooperation between all these interests is required for the future management of this valuable fishery. On the other hand, if each productive shallow bank produces its own post larval recruits, than each management unit can function independently. Unfortunately, there is no proven, definitive answer to this question. There are three possibilities:

- **A.** The long larval life of spiny lobsters in the oceanic currents of the Caribbean Sea and western north Atlantic allows distribution of the species in complex and probably variable patterns throughout this vast area.

Phyllosome larvae are widely distributed by oceanic currents during their extensive planktonic larval life. Annual, variable weather and tidal patterns create eddies and gyres and cause changes in surface, subsurface, and wind blown currents that may affect larval distribution in complex ways. Post larval lobsters that colonize particular areas probably originate from places many hundreds of miles away and may have traveled thousands of miles in oceanic currents before completing their larval life. According to this theory, most of the lobsters that colonize the Florida bank originate primarily in the Caribbean and travel the currents through the Yucatan Straits to Florida waters.

- **B.** Post larval lobsters return to the same general areas where they were spawned.

This may occur because the larvae are entrained in coastal and insular eddies and gyres that form about land masses and keep larvae within specific areas. It is also possible, and perhaps more likely if this theory is correct, that huge circular oceanic current patterns bring mature, last-stage larvae back to their point of origin at the proper time. It is also possible, but unlikely, that there may be a genetic and/or ecological "filter" that works against survival of post larval lobsters that happen to settle in areas other than their place of origin.

- **C.** The last possibility is some combination of the above two theories, which is sort of a cop-out, because the truth probably does lie somewhere between the two extremes.

Some Florida postlarvae must come from other areas, and some larvae from various areas probably do return near to their point of origin. The important thing is to determine, if possible, the source of the recruitment of the majority of the lobsters in each fishery most of the time.

Larval distribution is such an important factor in the biology and fisheries of the Caribbean spiny lobster that it deserves an expanded discussion. In order to understand and speculate on the possible patterns of larval distribution, however, one must know something of the major current patterns in the central western Atlantic. The surface currents in this vast area are complex and highly variable in position, volume, and speed. Winds, tides, water temperatures, salinities, upwellings, Coriolis effects (a force that deflects currents to the right in the Northern Hemisphere and to the left in the Southern Hemisphere), and great storms all interact to change the features of current distribution to a greater or lesser extent on a seasonal and annual basis. Figure 21, presented at the end of this discussion on larval distribution, describes the major currents and oceanic gyres that affect phyllosome distribution. Although the general patterns of the major currents are known, there is much yet to be learned about major and minor water flows in this vast area.

Since there is no definitive answer at this point on the origin of the spiny lobsters in any central western Atlantic fishery, let's take a look at what we do know, along with a little speculation, about the biology and distribution of Caribbean spiny lobsters.

(1) Female spiny lobsters spawn only on the offshore reefs near oceanic water flows. All scientific studies are in agreement with this statement. Reproductively active populations are found along the northeast coast of South America, throughout the Caribbean and the Bahamas, the Gulf of Mexico, as far north along the U.S eastern coast as the Savannah Snapper Banks (Ansley, 1983), and Bermuda.

(2) The phyllosome larva of spiny lobsters is adapted for life in an oceanic planktonic environment and does not normally occur or survive in inshore waters. Again, there is no disagreement on this point.

(3) Early stages of spiny lobster phyllosome larvae are found offshore of coastal areas that harbor adult populations, and middle and late stage larvae are found widely distributed in offshore waters. Spiny lobster phyllosomes are found in numbers in the waters of the Atlantic ocean east of the Bahamas and the Caribbean islands and in the Gulf of Mexico, the Caribbean Sea, the Florida Current, and the Gulf Stream (Sims and Ingle, 1967; Baisre and Quevedo, 1964, 1982; Lyons, 1980; Richards and Potthoff, 1980; Farmer, 1983; Farmer et al., 1989; Ward, 1989).

(4) The larval stage is quite lengthy, at least 6 months and perhaps as long as 12 months. Lewis (1951) suggested a period of 6 months based on the occurrence of early and late stages in the oceanic plankton offshore of Miami, Florida.

Warm water and abundant food organisms may shorten larval life, while cooler water and lack of food may lengthen it. Phyllosomes that remain in the Caribbean Sea under favorable conditions may have a larval life of only 6 months, while those that move into the central Atlantic may live as phyllosomes for a year. At this time, in the absence of any definitive, *in situ* data, my best guess for the length of larval life of the Caribbean spiny lobster in the Caribbean and Gulf of Mexico is 9 months, give or take a month. Farmer et al.,

(1989) speculated, on the basis of their research in the Bermuda area, that the period of planktonic development of *Panulirus argus* in the Sargasso Sea is about one year.

The scyllarid lobster *Scyllarides nodifer* has a phyllosome larva of size similar to that of the spiny lobster. This lobster occurs only northward of Yucatan and Cuba, with the center of abundance in the Gulf of Mexico and southeast Florida, and has a spawning season primarily restricted to June and July, although Hardwick (1987) reports some reproductive activity for this species in February and March in the northeastern Gulf. Lyons (1970) compared the times of spawning and the appearance of the postlarvae of this species and found the larval period to be 8 to 9 months. Although one can't conclude that the Caribbean spiny lobster also has a larval life of 8 to 9 months, it does show that phyllosome larvae of another species are long lived and are contained in the eastern Gulf of Mexico for the entirety of larval life.

The western Australian rock lobster *Panulirus cygnus*, similar in size and life history to the Caribbean spiny lobster, has a larval life of 9 to 11 months (Phillips et al., 1980). My own contained rearing of Caribbean spiny lobster phyllosome larvae (7th intermolt in 81 days) is also evidence of a long larval life.

Recent laboratory rearings of *Panulirus japonicus* in Japan (Kittaka and Kimura, 1989; Yamakawa et al., 1989) maintained phyllosoma for over a year before metamorphosis into the puerulus. Larval growth rates under laboratory and natural conditions are probably quite different, however, and much variation in larval growth rates is also to be expected under differing natural conditions.

(5) The last stage of the phyllosome larva becomes a puerulus postlarva in offshore waters and then, usually, swims to a shallow water, near-shore habitat (Sweat, 1968; Little, 1977; Lyons, 1980 b).

(6) The study by Lyons et al. (1981) presented a careful analysis of the time of spawning of spiny lobster off the Florida Keys. Egg-bearing females were first observed in April, rose to a peak in May and June, and declined thereafter with the last egg-bearing female occurring in September. The studies of Sweat (1968) and Little (1977) documented recruitment of postlarval spiny lobsters into shallow Florida Keys waters on the new moon during every month of the year. In both studies the largest numbers of postlarvae arrived in the months of December through March, six to nine months after the peak spawning period. Although it is quite possible that some of these postlarvae are returning to their birthplace in Florida waters, the presence of postlarvae in all months and the reduced spawning potential of Florida spiny lobster stocks argues effectively for substantial recruitment from other areas. Munro (1974) reports that egg carrying female spiny lobsters are found in all months of the year in Jamaican waters with no seasonal peaks.

Because of the intensive fishery, very few female lobsters in south Florida waters live to reach the peak of their egg production potential or even to produce any eggs at all. Lyons et al. (1981) considered the great reduction in spawning potential that has occurred in the intensively fished Florida spiny lobster populations and came to the conclusion:

"....it seems improbable that spawning contributions reduced to the level presently existing in the south Florida population could continue to produce sufficient recruits to maintain that population."

Despite this loss of reproductive potential, there is no indication that recruitment of postlarval lobsters to south Florida waters has declined. It is most likely, as Little (1977) points out, that the time of arrival of postlarvae is more affected by annual current patterns and other environmental factors than the time of spawning and length of larval life of Florida produced larvae. Ward (1989), in a study of patterns of settlement of spiny lobsters in Bermuda, found that peak settlement occurs in late summer with virtually no mid-winter recruitment. The year of greatest settlement during their study coincided with the occurrence of a Gulf Stream eddy (see Figure 21). He also found that although late-stage larvae are present in offshore Bermuda waters year round, there is little recruitment when water temperature is below 24°C.

Farmer (1983) looked for phyllosome larvae in plankton tows from the eastern Gulf of Mexico, the northern Caribbean, and the western Atlantic north and south of Bermuda. Dr. Farmer found large concentrations of middle stage (5,6, and 7) phyllosome larvae in the southern Sargasso Sea and the North Equatorial Current in the area between 20° and 25° north latitude and 50° to 65° west longitude. These larvae may have arrived at this location by spinning off Gulf Stream gyres and eddies and then moving southward through the Sargasso Sea to eventually join up with the North Equatorial Current. They may also become captured by warm core Gulf Stream Rings and be transported southward between the North American coast and the Gulf Stream for several months before reentering the Gulf Stream and resuming travels in the Atlantic gyres.

According to Farmer (1983), other potential paths include movement along the North Atlantic Drift off Newfoundland, along the Canary Current and the North Equatorial Current back into the Caribbean, and movement in the Gulf Stream past Nova Scotia, then turning southeast and south to follow the volume transport of warm, North Atlantic surface water.

These data on phyllosome larvae and observations of water movements support the concept of an oceanic pool of larvae with multiple points of origin. Current patterns that differ from year to year and season to season probably mix phyllosomes from various populations in different ways from year to year. In one year, for example, a large number of phyllosomes spawned off Florida may ride a countercurrent off the Keys back into the current loops in the Gulf of Mexico, or may move into the Sargasso Sea in eddies and water movements associated with a particularly large cold core Gulf Stream Ring, and eventually travel through the Sargasso Sea back to the Bahamas and the northern Caribbean. Specific, temporary current patterns such as these may result in a substantial contribution of post larvae back to a future annual recruitment of spiny lobsters in Florida populations. Such current patterns may not exist in another year, however, and all of Florida's lobsters for that year may come from Caribbean sources, while Florida's spawn for that year may be lost or may may wind up in Bermuda or the northeastern Bahamas.

But if phyllosomes of the Caribbean spiny lobster do distribute their species throughout the Caribbean, the Gulf of Mexico, and the northwestern Atlantic, then why doesn't the South American smoothtail spiny lobster, *Panulirus laevicauda*, also occur throughout these areas? It is quite common off the northeast coast of South America in the same areas that are also populated by *P. argus* and does occasionally occur on the Florida coast. In fact, in 1949, and only in 1949, *P. laevicauda* was almost as common off the coast of Palm Beach as *P. argus* (Moore, 1962). Assuming that both species have long-lived, planktonic larvae, there must be some reason that *P. laevicauda* does not also exist throughout the range of *P. argus*.

The smoothtail lobster, *P. laevicauda*, is not the only Brazilian species to have a distribution basically restricted to the northeastern coast of South America. The blunthorn spiny lobster, *Palinustrus truncatus*, occurs along the northeast coast of South America and through only the Windward Islands of the Lesser Antilles. The brown spiny lobster, *P. echinatus*, a sibling species to *P. guttatus*, occurs along the Brazilian coast and in the eastern central Atlantic and is not reported from the Caribbean. It is so similar in coloration to *P. guttatus*, however, that it may not often be recognized as a separate species in Caribbean areas. *Scyllarides delfosi*, a spe-

cies very similar to *S. aequinoctialis,* occurs along the northeast coast of South America but not, apparently, northward
into the Caribbean. So there are four species of tropical
lobster, all with long lived phyllosome larval stages, that
occur off the northeast coast of South America, but not at all,
or rarely, do they occur north of the Lesser Antilles.

It is possible that an oceanic gyre, bordered on the south
by the northern branch of the Southern Equatorial Current
and on the north by the Atlantic Equatorial Countercurrent,
entrains the larvae of these species (including a separate,
southern population of *Panulirus argus*) and maintains populations of these species along the northeast coast of South
America with little mixing with Caribbean, Gulf of Mexico,
and northwestern central Atlantic populations. Despite the
strong northwestern flow of the South Equatorial Current
along the northeastern South American coast and into the
Caribbean Sea, oceanic gyres that normally restrict larval
distribution between the Caribbean and the northeast coast
of South America seem to be the most likely explanation for
the separation of these lobster populations. It is also possible, however, that differing ecological requirements of the
postlarvae and juveniles may also be important.

Populations of *P. argus* off the southern coast of Brazil
between Recife and Rio de Janeiro may also be relatively
isolated, and their reproducive patterns may be contained
within a South Atlantic gyre formed by the southern branch
of the South Equatorial Current that becomes the Brazil
Current as it sweeps southward. Populations of *Scyllarides
brasiliensis* and *S. deceptor* may also share this coastal area
and may not maintain reproductive populations along the
northeastern coast of Brazil.

The possibility of discreet northern and southern stocks
of the same species separated at some point in the eastern
Caribbean is not unique to lobsters. There are evidently two
central western Atlantic stocks of dolphin, *Coryphaena
hippurus,* that show a similar distribution pattern (Oxenford
and Hunte, 1986). The northern stock migrates from the area

of Puerto Rico in January/February, to the area of North Carolina in June/July, to Bermuda in July/August, and then back to Puerto Rico. The southern stock migrates through the Lesser Antilles in February/March, northward to the Virgin Islands in April/May, and then begins a southeastward movement in the offshore Atlantic. The stocks differ significantly in electrophoretic properties of heart and liver extracts, rate of growth, size of eggs, time and place of spawning, and size at sexual maturity.

Another study done on queen conch, *Strombus gigas,* populations of the Caribbean and Bermuda (Berg et al., 1986) examined electrophoretic separation of 12 monomorphic and 10 polymorphic enzyme loci from conch taken from Bermuda, Belize, the Turks and Caicos, and the southern Grenadines. The results indicated that the Bermuda populations were isolated and self sustaining, that the Belize and Turks and Caicos populations were similar to each other, indicating seeding from common down stream populations, and the southern Grenadine populations (at the southeastern edge of the Caribbean) were differentiated from the northern populations, indicating a discreet southern Caribbean population that is, perhaps, an extension of populations on the northeastern South American coast. Both dolphin and conch spend only a few weeks as planktonic larvae. Conch settle out of the plankton and begin life on the bottom, while dolphin remain in oceanic waters but become relatively independent of current flows for individual movement. Their distribution and stock identity, however, provides more insight into patterns of biological populations in this complex area.

The only hard evidence for theory B, that each major population of spiny lobsters is reproductively separate and self sustaining, comes from the work of Bob Menzies of Nova University (Menzies and Kerrigan, 1979, 1980; Menzies, 1981). Dr. Menzies studied protein variation, a genetic trait, in populations of spiny lobsters from Florida, the Bahamas, Belize, Mexico, St. Thomas (Virgin Islands), Jamaica, and Trinidad. The results suggested that spiny lobster populations in Belize, Florida, and the Virgin Islands differ genetically; which indicates that these populations do not contribute significant numbers of postlarvae to each other. The results also indicated, however, that populations off eastern Mexico, Trinidad (at the southeastern corner of the Caribbean), and Key West were not significantly different and could be part of the same population. The Virgin Islands and Jamaica were different from each other and from all other populations. It is difficult to reconcile these results with what would be expected from the major current patterns and the known long larval period of spiny lobsters.

However, assuming that this tentative genetic based distribution pattern reflects actual postlarval recruitment, how would lobsters spawned off the Florida Keys return to their birthplace? The logical assumption is that all or most of these phyllosomes are swept northward by the Gulf Stream to be lost in the North Atlantic (Sims and Ingle, 1967).

It's possible, however, that they can ride the currents of the Gulf Stream toward the north Atlantic and then spin off into southern eddies, return southward through the Sargasso Sea, and pass into the Caribbean (Farmer, 1983); or as Menzies and Kerrigan (1980) suggested, a strong, summer counter current off the Florida Keys could carry early phyllosomes westward into the Gulf of Mexico where they would ride the Loop Current and drop out months later once again in south Florida. This coastal counter current is strongest and most persistent during the spiny lobster spawning season, and considerable numbers of Florida-spawned phyllosomes may be entrained into the Gulf of Mexico current systems. Bahamian phyllosomes could ride the eastern edge of the Gulf Stream, spin off into the Sargasso Sea, and then re-enter Bahamian waters with the North Equatorial Current.

The results of Dr. Menzies' alloenzyme analysis are still preliminary, and, as Dr. Menzies (1981) says:

"....it will be necessary to verify the stability of observed genotype frequencies in time to eliminate the possibility of observed differences being a result of high variance in reproductive success and chance variation in recruitment."

In other words, the analysis must be done many times over a long period of time to be sure that these genetic differences are consistent and really mean that the populations are reproductively separate.

Obviously, more research needs to be done. The situation is complex, and we need to investigate the distribution of phyllosome larvae in much greater detail with attention to where and when different stages are found. Much additional effort on the genetic differences between populations should also be done to extend the work of Dr. Menzies. Dr. Hardwick (1987) calculated intra-group variation of the isoenzyme band frequencies of the leg muscles of ridged slipper lobster, *Scyllarides nodifer*, from the Gulf of Mexico to determine if different populations were all of the same reproductive stock, which they were. Molecular techniques that compare isozymes and mitochondrial DNA (mtDNA) are now very useful for detecting variation within species (Powers et al., 1990). These genetic and molecular techniques are becoming more accurate and more useful in analysis of marine recruitment problems and an exhaustive study along these lines should be accomplished with the Caribbean spiny lobster.

Along these same lines, early work by the Cuban biologist Irma Alfonso and others indicate that the stocks of *Panulirus argus* on the southern coast of Cuba may be self-sustaining because of entrainment of the larvae in current patterns of the northern Caribbean. This conclusion is still speculative, however.

Farmer and Berg (1989) discuss oceanic circulation around islands and the possibilities of entrainment of larval forms in local areas. They point out that current patterns about each island system are different; thus dispersal patterns for each population must be studied separately. It is also important to keep in mind that current patterns on large and small scales may differ significantly from year to year and decade to decade. A pattern of larval dispersal that is determined to exist now may not occur in subsequent years. Entrainment in small gyres and current patterns that occur around relatively small islands may be sufficient to allow short term (two to three weeks) larvae of fish, mollusks, and some crustacea to return to the same shelf areas of their origin, but I doubt that larval forms with terms of six months to a year could consistently, or even commonly, be returned by such localized current patterns.

How is it possible that a tiny phyllosoma larvae can survive such extensive travels through vast expanses of the Atlantic Ocean? Well, there is another marine animal that does pretty much the same thing, the American eel.

In his classic paper, Dr. Johs. Schmidt (1925) describes the investigations that led to the determination of the spawning grounds for the American and European eel, *Anquilla rostrata* and *Anquilla vulgaris*. Adults of the American and European eel leave the fresh waters of their continents in the fall and swim to sea. In spring, vast numbers of small eels (elvers) come in from the sea and move into fresh waters to grow to maturity. For centuries, people wondered where and how eels reproduced. In fact, from Aristotle to the seventeenth century, eels were considered prime evidence for spontaneous generation. Since adults with active gonads were never found (eel reproductive systems do not develop until they are far out at sea), the elvers were obviously formed each spring from the mud of ponds and river banks.

When the myth of spontaneous generation was finally laid to rest, the spawning of eels was a great biological mystery. Dr. Schmidt found their spawning area by analyzing the growth stages of larval eels taken in plankton tows from throughout the north Atlantic. When he found the area that produced only the very youngest eel larvae, he had found the spawning grounds. And in his words:

"No longer subject to pursuit by man (after they leave continental waters), hosts of eels from the most distant corners of our continent can now shape their course southwest across the ocean, as their ancestors for unnumbered generations have done before them. How long the journey lasts we can not say, but we know now the destination sought: A certain area situated in the western Atlantic, northeast and north of the West Indies. Here lie the breeding grounds of the eel."

According to Dr. Schmidt, the larval life of the American eel is about one year, and the breeding grounds are located in a broad area of the Sargasso Sea south of Bermuda and to the northeast of the Bahamas. The American eel occurs in Puerto Rico, Hispaniola, Jamaica, Cuba, the Gulf of Mexico, and, of course, the eastern coast of the United States. The significant point is that these tiny, pelagic larval eels, in the leptocephalus stage, must move from the Sargasso Sea into the Caribbean to reach Jamaica and Cuba, and must either swim against the Florida Current around the tip of Florida (highly unlikely), or move southward into the Caribbean with the North Equatorial Current, and then through the Yucatan Straits to get into the Gulf of Mexico. They must also cross the Florida Current or the Gulf Stream to get to the eastern coast of the United States or, again, ride the currents through the Caribbean to be on the western edge of the Gulf Stream as it moves up the eastern coast. European eels cross the entire expanse of the Atlantic—a trip that takes three years to accomplish.

So here is another marine animal with long range dispersal of the larval form. In this case, however, we know that larval American eels are carried from the Sargasso Sea to the northern Caribbean, the Gulf of Mexico, and the eastern U.S. (unless, of course, there are undiscovered spawning areas in the Gulf and the Caribbean). Larval eels and phyllosome larvae are quite different creatures and have quite different innate swimming and navigational capabilities. One can't say that if eels can do it, lobsters can do it too. This is far too simplistic a conclusion. It is, however, a point to ponder when considering distribution and dispersal of lobsters.

In summary, I have to go along with theory A at this point. The evidence gathered from plankton collections and current patterns indicates that a variable mixing of the larvae of the major spiny lobster populations in the central western north Atlantic is the most likely reproductive pattern for spiny lobsters. The wide distribution of phyllosome larvae, long larval life, constant monthly recruitment to Florida waters, and the complex current patterns of the Caribbean and central western Atlantic argue effectively against isolation of various Caribbean spiny lobster populations, except, perhaps, for populations off northeastern South America. There is much work to be done on the problems of larval dispersal, however, and all possibilities should be vigorously investigated. We may find that some populations are more important as "seed" populations to the entire western central Atlantic than others, and that some populations receive greater return of spawned larvae than others, but I doubt that the reproductive potential of any major population will be found to be unimportant. **And as Doug Gregory Jr. (personal communication) points out, the only safe and responsible base for a fishery management plan is the assumption of a significant amount of self seeding in each exploited population. If every exploited population is managed as if it is dependent only on itself for all recruitment, then all populations will benefit equally.** Lola's larval travels may or may not be typical of Florida's spiny lobsters, but her route is quite plausible in light of our current knowledge.

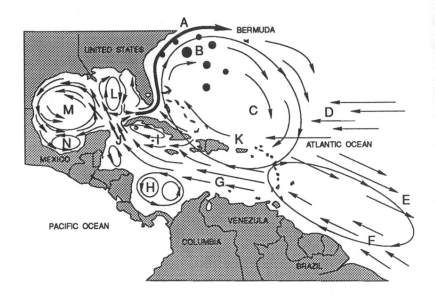

Figure 21. Typical current patterns of the western central Atlantic Ocean including the Caribbean Sea and the Gulf of Mexico. The current patterns of this broad oceanic area are very complex and variable. Most major currents, such as the Gulf Stream, are reasonably constant in presence, volume, and velocity. Others, such as the loop current in the Gulf of Mexico, vary seasonally in placement, volume, and velocity. Large gyres, formed and maintained by these currents vary seasonally and annually in size, volume, and even existence as the volume, temperature, placement, and interaction of the major currents also vary.

A. The Gulf Stream. The origin of the Gulf Stream is found in the Florida Straits between Cuba and the Florida Keys. Water flows from the Yucatan Channel and the Gulf of Mexico to form the Florida Current that flows around the tip of Florida, and then northward along the Florida shelf. The Antilles Current joins the Florida Current north of the Bahamas to form the Gulf Stream. The Gulf Stream flows northward until it reaches Newfoundland and then swings eastward toward Europe.

B. Gulf Stream Rings. The Gulf Stream moves about 4 billion cubic feet of water per second and attains speeds of 4 to 5 knots. It moves about 25 times more water than all the rivers of the world combined. The axis or jet of the stream is about 50 miles wide, but there are many meanders in its course. Some of these meanders become loops and projections that bud off the Stream and capture great volumes of cold coastal water or warm Gulf Stream/Sargasso Sea water that become giant eddies known as cold or warm core Gulf Stream Rings. These giant eddies or rings are 50 to 100 miles in diameter, although some may be up to 200 miles in diameter, and they move independently of the Gulf Stream. They often maintain their identity for several months, perhaps as long as a year. Cold core rings of captured coastal water and associated eddies of Gulf Stream water move down toward the Caribbean through the Sargasso Sea. The rings may eventually lose their identity and merge with the waters east of the Bahamas or may live long enough to join the Gulf Stream once again. The warm core Gulf Stream Rings and the eddies associated with cold core rings must capture planktonic organisms from the Gulf Stream, including lobster phyllosomes, and move them out of the Gulf Stream, often southward. Cold core rings move into the Sargasso Sea, and back toward the Bahamas and the Caribbean. Warm core rings tend to move southward between the Gulf Stream and the North American coast.

C. The Sargasso Sea. The Sargasso Sea is a vast oceanic area northeast of the West Indies and the Bahamas that is characterized by slow moving, calm water and great accumulations of floating Sargassum weed.

D. The North Equatorial Current. The North Equatorial Current originates north of the Cape Verde Islands and moves west across the Atlantic to merge with the northern branch of the South Equatorial Current and form the Antilles Current. The Northern Equatorial Current is between 600 and 900 miles wide and moves at about 0.5 to 2 knots. This is also the size and speed of all equatorial currents in the Pacific, Atlantic, and Indian Oceans.

E. The Atlantic Equatorial Countercurrent. There is a surface current that runs eastward along the equator between the North and South Equatorial Currents in both the Atlantic and Pacific oceans. The equatorial countercurrents are about 250 miles wide and travel at about 1 to 3 knots. The Atlantic Equatorial Countercurrent originates at some point between the merger of the northern branch of the South Equatorial Current and the North Equatorial Current. It then flows first southeastward far off the Brazilian coast and then eastward along the equator.

F. The South Equatorial Current. The Atlantic South Equatorial Current orignates off the west coast of Africa south of the Gulf of Guinea, and flows westward across the South Atlantic. It divides into two branches when it encounters the eastern protrusion of South America at Cape Sào Roque. The northern branch moves along the northeastern coast of Brazil, enters the Caribbean Sea as the Caribbean Current, and also joins with the North Equatorial Current to form the Antilles Current. The southern branch of the South Equatorial Current flows southward along the coast of Brazil and becomes the Brazilian Current.

G. The Caribbean Current. The Caribbean Current is formed from the northern branch of the South Equatorial Current and part of the North Equatorial Current and moves through the Caribbean Sea northward into the Yucatan Channel.

H. The Western Caribbean Gyre. A large gyre is often formed between Nicaragua and Columbia and has been reported as a single large counterclockwise circulation and as two smaller counterclockwise circulations. A similar smaller gyre forms off the coast of Belize and the Mexican state of Quintana Roo.

I. The South Cuba Gyre. The Caribbean gyre that circulates eastward along the southern coast of Cuba and then westward almost to the Cayman Islands is thought by Cuban biologists to entrain spiny lobster phyllosomes and make the southern Cuban populations of spiny lobsters almost a a self-seeding stock.

J. The Yucatan Channel. The narrow neck between Cuba and the Yucatan Peninsula funnels the flow of the Caribbean Current into the Gulf of Mexico to form the Loop Current and also sweeps eastward around Cuba to help form the Florida Current that later becomes the Gulf Stream.The speed of the core flow through the Yucatan Channel varies from about 4 knots in summer to 1 knot in the fall.

K. The Antilles Current. The branch of the North Equatorial Current that flows to the north of the West Indies and the Bahamas is known as the Antilles Current.

L. The Loop Current. As the Caribbean Current pushes through the Yucatan Channel, it invades the eastern Gulf of Mexico and also forms a more or less permanent eddy centered over the western Gulf. The Loop Current expands and contracts during the year bringing water from the Caribbean Current up into the northeastern Gulf in spring and summer and then retreating southward in winter. Large sections of the Loop Current bud from its northern sector, break off in late summer and fall, move toward the west with the Yucatan transport, and then gradually decay.

M. and N. Western Gulf of Mexico Circulation. The surface circulation in the western Gulf of Mexico is also seasonal in direction, speed, and volume. Gyres form and dissipate dependent on the flow of the Loop Current and seasonal winds.

10. **Phyllosome behavior.** Although phyllosomes are understood to be free swimming, planktonic creatures, there are reports of finding them riding on buoys, ropes, and even on oceanographic instruments. I have also observed young phyllosomes clinging for short periods of time to strips of fish and jellyfish in large aquariums. Phillips and Sastry (1980) document, with a photograph by J.G. Halusky, a large *Scyllarus* sp. phyllosoma riding on a moon jellyfish medusa, *Aurelia aurita*, off the coast of Bimini. Also, in an article in the National Geographic Magazine, Brower (1981) presents a night photo of an unidentified phyllosoma riding a small jellyfish. Post larval fish are attracted to floating objects, and

large phyllosomes may find it easy to obtain food organisms in the vicinity of jellyfish and floating debris—my speculation, not documented.

11. Phyllosome development. Lewis (1951) described 11 developmental stages of *Panulirus argus* phyllosomes and assumed that these represented 11 intermolt periods. Baisre (1964) also described 11 stages from larvae taken off Cuba. Although minor morphological variations are sometimes found, the 11 stages described by Lewis are used by lobster scientists as a good working model of the larval life history. Some individual larvae may only go through 9 intermolts, and others may experience 13 (possibly more than 20), depending on environmental conditions; based on existing evidence, 11 phyllosome stages appears to be the normal larval progression.

12. The puerulus. The puerulus stage has been collected in offshore oceanic waters and inshore waters; in shallow waters they have been taken near the bottom, at mid-depths, and on the surface. Sweat (1968) set up a series of three, 12-inch diameter plankton nets on Whale Harbor Bridge in the Florida Keys. The nets were fastened to a frame that lowered into the water and kept one net near the bottom (8 feet), one at mid-depth (4 feet), and one near the surface. The nets were fished over a two year period from 1966 to 1968, and a total of 595 transparent pueruli were collected. The mid-depth net took 418, the surface net 116, and the bottom net 61. All the pueruli were transparent, none had developed any pigment, which indicates that pigment formation does not occur until the puerulus settles for the final time. All the pueruli were also taken on the incoming flood tide. No pueruli were taken in any of the 88 ebb tide samples. This indicates that pueruli ride favorable flooding currents and drop to the bottom to wait out unfavorable ebbing currents. Only 34 phyllosome larvae were taken in this study, and only 10 of these were from the family of spiny lobsters. (The others were Scyllarid lobsters.) No late stage phyllosome larvae were ever taken from inshore waters. Sweat's study and that of Little (1977) and Little and Milano (1980) demonstrated that pueruli move into shallow waters in the Keys on the dark of the moon (new moon) and during all months of the year, although greatest recruitment occurred from January through April.

Calinski (1981) collected and observed thousands (2,751) of pueruli in the shallow waters of Manchoniel Bay, Carriacou, Grenada. Pueruli were collected 10 months of the year, although they were probably present year round. The largest numbers were collected in May, September, and December. Calinski found that pueruli maintained in glass aquaria never swam during the day and remained either clumped together or buried in the carbonate sand substrate of the aquarium. He also observed that almost all (86%) of 1,326 pueruli collected in measured equal nightly sampling efforts were collected in the first hour after occurrence of full darkness. He also observed that no pueruli that were collected swimming near the surface had the advanced pigment development of the first juvenile stage showing under the transparent puerulus exoskeleton. Calinski and Lyons (1983) also observed and described the swimming behavior of pueruli in the natural environment at this location (comment 13).

The Western Australian Rock Lobster, *P. cygnus*, has a larval stage very similar to the Caribbean spiny lobster, and it has been well studied. The early phyllosomes move out over the continental shelf in wind-blown surface currents and are distributed up to 1,500 miles offshore in the Indian Ocean. Once they reach the mid-larval stages, they drop down into deeper oceanic currents and are carried back towards the west Australian coast. There are no surface currents to carry them into coastal waters, so they metamorphose into pueruli and then swim about 25 miles (40 km) against the currents to reach the inshore waters (Phillips and Sastry, 1980). Phillips and Macmillian (1987) did scanning electron microscope studies of the antennal receptors of the puerulus and postpuerulus forms of *P. cygnus*. They found chemoreceptors (spines) and mechanoreceptors (pinnate and plumose setae) along the length of the antennae and postulated that the puerulus is able to sense vibrations, noise, and wave patterns caused by the interactions of ocean and coast. These vibrational clues, and to a lesser extent chemical clues, orient the puerulus toward the coast.

Transparent pieruli of the Caribbean spiny lobster gain pigment and soon molt into the first stage juvenile spiny lobster even when they are maintained in captivity. The average length of time pieruli are maintained before this first molt is 8 to 11 days (Sweat, 1968; Calinski and Lyons, 1983); however, the longest time between capture and first molt reported by Sweat was 26 days. Also, puerulus eye color changes from golden yellow to brown to black as the animal matures, and those pieruli that molt within 10 days or so are captured with black eyes. The length of the puerulus stage, then, is at least 15 days and, at least for some individuals, extends past 26 days. No puerulus captured and maintained in captivity, or even reared through the phyllosome stage in the laboratory and then into and through the puerulus stage (Kittaka and Kimura, 1989), has been observed to feed. Wolfe and Felgenhauer (1991) in an extensive scanning electron microscopy study of the developmental morphology of the mouthparts and foregut of the phyllosoma, puerulus, and juvenile of the Caribbean spiny lobster, found nothing that would prevent feeding, although mouthpart and foregut development appeared incomplete.

Quite probably, given time for travel to shallow coastal waters, the length of the puerulus stage is about 28 to 30 days, perhaps from new moon to new moon. Pieruli settle into the juvenile habitat on the dark of the moon. In fact, Phillips (1975) found that postlarvae of the western rock lobster, *P. cygnus*, no longer settled on their collectors when moonlight intensity rose above 10% of full moonlight.

13. Puerulus behavior. Nighttime swimming behavior in open water and daytime behavior in aquaria of spiny lobster pueruli was observed by Calinski and Lyons (1983). Their observations were made at Manchoniel Bay, Carriacou, Grenada in one meter of water about 25 meters from the shoreline. Calinski (1981) reported that he observed and collected a total of 2,751 pueruli during 185 hours of night-light collecting in this same area. In the light of a kerosene lantern, they were able to measure the swimming speed of pueruli and observe the reaction of these postlarvae to obstructions and turbulence in the water. The pueruli swam straight ahead with the antennae extended forward and the tail extended to the rear. The legs were folded under the body and the swimmeretts (pleopods) propelled the little lobsters at a steady 7 to 10 cm/second. The pueruli swam in the upper 2 cm (right under the surface) of the water in both calm and turbulent conditions. They also described alarm posture in the swimming puerulus when it encountered an object or an unusual turbulence: antennae spread, legs extended, tail fan spread, and slow sinking. The puerulus also exhibited a cautious approach behavior and a rapid backwards retreat. When retreating, the pueruli used their broad tail fan and rapid snaps of the abdomen to propel them backwards, just as juveniles and adults do when disturbed.

Most planktonic and larval stages of marine animals show a positive response to light, that is they move toward rather than away from a light source. Both Calinski (1981) and Rudlow and Little (1981) report that direct observations of swimming pueruli revealed no observed response toward or away from a light source. Rudlow and Little, however, tested lighted and unlighted collectors in the field and found that lighted collectors produced more pueruli by a margin of 3 to 1 than unlighted collectors. Thus collectors designed to produce pueruli for commercial applications may be more effective if equipped with a light source and even perhaps a source of low frequency vibrations.

Calinski and Lyons suggested that the pueruli may be able to detect turbulence from some distance and even distinguish types of habitats from the down-current turbulence patterns that form from various types of structures. During the day, pueruli maintained in aquaria were inactive and either clumped together or buried themselves in the sand with only their antennae extending from the sediments. The swimming behavior of the Caribbean spiny lobster puerulus is similar to the reported behavior of the Western Australian rock lobster and the California spiny lobster puerulus.

14. Juvenile habitat. In the mid 1960's, Ross Witham, a biologist with the Florida Board of Conservation (now the Florida Department of Natural Resources), noted that tiny postlarval spiny lobsters could often be found on marine fouling assemblages (Witham et al., 1964). It was difficult to find and sample these growths, however, so Ross began experimenting with artificial habitats that would attract and hold the newly settled postlarvae. After much trial and error, he found that a structure composed of "leaves" of nylon webbing material hung like the pages of book from a flat floating platform and located on the surface near the shore in shallow water was by far the most productive type of artificial habitat (Witham et al., 1968). Thus, most artificial

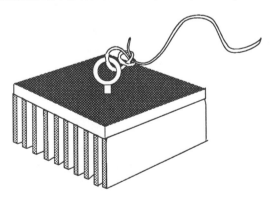

Figure 22. Structure of an artificial "Witham habitat" designed to attract and support settling pueruli and postlarval spiny lobsters.

habitats of similar construction used in spiny lobster research are termed "Witham Habitats". Since this early work by Ross Witham, there have been many reports of early postlarval lobsters being found on fouled buoys, untended boat bottoms, mangrove roots, grass beds, and even in algal masses on shallow lobster traps. The inshore development of most juvenile spiny lobsters is well accepted.

Jim Marx, while he was a graduate student at Florida State University and later as a biologist with the Florida Department of Natural Resources Marine Research Laboratory, studied postlarval lobsters in their natural habitat off Burnt Point on the Gulf of Mexico side of the central Florida Keys. He found concentrated populations of early juvenile lobsters, including newly settled pueruli, on shallow flats with heavy algal growth, primarily the red alga *Laurencia* spp., and large numbers of sponges, gorgonians, and calcareous green algae. These flats are common in the Keys and occur at depths of 2 to 3 meters. According to Jim's calculations, early juvenile lobsters occur in this habitat at a density of one animal for every 36 square meters. The entire area of the habitat, about 2 hectares (4.9 acres), could produce about 2000 juvenile lobsters per year assuming a growth rate of 4 mm CL per month (Marx and Herrnkind, 1985 a,b).

Another study (Herrnkind and Butler, 1986) demonstrated that settling pueruli and early juveniles actively preferred dark, complex habitat structure (clumps of *Laurencia*) over the lighter, simple structure of *Thalassia* seagrass shoots. Young lobsters may even select *Laurencia* as a juvenile habitat through chemical clues, a topic for further research. Algal clumps seem to be the choice habitat for other species of lobsters as well. These preliminary results indicate that small areas of the right kind of near shore habitat can produce large numbers of juvenile recruits to the lobster fishery, thus we should avoid disruption of this habitat through development and pollution. **Destruction of the juvenile habitat is the most permanent way to destroy a fishery resource.**

A population can usually recover from overfishing through management of the fishery, but elimination of the juveniles effectively destroys the foundation of the population. Even the spiny lobster population in the Florida Keys, which is apparently not dependent on its own reproductive potential, could not survive the destruction of the juvenile nursery habitat. Note that a marine habitat can be destroyed through both physical alteration such as dredging and filling and chemical alteration through increase of nutrients and discharge of chemicals (including petroleum spills and pesticide pollution) in the shallow, near shore waters. The overhanging prop roots of red mangrove, *Rhizophora mangle*, are a very important post-larval habitat, and the practice of clear cutting mangroves from the shore in various Caribbean areas may do great damage to the lobster populations.

Juvenile lobsters, however, are also found on offshore reefs. I see them myself with some frequency, and they are far too small, 20 mm CL, to have made the trip from the shoreline to the outer patch reefs. It is possible that the puerulus of some of these small lobsters settled on lobster trap buoys, navigational buoys, and other offshore surface structures and were then able to successfully make the transition to the bottom, or they may have settled directly in the offshore bottom growths instead of moving to the inshore waters. Spiny lobsters also occur on isolated sea mounts surrounded by deep Caribbean waters, such as the Rosalind Bank and Misteriosa Bank. In these cases, the pueruli must have settled in 20 to 60 feet of water. Thus, the spiny lobster is a hardy animal; it has to be to be able to survive a complex life history and intense fisheries. Although almost all pueruli do come to shallow, near shore waters, a few are able to settle and survive in the adult habitat.

15. Growth rate. Lola's growth rate for the first year is based on the observations of Witham et al. (1968), Sweat (1968), the analysis of Lyons et al. (1981), Davis and Dodrill (1989), and my own limited work with postlarval lobsters held in aquaria. Lobsters held under good conditions—abundant food, warm temperatures, and low population densities—grew at an average of 3 to 4 mm CL per month during the first year. It is important to note, however, that this is an average rate of growth and that the animals were maintained in captivity. Individuals showed a remarkable range of growth rates; some grew at only 2 mm CL per month and others at 5 mm CL per month. Growth rates in Florida Bay during 1978-80 (Davis and Dodrill, 1989) for first year lobster were about 3 mm CL per month, which were higher than natural growth rates reported from other areas. The highest growth rates reported by Lellis and Russell (1990) for small captive spiny lobster were about 4.4 mm CL per month at 30 °C. Mike Calinski (personal communication) field tested artificial habitats for postlarval lobsters at Key West, Florida, during the summer of 1983. He marked the post larvae that occupied his floating habitats by clipping a small part of the tail fan after they had spent a month on the habitat and were about 10 mm CL. The mark was distinguishable through the next two or three molts, and he was able to follow growth rates for several months in a "natural" habitat. He recorded growth rates for several individuals at about 8 mm CL per month, an average size of 32.5 mm CL four months after settling. These growth rates are much more rapid than any previously recorded and may be near the maximum for this species. Growth rate between the time of settling and the size at possible first capture in traps, roughly 40 mm CL (1⁹⁄₁₆ inches), is not well known and is evidently highly variable. Abundance of food, water temperature, and genetic potential combine in various ways to speed or slow actual growth. Average growth for a population of young lobsters may vary considerably from year to year depending on environmental factors and population densities. Lola's growth in the first year, 55 mm CL, may be a little below average for spiny lobsters in an excellent natural environment, but I believe that this rate of growth is representative of most of Florida's spiny lobsters.

16. Growth. Growth in spiny lobsters and other crustaceans can be achieved only by shedding the old exoskeleton,
a process called ecdysis or, more commonly, molting. This is
a complex and dangerous way to grow, but the hard, ar-
mored shell it allows the animal to maintain is well worth
the disadvantages. Molting allows growth, but growth does
not necessarily take place at each molt. The amount of
growth at each molt is dependent on environmental conditions and the health of the individual lobster. Molting is a
very complex physiological process in crustacea and involves every organ system. Most of the information on lobster molting and growth was developed through study of
the American lobster, *Homarus americanus.* There are a number of studies on molting in spiny lobster, such as Travis
(1954), Lipcius and Herrnkind (1982), Quackenbush and
Herrnkind (1983). Molting and growth in lobsters is discussed in detail by Aiken (1980).

17. Escape from traps. Do lobsters escape from wooden
slat, top entry traps once they enter them? Opinions range
between two extreme positions. First, there are those who
feel that lobsters can enter and leave traps as they wish—in
effect, using the trap as a daytime den. The other extreme is
that once in the trap, the lobster is caught for good and can
never leave alive. The correct answer, of course, lies somewhere in between, and the only way to find it is through
careful observation and scientific experimentation.

Miller and Sutherland (1978) observed the behavior of
short lobsters in standard wood slat traps with a remote
underwater television setup and observed actual escape
from the trap only when the lobsters climbed on the bait
containers adjacent to the entrance funnel. Lyons and Kennedy (1981) discussed the results of three previous studies
on escape rates of lobsters from traps and found that these
studies indicated escape rates of about 1% per day. The
observations for these studies, however, were conducted
during the day and did not eliminate the possibility that the

lobsters were leaving the trap to forage during the night and returning to the same trap during the day.

Further experimental work conducted by the Florida Department of Natural Resources (Hunt, 1981) with tagged lobster placed in traps and monitored night and day, showed that small lobster (CL less than 66 mm) escaped from the traps more easily (53% over a 5 day period) than larger lobsters. Sub-legal lobsters (CL between 66 and 75 mm) escaped at a lesser rate (20% over a 5 day period) and only 12% of the legal size lobsters escaped over the same 5 day period. The overall escape rate was 15%, a daily rate of about 3%. Obviously, some lobsters escape from traps, and the smaller lobsters have the best chance of escape. The evidence also indicates, however, that the majority of near legal and legal size lobsters do not escape but remain in traps until they die from starvation or are taken by the fishery (see comment 19).

18. Shorts in traps. The practice of using "short" (sub-legal size) lobsters for "bait" in south Florida is legal (early 1991) and practically universal among commercial fishermen. Short lobsters are placed in the traps because they are very effective at attracting wandering lobsters that are seeking the protective shelter of a den. The catch advantage of a trap "baited" with live, short lobsters over an empty or food baited trap occurs only during the initial precatch period before a lobster enters the unoccupied trap. In areas with large populations of lobsters, this initial precatch period is short. When the availability of lobsters in a particular area is low, short lobsters held in traps are most effective as attractants since the precatch period of an empty trap may be quite long. If trap numbers in the Florida Keys are greatly reduced by the new trap certificate program, then the advantage of traps baited with live, short lobsters over food baited traps should greatly diminish.

At present, given that sublegal and legal size lobsters are no longer abundant in the Florida Keys, the advantages to the fishermen of using short lobsters are quite significant. First, traps "baited" with already captured lobsters are most productive in intensively fished areas. Second, short lobsters are an available and inexpensive "bait" that do not attract stone crabs to the trap. And third, unfortunately, this practice gives those fisherman that break the law and sell undersize lobsters an excuse to legally keep 100 short lobsters (the maximum allowed (EEZ) by Federal law). The studies conducted by the Florida Department of Natural Resources Marine Reseach Institute in the 1980's indicated that use of short lobsters as attractors increased catches 3 to 1 over traps without shorts, that mortality of short lobsters used as attractors is close to 50%, and that perhaps as much as 50% of the average potential commercial landings are lost to the fishery by use of shorts in traps (Heatwole et al., 1988).

Obviously, the practice of using short lobsters as attractants is very harmful to the fishery. Fishermen are trading increased catches now for depletion of the resource in future years (and these "future years" are coming up quickly). Lyons and Kennedy (1981) and Hunt et al. (1986) figured that because approximately 500,000 traps are used in the south Florida fishery (current 1991 estimates are 800,000 to over 1,000,000 traps), over one million short lobsters are retained in traps at any given time during the entire season if no more than 3 shorts are used per trap. We can also figure that the life of a short lobster in a trap is two months (the average is probably much less than that) and take the length of the season as eight months (no one catches much the ninth month anyway). Thus, short lobsters are "turned over" in the traps about four times a season, an annual legal "use" of two to six million short lobsters.

This means that at least 25% to 33% (probably considerably more than 50% at the current number of active traps in the fishery) of the potential catch for the next season is held in traps to attract the legal lobsters of the current season. Now if these retained short lobsters suffered no injury and were all released to enter the fishery again when they reached legal size, then this would be a good practice, one that benefits the fisherman and does not damage the resource. If, however, these short lobsters die in traps or enter the illegal market, then the fishery is rapidly eating up its own future.

So what actually happens to these short lobsters that wind up as unwitting sirens to their elders? First of all, if a fisherman can make good, legal use of a short and increase his catch by keeping it in a trap, then a short lobster won't get tossed back into the sea unless it is dead or in a trap. If they are still alive when the trap is pulled, they are retained in the trap or perhaps placed in a different trap; thus, their fate is sealed unless they manage to escape from the trap.

This, in effect, creates a fishery with no minimum size since most of these shorts are lost to the future fishery. These undersize lobsters are, or can be, adversely affected by the following events.

1. Injuries sustained in handling.

2. Exposure to air or poor holding conditions during the time they are held aboard the boat.

3. Starvation and high densities in the trap.

4. Predation by triggerfish and octopi in the trap.

5. Loss to poachers.

Lyons and Kennedy (1981), Hunt et al. (1986), Heatwole et al. (1988), and Vermeer (1987) present data that help evaluate the effects of this practice. All of the above factors result in increased mortality of undersized lobster. In one experiment (Hunt et al., 1986), lobsters were held out of water for periods of ½ , 1, 2, and 4 hours and were then sealed in traps to prevent escape or entry of other lobsters. The traps were set out and checked each week for survivors.

Within one month, the average mortality rate for all lobsters held out of water for ½ hour or longer was 26.3%. About 42% of observed mortality occurred during the first week, indicating that exposure was the primary cause of death. Vermeer (1987) measured desiccation rates, hemolymph pH, lactic acid, and ammonia concentrations in spiny lobsters exposed to air for up to 2 hours. He found that lactic acid levels increased 11 fold, pH decreased from 7.91 to 7.40, and ammonia concentrations almost doubled. These conditions, very close to the lethal limits, reverted to normal 24 hours after the lobsters were replaced in water. However, the behavior of the exposed lobsters was abnormal and indicated that serious nervous damage had occurred. It may be this damage to the nervous system that causes the latent mortality associated with exposure, rather than the short term exposure itself.

Kennedy (1981) reports in a study on catch rates of lobster traps baited with shorts that the return rate of tagged and released lobsters not used as bait was 17.9%, whereas the average return rate of lobsters used as "bait" or "attractants" was 9.8%. The bait lobsters also grew significantly less (26.7%) than the non bait lobsters.

As of this writing, late spring 1991, the commercial fishery is still permitted to use shorts as attractants in traps, but the fishermen must now carry livewells on their vessels and maintain the short lobsters in seawater during the time they are kept on the vessel. A maximum of 50 short lobsters or one per trap whichever is greater, may be held aboard a commercial vessel in state waters, 100 per vessel in federal waters. A live well containing at least ¾ gallons of aerated, circulating seawater per lobster must be used for the shorts. When fishermen comply with this measure, it insures less immediate mortality and longer survival of short lobsters confined to traps. Warm salt water looses oxygen rapidly, so it is very important that the water in live wells is recirculated, and changed and aerated often. Lobsters die more quickly in hot, unoxygenated water than under a damp, shaded cloth. Although this measure is helpful, it does not resolve the problem of legal use and illegal harvest of short lobsters. The summary comment of Lyons and Kennedy (1981) is still valid.

"The evidence indicates enormous losses (63-83%, discounting recreational and unreported legal harvest) to the legal fishery attributable either to illegal harvest of shorts or to fishery-induced mortality. If both practices are abated, data indicate that approximately twice the number of lobsters should be available for legal harvest."

The future for Florida spiny lobsters, however, is getting a little brighter. The trap certificate program was established in Florida law as of July 1, 1991. It is the intent of the trap certificate program to greatly reduce the number of traps in the fishery, thus eliminating excessive fishing effort and restoring the resource. If the trap certificate program does not solve the problems in the fishery by August 1, 1998, then the laws on commercial fishing for spiny lobster may prohibit the use of shorts in traps as attractants, and a 2⅛ inch wide escape gap may be required in traps (see Chapter 6). The most recent Florida laws and regulations on the spiny lobster fishery are reproduced in Appendix A.

19. Starvation in traps. Lobsters, like all other animals, must eat to live and grow. There is very little for a trapped lobster to eat and eventually, in the absence of food, the lobster must use its own muscle tissue for energy, and when this happens the lobster soon dies. Starvation in a lobster is not very noticeable, however, because the hard exoskeleton of the lobster hides the loss of soft tissue. One cannot see a lobster's ribs or notice a shrunken belly or bone thin limbs. In July of 1982, shortly before the start of the lobster season, I was diving in shallow water just offshore of the middle Florida Keys. I came upon a trap, intact except for the loss of the buoy, that had obviously been in the water since at least the end of the season the previous March. The trap was still functioning, and there were 4 lobsters trapped within it. I opened the top and released and photographed the lobsters. Each lobster immediately went to a nearby bed of turtle grass and began running the blades of grass through their mouth parts, evidently feeding on tiny growths of hydroids and other organisms that occupied the surface of the grass blades. They were so intent on this feeding activity that they made little attempt to avoid positioning for photographs.

I found a similar trap in August of 1983 on the Gulf side of the Marathon area. This trap was also lacking a buoy and had also been in the water since at least the close of the season the previous spring. This trap contained three lobster, all legal size. I removed the top, left it next to the trap, and collected the lobsters. One of the lobsters swam actively around the inside of the trap before I caught it and then fell over and died when I placed it on the bottom near the trap. When the tail was split, the musculature of the abdomen was thin and wasted, a mere strip of muscle extending down the center of the abdomen—an apparent case of terminal starvation in the lost trap. I don't know how long it takes for a lobster to starve to death in a trap, there must be quite a range depending on size, initial condition, number of lobsters in the trap, location of the trap, and the amount of food that each lobster can find; but I would estimate that few lobsters can survive more than one or, at most, two months.

20. Regeneration of appendages. Lobsters, like other crustaceans, have the ability to lose a leg or an antenna, immediately seal off the injury, and survive to molt and grow back the lost appendage. This regeneration is costly, however. Energy that would have gone into growth, travel, and reproduction is channeled instead into creating a new leg or antenna. Loss of antennae, especially both at the same time, also deprives the lobster of its chief means of defense, and loss of legs limits mobility and even reproductive success if certain legs are lost. Lobsters are frequently injured by recreational fishermen that dive and attempt to capture lobsters by hand. They often escape a divers grip at the expense of one or both antennae and a leg or two. Davis and Dodrill (1980) examined 1,041 lobsters captured by recreational fishermen in the Everglades National Park and found that 78% were injured, with 57% sustaining multiple injuries.

Short lobsters captured and released by divers and bully netters also frequently lose appendages and may be captured and released several times in intensively fished areas. Injuries also occur in the commercial fishery, and injured shorts that escape from traps become part of the lobster population that has fishery caused injuries. Thus, there are three important questions concerning injured lobsters in an intensive fishery.

- 1. What percentage of the population sustains injuries?

- 2. How much more susceptible to predation and death are injured lobsters?

- 3. What is the effect of injury on the growth rate of lobsters that survive injury?

These are not easy questions to answer, and any bias toward exploitation or preservation of the resource can greatly sway opinion.

Davis (1981) and Lyons et al. (1981) explored these questions through scientific experimentation and analysis. According to these and other studies, the injury rate of lobsters in Florida waters is, as one might expect, least at the beginning of the fishing season and greatest at the end of the season. Also a common sense conclusion is that areas with intense recreational and commercial fisheries have a greater incidence of injured lobsters than areas seldom frequented by divers and commercial fishermen. Davis (1981) examined 7,643 spiny lobsters in southern Biscayne Bay from February 1976 to December 1977. He found that about 50% of the lobsters were missing several legs and/or antennae by the end of the open season in early April. The injury rate then fell to 30% by the time the season opened in August. In contrast, less than 25% of the lobsters examined in an area closed to all fishing (Dry Tortugas) had similar injuries.

These injuries were probably caused by natural predators or difficult molts (or perhaps, illegal fishing activity or movement of injured lobsters into the area). In the Lyons et al. (1981) study, a total of 19,180 spiny lobsters were captured between April 1, 1978 and March 31, 1979 at stations on the Atlantic and Florida Bay side of the Keys. Old injuries were observed at rates ranging from 22.4% in April to 7.7% in July (legal and sub-legal sized lobsters combined). Monthly rates of observed old injuries averaged 11.5% for sublegal lobsters and 9% for legal lobsters.

One very interesting observation in the Lyons study is that the injury rates for legal and sublegal lobsters were quite similar. Now if all legal lobsters that are caught are removed from the fishery, whether they are injured or not, and if all sublegal lobsters are returned to the water,

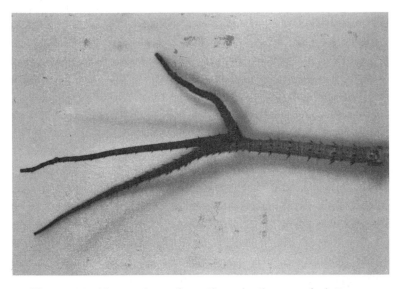

Figure 23. Unusual configurations in the exoskeleton sometimes develop if the bud where regrowth of the appendage occurs is damaged. Although such resulting malformations usually limit the survival of the lobster, some unsual specimens survive. In the above case, one antenna on a spiny lobster exibited a trifurcate tip.

whether they are injured or not, then the incidence of injured sublegal lobsters should increase significantly during
the fishing season, and this did not occur. The capture rates
for injured legal and sublegal lobsters remained in the vicinity of 10% throughout the study. **Thus, the data indicate
that sub-legal lobsters are removed from the fishery just
as rapidly as legal lobsters, and so, as far as the lobster
population is concerned, small lobsters are not protected
by a minimum legal size.**

Davis estimated that 22% of the injured lobsters died as
a result of their injuries. Obviously, severely injured lobsters
(loss of both antennae and several legs) are less likely to
survive than those that lose only one or two appendages.
There are no clear data, however, that can tell us what percentage of injured lobsters actually die in the wild because
of their injuries, and the use of sublegal lobsters by the legal
and illegal fisheries makes an estimation based on actual
data impossible to derive. There are figures, however, on the
effects of injuries on growth rates. Davis (1981) reports that
lobsters suffering minor injuries, loss of one or two appendages, and those surviving greater injuries, loss of nine or
more appendages, grew at the same depressed rate. Thus,
even a minor injury causes changes in growth patterns that
significantly reduce growth.

According to Davis' estimates, uninjured lobsters starting at 50 mm CL at 2 years of age in southern Biscayne Bay
grew at a rate of 0.51 mm CL/week and reached legal size in
51 weeks. Injured lobsters grew at the rate of 0.31 mm
CL/week and required 84 weeks to reach legal size—a
growth rate reduction of 33 weeks, about 40%. It should be
noted that these growth rates are rather slow when compared to other studies, but this population of lobsters was
stressed at the time of the study by an intensive fishery and
an extremely cold winter. An injured lobster that survives
can lose almost a year of growth and either reproduce at a
small size or delay migration to the outer reef for another
year.

21. Lobster movement. Herrnkind (1980, 1985) presents an excellent summary of patterns of movement of spiny lobsters. Spiny lobster movement has been studied by monitoring the commercial catch, tagging and recapture of individual lobsters, direct observation by divers, observations from submersibles and undersea habitats, ultrasonic telemetry, and even analysis of behavior of captive lobsters. Dr. Herrnkind has identified a pattern of spiny lobster movement he terms nomadism. This is more or less random movement, mostly by immature lobsters, but also exhibited by adults, where the individual lobster may move several miles or even a hundred miles in response to particular biological and/or environmental conditions. Although most spiny lobster movement takes place in nighttime hours, Glaholt (1990) reports observation of free ranging lobsters during daytime, mostly in the afternoon.

This type of movement is distinguished from migration in that it is not a cyclic movement of a large portion of the population. It is a behavioral pattern of roaming movement as contrasted to a pattern of residency in a particular area. Immature lobsters seem to commonly utilize nomadic behavior to move offshore from the juvenile nursery grounds. Ejection from a den by the activity of divers, intrusion of a predator or a competitor, and overpopulation of lobsters may induce nomadic movement. Large males may also use nomadic behavior to move inshore in the fall after the mating season. Herrnkind and Lipcius (1989) suggest that large lobsters may also move into shallow areas to molt. I have occasionally seen large males, 4 pounds or more, in shallow waters during this time of year.

22. Lobster migration. Caribbean spiny lobsters generally exhibit three migratory phases. The first is the movement of the transition stage, the puerulus, from offshore waters to the shallow, benthic nursery grounds. The second is the movement of the immature lobster to the deeper water patch reef and grass bed habitats, and the third is movement of mature and nearly mature lobsters to the offshore reefs where most mating and spawning takes place. One of the best ways to actually document the movement of a marine animal is to put a tag on it; record the date, size, and location; and release it to resume a normal life. With luck, and a cooperative commercial and recreational fishery, the tagged animals will be returned with information on where and when they were caught.

The marine scientist can then learn a great deal about the movement and growth of the animals and the intensity of the fishery when data from the returned fish or lobster is analyzed. Spiny lobsters are difficult to tag because when they molt, everything attached to, or painted on, their exoskeleton is discarded. Warner, Combs, and Gregory (1977) and Davis (1981) successfully tagged spiny lobsters with a spaghetti tag inserted into the abdominal muscle through the membrane between the carapace and the tail (abdomen). This tag usually remains in place during molting since the lobster leaves the old shell through the opening that develops at this point.

A total of 6,362 spiny lobsters were tagged from June 1975 to August 1976 during the Warner study. Of these tagged lobsters, 791 (12.4%) tags were returned by commercial and recreational fishermen. The return rate at the beginning of the season was 25%, a reflection of the great intensity of the spiny lobster fishery in the Florida Keys. Long distance movements (4.3 nautical miles or more) were described in this paper from four release sites: two north of Key West a few miles out in the Gulf of Mexico and two a few miles east of Key West in the Atlantic Ocean. One of the Atlantic sites was nearshore and the other was on an offshore patch reef.

The results were very interesting. The great majority (87%) of the long distance lobsters from the Gulf of Mexico sites moved rapidly and directly west-southwesterly toward the Atlantic reefs and the Dry Tortugas. The average length of movement was over 22 nautical miles. Tagged lobsters in the long distance category in the Atlantic moved offshore toward, and along, the reef tract in both westerly and easterly directions. The average length of movement was 9 nautical miles. This study demonstrated the movement of maturing lobsters from inshore and shallow bank environments toward the deep water reefs and identified the general pattern of movement for lobsters in the Key West area. Although it's a good bet that this pattern of movement is typical in this area, additional tagging studies conducted in other years and nearby areas are needed to provide better knowledge of spiny lobster movement in the Florida Keys.

Occasionally, in the fall of the year, great lobster "walks" are reported. Large numbers of lobsters gather together and move single file in long queues, moving with apparent purpose day and night toward unknown destinations. Fishermen who find lobsters during these walks strike a bonanza and are able to fill their trawls, traps, bags, and boats with this high priced crustacean. The occurrence of these walks has always stimulated speculation on why the lobsters walk and where they are going. In recent years, the physics, behavior, response to environmental stimuli, and patterns of movement of lobsters undergoing mass migration in these queues has been studied in a series of papers by Dr. William Herrnkind and his students at Florida State University.

Kanciruk and Herrnkind (1978) reported on field and laboratory studies of autumnal mass migrations of spiny lobsters at Bimini, Bahamas. They found that declines in water temperature due to passage of northern cold fronts, along with the wave surge that accompanies these stormy weather fronts, seems to act as the triggering stimulus for migration. The migrating lobsters form queues on the shallow Bahama banks and move westward toward the Gulf Stream edge and then southward during the 2 to 3 week period of migratory movement. The queues break up at the end of the migration, and the lobsters move individually out on the reef or back up on the banks. They also photographically documented a queue of lobsters forming a protective pod when disturbed by divers. In a later study in the vicinity of Lee Stocking Island in the eastern Bahamas, Herrnkind and Lipcius (1989) link the offshore movement of young adult spiny lobsters to onset of reproductive activity and summer molting that precedes reproductive maturity.

Bill and Herrnkind (1976) studied hydrodynamic performance of queuing lobsters and analyzed the benefits in drag reduction a queue of lobsters realized over movement of individual lobsters. Preserved lobsters were wired together to form queues, and the force required to pull these queues through a tank of water was measured. Drag reduction from queue formation was most prominent at speeds of 35 cm/sec., which is the speed that approximates the sustained walking speed of queuing lobsters. Their conclusion is that queuing conserves energy, and that this behavior developed during the evolution of *Panulirus argus* in response to a need for migration. Queuing may also function to keep migrating lobsters together, enabling the group to mount an effective defense against predators and to maintain the integrity of the group during the migratory period.

These migrations apparently do not serve to move the lobsters to the reefs before the spawning season, nor do they disperse the lobsters after spawning. According to Herrnkind and Kanciruk (1978) the most logical reason for these mass migrations:

"....is a concentrated seasonal movement adapted to moving the population from the shallow banks, subject to severe cooling, to the oceanic fringe where conditions are suitable to overwintering."

Especially in ages past, when lower water levels and severe winters accompanied glaciation, such seasonal movements would have had great survival value (Herrnkind, 1980, 1985). Even now, severe cold fronts may quickly drop shallow water (Florida Bay) temperatures below 53 °F, about the survival limit for spiny lobsters, and rapid movement to warmer offshore waters enhances survival of lobster populations.

23. Predation. Kanciruk (1980) provides photographic documentation of a triggerfish attack on a lone spiny lobster and also pictures defensive pod formation and describes this behavior as being effective against attacks by triggerfish. John Hunt (in preparation) describes predation on trapped spiny lobster by both grey and queen triggerfish.

24. Sound generation. Phillips et al. (1980) describe the structure and function of the sound generating organs in spiny lobsters and discuss the types of sounds generated and the apparent purpose of the various sounds. One species of spiny lobster, *Palinurus elephas*, produces a mating call during the mating season, but this type of sound has not been recorded for *Panulirus argus*.

25. Lobster, Morays, and Octopi. The relationship between moray eels, spiny lobsters, and octopi described in the text is speculative. Kanciruk (1980) describes such a relationship reported for an Indian Ocean spiny lobster and speculates that the Caribbean spiny lobster and the green and spotted moray may also enjoy this mutually beneficial association. He observes that spotted and green morays often share the same den with spiny lobsters, and although they are quite capable of feeding on spiny lobsters, they apparently do not. Aiken (1977), however, reports observing a spotted moray, *Gynothorax moringa*, preying on juvenile spiny lobster.

If such an association does exist, the spiny lobster gains a measure of protection, and the moray gains the possibility of a meal of octopus. The apparent relationship between these three species in Mediterranean waters is noted in the ancient writings of Aristotle, Pliny the Elder, Plutarch, Oppian, and Aelian. Even a mosaic discovered in ancient Pompeii depicts a struggle between an octopus and a spiny lobster—and a moray eel is observing the fight with great interest (Almog-Shtayer, 1988). Of course, ecological relationships on coral reefs are very complex and a real interdependence between morays and spiny lobsters may or may not exist. However, there is a strong enough association to make one very wary of reaching for a lobster without first looking for a moray.

26. Mating behavior. The description of mating behavior was drawn from personal observations of lobsters mating in 300 gallon tanks, 4 feet by 8 feet by 2 feet in depth, under laboratory conditions. Three females and one male were maintained, but only the largest female mated with the male. They were about the same size, approximately 85 mm CL, and the male usually made several unsuccessful attempts at grasping the female before he swung underneath her to complete the mating. It is quite possible that a large male may physically manipulate a smaller female into a position underneath himself to complete the mating. A light grey spermatophore was placed on the female, but she lost it after a few days.

Mating behavior in *P. argus* was studied by Lipcius et al. (1983) and Lipcius and Herrnkind (1985). Mating behavior of lobsters in Bahamian waters was observed and filmed in natural surroundings, and these observations correspond with observations of mating behavior in aquaria. Large males are apparently disproportionately important in the reproductive process in that they engage the females to the exclusion of smaller males. Mating was most frequent during times of long day lengths and warm temperatures. Although most mating interactions occur at dawn and dusk, there is substantial mating activity during daylight and night hours.

Sutcliffe (1952, 1953) observed that Bermuda spiny lobsters spawned at least twice each season. He was working with large, fully mature females, and repetitive spawning in favorable environments may be common in these large females. In the Florida Keys, I have observed large, mature ovaries in female lobsters that have recently spawned, and unless the mature oocytes were resorbed, a second spawning within a few weeks was probable.

27. How old is that lobster? This is one of the most common, and one of the most difficult questions to answer. Since spiny lobsters grow by molting, and since the growth increment at each molt is variable, and molting does not necessarily occur at regular intervals, size is not a reliable indicator of age. The hard parts of a lobster are also only as old as the last molt. The skeletal parts do not grow by increment, so there are no rings or layers to count to estimate age. When you add growth variables caused by injuries, sex, frequency of egg bearing in females, and differing environmental conditions, it's easy to see how individual lobsters can keep their age a secret. We can develop an estimate of growth rates of populations by repetitive sampling of age classes in the population, measurement of the growth increment after a molt, observations on the frequency of molting, growth of tagged individuals, and qualified observations on growth of captive individuals. Munro (1974) presents a good analysis of growth rates reported from many various studies, and Haughton and Shaul (1989) review growth rate studies and report on growth rates in Jamaican populations of spiny lobsters.

Lola's growth rate is a composite from studies using all these methods. I'm sure that lobsters settling during warm months in favorable locations grow more rapidly through the juvenile stage than those settling in colder waters with unfavorable food supplies. Uninjured lobsters also attain larger sizes more rapidly than injured lobsters, and males tend to grow faster then females. I feel that Lola's growth rate, based on existing scientific knowledge, is well within the central "average" range for Florida Keys lobsters and is representative of a "typical" lobster in this area.

CHAPTER TWO

TAXONOMY AND MORPHOLOGY
The Family Tree
Form and Function

The Family Tree

Let us begin at the very beginning. The oldest rocks known on Earth are about 3.8 billion years old. These ancient strata, found in Greenland, are so altered by heat and pressure that there is no evidence of any fossils that may have once been present. Fossil bacteria have been found, however, in rocks from South Africa that are 3.4 billion years old. Microscopic fossils in these early rocks show that simple life forms developed soon after the earth cooled and liquid water was present. For two billion years life on earth consisted only of simple cells similar to present day bacteria and blue-green algae.

At the end of that unimaginably vast stretch of time called the Precambrian Era, life had diversified into a limited number of soft-bodied animals: a few jellyfish, soft corals, and simple worms. Then, at the beginning of the Cambrian Epoch, 600 million years ago, the development of life suddenly accelerated. It was as if a type of critical mass had been achieved, and life suddenly exploded in a diversity of form and abundance. Within 10 to 20 million years—a

short time geologically speaking—precursors of all the
major phyla of invertebrates, and a few odd creatures that
have no modern descendants, appear in the fossil bearing
rocks. Even a lancelet-like animal, foreshadowing the cor-
dates, has been found in mid-Cambrian rocks from the Bur-
gess Shale deposits in Canada.

A group of animals called the Pseudocrustaceans are
present in early Cambrian rocks. They ranged in length from
½ to 4 inches (10 to 105 mm) and had appendages similar to
trilobites and stalked eyes similar to crustaceans. These animals were probably close to the stem that gave rise to both
trilobites and more advanced crustaceans. Fossils of primitive crustaceans are present in later Cambrian rocks in great
numbers and many types. The best known are the Trilobites—complex, three lobed Crustacea that were very numerous 550 million years ago in the mid Cambrian, hit their
peak in the Ordovician, diminished in the Devonian, and
finally died out in the great Permian Extinction.

To say that the fossil record is imperfect, especially as far
back as hundreds of millions of years, is quite an understate-
ment. For the most part, only shallow water, marine fauna
can fossilize; thus the fossil evidence tells us very little about
ancient deep water fauna. We can, however, put together a
probable evolutionary history of modern lobsters through
study and comparison of fossil and modern forms. Two
lines of ancient crustaceans, the Glypheoidea and the Penaeidea, entered the Permotriassic period about 230 million
years ago. This is the time of the great Permian Extinction
when life on Earth went through very great and very rapid
changes. For some reason, and there are a number of possibilities, about half the families of shallow water marine invertebrates became extinct within only a few million years.
Extinctions and development of many new species occurred
in all major groups. The earliest actual lobster fossils date
from this time.

There are four major families of modern shallow water
lobsters: the clawed lobsters (Nephropidae), the spiny lob-

sters (Palinuridae), the slipper lobsters (Scyllaridae), and the coral or furry lobsters (Synaxidae). The slipper, coral, and spiny lobsters are all closely related; all have the long-lived, phyllosome larvae; and all three families evidently arose from the Glypheoidea/Pemphicidae stem during the early Triassic period of extinction and regeneration. These early Triassic lobsters were known only from fossils and were thought to be long extinct. A new species of deep water lobster, however, *Neoglyphea inopinata*, was found in 1976 from a small area 190 meters deep just off the Philippines. The modern species of this ancient line is little changed from the exoskeletal remains found fossilized in rock.

The coral lobsters, Synaxidae, (also spelled Synaxiidae) are morphologically similar to some fossil genera, and they are considered the most primitive of modern lobsters. This family has only a single genus, *Palinurellus*, with two species. They were once included with spiny lobsters, Palinuridae, but since they have many characteristics in common with slipper lobsters and deep-sea Polychelidae as well as the spiny lobsters, they are now placed in a separate family. Robertson (1968 a) discussed the evolution of lobsters from the standpoint of larval morphology and considers *Palinurellus* to be derived from an ancestor that had already acquired the larval form characteristic of the slipper lobsters.

The earliest spiny lobsters appear in the Jurassic, and the earliest slipper lobsters are found later on in the Cretaceous. There is a fossil lobster that may be intermediate between the spiny and slipper lobsters because of its short, club-shaped antennae. This genus, *Cancrinus*, is found in the Liassic rocks, a hard bluish freestone from the oldest Jurassic strata found in Europe. Additional evidence of the relationship between the slipper and the primitive spiny lobsters can be found in their larval development. The most primitive genus of the spiny lobsters, *Jasus* of the Silentes group, and the slipper lobster genera *Scyllarides* and *Ibacus* first hatch into a prephyllosoma stage, the naupliosoma, before

quickly molting into the first phyllosoma stage. They also
have other larval characteristics in common. Thus, the slipper lobsters are probably derived from the primitive stem of
the spiny lobsters. Neoteny, the retention of larval or juvenile characteristics into the reproductively mature adult,
may have been the evolutionary mechanism that transformed an early palinurid *Jasus*-like species into the ancestor
of the scyllarids.

The clawed lobsters and their relatives developed from
the Astacidea, which have features in common with both
early stems, the Glypheoidea and the Penaeidea; thus the
origin of the clawed lobsters is uncertain, and few studies on
the evolution of the Nephropidae have been accomplished.
The fossil record of the Nephropidae extends back to the
mid-Jurassic and fossil remains do show that the genera
Metanephrops and *Nephrops* have been separate since the
Cretaceous.

George and Main (1967) studied the evolution of modern spiny lobsters from the Pemphicidae of the Triassic to
recent times. The tree of postulated palinurid evolution in
Figure 24 was modeled from their work. They postulated
that two major groups of modern spiny lobsters, the
Stridentes and the Silentes, developed from a primitive
pemphicid stock early in the Triassic. The primitive Silentes
are represented by the modern genera *Projasus* and *Jasus* and
lack the stridulating (noise making) apparatus of the
Stridentes. *Panulirus, Justitia, Palinurus, Palinustus,
Linuparus,* and *Puerulus* have a stridulating apparatus (see
Figure 18, p 69) and are capable of using sound for communication, an evolutionary advance.

Some spiny lobsters, especially the deep water genera,
have existed through immense periods of time with very
little change. *Linuparus* is a good example. There is a narrow
54 mile zone of fossil bearing rock in South Dakota that
dates back 90 million years to when the Gulf of Mexico
reached north into Canada. Fossils of *Linupaus* are common
in this area, and although only three species now exist, they

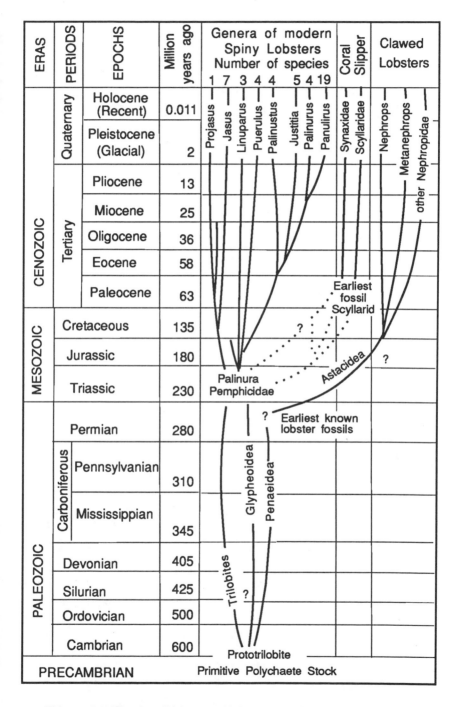

Figure 24. The fossil history of lobsters, as best we know it.

are little changed from their fossil relatives of 90 million years ago. *Panulirus,* the most recent genus of spiny lobsters, has 19 modern species and occurs in shallow waters where environmental changes are most significant. Separation of one population into two or more different species often occurs when a geological barrier develops and the range of a single species is divided. Different climatic and biological conditions may exist in each new area, and the separated populations may be pressured to evolve in different ways. If the separate populations become so biologically different that they can no longer interbreed, and if geological changes bring them together again, they may well become coexisting, separate species. And as separate but similar species, the process of natural selection pushes these species toward biological divergence or extinction.

The four species groups in the recently evolved genus of spiny lobsters, *Panulirus,* developed during the glacial Pleistocene Epoch and may reflect the four major glaciations of this period. Sea levels varied greatly during the glaciations, and shallow water populations were subject to geological isolation and extreme climatic changes during the Pleistocene. Thus the species that is the major focus of this book, the Caribbean spiny lobster, *Panulirus argus,* is a relatively recent species. It evolved during the glaciations of the Pleistocene less than 2 million years ago, within a genus that formed in the late Miocene, about 15 million years ago. The evolutionary history of its kind is rooted in the late Permian, 230 million years ago, and then stretches back to the Pseudocrustaceans at the dawn of the Crustacea in the early Cambrian. Knowledge of the evolutionary history of lobsters is very important, for it is fundamental to our understanding of the biology, ecology, and fishery of these tropical lobsters.

The Common and Scientific Name

In the Florida Keys, the Bahamas, and the English speaking Caribbean when one asks a friend to come along and look for bugs it usually means something quite different than when a New York City apartment dweller says the same thing. Likewise, a crawfish dinner in New Orleans, Louisiana, is not the same as a crawfish dinner in Key West, Florida. Besides bug and crawfish, the succulent spiny lobster is also called crayfish, rock lobster, common spiny lobster, Florida lobster, Caribbean spiny lobster, West Indian spiny lobster, Bahamian spiny lobster, langouste blanche (French), langosta (Spanish), aragosta (Italian), lagosta (Portuguese), jastog (Yugoslavian), langoesten (Dutch), langusten (Scandinavian), humrar (Icelandic), and a few other lesser known names as well.

To confuse the situation even more, different common names may be applied to the same species in different geographical areas, and the same common name may be applied to different species from the same or different areas. And when creative efforts from restaurant menus are tossed into the nomenclatural pot, there's no way one can know for sure what species is on the dinner plate from the name alone. Generally, however, people in one area use the same common name for a popular species, and confusion occurs mainly with geographical distance or as language changes over time. Confusion from common names is, well, quite common. A dolphin, for example, can be either a fish or a mammal. *Coryphaena hippurus*, however, can only be a specific species of fish, and *Tursiops truncatus* can only be a certain species of marine mammal.

Obviously, if we want to seriously study the natural history and biology of a plant or animal, we have to be absolutely sure that the name we use refers to the same species wherever and whenever it occurs. This is where Carolus Linnaeus and the science of taxonomy come into the picture. (Taxonomy, incidentally, is not taxidermy, which is the art of preserving animals in life-like pose.) Taxonomy is the science of classification of plants and animals and includes giving newly discovered species a scientific name. Latin is the basic language of taxonomy. Latin is used only because Linnaeus and other early naturalists wrote in Latin, but this tradition is very useful since Latin is not a modern language and is not subject to changes in meaning due to current usage.

A species may have many common names, but it can have only one scientific name. The scientific name of the Caribbean spiny lobster is *Panulirus argus* (Latreille). The scientific name is made up of the genus and species name and is always printed in italics. The name of the author of the original description of the species, in this case Latreille, follows the Latin name given to the organism. Parentheses around the author's name indicate that the organism is no longer classified under the genus of the original description. Sometimes the date of the original description (Latreille, 1804) follows the author's name.

It isn't easy to give an organism a scientific name. First, a detailed physical description of the new organism has to be written so that it can be recognized as a distinct species. Second, it has to be given a name that will not change in meaning or use despite any changes in modern language, and third, a normal specimen of the new species must be designated as the type specimen and placed in a museum collection where it will be available for study next year or a hundred years later. The scientific name and the description of the new species must also be published in the scientific literature and be accepted and used by modern science before the new species is considered valid.

Sometimes a scientist may write a description of a new species and give it a name without knowing that the "new" species had been previously described by someone else, or later research may show that the new species is just a different form of a previously described species. When this happens, and it is not an uncommon occurrence, the earliest name has precedence and is considered the valid name. Other scientific names that may have also been given to the species are considered synonyms.

Problems due to name and species confusion were great in the 17th and 18th centuries because there was no universally accepted system for cataloging and naming plants and animals. In the 10th edition of *Systema Naturae*, published in 1758, Linnaeus defined the basic system (known as the Linnaean hierarchy) that we follow today in giving scientific names to all species of living things. In theory, every species known to science has one, and only one, accepted scientific name. In practice, however, a couple of hundred years of developing names for newly discovered animals, often with inadequate biological and geographical information and a lack of communication between scientists of different times and different places, has resulted in some confusion in the scientific names of certain groups of plants and animals. Despite occasional mixups, and frequently more than one name for the same animal, this system brought order into the study of natural history and became one of the most important tools of modern biology.

The Linnaean hierarchy places organisms into groups based on their physical similarities, which reflects the closeness of their evolutionary relationship. Linnaeus, of course, didn't know about evolutionary relationships since this information wasn't available in the 1750's, so he, and other naturalists of the 18th century, used only the general appearance and physical characteristics of the organisms to determine the levels and groups of the hierarchy system. Even though we have a much greater understanding of the natural world today, the Linnaean system of classification works well and is still the basis of modern taxonomy.

The first few groups (each grouping is called a taxa) in this hierarchy are very large and include many organisms that are only distantly related. For example, bees, worms, spiny lobsters, and horses are all in the Animal Kingdom, but when you get down to the Family and Genus level, other kinds of animals are eliminated, and there are only types of bees, worms, spiny lobsters, and horses in each defined group. The basic classification listed below has only seven levels. Most modern scientists use classification schemes that include suborders, superfamilies, cohorts, and tribes— twenty-one or more levels to clearly define evolutionary separations between taxa. Family names always end in *idae*, and some other taxa above the genus level also have specific endings. The groups get smaller as the levels descend toward the individual species, and the organisms in each group are more closely related. Thus, the family of spiny lobsters, Palinuridae, contains only animals that look like spiny lobsters, and when we get down to the genus, *Panulirus*, there are 19 species throughout the world that look very much alike.

The scientific names given to these groups have meaning and describe the taxa in some way. The last name, however, the species name, functions only to identify the species and may or may not be descriptive of the organism. It may refer to a physical characteristic of the organism or the geographical area the organism inhabits. The new species name may honor the individual that discovered the organism, or it may be named after another individual that the author wishes to honor for some other reason. The basic classification of the spiny lobster looks like this:

Kingdom .   **Animalia** (multicellular organisms that ingest food, reproduce primarily through two different haploid gametes that join to become a diploid zygote which develops into a blastula stage, and are usually motile; Margulis and Schwartz, 1988)

Phylum . .   **Arthropoda** (jointed feet)

Class . . .   **Crustacea** (hard shelled)

Order . . .   **Decapoda** (ten legged)

Family . . . **Palinuridae** (after *Palinurus*, the pilot of Aeneas. In Greek legend, Aeneas, a Trojan, the son of Aenus, escaped from ruined Troy and wandered for many years before finding Latium.)

Genus . . . *Panulirus* (an anagram of Palinurus. An anagram is a word made by transposing the letters of another word. Thus, *Panulirus* may have been a mistaken spelling of Palinurus.)

Species . . *argus* (shining, bright. The giant *Argos* had a hundred shining eyes and upon his death, Juno placed them on the tail of a peacock.)

Thus if you know the classification and the scientific name of the Caribbean spiny lobster, you know that this particular organism is a hard shelled, invertebrate animal with ten jointed legs, a wandering habit, and bright, shining spots on its tail. Now you probably know more than you wanted to about the scientific name of the spiny lobster. This is important, though, because it is the foundation for understanding how different species of lobsters are distinguished and identified. Most folks know only two lobsters: the American or Maine lobster with the big claws and the tropical spiny lobster that doesn't have any claws.

Actually throughout the world there are about 163 species of living lobsters divided up into four major families and a few minor families. The Nephropidae are the clawed lobsters with 38 species, the Palinuridae are the spiny lobsters with 49 species, the Synaxidae has two species of coral lobsters, and the Scyllaridae have 74 species of slipper lobsters. We are concerned, however, with the tropical western Atlantic including the northeast coast of South America, the West Indies, the Caribbean Sea, the Gulf of Mexico, the southeastern coast of the United States, and the Bahamas.

Here we have only about 30 species representing six families. Most of these are small, rarely seen, deep water species. Only a few are fairly common and you will learn how to distinguish these from each other and from a few other less common lobsters in the next chapter.

Morphology

Morphology is the study of form, shape, and structure with little concern for function. Form and function go hand in hand, however, and we can learn much about the natural history of an animal by examining its morphology. Lobsters have all the basic organ systems and structures that characterize most other animals. They have a brain and nervous system, a heart and blood vessels (blood volume is about 20% of body weight and the blood pigment is copper based hemocyanin, which makes oxygenated lobster blood appear light blue), the senses of sight, chemosensitivity (taste and smell), touch and hearing, a hard exoskeleton, a reproductive system, a digestive system, gills and blood vessels for respiration, systems for excretion and salt regulation, a system of muscles (including the large abdominal muscles that we value so highly), and many other structures and chemical systems that adapt a lobster to its ecological niche.

We are most concerned at this point, however, with the physical structure (morphology) of the spiny lobster; for by knowing the proper terms for the basic parts we can correctly identify the various species and discuss the natural history, behavior, and fishery without confusion.

Lobsters are segmented animals and have 19 segments from head to tail. This is perhaps the fundamental characteristic of their body structure, one that they share with all the orders in the subclass Malacostraca, which includes shrimp, crabs, isopods, amphipods, mantis shrimps, opossum shrimps, and many other groups of small crustaceans. These segments, or somites, are not laid out as individually separate somites, each with one pair of appendages, as were the very earliest of this vast group of Crustacea. The somites have fused in certain areas and taken on specific functions as major body parts. The head, thorax, and abdomen are the three major regions. In lobsters and other decapods the head and thorax are united (the cephalothorax) and are covered by a hard outgrowth of the mandibular somite. This forms a strong dorsal shield over the head and thorax which is called the carapace. The head is composed of five segments, and the appendages of these segments are all present. These are the first antennae (antennules), the second antennae (the main or proper antennae), and the mandibles (jaws). The fourth and fifth segments are the accessory jaws (maxillula and maxilla).

The thorax is made up of segments 6 through 13. The appendages of the first three of these, the maxillipeds or jaw feet, perform functions associated with feeding and are actually mouth parts. The next five segments, 9 through 13, carry the walking legs (pereopods) variously developed into claws and legs, and these give the Decapods (10 footed) their name. The abdomen is composed of six segments, usually numbered 1 through 6, bringing the total number of somites to 19. Segments 14 through 18 carry the swimmeretts (pleopods) as appendages, and these have locomotive and reproductive functions. The last somite, # 19, has the uropods, which, along with the telson, form the tail fan. The telson is part of the abdomen but it is not a true somite. The tail fan, powered by the strong muscles of the abdomen, enables the lobster to swim rapidly backward for short distances. It is much easier to understand the structure of a lobster once you know that there are 19 segments in the body, each with two appendages, and that these segments have been fused and modified through hundreds of millions of years (eons) of evolution into particular body regions with specific individual functions.

Although all lobsters have the same basic body plan, there can be great differences between species. Some structures, such as walking legs and antennae, have evolved to perform very different functions and, although they are the same appendage, they may be very different in size and form. For example, spiny lobsters have long, cylindrical antennae while the same structure in the slipper lobsters is short, broad, and leaf-like. All the various body parts, prominent spines, and even specific areas of a lobster have a technical name. The seven jointed sections of the walking legs, from the body outward, are called the coxa, the basis, the ischium, the merus, the carpus, the propodus (also called palm), and the dactylus or dactyl. The coxa and basis in decapod crustaceans are often very short and may even be fused together. When a claw is present, the propodus and the dactyl combine to make up the pincers and are termed the movable finger and the fixed finger. The major areas of the carapace are the branchial region (the lower section of each side), the cardiac region (the central, dorsal, posterior part of the carapace), the gastric region (the central dorsal area), the frontal region (the anterior, dorsal section), and the orbital region (the lateral, frontal area around the orbits).

Generally, most body parts have one rather technical name and also several descriptive, non-technical names that may or may not be accurate and can cause confusion. For example, those long, pointed structures that the spiny lobster holds out in front are its antennae, or whips. They are not legs or claws or tentacles. Anemones and squid, and aliens from outer space have tentacles, lobsters do not. It isn't necessary to know all the technical names of every body part to understand and identify lobsters, but some terms are very important, and these are illustrated and defined. There are a few general terms that you probably know, but that are important. **Anterior** refers to the front of the animal. It may refer to the front edge of a part or a section or indicate a direction toward the front. **Posterior** refers to the rear of the animal. **Ventral** indicates the under surface, and **dorsal** refers to the upper surface. **Lateral** is to either side. **Distal** is toward the end and **proximal** is toward the beginning. The following diagrams and photographs will aid in identification of the basic parts of all lobsters—the spiny lobster in particular.

The chart that also follows (Figure 28) lists the tail length and total weight for particular caparace lengths (CL) of male and female lobsters. These values were calculated from equations graciously provided by John Hunt, Director of the Marathon Field Laboratory of the Florida Department of Natural Resources. These measurements for individual lobsters are variable, so the tabulated values are approximate, but far more accurate than gross estimates.

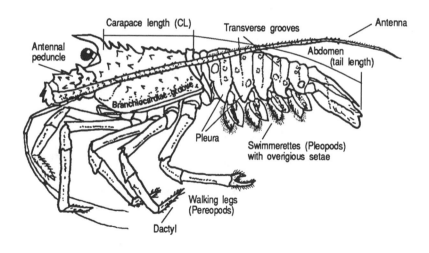

Figure 25. Terms and measurements of important body structures of the Caribbean spiny lobster, *Panulirus argus*. Lateral (side) view.

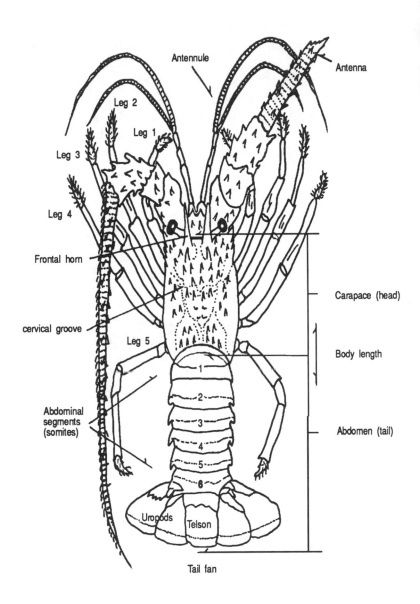

Figure 26. Terms and measurements of important body structures of the Caribbean spiny lobster, *Panulirus argus*. Dorsal (top) view.

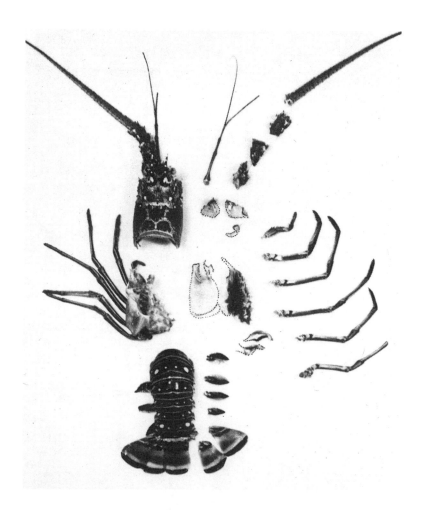

Figure 27. A photograph of an exploded molted exoskeleton of a male spiny lobster, *Panulirus argus*.The antennules (first anten-nae) are shown intact at the center top. The antennae (second antennae) are separated from the three major sections of the antennal peduncle. The internal gill structure in the branchial chamber under the carapace is shown with walking legs attached on the left and separated on the right. The single swimmeretts (pleopods) of the male lobster are shown attached (left) and sepa-rated (right) from the abdomen, and the uropods of the tail fan are also separated on the right side.

Carapace Length (Male & Female)		Male					Female				
		tail length		total weight			tail length		total weight		
inches	mm	inches	mm	lbs.	oz	gm	inches	mm	lbs.	oz	gm
1.5	38	3.0	77		2	56	2.9	74		2	59
2.0	51	3.8	96		4	125	3.8	97		5	132
2.5	64	4.5	115		8	234	4.7	120		9	247
2.75	70	4.9	124		10	298	5.2	131		11	317
3.0	76	5.2	133		13	374	5.6	141		14	397
3.25	83	5.6	143	1	0	476	6.1	154	1	2	506
3.5	89	6.0	152	1	4	576	6.5	164	1	6	613
3.75	95	6.3	161	1	8	688	6.9	175	1	10	734
4.0	102	6.7	171	1	13	836	7.4	187	2	0	893
4.25	108	7.1	180	2	2	978	7.8	198	2	5	1046
4.5	114	7.4	189	2	8	1134	8.2	209	2	11	1214
4.75	121	7.8	199	2	15	1334	8.7	221	3	2	1430
5.0	127	8.2	208	3	6	1523	9.1	231	3	10	1634
5.25	133	8.5	216	3	13	1728	9.5	242	4	1	1856
5.5	140	8.9	227	4	6	1989	10.0	254	4	11	2138
5.75	146	9.1	236	4	15	2231	10.4	265	5	5	2400
6.0	152	9.6	244	5	8	2491	10.9	276	5	14	2682
6.25	159	10.0	255	6	3	2817	11.3	288	6	11	3036
6.5	165	10.4	263	6	14	3118	11.8	299	7	6	3362
6.75	171	10.7	272	7	9	3438	12.2	309	8	3	3710
7.0	178	11.1	283	8	7	3836	12.6	321	9	2	4144
7.25	184	11.5	291	9	4	4201	13.1	332	10	0	4540
7.5	191	11.9	302	10	4	4653	13.5	344	11	1	5032
7.75	197	12.2	311	11	2	5063	14.0	355	12	0	5480
8.0	203	12.6	319	12	2	5497	14.4	366	13	2	5952
8.25	210	13.0	330	13	4	6031	14.9	378	14	6	6535
8.5	216	13.3	338	14	5	6514	15.3	389	15	9	7063
8.75	222	13.7	347	15	7	7021	15.7	399	16	12	7617
9.0	229	14.1	358	16	13	7644	16.2	411	18	4	8297

Figure 28. Length/weight chart. The tail (abdomen) length and total weight for male and female Caribbean spiny lobster, *Panilurus argus*, are listed for selected carapace lengths (CL).

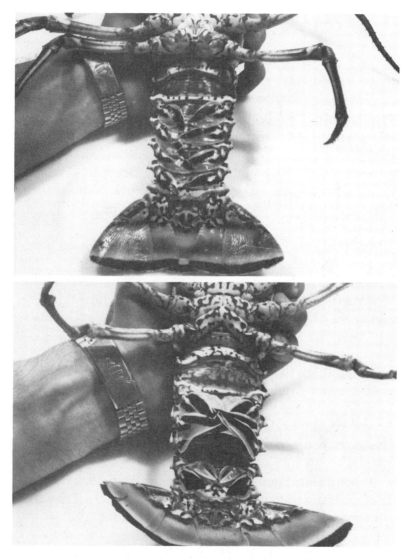

Figure 29. Ventral view of the male (above) and female (below) Caribbean spiny lobster. The male is characterized by the enlarged gonopores on the base of the fifth leg and the single swimmeretts (pleopods) on each abdominal segment. The second leg of older, mature males is also elongated (not shown). The female is characterized by the double set of swimmerettes (the endopod, the inner claw-shaped leaf modified to retain the eggs), the modified dactyl on the fifth leg, and the tiny gonopores at the base of the third leg.

Glossary of Technical Terms

Abdomen — The strong, flexible, segmented "tail".

Abdominal segments — The 6 somites of the abdomen, body segments 14 through 19, that make up the tail.

Antennae — Second antennae. Twin structures attached at the front of the carapace below the eyes. They may be long, thin, and cylindrical or short, flat, and broad.

Antennal peduncle — The five segmented base of the large, second pair of antennae.

Antennal scales — The scale-like structures that are present on the ventral surface of the antennal peduncle in certain clawed lobsters, Nephropidae.

Antennular peduncle — The three-segmented base of the small, first pair of antennae, the antennules.

Antennular plate — The flat surface below the eyes and between the antennae, usually with **spines**.

Antennular flagella — Two flexible extensions that protrude from the end of each antennular peduncle. They may be long or short, single strands or plumose.

Antennules — First antennae. Two small, thin, flexible structures that extend forward from between the eyes and the antennae.

Berry — A female lobster is "in berry" or "berried" when she is carrying eggs under her abdomen.

Biramous pleopods — The twinned pleopods on each side of the ventral surface of the abdominal segments of a female lobster. The exopod is the outer leaf and the endopod is the inner leaf.

Branchiocardiac groove — The groove between the branchial and the cardiac region that extends horizontally along the side of the carapace.

Buccal cavity — The cavity on the ventral surface of the body, under the head, where the mouth and mouthparts are located.

Carapace — The hard, usually spiny, outer shell covering the cephalothorax or head of the lobster.

Carapace length (CL) — The measurement between the anterior and posterior edge of the carapace, usually the key legal measurement. In spiny lobsters, it is measured from the ridge between the frontal horns back to the hard, posterior edge of the carapace. In clawed lobsters, it is measured from the base of the eye socket (not including the rostrum) to the posterior edge of the carapace.

Carina — A keel-like ridge or prominence, may be with or without spines.

Cephalothorax — The fused somites of the head and thorax, covered by the carapace, that form what is commonly termed the head of the lobster.

Cervical groove — The deep groove that cuts horizontally across the dorsal surface of the carapace at about the mid point and then extends forward on each side. It roughly separates the anterior and posterior sections, the cardiac and gastric regions of the carapace.

Chela — The organization of the two distal sections of the crustacean leg into opposing fingers that form a pincer or claw, a condition found on legs 1, 2, and 3 of the clawed lobsters.

Chelate — The condition of having chela.

Chelipeds — Large pincer claws, usually on the first walking legs of the clawed lobsters.

Claws — A term usually applied to the enlarged chela on the first legs of the clawed lobsters.

Crusher claw — The strong, massive claw used for holding and crushing when two claws are unequal in size.

Dactyl — dactylus, dactylopodite. The movable, distal section of the walking legs, usually relatively short and sharply pointed. The movable finger of the pincer.

Digestive gland — The hepatopancreas, the paired digestive gland found on either side of the stomach of the larval and adult lobster.

Ecdysis — The act of molting— shedding the old, hard exoskeleton that allows growth in Crustacea.

Embryo — The developing larva within the egg.

Endopod — The inner leaf of the double set of pleopods (swimmeretts) present on the abdominal segments of female spiny lobsters.

Exoskeleton — The hard, outer shell of lobsters and other crustaceans that serves as protection and firm attachment for muscles and other soft tissues. It is basically an external skeleton.

Eye stalk — The compound eyes of lobsters and other crustaceans are mounted on flexible, muscular stalks that allow the eye to extend, move laterally, and retract for protection.

False pincer — The first legs of the males of the longarm spiny lobster, *Justitia longimanus*, are greatly enlarged and end in apparent pincers. The movable finger, the dactyl, is enlarged but it moves against only a small ridge that acts as a fixed finger. This is a structure unique to this species and is not a true chela.

Fertilization — The meeting of the sperm and egg to form the early embryo, the zygote. In lobsters, mating occurs considerably before fertilization, and the female holds the viable sperm in a spermatophore until after ovulation and extrusion of the eggs, at which time fertilization occurs.

Finger — The propodus and the dactyl when these structures form a pincer or claw at the end of a walking leg in the clawed lobsters.

Flagella — The plural of flagellum. The long, flexible filaments at the end of the base of the first antennae, the antennules.

Front — Frontal part of the carapace.

Frontal horns — The two large, anteriorly directed, sharply pointed horns that curve up over the eyes in spiny lobsters.

Gills — Soft, branching, respiratory tissues found in the protected branchial chamber on the internal lateral surface of the cephalothorax (head).

Gonopore — The tiny openings at the base of the third leg on the female through which eggs are passed from the ovaries during spawning. The enlarged glands at the base of the fifth leg of male lobsters used to attach the spermatophore to the female are also termed gonopores.

Hand — The propodus and dactyl (the body and fingers of the claw) of the pincer-claw in the clawed lobsters.

Mandibles — The hard crushing jaws of the lobster. The appendages of the third somite of the head.

Maxilla — The appendages of the fourth and fifth somites, the accessory jaws. They function in positioning food for the mandibles.

Maxillipeds — The appendages of the first three somites of the thorax that function as mouthparts.

Mouthparts — All the appendages that are present in the buccal cavity and function in feeding.

Ocular peduncle — A technical term for the eyestalk.

Orbit — The circular depression in the front of the carapace that contains the eyestalk.

Orbital margin — The posterior and lateral edges of the orbit, usually with spines.

Ovaries — The paired reproductive organs of the female that lie just under the dorsal surface of the carapace. They are white when the female is not reproductively active and orange to red when yolk has formed in the eggs and the female is close to spawning.

Ovulation — The expulsion of the egg from the tissues of the ovary and the passage of the egg from the female reproductive organs.

Overigious setae — Long hair-like growths on the biramous pleopods (swimmeretts) of the female that function as a holdfast for the eggs and keep them under the abdomen of the female during incubation.

Palm — The body of the claw excluding the fingers, the proximal part of the propodus.

Pereopods — The walking legs, the appendages of the five thoracic segments, 9 through 13, that function in walking and climbing, and when chelate, in feeding and defense.

Phyllosoma, Phyllosome — The flattened, leaf-like larval form of the spiny, slipper, and coral lobsters.

Pincers — Chela. The opposing fingers formed from the dactyl and propodus at the distal end of the first three walking legs of the clawed lobsters.

Plane of autotomy — Fracture plane. A thin membrane extends across the leg at the third joint (the ischium). Here (near the base of the leg) the lobster can voluntarily break off the leg by spasmodic contraction of the muscles. The membrane seals the wound, and a bud that will grow into a new leg in future molts soon forms behind the membrane.

Plectrum — The antennal pad. A rounded area roughened with microscopic ridges on the base of the antennae that rubs on the rostral bar to create sound.

Pleopods — Swimmerettes. The flat, leaf-like appendages of the abdominal segments that function in locomotion and reproduction.

Pleura — The lateral, downward projecting extensions of the hard dorsal covering of the abdominal segments. The pleura act as a shield to help protect the ventral surface of the abdomen.

Plumose — Setae or flagella that are greatly branched and have a feathery appearance.

Postlarvae — The juvenile form that immediately follows the last larval molt.

Propodus — The next to the last leg segment. The dactyl is on the distal end of the propodus and the carpus (wrist) is on the proximal end. The propodus and dactyl form the pincer or claw when it is present.

Puerulus — The specialized postlarval form of the spiny lobster that functions to move the lobster from offshore, oceanic waters to the inshore, shallow algal flats.

Ripper claw — The lighter, thinner claw used for ripping and tearing when the two claws are unequal in size.

Rostral bar — The rostral file. A fixed ridge on the carapace at the base of the antennae that is roughened with microscopic scales. Sound is produced when the antennal pad on the antennal base is rubbed over the rostral bar.

Rostral spines — Strong spines, usually laterally directed, that occur on the rostrum of clawed lobsters.

Rostrum — A large, anteriorly directed horn at the central front of the carapace in clawed lobsters. The rostrum projects forward from between the eyes and usually ends in a sharp point.

Seta — A flexible, hair-like growth on various surfaces of the lobster. Setae (plural) may be long, short, soft, or stiff; a single filament, or twinned or feathered depending on function.

Somites — The individual segments that make up the body of the lobster.

Spawning — Spawning usually refers to the interaction of male and female (mating) and the immediate fertilization of the eggs. In lobsters, mating may occur days or weeks before fertilization of the eggs, so spawning is a lengthy process in lobsters.

Spermatophore — In spiny lobsters, the spermatophore is a grey to black, gel-like substance (tar) that contains sperm. The male attaches the spermatophore externally on the posterior sternal plates of the cephalothorax of the female. In other species, the female carries the spermatophore internally.

Spines — Hard, sharp outgrowths, small or large, of the exoskeleton that occur on the carapace and many other surfaces of the lobster.

Squamose — Scale-like. A sculpturing of the surface that resembles scales.

Stridulating apparatus — The structure composed of the plectrum on the antennae and the rostral bar on the carapace that creates sound in the Stridentes line of spiny lobsters.

Supraorbital ridges — Ridges above the orbits.

Swimmerettes — Pleopods. A non-technical term for the flat, leaf-like appendages of the abdominal segments.

Tail length — The length of the tail along the dorsal surface from the point where it meets the carapace to the end of the telson. An important legal measurement.

Tailfan — The broad, fan shaped structure a the end of the abdomen composed of the uropods and the telson. It functions in rapid backward swimming and moving water through the incubating eggs.

Telson — A broad, fan-shaped outgrowth from the last abdominal segment. The telson, and the lateral uropods, make up the tailfan.

Thorax — The central region of the lobster body, somites 6 through 13, that bear the walking legs.

Total length — The length of the tail and the carapace combined.

Transverse grooves — A groove, complete or incomplete, that extends from side to side across the dorsal surface of an abdominal segment.

Tubercle — A small, rounded discrete protuberance. Not a spine.

Uniramous pleopod — The single leaf-like appendages (pleopods) on each side of the abdominal segments of the male lobster.

Uropods — The fan shaped appendages on each side of the last abdominal segment of the lobster. The uropods and the telson make up the tailfan.

Walking legs — Pereopods. The appendages of the thoracic segments 9 through 13 that function in walking and climbing, and, when chelate, in feeding and defense.

CHAPTER THREE

IDENTIFICATION AND SPECIES ACCOUNTS
The Key to the Species

Suppose you have been studying a particular group of animals for many, many years. You have finally—after extensive collecting and intensive analysis of physical, biological, and ecological factors—been able to determine which populations are reproductively isolated from each other and represent distinct species. This is essential information for anyone studying the biology of these animals, the ecology of the area, or even the commercial exploitation of that group of animals. Now you must provide all these various interests with a clear, well documented account of your work that will tell them how and why each species was defined, and also enable them to quickly and easily identify each species.

Sometimes the characteristics that are unique to a particular species are very distinctive. The species may have a characteristic that allows no confusion about its identity, the red hourglass under the abdomen of black widow spiders, for example. On the other hand, like many parrotfishes, the color and shape of some species may change or differ with age and sex, or they may have characteristics that are very similar to those of other species; thus it may be very difficult to separate and identify closely related species.

So how do you summarize your work? How do you make it easy for others to distinguish these species without going through the laborious comparisons that took up so much of your life? Basically what you do is draw a map that will guide them from the specimen before them directly to the correct identification of that species.

This "map" is called an artificial key. The key provides a series of choices that must be made, usually about the physical characteristics of the specimens, that divide all the possible species into two or three groups at each point. The specimen in hand always provides the answer. The question may be—Is it black or red? Black sends you along one path and red, another path. All the black animals are now in one group and the red ones in the other. It is like starting with the trunk of a tree and making a decision at each fork on which branch to follow. Eventually you arrive at the twig that represents the species in hand. It is called an "artificial" key because it uses any characteristics that can accurately separate two or more species at any point without regard for any evolutionary or natural relationships between the species. There are two very important rules to follow when you use such a key.

First, be sure you understand all the terms used in the key. If you come across a word you don't understand, look it up. The glossary and the drawings in Chapter 2 explain the meanings of many common technical terms. A bad guess on the meaning of a word may easily give you the wrong identification.

Second, go through the key from the beginning, especially if your experience with that key is limited. You may miss the correct path by just assuming that the specimen in question has to be in a particular section of the key.

Development of a key to a group of species is almost always the result of years of dedicated effort, consultation with other scientists, trips to museums to examine type specimens, examination of hundreds of specimens, compilation and analysis of extensive listings of measurements and physical characteristics, and the intuition of a brilliant taxonomic mind. Did I do all this for this key?

No way! I went to the work done by the Food and Agriculture Organization of the United Nations in their FAO Species Identification Sheets, prepared by R.B. Manning (1978) and edited by Fisher; the Sea Grant Field Series Guide # 1 by Opresko et al.; and the work

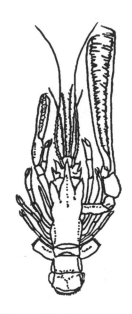

Figure 30. Thaumastochelidae

of other scientists: Williams (1984), Lyons (1970), Burukovskii (1982), and Holthuis (1969, 1974). I extracted the essential elements from their work, simplified the technical terms where possible, and compiled a key for the most common lobsters found in Caribbean, Gulf of Mexico, and Bahamian waters.

There are about 35 species of lobsters, classified into six families, in this broad oceanic area. Of these, only about 20 have a reasonable chance of coming to the attention of a fisherman, aquarist, diver, or beachcomber, and only about 10 of these are reasonably familiar to fishermen or divers working in any relatively shallow area of the tropical western Atlantic. The other species are small, rare, and usually found only in very deep waters. For example, one of these deep water species, *Thaumastocheles zaleucus*, a strange, small, white, blind lobster with fanged pincers almost as long as the body, is usually placed in a separate family, Thaumastochelidae. This family, and another deep-sea fam-

ily, the Polychelidae, are not
included in the key. The 20
species included in the key
are all illustrated with a
drawing and are described in
a brief species account.

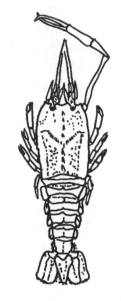

Several species from the
southwest Atlantic are mentioned in the key along with
the northern species that they
most resemble. Thus, the
most common species from
southern Brazil can also be
identified in the key al-
though they are not specifically designated in the
couplets.

Figure 31. Polychelidae

The key is presented as
an aid to identification of the relatively common lobsters of
this region for the student, fisherman, aquarist, diver, and
others with a general interest in lobsters. Identifications
made from this key should be considered tentative until
confirmed by reference to the scientific literature or through
consultation with an expert in lobster taxonomy.

Note that the family Synaxidae is spelled with a single i
in this book, the spelling most frequently found in the literature. The double ii spelling, Synaxiidae, occurs less frequently in the literature but may be the correct spelling.

Identification

The first thing is to be sure that you have a lobster and
not one of the other elongated crustaceans common to the
area. It is possible to confuse some shrimps with lobsters,
even though shrimps are generally much smaller than lobsters. If you have a shrimp, the pleura of the second abdominal segment will usually overlap the pleura of the first and

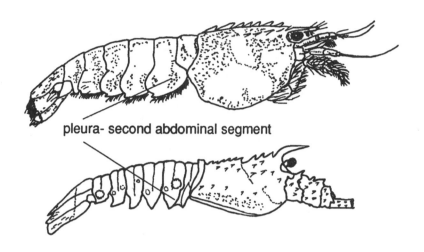

pleura- second abdominal segment

Figure 32. The body profile of the "reef lobster", *En-oplometopus*, Family Enoplometopidae, (not a "true" lobster) and the spiny lobster, *Panulirus*, Family Palinuridae. The structure of the overlapping pleura in shrimps and the pointed, separated pleura in lobsters is illustrated.

third, or just the third segment. In lobsters (Figure 32), the abdominal pleura **do not** overlap and usually end in a point. The pleura is the hard downward extension of the shell on the side of each abdominal segment that protects the underside of the abdomen. (The various illustrations in this chapter and in Chapter Two will help you identify important structures.)

Note, however, that this is not the case with the coral banded shrimp, an exception. Here the pleura of the first segment slightly overlaps the second, which in turn, slightly overlaps the third. The coral banded shrimp, note the illustration of *Stenopus hispidus*, Figure 33, also have massive

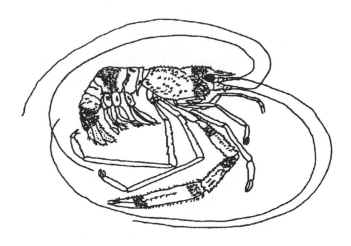

Figure 33. *Stenopus hispidus*, the coral banded shrimp.

claws developed from the third pair of legs and not the first pair as in lobsters. The exoskeleton (shell) of lobsters is hard and stony, except just after a molt, while the exoskeleton of shrimp is usually (there are exceptions) somewhat flexible. Some shallow water shrimps that could be confused as small lobsters are the banded coral shrimp, golden coral shrimp, scarlet stenopodid, brown snapping shrimp, common snapping shrimp, two clawed shrimp, bumblebee shrimp, and the mantis shrimps.

The lobster-like shrimps of the families Axiidae, Enoplometopidae, and, to a lesser extent, Callianassidae, can easily be assumed to be lobsters. The first walking legs are enlarged into massive, hairy (setose) pincers, and some of them are found in habitats where lobsters also occur—coral reefs and other offshore and deep water reef areas. These are uncommon, secretive crustaceans and are only rarely collected. They can be separated from the true clawed lobsters since only the first two pairs of walking legs have pincers (are chelate) while the first three pairs of walking legs of the Nephropoidea have true pincers.

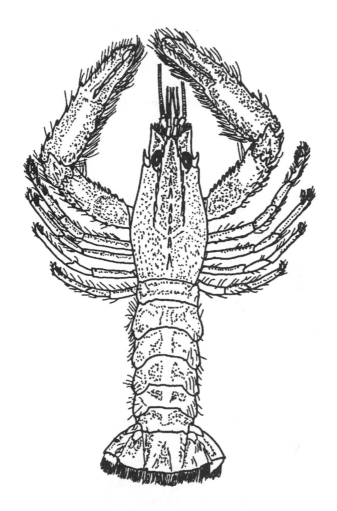

Figure 34. The flaming reef "lobster", *Enoplometopus antillensis*.

The flaming reef lobster, *Enoplometopus antillensis* Lutken, 1865, of the family Enoplometopidae is particularly significant in the Florida/Caribbean area. Holthuis (1983) recognized seven species in the genus *Enoplometopus*, two from the Atlantic and five from the Pacific. All are brightly colored, and the most common species are popular in the marine aquarium trade as "reef lobsters". The flaming reef lobster, note the illustration, is a very rare species and was previously known from only two specimens taken in the West Indies in 1865 and 1880. Filho (1970) described a third specimen taken off the northeast coast of Brazil in 1965.

The Family Enoplometopidae was recently established by de Saint Laurent (1988), and the genus *Enoplometopus* was placed in this new family. At the time of Filho's work, *Enoplometopus* was included in the family Nephropidae instead of the Enoplometopidae. Thus, the animal was at one time considered by scientists to be a lobster instead of a shrimp. Taylor (1984) presents a beautiful color picture of an unidentified six inch (150 mm) long "lobster" that is certainly *Enoplometopus antillensis*, taken in 30 feet (10 m) of water off St. Croix in the U.S. Virgin Islands. *E. antillensis* has recently been found in about 90 to 100 feet (27 to 30 m) offshore of the southeast coast of Florida between Ft. Pierce and Palm Beach. A diver, John Brady, from Sebastian, Florida, captured three specimens offshore of Singer Island on a small rock patch in 110 feet of water and made them available to scientific interests (Brady, 1991). Manning and Camp (1989) confirmed the identification and synonymized *E. dentatus* with *E. antillensis*, so now there is only one species of *Enoplometopus* recognized in the Atlantic and Caribbean area.

It is more difficult to confuse crabs with lobsters, but it can be done since many crabs have strong, hard, lobster-like claws. The abdomen of most crabs is small, flat, and permanently tucked up under the carapace (cephalothorax). If the carapace of the animal is roundish, squarish, triangular, or oval with the abdomen normally folded up underneath it, then it is probably a crab and not a lobster.

The anomuran crustaceans, Infraorder Anomura, of the family Galatheidae are also very lobster-like and are termed squat lobsters. Williams (1986) included two genera of squat lobsters, *Cervimunida* and *Pleuroncodes*, that are taken off the western coast of South America and are of economic importance, in his key to the lobster tails in U.S. trade. The abdomen of squat lobsters is not as tightly folded under the carapace as that of crabs, but is simply bent loosely under it, and the crustacean has the superficial body form of a lobster. The genus *Munida* in the western central Atlantic is particularly lobster-like. Only the first pair of walking legs are developed into pincers, and these are extended into great claws. No other legs are chelate, and of course, if the first three pairs of legs aren't chelate, it's not a clawed lobster. The central section of the tail fan (the telson) has a strong central notch that shapes it into two lobes, a feature that separates the galatheids from other lobsters. Some of the squat lobsters are found in shallow water, and many live in deep, offshore waters.

Hermit crabs, Superfamily Paguroidea, another group of anomuran crustacea, also have an abdomen that is not tightly folded under the carapace. It is soft, long, and a bit twisted, with sharp recurved spines (modified uropods) on the end. The crab uses its abdomen to hold itself inside a snail shell. Of course, one can't confuse it with a lobster when it's dragging a shell along behind it, but it is a strange sight without the shell, and it is possible for someone unfamiliar with marine life to think lobster when a large hermit crab is seen walking around without a snail shell on its rear end.

A couple of good general books to help sort out some of these creatures are *Seashore Life* by Voss (1980) and *Caribbean Reef Invertebrates and Plants* by Colin (1978), while *Shrimps, Lobsters, and Crabs of the Atlantic Coast* by Williams (1984), *An Illustrated Guide to the Marine Decapod Crustaceans of Florida* by Abele and Kim (1986), and *Marine Fauna and Flora of Bermuda* edited by Sterrer (1986) are excellent general technical references.

KEY TO THE FAMILIES OF LOBSTERS

Once you are sure you have a lobster, the next step is to place it in one of the four major families. The key below will do just this. Start with number 1 and decide if your lobster belongs to choice A or choice B, then go to the next step, number 2 or 3, whichever one your first choice indicates. The decision made at this next step will tell you the family of your lobster. A diagram of the family key is also presented on the next page to illustrate how your decisions move you along the path toward the proper identification. Once you know the family, then you can go to the key for that family and determine the species by following the species key in the same way.

---

1. **A.** Antennae as long or longer than the body
        go to ... 2

1. **B.** Antennae shorter than the body
        go to ... 3

---

2. **A.** Legs without pincers (claws). Two horns (sharp or blunt) on the anterior of the carapace. (Note: *Justitia* males have an apparent or false pincer on their enlarged first leg and females of all species have a false pincer on the fifth (last) walking legs that is used in egg care)...
        spiny lobsters, Family Palinuridae

2. **B.** First three pairs of legs with true pincers (claws). Single central horn (rostrum) at anterior of carapace...
        clawed lobsters, Family Nephropidae

---

3. **A.** Antennae cylindrical, half as long as body. Body cylindrical...
        furry (coral) lobsters, Family Synaxidae

3. **B.** Antennae short, flat, spade-like. Body flattened...
        slipper lobsters, Family Scyllaridae

Begin with a lobster from Florida, the Bahamas or the Caribbean

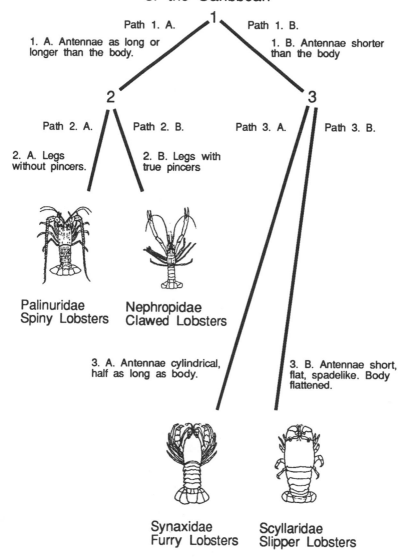

Path 1. A.

1. A. Antennae as long or longer than the body.

Path 1. B.

1. B. Antennae shorter than the body

Path 2. A.

2. A. Legs without pincers.

Path 2. B.

2. B. Legs with true pincers

Path 3. A.

Path 3. B.

Palinuridae
Spiny Lobsters

Nephropidae
Clawed Lobsters

3. A. Antennae cylindrical, half as long as body.

3. B. Antennae short, flat, spadelike. Body flattened.

Synaxidae
Furry Lobsters

Scyllaridae
Slipper Lobsters

Figure 35. Diagrammatic key to the families of lobsters in Florida, Caribbean, and Bahamian waters.

SPECIES LIST

Lobsters from the southeastern United States, Gulf of Mexico, Caribbean Sea, and the Bahamas, including major species from Brazil.

Nephropidae — clawed lobsters

Species included in key:
Acanthacaris caeca — Atlantic deep-sea lobster
Eunephrops bairdii — red lobsterette
Homarus americanus — American lobster
Metanephrops binghami — Caribbean lobsterette
Nephropsis aculeata — Florida lobsterette
Nephropsis agassizii — prickly lobsterette

Species not included in key:
Eunephrops cadenasi Chace, 1939 — deep water
Eunephrops manningi Holthuis, 1974 — deep water
Metanephrops rubellus (Moreira, 1903) — from Brazil
Nephropides caribaeus Manning, 1969 — deep water
Nephropsis neglecta Holthuis, 1974 — deep water
Nephropsis rosea Bate, 1888 — deep water

Thaumastochelidae

Species not included in key. Occurs in deep water.
Thaumastocheles zaleucus (Thomson, 1873)

Palinuridae — spiny lobsters

Species included in key:
Justitia longimanus — longarm spiny lobster
Palinustus truncatus — blunthorn spiny lobster
Panulirus argus — Caribbbean spiny lobster
Panulirus guttatus — spotted spiny lobster
Panulirus laevicauda — smoothtail spiny lobster

Species not included in key:
Panulirus echinatus Smith, 1849 — found along the
Northeast coast of South America.

Scyllaridae — slipper lobsters

Species included in key:
Parribacus antarcticus — sculptured slipper lobster
Scyllarides aequinoctialis — Spanish slipper lobster
Scyllarides nodifer — ridged slipper lobster
Scyllarus americanus — American slipper lobster
Scyllarus chacei — Chace slipper lobster
Scyllarus depressus — scaled slipper lobster
Scyllarus faxoni — Faxon slipper lobster
Scyllarus planorbis — Caribbean slipper lobster

Species not included in key:
Arctides guineensis (Spengler, 1799) — from Bermuda
Scyllarides brasiliensis Rathbun, 1906 — southern Brazil
Scyllarides deceptor Holthuis, 1960 — southern Brazil
Scyllarides delfosi Holthuis, 1960 — Guyana to Brazil

Synaxidae — furry (coral) lobsters

Species included in key:
Palinurellus gundlachi — copper (furry) lobster

Polychelidae

No species included in key. Occurs in deep water.
Stereomastis sculpta

FAMILY KEYS TO THE SPECIES

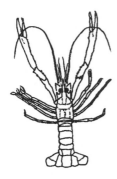

Key to the Nephropidae— Clawed lobsters

---

1. A. First pair of legs with massive, flattened pincers (claws or chelipeds), one developed as a larger crusher claw and one as a smaller cutting claw.
   American lobster, *Homarus americanus*

1. B. First pair of legs moderately enlarged into pincers (claws), equal in size and development.
   go to... **2**

---

2. A. Eyes white (no pigment).
   go to... **3**

2. B. Eyes black (with pigment).
   go to... **5**

---

3. A. Pincers (claws) long and slender with spines. Small scales present on the antennal peduncle (base of long, second antennae).
   Atlantic deep-sea lobster, *Acanthacaris caeca*

3. B. Pincers (claws) stout and hairy. No scales on the antennal peduncle.
   go to... **4**

---

4. A. Rostrum with one pair of lateral spines.
    Florida lobsterette, *Nephropsis aculeata*

4. B. Rostrum with two pairs of lateral spines.
    prickley lobsterette, *Nephropsis agassizii*

5. A. Carapace with several longitudinal ridges between the cervical groove and the posterior edge. Spines present between the rostrum and the cervical groove.
    Caribbean lobsterette, *Metanephrops binghami*

5. B. Carapace without ridges, posterior section evenly granular. Area between rostrum and cervical groove without spines.
    red lobsterette, *Eunephrops bairdii*

Note: The lobster-like shrimps of the Infraorder Astacidea or the Infraorder Thalassinidea, particularly the "flaming reef lobster", Enoplometopus antillensis, (Figure 34) in the family Enoplometopidae may key out at number 5 above if one assumes at the beginning of the key that the animal was a clawed lobster, family Nephropidae. The Axiidae, Enoplometopidae, and the Callianassidae, although superficially similar to clawed lobsters, differ from the true clawed lobsters, Nephropidae, in certain fundamental characteristics. They can be quickly distinguished from the clawed lobsters, however, because the third walking leg (pereopod) is never with pincers (chelate), while the third leg of the clawed lobsters is always with pincers. Only the first two legs of the flaming reef lobster are chelate, but the large pincers on the first legs are very lobster-like. The short, broad and relatively blunt rostrum and the two small spines on each central, lateral margin of the telson also distinguish the flaming reef lobster from the clawed lobsters.

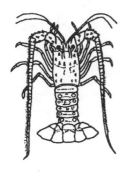

Key to the Palinuridae — Spiny lobsters

---

1. A. First pair of legs (greatly enlarged in males with apparent (false) pincers) with wide, red cross bands. Caparace with raised scale-like structures (squamous) on dorsal surface. Abdomen (tail) brick red with four or five strong transverse grooves on each segment.

longarm spiny lobster, *Justitia longimanus*

1. B. First pair of legs without wide, red cross bands and only a simple dactyl (single point) at the end, no trace of false pincers. No scale-like structure to surface of carapace. Tail variously colored, not brick red. Abdominal segments smooth or with only one transverse groove.

go to... **2**

---

2. A. Frontal horns over the eyes short and blunt, square in general outline. Flagella on antennules (first pair of antennae) much shorter than base segments (peduncle).

blunthorn spiny lobster, *Palinustus truncatus*

2. B. Frontal horns over the eyes long and sharp. Flagella on antennules longer than antennule base.

go to... **3**

---

3. A. Dorsal (upper) surface of abdomen (tail) smooth, without remarkable coloration. Abdominal segments without a transverse groove.

smoothtail spiny lobster, *Panulirus laevicauda*

3. B. Dorsal surface of abdomen with a conspicuous spotted coloration. Abdominal segments with a complete transverse groove.

go to... **4**

4. A. Four large conspicuous yellowish spots on the dorsal surface of the abdomen (tail), two on the second segment, and two on the sixth segment. Legs without numerous small yellowish spots.

Caribbean spiny lobster, *Panulirus argus*

4. B. Many small yellowish spots on abdomen, lacking four large conspicuous spots. Legs with numerous small yellowish spots.

spotted spiny lobster, *Panulirus guttatus*

Note: The brown spiny lobster, *P. echinatus*, found in the central and southwestern Atlantic, is similar in coloration, but larger than *P. guttatus*. It can be separated from *P. guttatus* by the incomplete transverse grooves on the dorsal surface of abdominal segments 2 through 5 and the striped rather than spotted first jointed section of the legs.

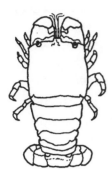

Key to the Scyllaridae— Slipper lobsters

1. A. Width of carapace greater than length. Side edges of carapace flattened and formed into sharp, thin, triangular projections.

> **sculptured slipper lobster,** *Parribacus antarcticus*

1. B. Width of carapace less than length in mature specimens. (Note: very young specimens, postlarvae, may have a wide carapace.) Sides of carapace more rounded, not flattened, with smooth to rough edges.

> go to... **2**

2. A. Front and usually side edge of flattened antennae smooth or with fine teeth, no large triangular projections. Adults large, up to 12 inches (30 cm) total length.

> go to...**3**

2. B. Front and side edge of flattened antennae with large, triangular, tooth-like projections. Adults small, less than 4 inches (10 cm) total length.

> go to... **4**

3. A. Dorsal surface of carapace with large protuberances (carina or "bumps") along the midline in the anterior and central areas. Second, third, and fourth abdominal segments with a central protuberance. Three to four dark markings, one in the center, on the dorsal surface of the first abdominal segment.

ridged slipper lobster, *Scyllarides nodifer*

3. B. Dorsal surface of carapace relatively smooth, without distinct protuberances. Second, third, and fourth abdominal segments smooth and rounded, without distinct protuberances. Two very distinct, large dark spots, one on either side of the center line, and two lighter, lateral spots on the dorsal surface of the first abdominal segment.

Spanish slipper lobster, *Scyllarides aequinoctialis*

Note: In the extreme southern edge of the Caribbean Sea, it may be possible to find a third species of *Scyllarides,* the three-spot slipper lobster, *S. delfosi.* The range of *S. delfosi* is further to the south, off the coasts of Guyana, Surinam, and Brazil. It is most like *S. aequinoctialis* in size and appearance. The most obvious difference is that *S. delfosi* has three large reddish spots, including one large median spot, on the dorsal surface of the first abdominal segment. *S. aequinoctialis* has four, including two large central spots on either side of the median line, and these spots are usually dark red to black rather than light red.

Scyllarides deceptor is found in abundance on the southern coast of Brazil (Salvador and Rio de Janeiro). It is similar to *S. aequinoctialis* and *S. delfosi,* but is easily distinguished by the presence of only two light red spots on the lateral dorsal surface of the first abdominal segment. *S. brasiliensis,* also found off southern Brazil, is smaller than *S. deceptor* and more closely resembles *S. nodifer.*

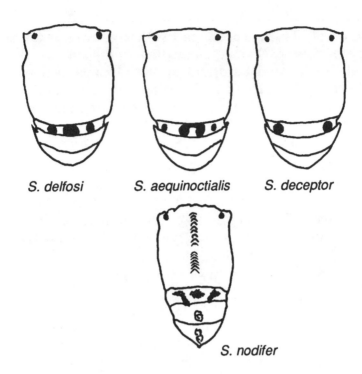

S. delfosi   S. aequinoctialis   S. deceptor

S. nodifer

4. A. Posterior edge of fifth abdominal segment with a large median (central) spine.

Faxon slipper lobster, *Scyllarus faxoni*

4. B. Posterior edge of fifth abdominal segment nearly straight and smooth or notched, without a median spine.

go to... **5**

5. A. Pleura of fourth abdominal segment sharply rectangular or pointed. Protuberances ("bumps") on carapace sharply pointed.

Scaled slipper lobster, *Scyllarus depressus*

5. B. Pleura of forth abdominal segment rounded on each side. Protuberances on carapace relatively blunt.

go to... **6**

6. A. Posterior edge of the first four abdominal segments with a strong, narrow, median (central) notch. Protuberances ("bumps") in the center of the dorsal surface of the carapace (just posterior to the cervical groove) divided into two lobes.
American slipper lobster, *Scyllarus americanus*

6. B. Posterior edge of the first four abdominal segments with a broad, shallow median notch. Protuberances in the center of the carapace formed into a single lobe, not divided.
go to... **7**

7. A. Inner orbital margin (edge of carapace behind eye) with two sharp teeth. Legs with dark bands, body with vivid orange-brown spots.
Chace slipper lobster, *Scyllarus chacei*

7. B. Inner orbital margin smooth. Legs not banded, body a uniform dark color without orange-brown spots.
Caribbean slipper lobster, *Scyllarus planorbis*

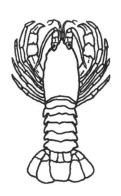

Key to the Synaxidae—
Furry (coral) lobsters

Only one species in the tropical, western north Atlantic.

furry lobster, *Palinurellus gundlachi*

SPECIES ACCOUNTS

Nephropidae — Clawed Lobsters

Figure 36.

Acanthacaris caeca (A. Milne Edwards, 1881)

Common names
   Atlantic deep-sea lobster
   Langoustine arganelle   Cigala de fondo

Distinguishing characteristics

Size: Relatively large, body length 15 inches (40 cm) maximum, commonly 10 inches (25 cm).

Color: Uniformly pink, an elongate white spot on the carapace behind the eye, eyes red, tailfan bright pink.

Form: Body is cylindrical, completely covered with small spines, median rostrum well developed. Antennae whip-like, longer than the body, with well developed scales. Legs long and slender, covered with sharp spinules, first pair longer than body, with smooth, equal pincers with several long teeth on inner edges.

Distribution

Gulf of Mexico, Caribbean Sea, and western north Atlantic. Deep water, 150 to 470 fathoms (290 to 860 meters).

Life History

Little is known of the life history of these deep water lobsters. What is known is developed from examination of the specimens themselves and associated fauna taken in trawlings and from photographs taken from deep-sea submersibles. The Atlantic deep-sea lobster lives in burrows formed in mud, grey ooze, and fine sand bottoms. Holthuis (1974) presented interesting photographs of this species in defensive posture before its burrow. Egg bearing females range in carapace length from 3.5 to 5.5 inches (99 to 140 mm), egg diameters are 2.0 to 2.5 mm.

Fishery

There is no fishery directed toward the Atlantic deep-sea lobster. The species is taken incidentally in deep trawling activities. Exploratory deep trawling has reportedly produced considerable numbers in deep Caribbean waters.

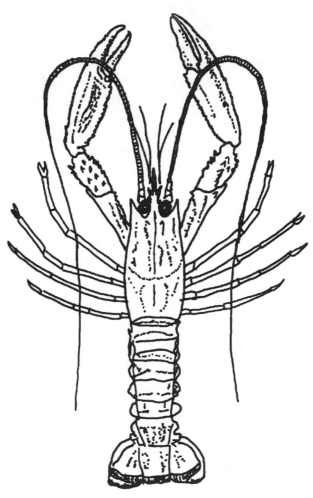

Figure 37.

Eunephrops bairdii Smith, 1885

Common names
  Red lobsterette
  Langoustine rouge   Cigala colorada

Distinguishing characteristics

Size: Observed carapace length for males ranges from 1.75 to 3.5 inches (44 to 90 mm) and for females, 1.75 to 2.75 inches (46 to 70 mm). Maximum body length is about 8 inches (20 cm).

Color: Generally an orange brown to red, legs are deeper red, spines are whitish to pink, tail fan is solid pale red, eyes black (pigmented) on a pink eyestalk, antennae and pincers are deep red.

Form: Body is cylindrical, the rostrum is well developed with two protusions, dorsal midline smooth without spines or teeth, a pair of spines present on the carapace just behind the cervical groove. Pleura of second abdominal segment square in shape rather than pointed. Each abdominal segment has a deep transverse groove. Eyes well developed and pigmented. The large pincers (chelipeds) on the first legs are usually equal in size and carry many small spines, but are not hairy or woolly.

Distribution

Apparently restricted to the southwestern Caribbean, off the coast of Panama and Colombia. Deep water, 125 to 220 fathoms (230 to 400 m).

Life history

No life history information available. Specimens have been taken on green mud bottoms and coralline, shell rubble bottoms. Females are apparently smaller than males.

Fishery

There is no fishery directed toward the red lobsterette. Specimens have been taken only during exploratory trawling operations.

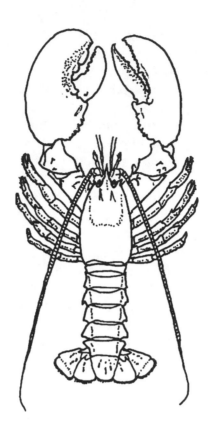

Figure 38.

Homarus americanus H. Milne Edwards, 1837

Common names
    American lobster
    Maine lobster
    Bogavante americano
    Homard americain

Distinguishing characteristics
    Size: A large lobster, 10 to over 40 inches (25 to 102 cm) body length. One of the largest American lobsters on record was 42 lb, 7 oz when taken in 1934.
    Color: Variable, yellowish red, dark red, greenish, and rarely, blue.

Form: Body smooth and cylindrical. Carapace has a strong, well developed median rostrum. Antennae long and whip-like. The true pincers on the first pair of walking legs are smooth and massive, one developed into a large crusher and the other into a slighter ripper claw.

Distribution

A lobster of northern, temperate waters. Only one record from Florida. Shoreline to 250 fathoms (1 to 480 m) usually 1 to 30 fathoms. This species is included because of its abundance and importance in northern waters. There is little chance of this species being found south of North Carolina; however, unusual range extensions can happen, especially in deep, cold waters where seasonal change is minor. On April 2, 1987, Richard B. Nielsen, Jr. was fishing traps for golden crabs in 138 fathoms (252 m) off Miami Beach, Florida. He caught a 3½ lb. (1.64 k) American lobster, 13.3 inches (34.1 cm) total length, a very unusual catch that extends the southernmost record for American lobster from South Carolina to south Florida. The water temperature was 43 °F (6.1 °C), far too cold and deep for spiny lobsters, but within the temperature and depth range for American lobsters.

Life history

Extensive research has been accomplished on the biology and fishery of this lobster. Williams (1984) presented a scientific summary of the information on this species and Taylor (1984) gave a popular account. It takes about 7 years for an American lobster to reach the minimum market size of 3³⁄₁₆ inches (81 mm) carapace length, a weight of about one pound. Abundance has increased in recent years, perhaps due to a warming trend in northern coastal waters.

Fishery

An extensive trap and trawl fishery exists along the northern U.S. and Canadian Atlantic coasts. Much mariculture research has also been accomplished.

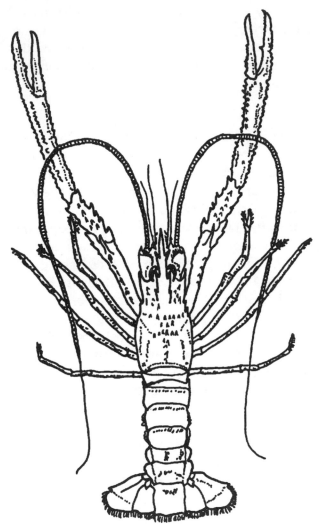

Figure 39.

Metanephrops binghami (Boone, 1927)

Common names
   Caribbean lobster
   Cigalla del caribe   Langoustine caraibe

Distinguishing characteristics

Size: Small to medium, body length ranges to 6 inches (16 cm), commonly 4.6 inches (12 cm).

Color: The carapace is pink to pale orange with a bright white rostrum. The cervical and post cervical grooves are white, especially in juveniles. The dorsal abdomen is pink to orange, and the tailfan is red with a broad white band along the posterior margin.

Form: Body is cylindrical with a spiny carapace. Strong median rostrum with lateral and ventral teeth. No tubercles or spinules are present between the supraorbital ridges (*M. rubellus*, a more southern species, has scattered tubercles or spinules between these ridges). Eyes are well developed and pigmented. Tail is strong with a well developed fan, and abdominal segments are smooth, without transverse grooves. Pincers on first legs are long and slender, square in cross section with rows of spines along the ridges.

Distribution

Northern Bahamas and south Florida, Gulf of Mexico, Caribbean Sea, northern South America. Deep water, 125 to 382 fathoms (230 to 700 m). Commonly found on level bottoms in 130 to 325 fathoms (250 to 600 m) in Caribbean Sea.

Life history

Found on flat sand, shell rubble, coral rubble bottoms. The eggs, 2.0 to 3.0 mm, are carried on the abdominal appendages of the female and are at first bright blue changing to green and finally to yellowish red. Eggs are carried throughout the year. Abundance is greatest in water of 54 °F, but *M. binghami* ranges from 43 °F to 65 °F.

Fishery

Taken in commercial quantities during exploratory trawling in 160 to 190 fathoms off the coasts of Nicaragua and Colombia; 40-foot flat trawls produced 2 to 15 pounds (10 kg) per hour (Roe, 1966).

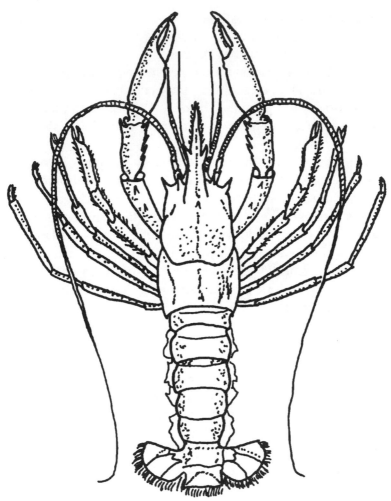

Figure 40.

Nephropsis aculeata Smith, 1881

Common names
  Florida lobsterette
  Danish lobsterette
  Cigala de Florida   Langoustine de Floride

Distinguishing characteristics

Size: Small, body length commonly about 3 inches (8 cm) and maximum 4 inches (10 cm).

Color: Variable, reddish pink, pink to pale red, sometimes dorsal area of carapace is pale orange or brown, white spot present over the orbit, and a whitish band occurs along the base of the pleura. Eyes are very small, white on a pink eyestalk.

Form: Antennae are long and whip-like with no antennal scales. Rostrum strong with only one pair of lateral spines. Anterior edge of second abdominal pleura smooth with no forward directed spines. Pincers are well developed with woolly-like setae on the fingers.

Distribution

This species occurs throughout the Gulf of Mexico, the Caribbean Sea, and the Bahamas. The total range extends north to New Jersey and south to South America. Depths range from 70 to 454 fathoms (130 to 830 m), usually found between 164 and 273 fathoms (300 to 500 m).

Life history

Found on mud or fine sand bottoms. Eggs are carried on the abdominal appendages of the female and range from 1.5 to 2.5 mm in diameter. Newly spawned eggs number 100 to 300, are bluish at first, and become yellowish red as the embryos develop. *N. aculeata* is most abundant in water of 51 °F, but is found in a temperature range of 45 °F to 54 °F.

Fishery

Large catches of the Florida lobsterette have been made in 160 to 220 fathoms off St. Augustine, Florida, in 210 to 240 fathoms near the Dry Tortugas, and in 220 to 240 fathoms off the Mississippi River Delta. Catches of 2 to 10 pounds per hour (heads on) have been produced with 40-foot trawls and up to 80 pounds per hour (heads on) with 65 foot trawls. Average size was 18 individuals to the pound (Roe , 1966).

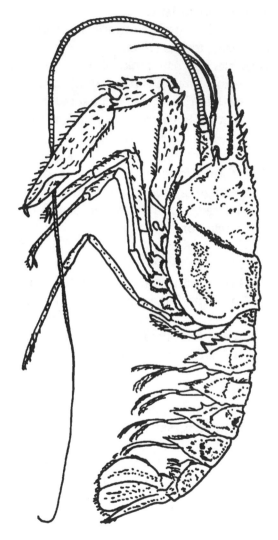

Figure 41.

Nephropsis agassizii A. Milne Edwards, 1880

Common names
   Prickly lobsterette
   Langoustine epineuse   Cigala de grano

Distinguishing characteristics

Size: Small, carapace length ranges from 0.75 to 2.25 inches (20 to 56 mm) and maximum total length is about 4.75 inches (12 cm).

Color: Basic color is bright pink, the rostrum and anterior portion of the carapace is a darker red and the appendages, mouth parts, legs and uropods are bright red. The eye stalk is reddish and the eye (cornea) is white.

Form: The well developed median rostrum has two pairs of strong lateral spines. Antennae are long and whip-like with no antennal scales. Pleura of the second abdominal segment with two forward projecting spines on the anterior edge. Pincers well developed with long hair-like setae (not woolly) on most of the leg and pincers.

Distribution

Throughout the Caribbean, the Bahamas, the northern and eastern Gulf of Mexico, and south to Brazil. It occurs at depths from 328 to 1,399 fathoms (600 to 2,560 m), but is usually taken between 437 and 710 fathoms (800 to 1,300 m).

Life history

Females are slightly smaller than males. Eggs are incubated on the abdominal appendages and are 2.6 mm in diameter. Found on mud bottoms with organic detritus.

Fishery

Not fished commercially. Taken sparingly in the northwestern and north central Gulf of Mexico at 500 to 1000 fathoms by exploratory fishing vessels.

Palinuridae — Spiny Lobsters

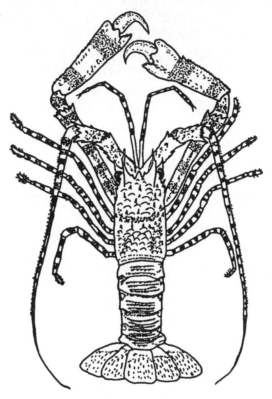

Figure 42.

Justitia longimanus (H. Milne Edwards, 1837)

Common names
Longarm spiny lobster
Langousta caribe   Langousta de muelas

Distinguishing characteristics
   Size: A small spiny lobster, maximum total body length
6 inches (15 cm), usually about 4.5 inches (11 cm).
   Color: Tail is brick red, body also brick red but variously
spotted with yellow. First pair of legs with wide red cross
bands.

Form: Carapace is rounded and spiny with scale-like sculpturing, a strong central spine present between the twin frontal horns. In males, the first pair of walking legs are greatly enlarged and the dactyl is strongly curved and forms an apparent (false) pincer. The dorsal surface of each abdominal segment crossed by four or five transverse grooves.

Distribution

An uncommon species, found from Bermuda and south Florida, through the Bahamas, and along the Caribbean Antilles island chain to the coast of South America. Depth ranges from 1 to 164 fathoms (2 to 300 m), usually found between 25 and 50 fathoms. Divers may encounter this species on deep Florida Keys reefs, 80 to 150 feet (25 to 45 m).

Life history

Not much is known about this species. The larval stages, presumed to be of *J. longimana*, have been described by Robertson (1969) from phyllosoma larvae collected in plankton samples from the Florida Straits and the Atlantic north of the Bahamas. (Note: Robertson uses the species name *longimana* over *longimanus*.) The distribution of the larvae is most likely similar to other palinurid lobster larvae in this area; however, the apparent restriction of occurrence of adults to the eastern edge of the Caribbean raises some interesting questions. Since the enlarged first walking legs with the false pincer are found only in males, it is possible that this unique appendage has a mating function. Like other spiny lobsters, the longarm spiny lobster is hidden deep in the reef during the day and emerges at night. Life history is probably similar to that of other spiny lobsters.

Fishery

Rarely taken in the commercial fishery. May occur in traps set on the deep outer slopes of reefs. Sometimes taken by collectors for the marine aquarium industry and, rarely, found in aquarium shops.

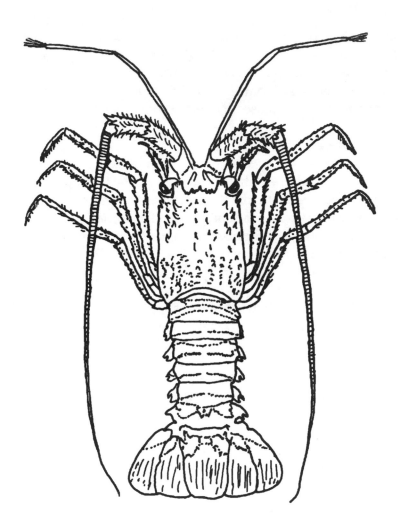

Figure 43.

Palinustus truncatus A. Milne Edwards, 1880

Common names
  Blunthorn spiny lobster
  Langouste aliousta   Langosta nata

Distinguishing characteristics

Size: A small spiny lobster, maximum size at least 4 inches total length (10 cm).

Color: Pale brown body with scattered reddish brown spots. Legs cream color with reddish bands.

Form: Carapace rounded and covered with strong spines. The frontal horns over the eyes are strong and very blunt with toothed anterior edges. No strong central spine on anterior edge of carapace. No spines on the antennular plate between the antennae bases. Antennules slender, their flagella much shorter than their bases. Each abdominal segment with a transverse groove that is interrupted at the midline.

Distribution

Type specimen taken at Cariacou, Lesser Antilles. Known also from the northern coast of South America (Surinam to Brazil). Depth ranges from 54 to 546 fathoms (100 to below 1000 m).

Life history

A rare species. Nothing known of its life history. Phylosoma larvae not identified.

Fishery

No fishery exists.

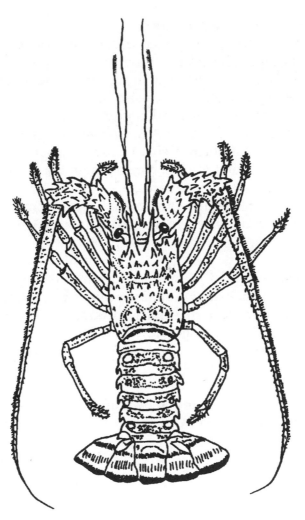

Figure 44.

Panulirus argus (Latreille, 1804)

Common names
> **Caribbean spiny lobster**
> Florida spiny lobster   Common spiny lobster
> Langouste blanche   Langosta comun
> (See Chapter 2 for additional common names)

Distinguishing characteristics

Size: Caribbean spiny lobsters have the capability of living long and growing very large. In unfished areas, generally deeper waters, individuals over 15 pounds and four feet long (including antennae) can be found. These very large individuals may be as old as 15 to 20 years. The largest spiny lobsters in Florida, 10 pounds and up, occur on the northeast coast, Melborne to Savannah, Georgia. Large lobsters, up to 9 pounds, are often found on the Middle Grounds in the northeast Gulf of Mexico. Males reach a larger individual size than females. Maximum size is typically considered to be 18 inches (45 cm) total body length. Average weight of individuals from lightly fished populations in the Caribbean and Bahamas may be at least 3 to 5 pounds. According to Fonteles-Filho (1990), the asymptotic length (which is about as big as they grow in the population under study) of the *P. argus* stocks off Brazil is 17 inches (43.8 cm) and the asymptotic weight is 7 pounds (3.2 kg). Average length in this population is reported at about 8.5 inches (21.6 cm); average weight is about 14 ounces (404 g).

In the Florida Keys, average size is probably below the legal size of 3 inches carapace length (76 mm), but average size varies with the intensity of the fishery. The more intense the fishery, the smaller the average individual size. Figure 24 in Chapter 2 shows the relationships between carapace length, tail length, and total weight for males and females in English and metric units.

Color: Base color variable. Inshore, smaller specimens often dark greenish purple while offshore, deeper water specimens often a brilliant dark red. Brown is also a common background color. The four large, cream colored spots on the dorsal surface of the abdomen, two on the first and two on the sixth abdominal segment are characteristic of this species. Smaller cream colored spots are usually present on other abdominal segments. Legs have light and dark longitudinal markings.

Form: The single transverse groove on the second to fifth abdominal segments is interrupted in the middle. Legs are without pincers except for the false pincers on the female's last pair of walking legs that are used in fertilization and egg care during repoduction. Carapace rounded and spiny with two strong, sharply pointed horns above the eyes. Antennae long and whip-like with many forward pointed spines. Antennule flagella are longer than the antennule pecuncles (base). Two pairs of strong spines present on the antennular plate below the eyes.

Distribution

Widely distributed. The southeastern US from North Carolina and Bermuda throughout the Bahamas, Gulf of Mexico, and the Caribbean Sea, south to the northern coast of South America down to Rio de Janeiro, Brazil. A shallow water species, depth ranges from a few inches (early juveniles) to over 50 fathoms (1 to 100 m), but commonly found in 1 to 25 fathoms (2 to 45 m). *P. argus* is very abundant throughout the Bahamas, on suitable habitat in the Caribbean Sea, and along the southeast Florida coast, the Florida Keys, and Florida Bay. Divers (Kevin Bruington, personal communication) often find spiny lobsters in the Gulf of Mexico off St. Petersburg, FL, at depths of 40 to 90 feet (12 to 27 m). They are seldom found in relatively near shore waters north of Clearwater, FL, although one 8 pound lobster was taken off Tarpon Springs on April 1, 1987. They seem to move into these waters in April and are absent from the area during December through February. They usually occur in groups of 4 to 6 individuals; one large male and several females constitute one unit. Females commonly carry eggs. Spiny lobsters are not abundant, but are common on the humps in the Florida Middle Grounds from 80 to 90 feet (24 to 27 m) and down to 120 to 130 feet (36 to 40 m). Females with eggs are also common on the Middle Grounds. As an estimate of abundance, 5 divers in a total of 30 dives (6 dives each) may find 15 lobsters on a typical Middle Grounds trip.

Life history

P. *argus* has a long and complex life history. Spawning occurs throughout the year in the southern areas of the range and only from April into August in the northern areas. The phyllosome larva spends 6 to 9 months in oceanic currents feeding on other planktonic animals before metamorphosing into an intermediate form, the postlarva or puerulus, which swims rapidly and directly toward the coast. Once shallow water (or an appropriate habitat) is reached, another molt transforms the puerulus into a juvenile lobster. The tiny lobster feeds on small mollusks, worms, and other organisms in shallow algal flats or other nursery habitats and grows through periodic molts of the hard exoskeleton. After two to three years in shallow water, the spiny lobster reaches adult size and migrates to the offshore reefs for spawning. Some of these adult lobsters return to shallow water after the spawning season. Life history is described in Chapter 1. There are other excellent accounts of the life history of the Caribbean spiny lobster: Williams (1984), Marx and Herrnkind (1986), and The Fishery Management Plan for the Spiny Lobster Fishery of the Gulf of Mexico and South Atlantic produced by the Gulf of Mexico and the South Atlantic Fishery Management Councils in 1981.

Fishery

Fisheries for the Caribbean spiny lobster vary from the intensive trap fishery of the Florida Keys, to the extensive spear fishery in the Bahamas, to spear fisheries based on artificial habitats in Mexico, and the wire trap fishery in Cuba. Wherever people and spiny lobsters coexist, there is a fishery, be it primitive or modern, commercial or recreational. The fishery off the northeast coast of Brazil began in 1955 and produced an average of 5,280 metric tons per year during the period 1965 to 1987. The fishery for P. *argus* is described in greater detail in Chapters 5 and 6.

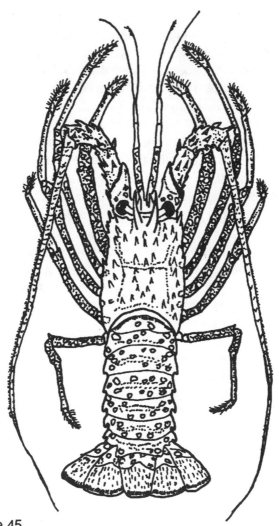

Figure 45.

Panulirus guttatus (Latreille, 1804)

Common names
    Spotted spiny lobster   Guinea chick lobster
    Chicken lobster   Star lobster
    Langouste bresilienne   Langousta moteada

Distinguishing characteristics

Size: Generally smaller than *P. argus*. Maximum body length is about 8 inches (20 cm), and 4 to 6 inches (10 to 15 cm) is common.

Color: The coloration of *P. guttatus* is very distinctive. The background color is purple to dark reddish brown. The tail may be a bit greenish. The entire lobster is covered with small yellowish to cream-colored spots. All but the last segment of each leg is also covered with these spots.

Form: Carapace rounded and covered with many spines. Frontal horns over the eyes are sharp and pronounced. Only one pair of strong spines present on the wide antennular plate. Each abdominal segment with a complete transverse groove.

(Note: The brown spiny lobster, *P. echinatus* is very similar to *P. guttatus* and was only recently recognized as a distinct species (Holthuis, 1961). *P. echinatus* differs from *P. guttatus* most noticeably by having the transverse grooves on abdominal segments 2 through 5 interrupted in the middle. It is generally not found north of Brazil.)

Distribution

Found from Bermuda and the southeast Florida coast, throughout the Bahamas and southward throughout the Antilles island arc to the northern coast of South America down to Brazil. A shallow water species, common on near shore jetties and shallow reefs down to 40 feet (12 m). Maximum depth probably less than 100 feet (30 m).

Life history

Generally, the life history is similar to *P. argus*, but there are many fundamental differences. Not known to have migratory habits and usually found only on shallow, offshore reefs and rocky, nearshore jetties. The postlarva settles directly on the shallow coral reefs under the ledges and in crevices in the roofs of caves that are also the adult habitat. William G. Lyons (personal communciation) reports that artifical habitats designed to collect newly settled pueruli catch *P. guttatus* and not *P. argus* when set in offshore reef structures. Conversely, *P. guttatus* pueruli are not taken in these habitats when they are set in shallow, near shore waters where *P. argus* pueruli are found. *P. guttatus* is found on shallow reefs also occupied by *P. argus*, but they are much more secretive and are found deep in the reef structure and far under coral heads during the day. Females generally hide deeper in the reef than males.

Sutcliffe (1953) reported that the numbers of males on the reefs exceeded females by 10 to 1. This unusual sex ratio may have been a result of females not entering traps, since Florida studies, Chitty (1973) and Beardsly (1973), reported overall sex ratios reasonably close to 1 to 1. They emerge at night and wander over the reef structure seeking food. They do not leave the reefs to feed on the nearby sand and grass flats as do *P. argus*. The ratio of *P. guttatus* to *P. argus* on shallow reefs has been estimated at 1 to 20 on offshore reefs in Bermuda (Sutcliffe, 1953), but *P. guttatus* is more abundant on man-made jetties.

Sutcliffe (1953), Caillouet et al. (1971), Chitty (1973), and Beardsly (1973) presented biological information on this species. First spawning takes place at a carapace length of about 1.5 inches (38 mm). In south Florida, peak spawning takes place in June. Eggs are incubated by the female for about 30 days at a temperature of 77°F (25°C). Females carry between 40,000 and 140,000 eggs depending on size and condition. The phylosoma larva is very similar to *P. argus*. Hatching occurs at night.

Fishery

A separate fishery for this species does not exist. Large specimens are taken incidentally in the *P. argus* lobster trap fishery, and large specimens are occasionally taken by spear in other fisheries. The small size of this lobster usually excludes it from the commercial trap fishery. Males are larger than females and are more likely to appear in the commer-

cial catch. Commercial marinelife specimen collectors frequently capture this species for the marine aquarium market. The spotted spiny lobster is rather common on the
jetties of Florida southeast coast inlets and sometimes up to
100 per hour can be taken by divers at night. This species is
not protected by law since it is not important to the commercial fishery, but to preserve the current stocks, females carrying eggs still should not be taken .

Figure 46. *Panulirus guttatus* (left) and *Panulirus argus* (right).
This photograph illustrates the distinguishing color patterns of
each species.

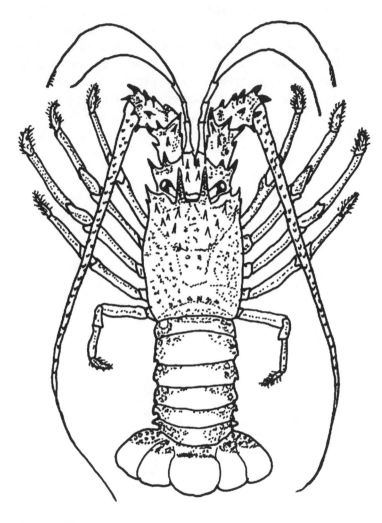

Figure 47.

Panulirus laevicauda (Latreille, 1817)

Common names
  Smoothtail spiny lobster
  Brazilian spiny lobster
  Langouste indienne   Langosta verde

Distinguishing characteristics

Size: Maximum total body length for *P. laevicauda* taken off Brazil (asymptotic length), reported by A. A. Fonteles-Filho (1990), is about 15 inches (38.0 cm), with average length at about 7 inches (18.2 cm). Maximum total weight (asymptotic weight) is reported as about 4 lbs (1.8 kg), with the average total weight about 8.6 oz (247 g)

Color: Variable, background may be greenish or yellowish with purple overtones. White spots present near the edge of the carapace and along the edges of the abdominal segments.

Form: Strong frontal horns over the eyes are red with white markings. Legs have longitudinal white and purple streaks. The carapace is rounded and spiny. The antennular plate has two pairs of strong spines. The dorsal surfaces of the abdominal segments are smooth, no transverse grooves present, with no conspicuous markings—a physical characteristic that provides the basis for the common name.

Tail surface: *P. argus*

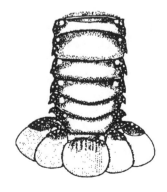

Tail surface: P. *laevicauda*

Distribution

Found from Bermuda and the southeast and southwest coasts of Florida, along the Antilles island arc, probably throughout the Caribbean Sea, and along the northern coast of South America including the Brazilian coast. It is rare in the northern portion of the range, with occasional exceptions. Moore (1962) records *P. laevicauda* as common off West Palm Beach, Florida, in the year 1949, and specimens of this species are occasionally taken along the continental coast of south Florida. This species is very common off the northeast coast of Brazil, and is second to *P. argus* in the commercial landings. The seafood restaurants of Rio de Janeiro sell considerable quantities of this species that are taken in local waters. *P. laevicuda* is a shallow water species, although the maximum depth ranges out to about 328 feet (100 m). It is most common on the inner shelf area, while *P. argus* is found over a much wider area. Both species are found on the rock and coral reefs in the shallow 50 foot (3 to 15 m) coastal areas off northeastern Brazil.

Life history

Life history is very similar to *P. argus*. The two species may be able to coexist only because competition for breeding and nursery sites is minimized since they are occupied by each species at different times of the year. There may also be subtle differences in the ecological requirements of each species that reduces interspecific competition. If so, some ecological parameter common to the Brazilian coast but absent in the Caribbean sea and the Gulf of Mexico may explain the relative absence of *P. laevicauda* in these more northern areas. Current patterns that may reproductively isolate lobster populations along the northeastern coast of Brazil from more northern populations (see comment 9 in the addendum to Chapter 1) may also prevent *P. laevicauda* from establishing northern populations.

Off the northeast coast of Brazil, breeding occurs in late winter and spring, and molting occurs twice a year in January and in July/August. *P. argus* and *P. laevicauda* are very abundant off the northeast coast of Brazil, perhaps because the offshore coastal area is very stable with little annual change in temperature and salinity. Patterns of larval distribution and migration have not been studied. Current patterns must exist, however, that allow the larvae of *P. laevicauda* (and also *P. argus* and *P. echinatus*) to return to the waters off Brazil. Paiva and da Costa (1968) present a review of the biology of this species. Fonteles-Filho (1990) reports the growth rate of *P. laevicauda* in the populations off the northeast coast of Brazil to be 1.05 inches per year (2.7 cm/yr). He also reports that this species carries an average of 141,235 eggs per female, and the average number of eggs per gram of body weight is 579. The growth coefficient (K) for this population is 0.163.

Fishery

Occasionally taken in fisheries for the Caribbean spiny lobster. Rarely found in the Florida Keys but occasionally taken along the southeast Florida coast. Fishermen usually recognize it as a separate species although some may consider their catch a "sport" or mutation of *P. argus*. *P. laevicuda* supports an important fishery off the coast of Brazil. Landings of *P. laevicauda* for the period of March though November of 1987 totaled 5,356 tons. More information on this fishery is included in Chapter 6.

Scyllaridae — Slipper Lobsters

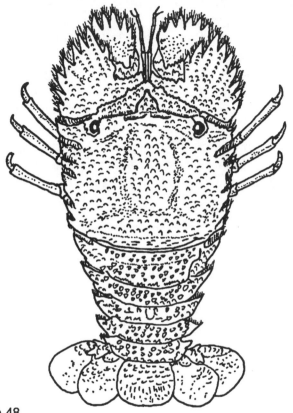

Figure 48.

Parribacus antarcticus (Lund, 1793)

Common names
Sculptured slipper lobster   Slipper lobster
Cigale savate   Cigarro chineso

Distinguishing characteristics
Size: Maximum size is about 8 inches (20 cm) total
length. Commonly found at 5 to 6 inches (12 to 15 cm).

Color: Body tan to gray, mottled with red but with no remarkable stripes or spots.

Form: Carapace and abdomen greatly flattened, carapace broader than long, its sides thin with sharply toothed triangular projections. Stiff hairs occur between these triangular projections. Body surface with a pebble-like sculpturing. No pincers on legs. Antennae broad and flattened with strong, toothed projections.

Distribution

South Florida, throughout the Bahamas, reef areas in the Caribbean Sea, and along the Antilles island arc to the coast of South America to Brazil. A shallow water species usually found on offshore reefs, 20 to 100 feet (6 to 30 m).

Life history

A secretive species, seldom seen by daytime divers. Usually found at night moving about the reef or occasionally taken in traps by commercial fishermen. Spawning seems to occur from April to August, and, as in all the Scyllaridae lobsters, a long lived phyllosoma larval stage aids distribution of the species. Sims (1965) described 12 larval stages of *Parribacus* sp., almost certainly *antarcticus*, developed from a collection of 1,579 specimens taken in plankton tows in the Yucatan Straits and near the Florida Keys. Note that 1,306 of these were taken at one station in the Keys during August of 1963 and were mostly representative of the first five stages. Robertson (1968 a) also described the phyllosome of *P. antarcticus* (see illustration) and mentioned that the stages 11 and 12 described by Sims (1965) are most probably *S. nodifer* and not *P. antarcticus*. Because of its secretive habits and apparent scarcity, little is known of its life history.

Fishery

No commercial fishery. Occasional individuals taken in the spiny lobster fishery may be sold as specimens for marine aquariums.

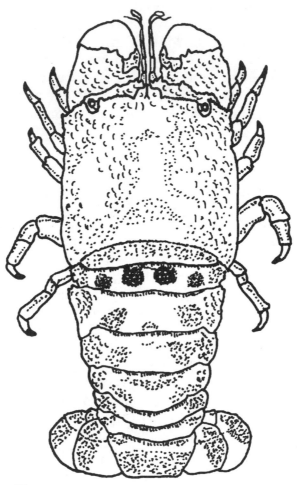

Figure 49.

Scyllarides aequinoctialis (Lund, 1793)

Common names

Spanish slipper lobster	Buccaneer crab
Shovel nosed lobster	Gollipop
Bulldozer lobster	Locust lobster
Dozer	Rock lobster
Cigale marie-carogne	Cigarro espanol

Distinguishing characteristics

Size: A large slipper lobster, total body length can exceed 12 inches (30 cm).

Color: Overall color is a mottled reddish orange to tan and brown. The underside is more yellowish brown, and the legs are yellow with brown to red spots. The dorsal surface of the first abdominal segment is conspicuously marked with four dark red to black spots. Two are on the sides of the abdominal segment, and two are on either side of the central line. The center two spots are often joined by a bar of dark color just under the edge of the carapace. A small fifth spot may occur at the median line where the first and second abdominal segments overlap. As with most lobsters, intensity of color can vary with environment and other factors.

Form: The body is flattened with a rounded dorsal surface. The carapace is longer than it is wide, with relatively smooth edges, and the dorsal surface of both carapace and abdomen is finely pebbled. There are no ridges or projections on the carapace. The antennae are composed of four movable segments and are flat, broad, and strong with smooth front edges. The legs are short and strong without pincers, except for the false pincers on the last walking legs of the female used in egg care during reproduction. Eyestalks are short, stout, and striped. The abdomen is strong and stout with no dorsal ridges or projections. Lyons (1970) presents a detailed morphological description of this species.

Distribution

Bermuda, East coast of the United States, Florida to South Carolina, the Florida Keys, throughout the Bahamas, western Gulf of Mexico, Caribbean Sea, and the Antilles island arc to South America. Not found, or rare, in the eastern and northern Gulf of Mexico. A shallow water species found on coral reef formations, 10 to 100 feet (3 to 30 m), but recorded as deep as 590 feet (180 m). Not uncommon on deep reefs along the coast of northern Florida and Georgia.

Life history

Despite the wide range and relatively common occurance on coral reefs, not much is known about the life history of this species. *S. aequinoctialis* hides during the day deep under the reef structure. They can be found clinging tightly to the roofs of coral rock caves and far under coral heads during the day. I have seen them emerge from the reefs at twilight and begin to move about the sandy bottom near the reefs. They do not seem to be as gregarious as *S. nodifer*, as they are usually solitary on the reefs, but they do aggregate when held in captivity.

We attempted to rear this species when Aqualife Research Corporation was based near Marathon in the Florida Keys, and some of this information is valuable in a life history context. Chapter 4 contains more details on the rearing experimentation. A large, gravid female *S. aequinoctialis* was taken by Forrest Young on April 30, 1978 from under a deeply recessed ledge in about 15 feet of water at the 7 mile bridge west of Marathon and was maintained in a large tank at our hatchery. The eggs were bright yellow, undeveloped with a small, translucent section at one pole where the embryo was just beginning to develop. The eggs were 700 microns (.7 mm) in diameter and only about 40% of the eggs the female carried developed to hatching. This could have been due to incomplete fertilization or due to environmental conditions in the holding tank. Hatching occurred on the night of May 18, 1978 at 22:30 hours.

The female fanned her swimmeretts over the eggs and slowly flexed and extended her abdomen. Many thousands of larvae were hatched. The hatched larvae retained the ball-like form from the egg with their legs tightly tucked. Only the swimmeretts on the extended antennae of the larvae moved the larvae upward in the water column. The legs were extended with jerky movements after about 10 to 15 minutes, and the larvae took on the typical phyllosome form and movements. The female retained the undeveloped eggs for several days and then shed them on the tank bottom. She produced another spawn on May 30, but the eggs did not develop. No spermatophore was observed, but fertilization is apparently internal in *S. aequinoctialis* as in other *Scyllarides*. The larvae first molted on the night of May 27, nine days after hatch. They did not survive to the next molt.

Robertson (1968 a) reared *S. aequinoctialis* from laboratory hatched eggs at 24 °C to stage 10 and presents an excellent description of the larval stages from both reared and plankton caught specimens. Larvae reared at 5 °C above and below 24 °C did not survive to stage 3. It took 94 days for the larvae to reach stage 8. All but three of the larvae died after stage 8. The survivors did not change morphologically when they entered stage 9 and measured 6 mm total length at that point. The duration of the intermolt periods began at

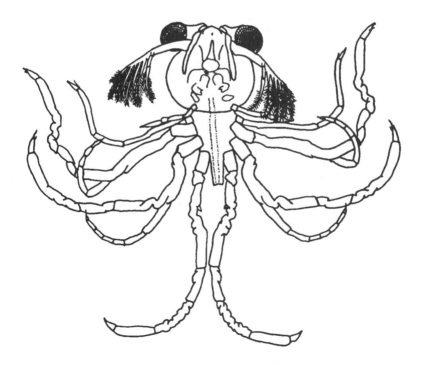

Figure 50. Naupliosoma stage of *S. aequinoctialis* from Robertson (1968).

8 days and extended to 14 days at the last surviving molt. Robertson noted that the larvae first hatched into a naupliosoma stage (Figure 50) which occurs in *Jasus, Ibacus,* and *Scyllarides,* but not in *Scyllarus* or *Panulirus*. The naupilosoma stage is quite different from the first phyllosome stage, with natatory setae (swimming hairs) on the antennae and not on the legs. The naupliosoma stage lasts only a few minutes, and then quickly molts into the first phyllosome stage. It is possible that the naupliosoma stage allows the larvae to swim upward off the bottom more quickly than the typical phyllosome form, which is more adapted for horizontal movement.

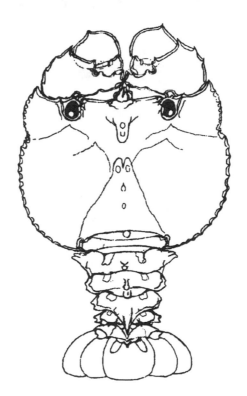

Figure 51. Dorsal view of the postlarva of *S. aequinoctialis* from Lyons (1970).

The period of larval development, based on rearing observation of the first stages and estimates from other scientists (Lyons, 1970), is apparently 9 months to a year.

The postlarvae ranges in total length from 26 to 29 mm and has a large flattened, disk-shaped carapace and a smaller abdomen. The postlarva of *Scyllarides* serves the same purpose as the puerulus stage of *Panulirus*—to move the animal from the offshore, planktonic larval environment to a benthic (bottom) habitat. They are probably capable of extensive swimming behavior, clinging to floating objects, and hiding in a benthic substrate during the course of their journey. Once they have settled and become juveniles, there is no indication that *S. aequinoctialis* undergoes any migratory movement. Reproductive behavior and food and feeding is not known.

Fishery

Because of the large size and sweet flavor, *S. aequinoctialis* is highly favored by commercial and recreational fishermen. A small fishery for this species exists in Puerto Rico, but in most other areas it is taken in traps along with spiny lobsters, found on the reefs by divers, and often taken in shrimp trawls. Since the catch is small, most marketing is done to restaurants although a few occasionally turn up in fish markets. This species is sometimes taken in the recreational lobster fishery on deep reefs offshore of the northeast Florida and Georgia coasts. They are typically found under ledges and in small rock caves.

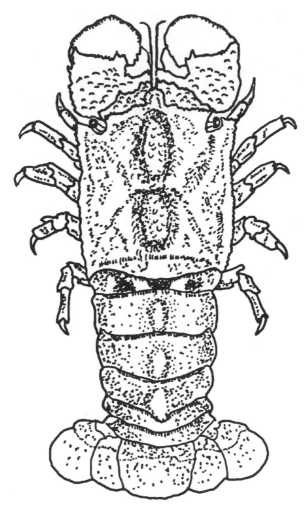

Figure 52.

Scyllarides nodifer (Stimpson, 1866)

Common names
Ridged slipper lobster   Spanish lobster
Bulldozer   Dozer
Shovel nosed lobster   Sand lobster
Cigale chambre   Cigarro de quilla

Distinguishing characteristics

Size: A moderate sized lobster, rarely exceeds 12 inches (30 cm) total length, weight is 200 to 300 g. Maximum recorded carapace length, excluding tail, is 5 inches (127 mm).

Color: Body generally reddish brown but varies from tan to orange. Newly molted adults are bright orange with white patches. Red tubercles and darker reddish spots are present over the body. Legs are yellowish with bright red bands. Antennules are purple. The dorsal surface of the first abdominal segment has a large median red spot with two smaller reddish spots in the center of each side.

Form: The body is flattened but strongly rounded in dorsal aspect. The carapace is longer than it is wide, and the dorsal surface of the carapace and abdomen is roughly pebbled. The edges of the carapace are finely toothed. A broad, heavy ridge extends along the center line of the carapace and the second, third, and forth abdominal segments also have a strong, raised ridge. The antennae are short and broad with smooth front edges. The legs are strong and short, without pincers. The fifth (last) walking legs of the female have a set of false pincers used for egg care during reproduction. The abdomen is broad and strong. Williams (1984) presents a complete description of this species, and Lyons (1970) provides detailed information on populations in the eastern Gulf of Mexico. Hardwick (1987) provides extensive biological and fishery information on this species in a doctoral dissertation from the University of Alabama.

Distribution

S. nodifer is found in the Gulf of Mexico, the Florida Keys, along the southeast coast of the United States from Florida to North Carolina, and Bermuda. The center of abundance is the Gulf of Mexico, and distribution along the southeastern U.S. is apparently due to the dispersal of the pelagic phyllosome larvae along the path of the Florida Current and the Gulf Stream. There is only one record of this species south of the Florida Straits. An unpublished report described by Hardwick (1987) mentions a single *S. nodifer* observed in Abraham's Bay at Mayaguana Island in the southern Bahamas.

Depth of occurrence ranges from 6 to 300 feet (2 to 91 m). It is possible that a large population of this species may be present in depths greater than 54 fathoms (100 m), but fishing gear that will take *S. nodifer* at these depths has not been utilized. Shipp and Hopkins (1978) made observations from a research submersible along the northern rim of the De Soto Canyon and reported numerous *S. nodifer* on limestone block ridges. Greatest abundance in the eastern Gulf of Mexico is 100 to 138 feet (30 to 42 m) (Lyons, 1970). The four areas where the ridged slipper lobster seems to be most abundant in the Gulf of Mexico are west of Fort Myers in 65 to 196 feet (20 to 60 m), the Florida Middle Grounds west and north of Tampa, along the northwest Florida coast from Apalachee Bay to Panama City, and along the shell bank areas offshore of Alabama, Mississippi, and Louisiana. They have also been reported in the Bay of Campeche and on the underside of drilling platforms off Texas.

Hardwick (1987) compared isozyme analyses (a method of comparing muscle extracts for statistically significant genetic differences) from different Gulf of Mexico populations of *S. nodifer*. He found no significant differences and considers the stocks of ridged slipper lobsters in the eastern Gulf to be one population, the result of a single gene pool. Specimens from Texas, Yucatan, and the east coast of the U.S. were not tested and compared.

Life history

A number of studies have been done on the fishery and biology of *S. nodifer*. Its center of abundance in the eastern and northern Gulf of Mexico places it close to recreational diving, commercial fishing (shrimp trawling) activity, and also within the sphere of interest of several universities and marine research institutions. Although much is yet to be learned, we do have a growing body of information on this species. Fertilization is internal, and spawning occurs from late May to early August (Lyons, 1970). Hardwick (1987) reports that the spawning period for *S. nodifer* in the northeastern Gulf of Mexico extends from early February through August. The male apparently extrudes a spermatophore and then places it externally on the female. She then moves the spermatophore to an internal position. The female extrudes and fertilizes the eggs some time after mating and then carries the fertilized, developing eggs under her abdomen until they hatch, a period of several weeks.

A sibling species, *Scyllarides latus*, the Mediterranean locust lobster, carries up to 350,000 eggs, and *S. nodifer* probably carries about the same number. The false pincer on her last pair of walking legs is used to groom and ventilate the eggs. Postlarvae are found in the eastern Gulf and in the Florida Keys from six to ten months after the spawning season, which provides a good indication of the length of the larval period, since there are no Caribbean populations of this species and since the spawning season is limited. Postlarvae have been found at considerable depths in the eastern Gulf, and this indicates that the postlarvae may settle in deep as well as shallow water.

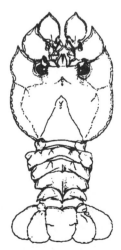

Figure 53. Dorsal view of *S. notifer* postlarva from Lyons (1970).

Recreational fishermen report that *S. nodifer* is common
on the Florida Middle Grounds, offshore of the central Florida west coast, and offshore of the northwest Florida coast.
Like other spiny and slipper lobsters, *S. nodifer* moves about
and feeds at night and spends the day hiding quietly in a
protected den. Divers often find them aggregated far up
under ledges and in rock caves in numbers of 10 or more.
They are seldom found in the open during the day, prefer-
ring to hide in caves, crevices, and under ledges, often clinging to the roof of their shelter. Metal shipwrecks, airplane
wrecks, old automobile tires, and other artificial structures
are also common daytime habitats. It is not uncommon for a
diver to collect 20 to 30 per dive. They are found on most
bottom types in the eastern Gulf if suitable rocky shelter is
nearby. *S. nodifer* shares the same general habitat and seems
to be more abundant than *S. aequinoctialis* in the Florida
Keys.

S. nodifer appears to be an opportunistic omnivore. They
are common in scallop grounds and feed avidly on squid,
clams, shrimp, mussels, and oysters in aquaria. They can
easily open living clams and oysters, capture and eat live
scallops, and will even eat hermit crabs. Bivalves are opened
with the first two pairs of walking legs by forcing the sharp
dactyls between the shells and then cutting the abductor
muscle by insertion of a single dactyl. The lobster supports
itself on the last three pairs of walking legs and its tail
during this process. Sea lettuce, the alga *Ulva*, is also in-
cuded in the diet. Their major predators are groupers and
sharks, and their defense mechanisms are simple. They usually den in inaccessible areas during the day, and their body
is so camouflaged in color and form that they are difficult to
distinguish when motionless. They also cling tightly to the
substrate exposing only a smooth, rounded dorsal aspect to
a potential predator. They may also burrow into soft sub-
strates, but this has not been observed.

S. nodifer and other scyllarid lobsters have a capacity for
movement through swimming and gliding behavior. The

strong abdomen and broad tail fan provide the propulsion, and the convex dorsal and flat ventral surfaces provide hydrodynamic lift. The flat antennae trim the glide and give the lobster some control over the direction of its movement. Slipper lobsters released in mid-water, or at the surface, swim in this fashion, but it is not known if they use this method of locomotion commonly, or at all, under normal conditions. Since they tire easily from swimming activity in captivity, it is likely that swimming in the wild is limited to escape reactions. There is some evidence for migratory behavior in this species, a movement into shallow water in the early spring for reproduction and a possible southward movement during the summer, but this has yet to be proven.

Fishery

A significant fishery for *S. nodifer* has developed in the eastern Gulf of Mexico, the "Big Bend" area, offshore of Carrabelle, Florida. Slipper lobsters are taken primarily by shrimp trawls, but also in traps and by divers. Shrimp trawlers have found specific areas, "hang-free corridors", where they can trawl their nets without fouling them on rocks and coral and where, during the spring, knowledgeable shrimpers can catch up to 2,000 pounds (909 k) of *S. nodifer* in 3 to 4 night's fishing effort. The total catch from this area has gone from 8,000 pounds in 1980 to 75,000 pounds in 1985. This species is now in considerable demand in markets and restaurants in northwestern Florida. The Fort Myers area is a close second with production of 30,000 to 50,000 pounds per year since 1982. Over 100,000 pounds (45,455 k) of ridged slipper lobster were taken from Florida waters in 1983 and 1985. The indication from fishery statistics is that the fishery is still underexploited, but care must be exercised to prevent overfishing. In other areas, the Florida Keys and the southeast coast of the United States, the fishery is not as intense and the catch is mixed with *S. aequinoctialis*. This fishery for *S. nodifer* is discussed in greater detail in Chapter 6.

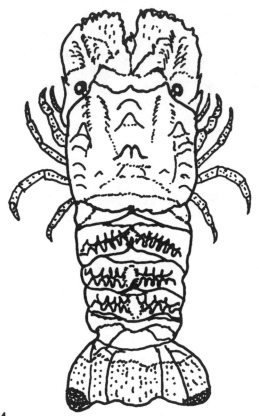

Figure 54.

Scyllarus americanus (Smith, 1869)

Common names
　　American slipper lobster　　　　Sand lobster

Distinguishing characteristics
　　Size: A small lobster, total length about 3 inches (75 mm).
　　Color: Gray to tan, legs are thin and banded.

Form: Carapace with scale-like sculpturing on the dorsal surface. Mid-dorsal ridge with bilobed protuberance just posterior of the cervical groove. Two fused, blunt spines over each eye. Rostrum short and rounded. Antennae short and flat, square in outline with triangular projections on the front edge. Abdomen strong and stout, transverse grooves on segments two, three, and four with branching furrows. First to fourth abdominal segments with a narrow, deep notch at the center of the posterior margin. Williams (1984) presents a comprehensive description of this species.

Distribution

Found in the near shore waters from North Carolina to the Florida Keys, the eastern Gulf of Mexico, the Bahamas, and the Caribbean and off the coast of Venezuela. It is the most common scyllarid lobster along the southeast Florida coast. Depth ranges from the shore line to 150 feet (46 m).

Life history

This is one of the very few species of tropical lobsters that have been reared through the phyllosome larval stage in the laboratory. As reported in several studies, the genus *Scyllarus* has internal fertilization. Spawning in Florida waters apparently occurs at all times of the year, but peak spawning occurs in late winter and early spring. Females carry the eggs for two to three weeks before hatching, which occurs at night. The larvae are typical phyllosomes and develop for 40 days through six or seven stages at 25°C before metamorphosis into postlarvae. In the laboratory, the larvae were able to survive solely on a diet of brine shrimp even though this diet has not been successful in rearing other species of tropical lobsters. Robertson (1968 b) presents an account of the rearing techniques and detailed descriptions of the larval stages. Some of the larvae metamorphosed into postlarvae from larval stage six, and others went through stage seven before becoming postlarvae. The relatively short larval development takes place in shallow coastal waters, so the postlarvae may settle not far from the breeding adults. The adults are found on many different bottom types and are usually taken in large numbers by bait shrimp trawls. They are active at night and usually hidden during the day. Feeding habits not reported.

Fishery

S. americanus is common in the catches of offshore shrimp boats and nearshore bait shrimp boats. They are not used for food or marketed due to their small size. They rarely turn up in the marine aquarium market. They may occasionally be used as bait. In the Mediterranean, a similar small scyllarid lobster, petite cigale, is used in fish soups, but no common food use is made of them in the western Atlantic. Although not now used as food, the relatively short larval period may make this species a candidate for controlled mariculture. If large numbers can be reared easily and inexpensively, a market for these small slipper lobsters may be created.

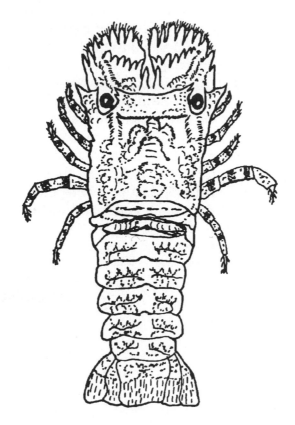

Figure 55.

Scyllarus chacei Holthuis, 1960

Common names
    Chace slipper lobster

Distinguishing characteristics
    Size: A small scyllarid lobster, total length less than 2½ inches (60 mm) with a carapace length of 21.6 mm for the male and 24.2 mm for the female.

Color: The entire lobster is usually an olive green with conspicuous orange-brown spots. The dorsal surface of the first abdominal segments has two distinct, small spots near the midline and two fainter spots near the lateral edge.

Form: Carapace with scale-like sculpturing on the dorsal surface. Protuberances on the mid dorsal ridge large and rounded, not bi-lobed. Two fused, blunt spines over each eye. Rostrum short and rounded with parallel sides. Antennae short and flattened with distinct, triangular projections along the front edge. Stiff hairs occur on the edges of the antennae. Abdomen is strong and slightly tapered. The dorsal surface of the second, third, and fourth abdominal segments with branching furrows off the transverse groove. The median notch at the midline of the posterior edge of the first to fourth abdominal segments is very shallow. Williams (1984) presented a comprehensive description of this species.

Distribution

Lyons (1970) considered *S. chacei* as one of the most common and wide ranging of the small scyllarid lobsters in the western Atlantic. It generally occurs in deeper water than *S. americanus*. Its range extends from North Carolina through the Gulf of Mexico and the Caribbean Sea, the Bahamas and south to Brazil. It is apparently quite common off the northeast coast of South America. The depth range is 6 to 180 fathoms (36 to 329 m), but it is seldom taken in depths greater than 100 fathoms (183 m).

Life history

As in other *Scyllarus* species, fertilization is internal. Robertson reared phyllosomes of *S. chacei*, that were collected in the plankton, through to metamorphosis. The larval stages were indistinguishable from those of *S. americanus*. Lyons (1970) reported collecting a female with bright yellow eggs in late January. Hatching occurred 15 days later which indicates that development in the egg may take less than three weeks. *S. chacei* is also reported reproductively active in March, July, August, September, and November from various areas of its range, so spawning probably occurs primarily during the warmer months in the northern areas, and year round in the southern areas. It is usually found on silty bottoms with sponge, shell, and coralline algae. In contrast, *S. planorbis*, a very similar, but smaller, species, is found on harder bottoms of shell rubble, sand, and some mud.

Fishery

No fishery for this species exists. It is taken by shrimp trawlers and usually discarded with other bottom "trash".

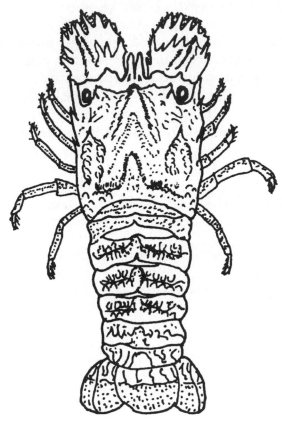

Figure 56.

Scyllarus depressus (Smith, 1881)

Common names
  Scaled slipper lobster

Distinguishing characteristics
  Size: A small scyllarid lobster, about 3 inches (75 mm) total length. Carapace length about 24 mm.
  Color: Cream to tan with darker mottled markings. No red or dark spots on the dorsal surface of the first abdominal segment.

Form: Dorsal surface of the carapace with scale-like scupturing, but only on the ridges and the sides. Lateral and dorsal protuberences on the carapace sharply pointed. Two spines over the eyes fused at their base. The rostrum is short and pointed. Antennae short and stout, rounded in outline with the front edge formed into triangular projections. Stiff hairs occur on the edges of the antennae. Abdomen is strong and stout. The first to fifth abdominal segments with branching furrows off the transverse groove. First to fourth abdominal segments with a deep, narrow notch in the midline of the posterior margin. Williams (1984) presented a comprehensive description of this species. *S. depressus* is often found in recent literature under the name *S. nearctus* Holthuis.

Distribution

A widely distributed species. Found from offshore North Carolina (one postlarval specimen, the type specimen, was taken from Massachusetts, off Martha's Vineyard), along the east coast of the United States, the Gulf of Mexico, the Caribbean, and northern coast of South America, south to Sao Paulo, Brazil. Found at moderate depths, range 16 to 144 fathoms (29 to 263 m), but most commonly found within 27 to 82 fathoms (50 to 150 m).

Life history

Fertilization is internal. Spawning is recorded off Florida in October and January and off North Carolina in June and November. Robertson (1971) reared the phllosomes of this species from hatching through the first seven stages and then reared wild caught phyllsomes through the last few stages into postlarvae. Robertson's work shows that spawning occurs in Florida waters during fall, winter, and spring. Robertson reported that females carrying eggs were taken at about 55 fathoms (100 m) in January near the edge of the Florida Straits and were held in small laboratory tanks. They lost their eggs but soon spawned new batches of fertile eggs.

The eggs were bright yellow and measured 0.37 to 0.43 mm in diameter. They hatched in 3 to 4 weeks at a temperature of about 20°C. The phyllosomes were hatched in the first free swimming stage and can be easily distinguished from the phyllosomes of *S. americanus*, *S. chacei*, and *S. planorbis*. There are about ten larval stages, and the length of larval life was estimated at 2.5 months at water temperatures of 25°C. Postlarvae are usually taken at depths inhabited by adults, so developmental migrations are not indicated. The deeper water distribution of *S. depressus* puts it on bottoms with few sponges but heavier growths of coralline algae and more silt than the inshore bottoms where *S. chacei* is found. As with other scyllarid lobsters, Lyons (1970) presents a good summary of biological and morphological information.

Fishery

No commercial fishery exists. This species may be taken in shrimp trawls but is discarded with most of the other incidental catch.

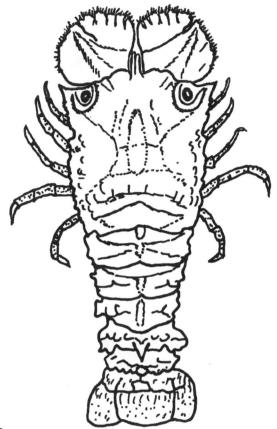

Figure 57.

Scyllarus faxoni Bouvier, 1917

Common names
    Faxon slipper lobster

Distinguishing characteristics
    Size: A small, deep water scyllarid lobster, about 2⅛ inches (54 mm) total length. Carapace length is about 16 mm in the adults.

Form: Carapace with scale-like sculpturing on the dorsal surface, no prominent dorsal ridges. Lateral carapace ridges ending anteriorly in a sharp, forward spine. Rostrum is short and tubercle-like. Antennae are broad and flattened, rounded in outline, and with dense feathered hairs on the edges. The distal edges of the antennae are notched into lobes rather than sharp triangular projections. The abdomen is tapered from the carapace and the dorsal surfaces of the abdominal segments are deeply furrowed. A strong spine is present at the posterior midline of the posterior margin. Legs are slender. Lyons (1970) presents a detailed description of this species.

Distribution
Northern Bahamas to the Caribbean coast of Costa Rica and Guadeloupe, West Indies. Depth ranges from 125 to 250 fathoms (229 to 457 m).

Life history
The small size and deep water habitat of this lobster have prevented gathering of much life history information. There are no reports of any reproductively active females in the literature.

Fishery
No fishery for this species.

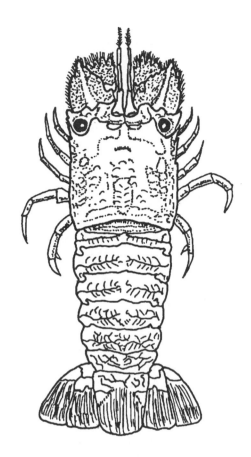

Figure 58.

Scyllarus planorbis Holthuis, 1969

Common names
   Caribbean slipper lobster

Distinguishing characteristics
   Size: A very small species of scyllarid lobster, about 1½ inches (35 mm) total length. Egg carrying females have a carapace length of only 7 to 12 mm.

Color: The body is olive green, marbled with brownish streaks and spots. The dorsal surface of the first abdominal segment has no pattern of spots. Legs are not banded.

Form: The carapace has scale-like sculpturing, and the dorsal protuberances are low and blunt. The rostrum is short and blunt. The inner margin of the orbit (eye socket) is smooth, without spines. Antennae are short and broad with irregular deeply notched projections on the front edges. Feathered hairs cover the edges of the antennae. The abdomen is strong and truncate, slightly tapered, the first abdominal segment with a complete transverse groove. There are no ridges or protuberances on the abdominal segments. The first four abdominal segments have a shallow median notch on the posterior margin. Holthuis (1969) presents a complete description of this species.

Distribution
Found off the northern coast of South America and in the southwestern Caribbean. Depth ranges from 16 to 53 fathoms (29 to 97 m), but most specimens have been taken between 19 and 38 fathoms (35 to 70 m).

Life history
Females with eggs were taken in March, July, and August. The eggs were numerous and small, 0.40 mm in diameter. Robertson (unpublished) reared the larvae from eggs hatched in the laboratory. The larval period is short, probably similar to *S. chacei*. Although *S. chacei* occurs throughout the range of *S. planorbis*, the two species are not found together, thus probably inhabit different ecological niches.

Fishery
No fishery exists for this species.

Synaxidae - Furry Lobsters

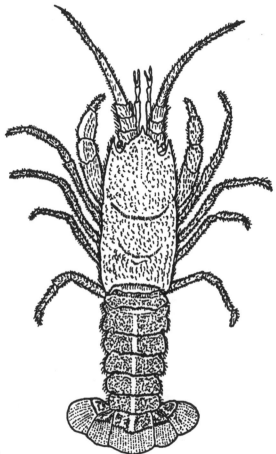

Figure 59.

Palinurellus gundlachi (von Martens, 1881)

Common names
　　Furry lobster
　　Copper lobster (Aquarium trade common name)
　　Coral lobster
　　Cacahouete　　　　　　　　　　Langosteta

Distinguishing characteristics

Size: A moderate to small lobster, maximum total length about 6 inches (15 cm).

Color: Overall bright orange, the ventral surface lighter than the dorsal.

Form: The carapace is long and rounded and completely covered with small tubercles and short hairs. No large ridges or spines present on carapace. Rostrum is small and triangular. Antennae are shorter than the carapace and covered with short hairs. Abdominal segments are also hairy, do not have transverse grooves, and have a low, dorsal midline ridge. Legs without pincers, but the first pair of legs are stout, perhaps twice the thickness of the second pair.

Distribution

Found from Bermuda, the southeast coast of Florida, Yucatan, and the Caribbean island arc. Found on coral reefs in moderate to deep waters for divers, maximum depth is about 115 feet (35 m).

Life history

The primitive lobster, *P. gundlachi*, is quite rare throughout its range in the tropical western Atlantic. Like other lobsters, it is nocturnal and hides deep in the reef during the day. The presence of first and last stage phyllosomes of this species in plankton collections (Sims, 1966) indicates that spawning occurs in summer and early fall and that the period of larval life is about 10 months. Sims (1966) describs twelve larval stages. The phyllosomes are quite distinctive with a fore-body that overlaps the mid-body. The phyllosoma also has a prominent triangular rostrum, a feature characteristic of the adult. As determined from plankton collections, the larvae follow the typical pattern and are near the surface during the night moving to deeper water during the day. The phyllosomes of this species are rare, which agrees with the rarity of the adults. *P. gundlachi* has been

Stage 1 phyllosome of *P. gundlachi* (after Sims, 1966).

Stage 3 phyllosome of *P. gundlachi* (after Sims, 1966).

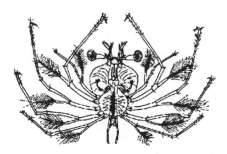

Stage 4 phyllosome of *P. gundlachi* (after Sims, 1966).

Figure 60. Phyllosome larval stages 1, 3, and 4 of the furry lobster, *Palinurellus gundlachi*, after Sims, 1966.

observed on the reef at night feeding on the tail of a spotted spiny lobster (Colin, 1978).

Fishery

There is no fishery for this species, although collectors of marine life for the marine aquarium trade almost always collect them when they are observed. On rare occasions, *P. gundlachi* may turn up in the lobster traps set on and near the reefs, and divers occasionally find a single specimen. This species occasionally turns up in the marine aquarium market as the Atlantic copper lobster.

CHAPTER FOUR

LOBSTER CARE AND CULTURE
Aquarium, Hatchery, and Farm

Aquaculture (freshwater) and mariculture (saltwater) have become big business all over the world in the last few decades. In some areas of the world, culture of aquatic organisms has always been a big, traditional, people-based, low-technology industry; and in other areas, modern technology has made it possible for industrialized cultures to economically breed and culture fish and invertebrates that were traditionally fished from wild populations. Lobsters, now an intensively fished, highly valuable resource wherever they occur, have been the subject of intense mariculture research, past and present. There are many problems, however, and although it is possible that the culture or farming of tropical lobsters may become an industry at some future time, the short term possibilities for the large scale culture of tropical lobsters are bleak. Lobsters are interesting animals for marine aquariums, however, and many species are part of the world wide market of live marine organisms for marine aquaria. Note that whenever the term spiny lobster is used in this chapter, it refers to the Caribbean spiny lobster, *Panulirus argus*, unless otherwise stated.

Aquarium Maintenance and Care

Although we know that mullet and other marine fish were kept by the ancient Romans in tidal ponds about 200 BC, the first records of real seawater aquaria, marine organisms kept in small glass bowls, date from the 1840's and 50's. "Aquarinists" in England in those days recorded and published experiments on keeping various invertebrates, temperate small crabs, and sponges. Freshwater organisms were much easier to keep with limited technology, however, and the marine aquarium hobby did not really get started until after WWII. An understanding of the nitrogen cycle (the bacterial processing of nitrogenous wastes) in marine aquaria, the wide availability of artificial sea salts, and the manufacture of all-glass aquaria constructed with silicone sealers all came together in the early 1960's, and the modern marine aquarium industry was born.

In the United States, keeping marine aquaria has become an important hobby over the last 20 years. The hobby now supports a multi-million dollar industry dealing in specialized equipment manufacture and sale, fish and invertebrate capture and transport, culture of marine plants and animals, and publication of books and magazines; and the marine end is still only a shadow of the freshwater side of the aquarium industry. Until about 1985, most marine aquarists were able to successfully maintain only marine fish and a few large invertebrates. Recent advances in marine aquarium technology made it possible for marine aquarists to keep many kinds of marine invertebrates and plants in a balanced, dynamic display of coral reef life.

The technological base for these new sophisticated "reef system" aquariums includes trickle filtration, intense broad spectrum lighting, "live rock" (porous rock from the sea with natural bacterial growth), strong water movement, and protein skimmers. The older "traditional" type of marine aquarium system uses undergravel filters and auxiliary power filtration along with less intense lighting. Although marine fish and large mobile invertebrates do well in traditional marine aquariums, corals, anemones, sponges, certain algae, and other coral reef creatures thrive only in well maintained reef system aquariums.

Spiny lobster, and other species of tropical and subtropical lobsters, survive quite well in both types of modern marine aquarium systems; but like most marine organisms,

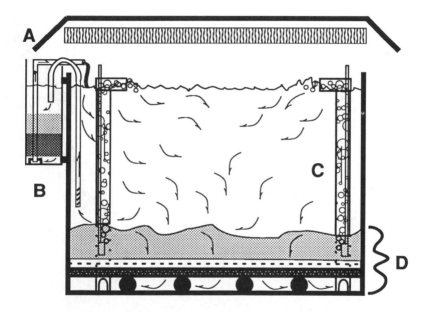

A. Lighting. Shop light with 2, two or four foot fluorescent bulbs or a standard aquarium light hood.

B. Auxiliary filter. A small external filter with floss for mechanical filtration and activiated carbon for chemical filtration.

C. Air lift assembly. One inch diameter lift tube powered by air stone or powerhead pump.

D. Undergravel filter. One to two inches of filter media held above the filter plate with a fine screen. The filter plate is supported above the bottom by marbles or other solid supports.

Figure 61. Structure of a simple marine aquarium system with an undergravel biological filter.

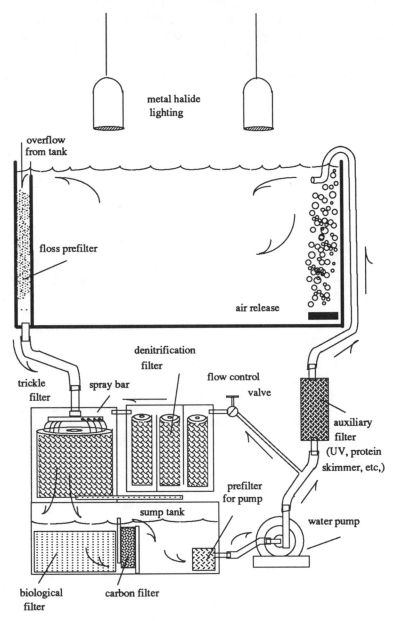

Figure 62. General structure of a reef tank system, after Moe (1989).

they really thrive in reef system marine aquaria. The following section provides some basic information specifically on keeping spiny lobsters in marine aquaria. The techniques and technology of marine aquarium keeping is far too broad a subject to include much detail in this book. There is, however, a great deal of information now available on establishing and maintaining marine aquariums, and those who wish to delve more deeply into this subject are directed to the following references: de Graaf (1982) and Moe (1982, 1989) are good basic books, and Adey and Loveland (1991), Spotte (1970, 1979) and Thiel (1988, 1989) are more technical works. Debelius (1984) discusses the maintenance of many species of decapod crustacea and includes excellent color photographs of most species popular with marine aquarists. The typical structure of the traditional and the reef type marine aquarium systems is shown in Figures 61 and 62.

Populations of large spiny lobsters throughout the world are primarily food fishery resources. Thus, the laws and regulations that control spiny lobster fisheries are designed to regulate intensive commercial fishing efforts in order to sustain the reproductive capacity of the lobster population and assure continued survival of the resource. Most of these regulations protect small lobsters from capture and sale for any purpose, so many species of spiny lobsters, although naturally abundant, seldom find their way into the marine aquarium market. Although such regulations are necessary, it is unfortunate that so few species are available to marine aquarists.

Small spiny lobsters make very interesting aquarium animals, and keeping small lobsters greatly expands the knowledge and appreciation of these animals among the general public. Use of spiny lobsters as a consumptive resource should not preclude their use as an educational resource, especially since the number of animals taken for the aquarium market is so small when compared to their exploitation as a food fishery. In reality, however, it is seldom, if ever, possible to include a small, non-consumptive use of undersize animals in the development and enforcement of fishery regulations for a major resource. The potential for abuse, and complications in enforcement of fishery regulations, seem to preclude the educational and economic advantages of aquarium use of an important resource.

Fortunately, most species of tropical lobsters do not support large, regulated fisheries, and these smaller species are occasionally available to marine aquarists. They are also usually more brightly colored than their larger, commercially valuable relatives. The spiny lobsters, family Palinuridae, like the shrimps, are more openly active and responsive to their environment than slipper lobsters, family Scyllaridae; and because of their higher activity level, they are generally more interesting in an aquarium. The Atlantic species of greatest interest to aquarists are the longarm spiny lobster, the spotted spiny lobster, the copper or furry lobster, and, more rarely, the sculptured slipper lobster, the Spanish slipper lobster, and the American slipper lobster. The spotted spiny lobster, *Panulirus guttatus*, from Florida and Caribbean reefs is a beautiful small species and is not uncommon in the aquarium trade. Additional information on these species can be found in Chapter Three.

There are many species of Pacific and Indo-Pacific lobsters that are interesting aquarium inhabitants. One of the most common in the aquarium trade is the painted rock lobster, *Panulirus versicolor*, from the Philippines. The green tail is brightly banded with light and dark stripes, and the antennal flagella are brilliant white. They remain in the reef structure during the day, but usually position themselves near the edge and expose their antennae to the open water, so they are easily observed. Although it grows to a fairly large size, total body length of about 15 inches (40 cm) or more, small specimens often enter the marine aquarium market because of the intensive live specimen collecting industry in the Philippines. This species may also enter the market from the Red Sea. Other species that may occur in the aquarium trade are the ornate rock lobster, *Panulirus ornatus*, from the Indo-Pacific and the Red Sea; the Hawaiian lobster, *Panulirus marginatus*; and the double spined rock lobster, *Panulirus penicillatus*, from the Indo-Pacific. The Pacific slipper lobster, *Arctides regalis*, a brightly colored species with red margins around the flat, shovel shaped antennae is probably the most common of the slipper lobsters in the aquarium trade.

Juveniles and small specimens of large species are most preferred for small aquariums. A large aquarium, 150 gallons or more, is required to house a large adult spiny lobster. Large slipper lobsters require a little less area since they are less active than spiny lobsters, but even so, adult specimens of many species of slipper lobsters are relatively large aquatic animals. If a small specimen of a large species of lobster is purchased for a small reef or traditional marine aquarium set up, it is important to include the consideration that the lobster will probably require a larger tank in a year or two if all goes well.

Juveniles and small species seldom require special care in a marine aquarium, especially in a reef type aquarium with extensive rock habitat and plant and invertebrate growth. Lobsters, especially spiny lobsters, are opportunistic feeders, so if an aquarist maintains various corals and other sessile invertebrates, it is important to observe the feeding habits of the lobster closely, especially at night, to be sure that the lobster does not damage or feed upon other valuable invertebrates. Large spiny and slipper lobsters do require attention to their needs for shelter and food. Although it may not be observed in their behavior patterns, a lack of appropriate shelter in the aquarium can create substantial physiological stress in the lobster.

Different species of lobster, especially those from the same geographical area, must differ in fundamental ways, such as choice of habitat, selection of food organisms, reproductive behavior, depth range, and other basic characteristics. If such inherent differences did not exist, the species could not coexist. One conflicting species would displace the other, and eventually only one species would exist in that area. However, in the short term (the lifetime of one individual), the basic living requirements of most species of lobsters, and most decapod crustaceans in fact, are so broad that few species have any difficulty living in a well managed marine aquarium. If there is adequate food, some shelter, and an absence of predators, most lobsters can survive quite well even if the habitat is different from their natural ecological niche. In other words, almost all species of tropical lobsters can survive quite nicely in all the basic types of modern marine aquarium systems. Be aware, however, that large slipper lobsters may move rocks that are neatly stacked in the aquarium, and that large spiny lobsters may catch and eat other organisms in the aquarium, including rather large fish.

Juveniles prefer a network of interconnected sheltered areas, while larger lobsters can get along with one or two areas that totally accommodate their body mass. Small slipper lobsters appreciate some substrate that will allow them to burrow, although rock lobsters like *Scyllarides aequinoctialis* (the Spanish slipper lobster) and *Scyllarides nodifer* (the ridged slipper lobster) do well in a rocky reef tank. Slipper lobsters that frequent rocky reefs spend the day hiding, often clinging upside down to the roof of a cave, and then forage the reefs and nearby rubble areas during the night. Smaller sand slipper lobsters often bury themselves in the sediments during the day and then forage over rocks, sand, and grasses during the night. One species, an unnamed scyllarid species of *Thenus* from Australia, has developed a laterally extended and compressed carapace and reduced antennae, and apparently swims several hundred meters during forging periods to find new feeding areas where prey may be more abundant. So although lobsters can appear to be very much alike, they are very different in many subtle ways, and they are very interesting and rather easy aquatic creatures to maintain in aquaria.

Aquarium considerations

Water quality. The traditional type of marine aquarium with an undergravel filter, relatively low lighting, limited auxiliary filtration (i.e., some carbon and extra mechanical filtration), and limited water flow is adequate for most species of tropical lobsters provided frequent water exchange is performed. Waste nitrogen in the form of ammonia and nitrite is well processed in this type of aquarium and is instantly transformed to nitrate by the nitrifying bacteria in the filter bed. So although ammonia and nitrite are usually near zero, nitrate can accumulate fairly rapidly to levels above 50 parts per million (ppm).

The gradual accumulation of nitrate to, and slightly above, this level seems to have little effect on most marine fish. Decapod crustacea, including tropical lobsters, however, are variably stressed by the accumulation of nitrate, and associated organics, above 20 to 30 ppm nitrate. This stress is exhibited by increased susceptibility to disease, lethargy, disinterest in feeding, and difficulty in molting. Therefore, it is important to conduct frequent water changes or operate a denitrifying filter to keep nitrate levels below 20 ppm for best maintenance of tropical lobsters and other crustacea. Salinity is best maintained at or just below the oceanic level of 35‰ (a true specific gravity of 1.0260 at 59 °F (15 °C); 1.0235 at 80.6 °F). Moe (1982) has a complete discussion of salinity in marine aquaria. Although marine fish are better off at salinities that are a bit lower, crustacea are better off at salinities that are closer to natural oceanic seawater. Given monthly water changes of 10% or more, trace elements and carbonate hardness should always be present in adequate amounts. Low iodine levels may develop if the system has extensive algal growth and very effective protein skimming. Low iodine can cause molting difficulty in some crustacea. Moe (1989) discusses low iodine and includes a formula for dosing marine aquaria with iodine when necessary. Refer to Moe (1989) also for a complete discussion on water quality in marine aquaria.

Physical requirements. Unlike corals, algae, and sponges that have specific requirements for quality and intensity of light, most crustacea can do quite well under a variety of lighting conditions. Many are nocturnal animals that hide from intense light during the day and do not need direct intense lighting. Also, those lobsters that inhabit deep water, over 50 to 100 feet, never receive intense sunlight, even during the day. Subdued lighting, therefore, is adequate for a lobster tank. A rocky environment is best for most lobsters, although small sand slipper lobsters are appreciative of at least a small section of sandy substrate. The rocks should be placed so that there are caverns and caves large enough to shelter the lobsters. Careful positioning of the rocks can allow shelter for the lobsters and still preserve observation opportunity for the aquarist. Water flows need not be strong, for unlike corals, anemones, and other sessile invertebrates, lobsters can move about and find areas where conditions are to their liking. A gentle water flow throughout the tank is necessary, however, to prevent stagnant areas from developing in the tank. For tropical lobsters, temperatures can vary from 65 to 90°F (18 to 33°C). The extremes of this range, however, allow only survival. The broad range of about 72 to 82°F (22 to 28°C) provides a much better environment for growth and reproduction.

Food and feeding. Most lobsters are opportunistic carnivorous feeders. Many species will occasionally consume algae, but this may be incidental to feeding on epiphytic animals (small animals attached to algal surfaces). Coralline alga, however, is consumed directly by small lobsters and may be an important source of calcium for their exoskeleton. Small gastropods (snails) are eagerly eaten by small spiny lobsters as are small bivalves, benthic copepods, and other small marine animals. Lobsters in reef tanks, where the ecology of the tank produces many small copepods, amphipods, marine worms, and other life, are very easy to feed since they may or may not require supplemental feeding.

The amount of supplemental feeding required depends on the size of the tank and the amount of biomass present, and the number and size of the lobsters. Obviously, large lobsters in relatively bare tanks require daily primary feeding. For best results, the animal protein fed to spiny and slipper lobsters should be of marine origin. Terrestrial meats with saturated fats are not a good basic food for marine animals. Lobsters should be fed organisms such as shrimp, clams, oysters, scallops, and fish, although fish flesh is often oily and unsuitable for sustained feeding in a closed system marine aquarium. Food organisms do not have to be live or even whole, but should be fresh or fresh frozen. The pieces should be the proper size for the size of the lobster. A spiny lobster feeds by manipulating the food organism with legs, maxilla, and maxillipeds, and then crushing and grinding with the mandibles or jaws. Thus, the food particle should be big enough to allow the lobster to handle it, but not so big that it can't carry it away or so small that it cannot be easily grasped. When in doubt, make the food particle about the size of the telson of the lobster being fed. Food mixes for marine animals are often created in a blender, stabilized with gelatin or agar, frozen in cubes or flat trays, and then thawed and fed as required. Such prepared food can carry additional vitamins and minerals and can be easily processed to the proper size. Moe (1982, 1989) discusses the preparation of such food mixes.

Capture and handling. Various species of lobsters from all tropical ocean areas are occasionally available in the marine aquarium market. A good specimen has all its legs and antennae and is active and responsive. A spiny lobster readily moves about the aquarium, and a slipper lobster will move about when disturbed. A lobster that sits out in the open and moves only slightly when disturbed is not a safe buy. A loss of one or two appendages, while not desireable, does not necessarily mean that the lobster will not survive. If the animal has strong color, moves about readily, and feeds well, it will probably survive and replace the lost appendages at the next molt if it is placed in a good environment.

Lobsters destined for aquaria are usually caught by hand by diver collectors or in traps along with other species destined for the fish market. Night diving is an efficient method of hand capture of lobsters, since most lobsters are more active at night than during the day. The sudden application of a bright light at night usually transfixes the lobster and makes it easy to collect the animal in a net. Some specimens can be taken alive and undamaged as a byproduct from the trawls of bait and food shrimpers, but many specimens so caught are damaged by the action of the trawl.

A push net operated on shallow tropical grass flats often catches small spiny and slipper lobster without injury. A push net consists of a square or rectangular frame about 3 or 4 feet around with a rounded bottom and loose netting attached around the frame. The netting may be ⅛ or ¼ inch mesh, not so fine that sand and silt clog the net, but small enough to catch the tiny animals of the grass flats. The top of

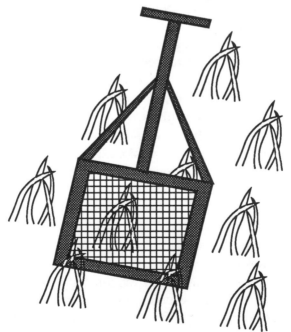

the frame has a handle like an old fashioned lawn mower handle firmly attached to the center of the top and bottom of the frame. In operation, the push net is tilted at about 45° and pushed over the grass bed. The rounded bottom glides over and pushes the grass blades down, and the small animals in the grass beds are swept over the bottom of the frame and into the net. Push net collections taken at night would be most likely to catch small spiny and slipper lobsters in tropical areas.

Perhaps the most efficient way to capture small spiny lobsters is with an artificial habitat. The Witham habitat is discussed and illustrated in section 14 of the Addendum to Chapter One, and further discussion occurs in the lobster farming section in this chapter. The structure and placement of such habitats determines to a great extent what species is captured. Research by the Florida Department of Natural Resources Marine Institute Field Station in Marathon, Florida, indicates that pueruli of the spotted spiny lobster, *P. guttatus*, are captured when artificial habitats are placed down in the offshore reef structure, and the pueruli of the Caribbean spiny lobster, *P. argus*, are captured when habitats are placed at the surface in shallow, near-shore areas.

It is possible that different habitat designs placed in particular types of areas may capture juveniles of other species of lobsters in the Caribbean and other oceanic areas. A lot of research is needed, however, before such methods could be productive. There is always the threat of injury to lobsters, large or small, during capture and handling. It is very easy to catch an appendage in the net, and if a little of the wrong pressure is applied to the leg, the lobster will quickly break it off. Care must be taken whenever a lobster is handled, to free all appendages from rocks or nets. Never use undue force to pull a lobster free from its attachment. A lobster is an aquatic animal that obtains it oxygen from the water. Even though it is able to crawl about on land to some extent, it is strictly aquatic and will die or suffer sever damage from lack of oxygen and carbon dioxide accumulation if kept out of water for any length of time. Although lobsters can sustain being out of water considerably longer than fish, it is best to limit a lobster's air time to only a few minutes. The smaller the lobster, the less tolerant it is to loss of the aquatic environment.

Shipping and holding. Most lobsters have sharp points on spines and at the end of their legs. Unless the lobster is very small, these spines can easily puncture plastic shipping bags. A good precaution to prevent puncture and loss of water and oxygen is to use two bags, one inside the other with several layers of newspaper between the bags. This way if the inner bag is punctured, the spine will not go through the layers of paper and the outer bag will still hold the water and oxygen. Holding spiny and slipper lobsters for shipment is not difficult since cannibalism is rare in these species, although small newly-molted lobsters may be attacked by larger lobsters when held in close quarters. Shallow invertebrate trays or compartments are fine for brief holding periods, but care should be taken that water flows are adequate and that the animal can submerge all of the antennae, carapace, and telson.

A Spiny Lobster Hatchery

So you want to grow spiny lobsters and make many millions of dollars. That sounds like a good idea. Unfortunately it won't work. At least not within the usual system of keeping brood stock, hatching eggs, and rearing the hatched young to market size. I know it can't be done. I tried it. OK, sure, nothing is impossible. A 747 actually flies, we've been to the moon, and we can send moving pictures, even in color, through air and space. So who's to say the commercial hatching and rearing of spiny lobster is impossible?

Well, maybe it isn't impossible, but it sure won't be easy, or inexpensive. A commercial hatchery/farm for most marine organisms includes brood stock maintenance and spawning facilities, a larval rearing facility, an expansive juvenile grow-out area, a laboratory, a kitchen or feed preparation area, algal and larval food cultures, an engineering support section, administration and offices, and numerous other extensive and expansive support structures, including one labeled "abundant money supply for numerous unforseen needs and calamities".

During most of the 1970's and 80's I worked with spawning and rearing marine tropical fish for the aquarium industry. It was a difficult technology to develop, but the price per pound for aquarium fish was far greater than that for food fish, and it seemed that a small hatchery for marine aquarium fish had a much greater chance of success than a huge food fish hatchery. We developed a hatchery technology for anemone fish (clownfish) and neon gobies and then moved to the Florida Keys under the name Aqualife Research Corporation to try our hand with the ultimate marine aquarium fish, marine angelfish. We established a small marine fish hatchery just east of Marathon in the middle of the Florida Keys in early 1975. Our trials and tribulations with this venture could fill another book someday. Now, however, I will briefly relate our experiences in attempting to hatch and rear spiny and slipper lobsters.

The term phyllosome refers to the larval form of spiny and slipper lobsters. The larvae of spiny lobsters and slipper lobsters are quite different in form from the adult. The larvae are tiny, flattened, spider-like creatures that have no resemblance to the juvenile or adult lobster. They are so different, in fact, that they were thought to be a distinct species when they were first discovered, and were given the name *Phyllosoma* (Leach, 1816). It wasn't until the early 1900's that the eggs of spiny lobsters were hatched, and biologists discovered that *Phyllosoma* were actually the larvae of spiny lobsters. Although no longer a valid scientific name, the term phyllosome came to refer to a specific larval form most characteristic of spiny and slipper lobsters.

During my years in the Florida Keys, I enjoyed recreational diving for spiny lobster as frequently as possible; and as a marine biologist with a bent toward spawning, rearing, and farming marine organisms, I also developed a professional interest in these animals. (Of course, the thought of making millions of dollars spawning and rearing spiny lobsters never entered my head.) We kept a half dozen adult spiny lobsters in a large tank used for occasional maintenance of angelfish and watched the lobsters feed, mate, and molt. I was quite aware of the difficulties of rearing the phyllosome larvae of spiny lobsters and of their extended period of planktonic larval life.

Nevertheless, because of the ease of holding and spawning spiny lobster brood stock, and the fact that juveniles can be held together and grown out to market size with little difficulty, a good try at larval rearing seemed to be in order.

A great effort was underway at that time in commercial rearing of the American lobster, *Homarus americanus*, and some remarkable success had been had in rearing this lobster. Bardach et al. (1972), Kensler (1970), Hughes and Matthiessen (1962), and Hughes (1973) are good general references to the culture biology and the problems and potential of culture of American lobster. Maintaining brood stock of the American (or Maine) lobster was not particularly difficult, and spawning the adults and hatching and rearing the larvae was almost a routine task. Of course, "easy" and "routine" describe the process only after all the unknown problems and techniques are worked out. Hughes (1973) found that American lobster females produced fertile eggs only if the spawning tank contains water at least 46 cm (18 inches) deep. For some unknown reason, the female requires at least this depth of water to successfully lay and fertilize the eggs under her abdomen. She supports herself in a tripod position with her claws and the tip of her tail when the eggs are extruded onto her abdomen, and apparently if the water is less then 46 cm in depth, this process cannot occur successfully.

The larvae spend only about three weeks and three molts as a planktonic creature, and they readily feed on

ground clams, frozen brine shrimp, and other easy-to-pro-
vide foods. Survival through the larval stage is up to 30%.
After the fourth molt they leave the plankton and seek a
bottom habitat. It would seem that with the exceptional
demand and high price that American lobster enjoy, they
would be ideal marine animals for contained culture. Unfortunately, they like to eat each other, and like most other cold
water Crustacea, grow very slowly. It is possible to grow
them to market size in three years or less, instead of the
normal 5 to 8 years that it takes in the wild, by maintaining
water temperature at 70 °F year round; but lobster culturists
have not yet been able to curb a young lobster's appetite for
a newly molted tank mate. Many millions of dollars have
been spent developing devices and methods for circumvent-
ing the cannibalistic nature of American lobsters. Although
it is possible to rear American lobsters to market size in
isolation, it is very expensive, and this is the greatest imped-
iment to the economical culture of American lobster.

Spiny lobsters, on the other hand, can be reared together
without significant cannibalism; and with good water quality, abundant food, and high to moderate water temperatures, postlarval spiny lobsters can probably grow to a good
market size in about 18 months to two years. The only
problem is that pesky phyllosome larval period. Well then, I
thought, all we have to do is to develop an adequate pelagic
type environment, shorten the larval period, and find a
good food for the phyllosome larvae, and we've got it made.
So, on August 8, 1976, we obtained a gravid spiny lobster
from a commercial fisherman and maintained her until the
eggs hatched on August 13.

Our experimental rearing work with spiny lobsters was
a serious effort, but our major project was rearing marine
tropical fish, and all other work was secondary to this primary purpose. I knew that the possibility of developing a
practical technology for rearing spiny lobster larvae was
slim, at best, but there were a few tricks I wanted to try, and
I was sure we could learn something from even a part time

attempt. All the past rearing efforts on spiny lobster were done on a laboratory scale, with larvae kept individually in small compartments or a relatively small number of larvae kept in small tanks and fed with brine shrimp or tiny food particles two or three times a day. These efforts almost always failed after three to six weeks of rearing, when the larvae are in the second or third intermolt; although recently (Kittaka and Kimura, 1989 and Yamakawa et al., 1989) have succeeded in rearing the Japanese spiny lobster, *Panulirus japonicus*, through the phyllosome, puerulus, and into the juvenile stage after 307 to 391 days as phyllosome larvae. These, and other published experimental rearings, are discussed at the end of this section to provide a little insight into the history of phyllosome rearing attempts.

We set up two tanks: a 250 gallon, black polyethylene tank, and a 75 gallon glass tank, for exclusive rearing of phyllosome larvae to experiment with various larval foods. About a thousand phyllosomes were placed in each tank, and most of the remaining phyllosomes were released to the sea. The water was the same processed natural sea water we used for rearing marine larval fish; a weak turbulence in the tank was provided by a couple of air stones; and lighting was provided by two 40 watt natural spectrum fluorescent bulbs. As with the marine tropical fish, lighting over the tanks was maintained 24 hours a day, and some level of food organisms were always present, although high levels were maintained only during daylight hours. I wanted to see if perhaps feeding, growth, and molting could be enhanced by eliminating the night hours, thus allowing the larvae to feed at will at all times. A trickle change of water was provided several days into the rearing experiment. All the standard larval rearing foods for marine fish were added to the tank to see if the phyllosome larvae would accept any of them. These included new-hatch brine shrimp (*Artemia*), cultured rotifers (*Brachionus plicatilis*), cultured copepods, and wild plankton sieved to below 150 microns, along with some cultured algal cells. Phyllosomes have tiny mouth parts, and it was assumed that they would feed on very small organisms.

The results of these first experimental rearings were basically negative. Most of the larvae did not feed and died out after 6 to 8 days, just before time for the first molt. A few did make it through the first larval molt, but did not survive more than a few days after the molt. Even though there was a large initial population of larvae in these tanks, the long legs and fragile swimmeretts did not cause them to become entangled into large balls as predicted by some culturists. Probably because of overfeeding, strands of bacterial slime developed in the 250 gallon tank, and many phyllosomes became entangled in these strands. We did observe some larvae feeding on newly hatched brine shrimp, but no phyllosomes were observed to feed on anything smaller that was available, such as rotifers or copepods. The phyllosomes maintained in the 75 gallon glass tank had the better survival rate, but many of the older larvae in this tank developed growths of tiny red algal cells on their legs (perhaps due to the constant lighting) that became quite heavy and seemed to contribute to mortality.

Larval feeding. The most interesting results of these first experimental rearing attempts were achieved as a result of casual curiosity. The newly hatched phyllosomes gathered densely in the corners of the 300 gallon hatching tank, especially if a light was placed over the corner, and this made collection of the larvae into a bucket very easy. All the tiny, transparent larvae could not be caught, however, and a few hundred newly hatched phyllosomes remained scattered in the hatching tank after the remainder of the spawn was released. We were also working with marine angelfish and mangrove snapper spawns at the time, and these fish larvae were two to four days old and feeding well. I collected some of the newly hatched phyllosome larvae that remained in the 300 gallon holding tank and placed about 10 to 20 in one of the snapper tanks and one of the angelfish tanks. These were large glass tanks, and observations could be made through the sides of the tank. My thought was to see how the phyllosomes behaved in a tank with low densities of phyllosomes and in surroundings a little closer to the natural planktonic environment.

That evening, on the day of hatch of the spiny lobster larvae, I was crouched down in front of the angelfish larval tank with my head under the black plastic tank cover and my nose pressed against the glass (a very natural position for one who cultures marine organisms), and I observed something I did not recognize or understand. Two tiny black dots were moving through the tank side by side. They were obviously swimming in close formation since they followed the currents around the tank, sometimes moving with the flow and sometimes against the flow. There were no fins or tails on these little black dots—they looked like the pupils of the eyes of some huge (on a planktonic scale), absolutely invisible planktonic creature.

Upon close examination, I saw about a half dozen of these strange creatures, and also a few single dots moving about the tank. I got a small fingerbowl and managed to capture one of these strange things and looked at it under the dissecting microscope. And there, looking up at me through the microscope lens, was a tiny, transparent phyllosome larva rapidly treading water with its swimmerettes, and, with the tiny spines on the end of each of its third legs, holding two very dead, half-eaten, larval angelfish. As I watched, the little phyllosoma drew up one of these third legs, munched on the angelfish larvae for while, and then dropped the leg down into swimming position and moved off to investigate the edge of the fingerbowl. Even though the grey angelfish larvae (which are black at this stage) were as big as, if not bigger than, the tiny lobster larvae; the lobster larvae could easily catch, kill, and transport for later consumption, not one, but two fish larvae, and on the day of hatch, no less. The digestive gland in the center of the phyllosome's body was a dirty grey, the only sign (aside

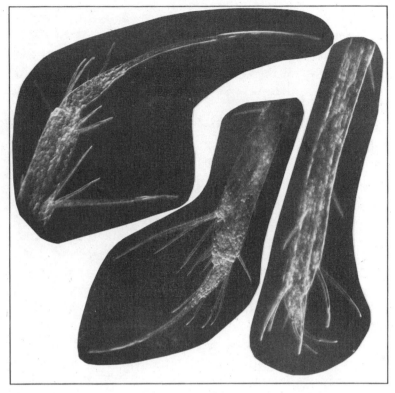

Figure 63. Photomicrograph of the sword-like spines on the tips of the first, second, and third legs of a first stage phyllosoma larva of the Caribbean spiny lobster, *Panulirus argus*.

from the two dead larvae in tow underneath it) that it had been feeding on the dark grey angelfish larvae.

I went over to a tank with mangrove snapper larvae, where a number of spiny lobster phyllosomes had been placed, and watched carefully. Mangrove snapper larvae are mostly transparent at that age, and it was more difficult to see what was going on. (As soon as your eye is trained to see something, however, it becomes much easier to discern and identify vague objects and activities.) I could then see the swimming phyllosomes when the light caught them at the right angle and even watch their feeding behavior. Careful observation revealed that the snapper larvae population in

that tank was decreasing just as rapidly as were the angelfish larvae in the other tank.

I watched this almost microscopic predator/prey interaction with great interest and intensity as the phyllosome
larvae fed in both tanks over the next few days. They would
swim over the top of a fish larvae and then descend down
onto it with their sword tipped legs stabbing and thrusting
at the larva. The larva was usually impaled on the end of the
first or second leg and then transferred to the holding claw
on the end of the third leg. The phyllosomes in the fish
larvae tanks were much stronger and seemed larger than the
phyllosomes in the tanks dedicated to the lobster larvae.
Although I observed a few brine shrimp taken by the phyllosomes in the tanks with the fish larvae, the lobster larvae
fed almost exclusively on the fish larvae in these tanks. After
about 7 to 10 days, however, it became very difficult to find
phyllosomes in any tank, and we expended no further effort
on this spawn.

Even though we were working intently on developing
rearing techniques for marine angelfish, another lobster
spawn was obtained and set up on August 30, 1976, and we
ran a few more rearing experiments based on the findings of
the first rearing run. Keeping the phyllosomes on a regimen
of 24 hours of light seemed detrimental, since they molted at
night, so we set up the new spawn with a photoperiod of
about 14 hours light and 10 dark. Developing an acceptable
food was the main effort of this experimental rearing. Although the early phyllosomes would take newly hatched
brine shrimp, it was obvious that the phyllosomes preferred
fish flesh, so we worked on ways to provide fish flesh in a
form that the phyllosomes could handle.

Processed larval lobster diets. We used dolphin flesh
(the fish, *Coryphaena hippurus*) since dolphin larvae are common in open sea plankton and are probably a common
organism in the natural diet of spiny lobster phyllosomes
(they're also a lot of fun to catch). We tried processing fresh
fish fillets in a blender and feeding the resulting mash to the

phyllosomes. This resulted in few particles large enough for the larvae and a lot of tank pollution. Boiled dolphin fillets produced a slightly better mash, but this was still unsatisfactory. Boiling the fish flesh denatured the protein and decreased its solubility, which decreased the pollution of the tank water and made the particles more solid and discrete. They sank faster, however, and the particles were still too tiny for the phyllosome larvae. A very short burst in the blender produced a better size particle, but also produced too many particles that were far too large, and numerous sticky clumps of tissue. We finally found a way to create fish particles that were best in size, buoyancy, and attractiveness to the phyllosome.

A fresh fillet was first stripped of all possible connective tissue, bones, and skin. These carefully cleaned fish pieces were then wrapped in freezer wrap and frozen hard. At feeding time, a frozen fish piece was removed from the freezer and hand grated with light strokes over a bowl of cold water. The cold water kept the tiny grated pieces from sticking together, and pouring the contents of the bowl through a 1 mm sieve (plastic window screen) eliminated the larger pieces and strings of connective tissue. The grated fresh fish was then added to the phyllosome tanks three to four times a day. We also tried the same technique with boiled fish flesh, but the dense white particles seemed rather heavy and sank quickly. The phyllosomes fed on both boiled and fresh fish particles, but seemed to prefer the fresh fish. The phyllosomes grabbed the particles of fish just as they did the fish larvae and seemed to feed on them the same way.

Even in fresh form and with increased turbulence in the tank, the particles did not remain in the water column very long, and it was only while the food particle floated about the tank that the phyllosome larvae would take it. We had to feed quite frequently in order for most of the phyllosomes to get sufficient food, and this resulted in a nasty deposit of decaying organic matter on the tank bottom. Thus, the tank bottom had to be carefully siphoned at least once a day with a small bore siphon to avoid removal of the tiny phyllosomes, a time-consuming chore. We tried dangling a small piece of fresh fish in the tank on a string, since phyllosomes had been reported clinging to objects in culture and in nature. The idea was that the phyllosome would hook onto the fish piece, feed a while and then drift off to grow fat and molt often. A few phyllosomes did hook onto the fish strip, but none appeared to feed, and some could not disengage from the fish and died.

The best feeding method for fresh fish was the frequent application of tiny grated particles. This food source, along with newly hatched brine shrimp, was the best feeding regimen we could develop at that time. Even though this rearing method was inadequate and inefficient, it allowed several hundred phyllosomes to survive for three to four weeks and develop up to the fourth intermolt. This rearing environment brought about 20% of the phyllosomes into the third intermolt period in 13 to 15 days, a considerably faster rate of growth during this early period then had been reported in the literature. (The first and second intermolt period were each about seven days.) The first cannibalism I noticed occurred after the third intermolt. Phyllosomes that were strong third intermolt larvae attacked larvae that were in the process or had just molted into their third intermolt. Although the phyllosomes were not wildly cannibalistic, this behavior did appear to contribute significantly to mortality in the tank.

Phyllosomes were no longer observed in the rearing tank after September 24, 1976. Other causes of mortality were entanglement in strands of *Enteromorpha* (a tiny filamentous green alga that entered the tank through the water system), and a fungus that appeared on their legs. New hatched brine shrimp were added to the tank regularly to keep a constant food source available to the larvae. Although attractive and apparently nutritious to the phyllosomes, the brine shrimp nauplii contained a heavy, oily orange yolk, and this yolk material coated the spines and hairs on the legs of the phyllosomes. Fungus seemed to grow on this yolk residue and either prevented the phyllosome from feeding or actually penetrated the endoskeleton of the phyllosome. Phyllosomes with this yolk/fungus growth were weak and did not survive long.

Our rearing experiments with spiny lobster larvae ended at this point since we became very involved in marine angelfish culture. We did, however, resume experimental work on rearing phyllosomes of spiny and slipper lobsters at a later date.

Slipper lobster. On April 30, 1978, Forrest Young, a biologist on our staff at that time, brought in a large, gravid Spanish slipper lobster, *Scyllarides aequinoctialis*, that he had found under a deep ledge by the 7 mile bridge west of Marathon. The bright, yellow eggs were attached under the female's abdomen. A sample of the eggs were removed and examined under the microscope. The eggs were about 700 microns (0.7 mm) in diameter and almost entirely yolk at this point. A tiny clear spot at one pole contained the first few cells of the developing embryo. We maintained the female Spanish slipper lobster in a 300 gallon holding tank. She stayed hidden during the day, roamed the tank at night, and ate small pieces of shrimp and conch (queen conch, *Strombus gigas*). Her eggs were sampled and examined again on May 17. Only about 40% of the eggs had developed, and these appeared very close to hatching. The remainder of the eggs were completely undeveloped and were still bright yellow, no apparent change in color or development had occurred since she was first captured. There was no apparent pattern to the distribution of the developed and undeveloped eggs in the egg mass. The developed eggs were randomly scattered among the undeveloped eggs.

The Spanish slipper lobster hatched her eggs the next night, May 18, at about 8:30 PM. She stood on the bottom of the tank and fanned her swimmeretts over the eggs and moved her abdomen back and forth giving the egg mass an accordion-like motion. The tiny larvae rose to the surface of the tank still shaped as a tight ball with only a few swimmeretts extended and moving. Their legs were still tucked around the body as they were in the egg. After about 10 to 15 minutes, the tiny larvae extended their legs in jerky movements and took on the typical phyllosome larval shape. Although we did not examine the newly hatched larvae under a microscope, the behavior of the early larvae that we observed is consistent with Robertson's (1968 a) observation of a short duration (10 to 15 minute) naupliosoma stage that occurs at first hatch.

The female shed the undeveloped eggs on the tank bottom after a few days. She spawned another batch of eggs on May 30, but none of the eggs in this second spawn hatched.

We obtained a female Caribbean spiny lobster carrying eggs on May 20, and these eggs hatched on May 22 at about 2:00 AM. We now had four tanks set up with slipper lobster phyllosomes, two 250 gallon black polyethylene tanks and two 60 gallon glass tanks, and one black 250 with spiny lobster phyllosomes. They were kept on 12 hour light and 12 hour dark photoperiod, and the water handling was the same as the previous lobster rearing attempts. We experimented with foods for the phyllosomes. Brine shrimp were grown for several days to a week before feeding to reduce the problem with the sticky yolk, and this seemed to prevent that problem. Finely grated fresh conch and fresh fish were the other foods in the experiment, and one tank also received some larval jewelfish (*Microspathodon chrysurus*) and larval coral banded shrimp (*Stenopus hispidus*).

Spanish slipper lobster phyllosomes were observed feeding on all offered foods by noon on the day after hatching. The slipper lobster phyllosomes first molted on May 30, 12 days after hatching. They did not do as well as the spiny lobster phyllosomes, and their numbers diminished from a couple of thousand in the 250 gallon tanks to a few hundred over the first 10 days. A tiny hydroid-like growth appeared on the legs and swimmeretts of the larvae after the first 4 or

5 days and apparently caused mortality in the phyllosomes that did not molt within 10 or 11 days. The slipper lobster phyllosomes died out by June 3 before any were observed to have molted the second time.

The spiny lobster phyllosomes survived well into the third intermolt, but their numbers also gradually declined, and this rearing experiment was also abandoned by about June 10. Finely grated fish and conch were well accepted by the phyllosome larvae of both species, but feeding was greatly limited by the relatively short period of availability of the food particles before they settled out onto the tank bottom. The accumulation of food particles on the bottom also made it difficult to maintain proper water quality. Careful and continuous water changes were required early into the rearing period, and frequent siphoning of the tank bottoms was also required.

Caribbean spiny lobster. Our most serious attempt at rearing the phyllosomes of spiny lobster began on August 20, 1979. Forrest and I dove in 80 feet of water just east of Delta Shoals and found one large female spiny lobster with late-stage eggs. We had the proper permits from the state for experimental lobster rearing and brought her back to the lab and set her up in a holding tank. The eggs hatched on the nights of August 23 and 24. Many, many thousands of phyllosomes were hatched on both nights, far more than we could use, and most were released back to the sea. We set up four tanks, three black 250 gallon rearing tanks and one 60 gallon glass tank, for feeding and behavioral observations.

One tank was set up with an experiment that I thought might be very interesting. I wanted to see if it was possible to shorten the total time of the intermolt period by providing the phyllosomes with abundant food and giving them two periods of light and dark within one 24-hour period. Two 8 hour days and two 4 hour nights, for example, within a normal 24 hour day/night period. I reasoned that if the sequence of day and night had any effect on the length of the intermolt period, then increasing the number of "days" might decrease the time between larval molts and shorten the entire larval period. The other tanks were set up on a normal day/night photoperiod. One of these was fed primarily live foods including new hatch brine shrimp, half grown brine shrimp, jewelfish larvae, and wild plankton. The other tank was fed mostly dead foods including shaved conch and fish particles, and hanging strips of jellyfish (*Cassiopea*), conch, and fish. The jellyfish were fed only as hanging strips since they could not be broken up into fine particles. The food strips were changed twice a day, and the particulate food was fed three times a day. The larvae in the double photoperiod tank were also fed primarily on the dead food regimen since live food was more difficult to provide than dead food.

Things started off very well. The lobsters fed in all tanks and began their first molt in the usual 6 to 7 days. There may well be gods and fates that are beyond the ken of mortal humans, and if so, there is certainly something in our feeble attempts to rear marine creatures that seems to tick them off mightily. Hurricane David blew up in the Caribbean with 150 mile an hour winds and took aim at the Florida Keys. Thankfully, David blew by offshore with very little effect during the first couple of days in September, but our routine tank maintenance was disrupted by hurricane preparations, and the offshore waters were roiled for many days.

Hurricane Fredric followed on the heels of David, and our plans for extensive live food in the form of jewelfish larvae and wild plankton were severely limited. On September 4, after the threat from David, the phyllosomes were in the best condition in the tank that received live food and in the double photoperiod tank. Phyllosomes in these tanks molted for the second time and entered the third intermolt on day 15 or 16, about September 9. After 20 days, there were only a few phyllosomes left in the tanks that received dead foods. These phyllosomes were in the third intermolt period, however. The larvae that were given the double photoperiods each 24 hours did not grow and molt any faster than those given the normal photoperiods. Their intermolt periods seemed to be the same as those in the normal photoperiod tanks. (It might be worthwhile to try this again under better rearing conditions.)

The most numerous and strongest phyllosomes were in the tank where they were fed mostly with half grown brine shrimp, even though other foods that might have enhanced survival were not available due to stormy weather conditions. Although the phyllosomes seemed to readily accept the dead particulate foods, they did not survive well in the tanks where the larvae were fed predominately on grated conch and fish. These particulate foods quickly drifted to the bottom and were available to the larvae for only a short time after each feeding. Also, the build up of old food on the bottom seriously degraded water quality. The hanging strips of food material were not utilized well by the larvae and were soon discarded. The most effective food was half grown brine shrimp, since they appeared to meet at least the minimal dietary requirements of the phyllosomes when marginally supplemented with other food items. However, as Provenzano (1968) points out, brine shrimp are not a natural food for phyllosome larvae and evidently are not adequate as a sole diet after the first few larval stages.

Mortality in this, and other rearing runs, seemed greatest a few days before, and at the time of, the third molt (the end of the third intermolt period). This is probably the time when a diet change is needed, and it is also the point when hydroids begin to develop on the tank sides and bottom, and when hydroids and fungus attack the weaker phyllosomes. The development of hydroids on the sides and bottom of the rearing tank became a major problem that extended beyond the third molt. Many phyllosomes became entangled and stung by the hydroids, and this was a direct cause of mortality. But even more important, the hydroids quickly removed food organisms and food particles from the water. The presence of the hydroids required more frequent feeding, which encouraged hydroid growth, which

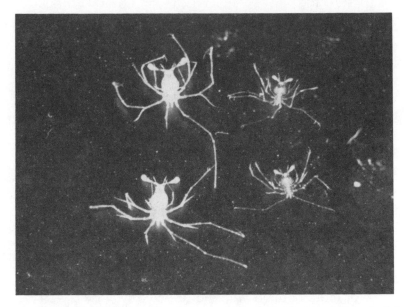

Figure 64. Phyllosome larvae of *Panulirus argus*. New hatch larva on the right and third intermolt larva on the left.

then required more abundant and frequent feeding, which encouraged more hydroid growth, which—anyway, I'm sure you get my point here.

We had about 100 phyllosomes remaining on September 20, and these had gone through their third molt and were in the fourth intermolt period. We carefully captured these phyllosomes in beakers (nets only entangled them), and moved them to a clean tank. We continued to feed them half grown brine shrimp, fish larva when possible, and occasional particles of shaved conch and fish.

The phyllosomes were now fairly large, over a quarter inch long, but still very transparent, and it was quite difficult to see them in the large, black tanks. Body size and number and length of the appendages increased noticeably after each molt, so we were able to tell when molting took place by carefully observing the phyllosomes each day. The numbers of phyllosomes gradually decreased, and it became harder to find them in the tank as the days went by. On

October 8 the remaining phyllosomes were 46 days old and were in their 5th intermolt period. We had some distinguished visitors at the laboratory on November 12, 1979, and two of the phyllosomes were removed from the tank and placed in a finger bowl for observation. They were quite large, about a half an inch long (12 mm), and were well into the seventh intermolt period. The phyllosomes were returned to the tank, but after a few days we could no longer find them in the tank. We moved on to other things at that time, since it was obvious that rearing spiny lobsters through the phyllosome larval stage did not have great commercial potential. We did, however, rear spiny lobster phyllosomes into the seventh intermolt period in less than 81 days, and that was an accomplishment in itself.

Although our lobster rearing projects were not done as conventional laboratory science and lacked proper controls and documentation, the results were interesting and the above description of the work may be helpful to those with an interest in rearing phyllosomes. Note that a molt is not necessarily equal to a "stage" in phyllosome development. A stage has a particular constellation of characteristics that identify a particular developmental point common to all the phyllosomes of that species. For example, Lewis (1951) identified eleven developmental stages of phyllosome larvae of the Caribbean spiny lobster, *Panulirus argus*, from the plankton. In culture, it may take several molts for a phyllosome to move from one recognized stage to another, or this may be accomplished in only one or two molts. In some instances, a phyllosoma may molt and show no morphological changes at all. Morphological changes from molt to molt probably depend greatly on the environment, including temperature, available food, and perhaps light, in both the natural and culture environment. We did not maintain the phyllosomes as individuals and did not closely examine the phyllosomes to identify the specific stages that they achieved. Thus, our rearing work lacks scientific exactitude and our results are reported only anecdotally.

Laboratory rearing work

There has been a great deal of work done in laboratory rearing of various phyllosome larvae all over the world. Provenzano (1968) reviewed much of the important work through mid-1960 and is a good reference to the state of the art in rearing phyllosomes at that time, which, except for the recent Japanese work, isn't much different from the present time. Tamm (1980) presents a more recent comprehensive review of the state of spiny lobster culture and concludes that "culturing of spiny lobsters is not yet a viable alternative to natural stock management." He also suggests that any serious attempt to establish a spiny lobster culture facility begin with juvenile culture rather than begin with work on the larval stage.

Dexter (1972) worked with the California spiny lobster, *Panulirus interruptus*, and succeeded in rearing them through six stages in eight molts. The maximum larval life was 114 days. Johnson (1956) identified eleven phyllosome stages for *P. interruptus*, and Dexter used Johnson's work to establish the stages she encountered with the cultured phyllosomes. Dexter attempted mass culture with 20,000 phyllosomes, multiple culture with 5 to 15 phyllosomes per dish, and individual culture with phyllosomes in compartmentalized plastic trays. Maximum survival was achieved with those phyllosomes living in individual containers. She also found that *Tubifex, Mytilus* gonad, and sea urchin eggs (*Lytechinus* sp.) apparently did not contain proper nourishment for the phyllosomes. Chaetognaths, ctenophores, and fish larvae were excellent food sources, but could not be obtained continuously during a lengthy rearing run. Brine shrimp naupliar and metanaupliar stages were used as the major food because of the ease of culture and constant availability.

Batham (1967) reported on rearing work done with a New Zealand spiny lobster or crayfish, *Jasus edwardsii*. He found that *Jasus edwardsii* first hatched into a naupliosoma stage. Robertson (1968a) states that the naupliosoma of *Jasus*

Figure 65. The naupliosoma stage of *Jasus edwardsii* (after Batham, 1967).

closely resembles the naupliosoma of *Scyllarides aequinoctialis*. This preliminary larval stage is called the naupliosoma because it is generally considered to be a modified nauplius larva. The nauplius is the first stage swimming larva of many crustaceans, and the naupliosoma stage in most spiny lobsters is probably completed in the egg before hatching. The first phyllosome stage is the first larval stage in a normal hatch of *Scyllarus* and *Panulirus*.

An even earlier stage termed the prenaupliosoma stage has been observed in *Jasus lalandii*. The prenaupliosoma and naupliosoma stages may, in some instances, be a result of premature hatching of the egg. In some species, these earlier stages do not even have the ability to swim. Robertson (1968a) points out that a naupliosoma stage has been reported in *Jasus*, *Ibacus*, and *Scyllarides*, and that in this stage the antenna is specially adapted for swimming and may function to rapidly transport the larva upward off the bottom and into the upper water column. Apparently, the naupliosoma stage is a normal adaptation in some species and is passed in the egg in others.

Batham (1967) reared *Jasus edwardii* into the second phyllosome stage. The five larvae that survived the first phyllosome stage molted into stage 2 in 19 to 25 days after hatching. They were offered a variety of foods: brine shrimp nauplii, *Obelia* medusae, calanoid copepods, crab zoeas, trochophore veliger larvae, *Mytilus* muscle, and an ascidian tadpole larva. The phyllosomes did not feed on any of these organisms. The larvae did feed "purposefully" on pieces of a Capitellid polychaete, *Heteromastus filiformis*, found in nearby sand bottoms. They also fed on small pieces of fish flesh, the yellow-eyed mullet. Because the phyllosomes fed actively on Capitellid polychaetes and ignored most other foods, and because these phyllosomes lack a feathery exopodite on the third maxilliped, Batham postulated that perhaps *Jasus edwardsii* phyllosomes were benthic rather than planktonic feeders. I doubt that any phyllosome is a benthic feeder, but this is a point to ponder.

The Japanese have been most successful in rearing the long lived phyllosomes of the genus *Panulirus*. Nonada, Oshima, and Hirano (1958) were apparently the first to use *Artemia* nauplii as food for laboratory cultured phyllosomes of *Panulirus*, and they succeeded in rearing the phyllosomes into the third stage. Inove and Nonaka (1963) reared the phyllosomes of *Panulirus japonicus* on brine shrimp into stage seven in 48 days. They experienced great mortalities after stage 4, but did rear a few into stage seven. Inove (1981) then reported rearing *P. japanicus* to the last phyllosome stage in 253 days, but the individual did not become a puerulus.

The first successful rearing of a *Panulirus* phyllosome to the juvenile was reported by Yamakawa et al. (1989). They reared one *Panulirus japonicus* from the egg through the puerulus stage and into the juvenile stage. Food consisted of *Artemia* nauplii (new hatch brine shrimp) for the first few stages and partly grown brine shrimp fed on *Phaeodactylum* sp. was fed after the third instar (the intermolt form). Finely chopped gonads of the mussel, *Mytilus edulis*, was fed after the tenth instar. Seawater in the rearing bowls was changed twice a day, and the water temperature was kept at 26 °C up to day 296 and at 24 °C thereafter. After 28 molts, one individual metamorphosed abruptly into a puerulus 307 days after hatching. This individual did not feed as a puerulus and metamorphosed into a juvenile 13 days later.

Kittaka and Kimura (1989) also report successful rearing of *P. japonicus* from egg to juvenile. They began with about 20,000 first stage phyllosomes and reared them initially on brine shrimp nauplii and later on *Mytilus edulis* ovary at temperatures of 24 to 28°C. At 200 days after hatch, five phyllosomes reached stage eight. Three individuals molted into the final phyllosome stage at 328, 379, and 396 days after hatching. Two individuals metamorphosed into pueruli at 340 and 391 days, and these two pueruli metamorphosed into juveniles at 355 and 403 days after hatch. The puerulus did not feed, but the new juveniles immediately fed on the mussel, *Mytilus edulis*. Molt intervals varied for individual phyllosomes in Kittaka and Kimura's work, but the molt interval for phyllosomes kept at a light intensity of 140 lux was 11.1 to 11.8 days and 13.8 to 16.7 days for those kept at high light intensities of 540 lux. Another interesting observation was that some of the phyllosomes kept under high intensity lighting molted repeatedly without morphological change. Tamura (1970) reviews the earlier work on rearing *Panulirus japonicus* in detail. One interesting observation that Tamura includes is that the most favored food of *P. japonicus* phyllosomes is the flesh of ise-ebi. "Ise-ebi" is the Japanese common name for *Panulirus japonicus*.

A Japanese worker, Jiro Kikko, has even obtained a patent on rearing phyllosomes. The title is *Cultivation of Spiny Lobster Larvae* under JC 11.2 (Agriculture—Marine Products) (89.04.25 Sect. C, Section No. 589: Vol. 13, No. 174, Page 111). The purpose of the patent is to enable multiplication and cultivation of spiny lobsters by feeding a liquid of densely propagated unicellular algae (diatoms at about 400,000 to 1,500,000 cells/ml or green algae at 6,000,000 to 25,000,000 cells/ml) and minced meat of brine shrimp nauplii and hard shelled mussels as feeds. An appropriate flow rate of water is provided at the edge of the tank. *Panulirus zainus* is cultured at 18 to 20 °C, and *P. japonicus* is cultured at 25 to 28 °C.

Igarashi et al. (1990) report on the effect of various species of marine bacteria in phyllosome culture of *Jasus edwardsii*. Survival rates and activity levels of phyllosomes were observed to be affected as the color of the water changed in the rearing tanks. Cultures of the alga *Nannochloropsis* sp. are routinely used in larval rearing tanks to control water quality through utilization of animal and bacterial metabolites, and to provide food for various micororganisms. It was observed that the color of the culture water for phyllosomes varied from green at the beginning, to white turbid, to transparent. Phyllosome mortality increased when the water was white turbid and decreased as the water became transparent. Obviously, the successional changes in the microflora of the culture were affecting molting frequency and survival of the phyllosomes. A total of 180 bacterial strains were isolated from green, white turbid, and transparent culture water. *Pseudomonas* was the most dominant genus in green water, but *Moraxella*, *Aeromonas*, and low numbers of *Vibrio* and *Cytophaga-Flexibacter* were also present. In white turbid water, the above bacteria remained in the culture, but *Staphylococcus*, *Micrococcus*, and *Acinetobacter* were also present. *Vibrio* was the predominant bacterial group in transparent water. Experimentaton with isolation and effects on culture water of the various bacterial strains showed that the changes in water color were caused by the lyses of *Nannochloropsis* cells by *Vibrio* bacteria. Although phyllosomes survived in water dominated by *Pseudomonas* and *Vibrio*, survival and molt frequency was better when *Nannochloropsis* was dominant, which may have been because pH (8.24) was closer to normal oceanic water. Selection of bacterial strains as well as algal strains may significantly improve culture success for phyllosomes.

Some species of slipper lobsters, family Scyllaridae, are much easier to rear than spiny lobsters. Unfortunately, the larger species in the genus *Scyllarides* have long-lived phyllosome larvae similar to spiny lobsters, and these species are no easier to rear than spiny lobsters. The smaller species in the genus *Scyllarus*, however, have a much shorter phyllosome larval period, and several species have been reared through this larval stage. Robertson (1968a, 1968b, 1971) worked with rearing several Florida Scyllaridae species and was most successful with the sand lobster, *Scyllarus americanus* (Robertson 1968b). This species went through six or seven phyllosome stages in 32 to 40 days. (See Chapter 3 for more information on Robertson's work.) Robertson (1971) also reared the first seven stages of *S. depressus* in the laboratory and completed the 10-stage series for this species with specimens caught in the plankton and postlarvae obtained from metamorphosis of final stage phyllosomes also taken

Figure 66. The ridged slipper lobster, *Scyllarides nodifer*, (bottom) and the American slipper lobster, *Scyllarus americanus* (top). Both specimens are mature adults. The American slipper lobster is about three inches in length.

in the plankton. Robertson estimated the larval life of *S. depressus* as about 2.5 months. Recently, Ito (1990) reared the Australian and Indonesian scyllarid lobster, *Scyllarus demani*, from egg to postlarva in 42 to 53 days. The phyllosomes were fed brine shrimp nauplii and a chopped bivalve, *Gafrarinis*. There were eight phyllosome instars and a postlarval nisto instar.

Obviously, the outlook for a commercial hatchery for spiny and slipper lobsters is bleak. Low larval survival and an extremely long and difficult to culture larval life combine to make investment in such a project akin to going into real estate sales on lunar properties. The only glimmer of a commercial possibility, in my opinion, lies with the small *Scyllarus* species. These animals are valued food species in many parts of the world, and they may have value as small rock lobsters if price and size are proper. The petite cigale, *Scyllarus arctus*, for example, is a valuable food species in the Mediterranean area. A good bit of research is required, however, on larval rearing and grow out of the postlarvae before the possibilities of commercial hatching and rearing of these species can be accurately evaluated.

Farming Spiny Lobsters

If it were possible to rear spiny lobsters through the larval stage in great numbers, then the relative ease of rearing them to market size would assure the development of a multimillion dollar industry. Well now, if a good marine culturist/biologist can't solve a problem head on, he or she tries to figure out a way to get around the problem. And as it turns out, there is a way of getting around the technical problems of rearing spiny lobster from the egg and still being able to rear thousands of spiny lobsters for an insatiable worldwide market. However, although the biological and engineering problems in this little detour can be solved, the political and legislative difficulties are more than formidable. Basically, the trick is to let nature rear the phyllosomes and then capture and rear the juveniles from the settled puerulus stage to market size.

Female spiny lobsters in any fairly large population that allows females to spawn at least once or twice, produce billions and billions of new-hatch phyllosome larvae. The sea is cold and cruel, and it's a lucky, lucky larva that survives the phyllosome larval stages to become a puerulus, but even so, millions and millions of spiny lobster pueruli survive to settle and become juvenile spiny lobsters. In some years, when the sea is almost kind, the numbers of settling pueruli are very high—and in other years, only a relatively few pueruli come to the shallows along the shore. Even in years with poor settlement, however, the numbers of new juvenile spiny lobsters are usually far greater than the available number of niches in the habitat. Natural predators take their toll of the tiny lobsters, and only a very few of the lucky pueruli that settle and become juveniles survive to enter the fishery. As the saying goes, it doesn't take a rocket scientist to see the possibilities in collecting these surplus pueruli, sheltering and feeding them through the difficult early months, and then selling them when size and market come together at the most profitable point.

In Florida, Ross Witham's work in the 1960's (Witham et al., 1964, 1968) and Don Sweat's work at Key West (Sweat, 1968) made Florida's marine scientists aware of the number and location of settling spiny lobster pueruli and the ease of early grow out of juvenile spiny lobsters. This work stimulated a lot of speculation on the possibility of culturing spiny lobster from the first juvenile stage. Ingle and Witham (1968) were the first to put it in writing. In a short paper, they explored this possibility for Florida spiny lobsters including both rearing the juveniles to market size and releasing the lobsters to public waters after growth through the first few most dangerous months.

This concept is by no means unique to Florida. Tamura (1970) describes this process in Japan as "storage culture". Bardach et al. (1972) discusses this concept and describes early efforts in Australia, Japan, and California to rear captured juveniles. The Australian work with *P. longipes* achieved a food conversion ratio of 6 : 1 feeding fish and abalone flesh (6 pounds of food produces 1 pound of lobster), which is quite good for crustaceans. Serfling and Ford (1975) worked with the California spiny lobster, *Panulirus interruptus*. They reared this spiny lobster through the juvenile stages at constant temperatures of 22 and 28 °C in closed system aquaria. The growth rates achieved, 3.3 mm and 4.5 mm per month in carapace length at these respective temperatures, are about two and three times greater than estimated natural growth rates. The increased rate of growth was a result of an increased number of molts rather than increased size per molt.

Phillips (1985) discusses several Australian studies done on the biology and culture of the western rock lobster, *Panulirus cygnus*. Phillips reports that studies done by himself and Dr. R. G. Chittleborough in the 1970's suggested that settlement of pueruli in some areas was often in excess of the carrying capacity of the natural environment. They explored the possibility of "cropping off" the excess settlement for stocking under populated reefs or rearing them in captivity. Postlarval rock lobsters are collected in habitats of artificial seaweed placed near the shore. The young lobsters, about 3 cm long, are taken from the seaweed collector and transported to a hatchery. They are reared at a constant temperature of 25 °C and fed trash fish or, if possible, a diet of mussel, *Mytilus edulis*, cultured on rafts just for this purpose. Fleshy and coralline algae are also suggested as an important part of the diet of this species of spiny lobster. At a conversion ratio of 3.6 : 1, it would take about 1.4 kg (3.08 lbs) to rear a western rock lobster to legal size (76 mm CL, 390 g). Thus, a relatively inexpensive food source is required to make grow-out of this, and probably other species as well, economically feasible.

Phillips also reports that it is possible to hold about 25 kg (55 lbs) of western rock lobster per square meter of tank surface and proposes a tank system with vertical stacking trays to take advantage of the vertical water column in large tanks. As Phillips points out, the costs of such a commercial lobster "farm" are quite high. Aside from the capital costs of construction, and the unknown costs of assuring a supply of postlarvae, there are also the operating costs of labor, temperature control, water quality control, and many other costs. Phillips wisely councils the development of a pilot plant before planning out a major commercial facility. On a positive note, however, Phillips reports that taste panels agreed that tank reared western rock lobster compared favorably with wild lobsters and were even more tender than their wild caught cousins. Culture of cold water palinurid species has even less mariculture potential.

Pollock (1973) studied the growth of the South African rock lobster, *Jasus lalandii*, on the breakwater wall off Cape Town and developed a lot of biological information on this species. He found that recruitment of juvenile rock lobsters to the offshore fishing grounds from the inshore nursery areas occurs at a size of about 6 cm (2.3 inches) CL, four years after settlement of the puerulus. The male South African rock lobster may not reach the legal size of 8.9 cm (3.5 inches) CL until nine years after settlement.

The Harbor Branch Oceanographic Institution in Fort Pierce, Florida has long been interested in rearing and farming spiny lobster. Lellis (1990, 1991) presents a comprehensive review of their experimentation in capture and grow out of postlarvae. A one-year study of spiny lobster recruitment around the island of Antigua in the British West Indies produced about 30,000 pueruli. Some of these postlarvae were used to experiment with grow out methods for spiny lobster. Groups of 500 to 1000 postlarvae were contained in tanks with bricks for shelter and were fed ground fish and postlarval shrimp feed. Survival was poor.

Control rearings showed that mortality was the same for groups and for lobsters maintained as individuals. A wide variety of diets was then offered to find a diet that gave good early survival. The experimental diets included live and frozen adult brine shrimp (*Artemia*), ground clams, fish, several post larval commercial shrimp diets, salmon starter feed, BioKyowa Fry Feed-C, BML-81S, HFX-CRD, HFX-EXD, a shrimp maturation diet, a lobster storage diet, a crawfish diet, and a diet composed of herring and blue mussels. Interestingly, only the adult brine shrimp diet proved satisfactory for the first stage postlarvae. Adult brine shrimp worked only until the third molt (350 mg live weight), and then the BioKyowa-C diet was acceptable. The juvenile spiny lobsters fed on ground fish or fish meal had a high mortality rate during the first few molts.

As with other marine organisms, there was a wide variation in individual growth rates among the postlarval lobsters. Subsequent experiments resulted in the best growth at 30 °C, but best food conversion was at 27 °C. After about 10 weeks, the remaining lobsters were grown out at 29 °C on a diet of ground fish, shark, clam, squid, shrimp, and macroalgae. The lobsters averaged 544 grams (about 1 lb, 3 oz), with a range of 118 to 884 grams at the end of 18 months. Lellis concludes that spiny lobsters can be grown, at least on an experimental basis, from puerulus to a market size of 454 grams (about 1 pound) in less than 18 months. The major problems to be resolved in a commercial operation are lack of an economical grow out diet and availability of postlarvae.

Another intensive effort in Florida to research the farming of spiny lobsters through rearing captured juveniles was mounted by a young marine biologist named Mike Calinski. Mike is one of those individuals who is often characterized by the term "unconventional". Mike approaches problems with great energy and intensity under his own terms and in his own way. Like Tom Edison and Henry Ford, this can sometimes result in great success, and sometimes not. Mike developed his interest in spiny lobsters as an instructor at the Carriacou Marine School, Carriacou, Grenada, in the West Indies. His observations and experiments caught the ear of William Lyons of the Florida Department of Natural Resources Marine Research Laboratory, and William aided Mike in describing, quantifying, and publishing these observations on swimming behavior of *Panulirus argus* pueruli (Calinski and Lyons, 1983).

Mike subsequently earned a degree in marine biology from New College of the University of South Florida in Sarasota, Florida, all the while pursuing with great vigor his interest in the farming and open culture of spiny lobsters and other valuable marine organisms. Mike's most intensive work with spiny lobster revolved around the development and testing of large, floating artificial habitats. These structures were designed to attract settling pueruli and to provide them with shelter and food in the form of growing communities of small marine organisms. After a couple of months in the habitat, they are large enough to survive on grass and rubble bay bottoms or in the rearing tanks or ponds of a commercial lobster farm.

Getting inspiration from the small settlement sampling device for pueruli first designed by Ross Witham, Mike built a much larger structure constructed of resin impregnated plywood, polypropylene rope, and floats. The flat 4 by 8 foot plywood sheets were layered one on top of another about 9 inches apart. Tufts of unravelled polypropylene rope were inserted a few inches apart on each board and extended several inches upward and downward to provide the complex fouling surface that attracts the settling pueruli. The total volume of these artificial habitats was 2.4 cubic meters. Three of these habitats were placed in the water in the Key West area on March 14, 1983. Mike designed the artificial habitat apparatus so that a fine, plastic window screen cage could be placed around the habitats. Then the entire apparatus could be hoisted from the water every few weeks at the time of new moon, washed with salt water, and the juvenile lobsters that had settled on the habitat could be removed and collected without harm. He could then count, measure,

Figure 67. The basic structure of Calinski's large puerli settlement and juvenile shelter habitat.

Figure 68. Left: Deployment of Calinski's habitats off the end of
a dock in Key West, FL. Right: The same habitats pulled to the hoist
and waiting for wash down and sampling of the small lobsters.

Figure 69. Beginning the task of hoisting the artificial habitat from the water before flushing the lobsters into a screen collector.

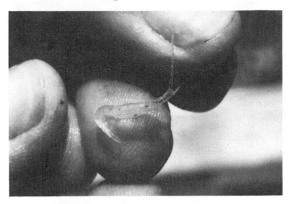

Figure 70. A newly settled Caribbean spiny lobster still in the transparent puerulus stage.

Figure 71. Tiny lobsters taken from Calinski's habitat. The lobsters on the left are a month old and those on the right are the first stage juveniles, newly molted from the puerulus stage.

and tag them, and then return the tiny lobsters to the habitat that had been replaced in the water.

Mike sampled and worked with these habitats for about seven months during summer and fall of 1983. As was to be expected, he had many problems with this initial effort. It was difficult and time consuming to harvest the huge habitats of all the tiny lobsters. Mortality was greater than expected, perhaps due to a school of about 200 mangrove snappers that took up residence within and around the artificial habitats. The flat plywood plates, at about 9 inches apart, were too far apart, and predators could enter the habitats with ease. The plywood plates also warped and closed up one end of the habitats while opening wide at the other end. Drifts of seaweed often clogged the habitats. Despite these and other difficulties, Mike did develop some data on settlement and growth of spiny lobster. Growth attained by tagged (tail notched) postlarvae in Mike's habitats was from a CL of 6 mm (the size of the first juvenile stage after the puerulus) to an average (mean) CL of 32.5 mm in four months. Growth in the first month was to about 10 mm CL; second month's growth was to about 16 mm CL, and growth was to 22 mm CL in the third month. This is very rapid and probably represents growth under good conditions of temperature and food availability in a "natural" (as opposed to a tank) environment. Numbers of pueruli that settled on the habitat were counted at 462 the first month followed, by 68, 88, and 119 on subsequent months. The habitats were sampled on the new moon of each month.

Mike's work was not sponsored by any government or private research organization, although the Florida Department of Natural Resources did give him permits to do the work, and monitored and encouraged his efforts. Although his work has not yet resulted in a large commercial lobster farm or a government contract to build and set juvenile lobster habitats to enhance natural lobster populations, he has added to our understanding of lobster biology and opened the door to some intriguing possibilities.

General considerations on spiny lobster farming

So it is within the realm of possibility to create a farm to rear spiny lobsters from the early juvenile stage to market size. I didn't say it would be easy, or inexpensive, or without problems, just within the realm of possibility. The biological and engineering problems are impressive, but even these are dwarfed by the political and legal obstacles. In the wild, a spiny lobster is government property, and the government has the power to say where, when, and how that lobster can be taken. Almost every population of spiny lobsters is subject to fishery regulations that protect lobsters during the reproductive season, lobsters carrying eggs, and lobsters under a particular size. It is the intent of these regulations to preserve the spiny lobster resource and provide a continuing supply of lobsters each year for recreational and commercial fisheries. Different governments often have different regulations, and lobsters taken under one set of regulations cannot be shipped to other areas with different laws unless many customs and fishery department requirements are carefully followed.

Biologically, it is far easier to establish a spiny lobster farm in an area where there is a large spiny lobster population. In such an area, postlarval lobsters must be available, and ambient temperatures will be acceptable for most, if not all of the year. Some natural foods will also be available from the environment or perhaps from fishery industry waste. However, also in such an area the local government and the local spiny lobster fishery must be persuaded that the capture of postlarval lobsters will not deprive the recreational and commercial fishery of recruits, and that sale of farmed lobsters will not depress the local fishery. The market size of farmed lobsters will also probably have to be the same as the local legal size. Selling farmed lobsters smaller than the local legal size and/or out of season would open the door to many enforcement difficulties with regulations on wild stocks. One has only to investigate the history of green turtle farming to gain an appreciation of the legal difficulties in farming protected marine species.

This is not to say that a spiny lobster farm is necessarily detrimental to local lobster populations or fisheries. If it can be shown that there is usually a settlement of pueruli in excess of the carrying capacity of the environment, then a spiny lobster farm can be quite beneficial to the area. Little and Milano (1980) investigated methods and techniques to monitor recruitment of postlarval lobsters, but this is still a dynamic field of study. In addition to the positive economic ramifications of increased local revenues and jobs, the spiny lobster fishery can be enhanced by a greater biological knowledge of the resource, and through the agreed upon release of a certain percentage of half grown lobsters each year to augment the natural populations. The state may also wish to charge a small fee for each postlarval lobster removed from the environment, to help pay for administrative costs. All farm production could also be exported to other world wide markets so as not to interfere with marketing of local fishery products. Finding a market for spiny lobsters is not anticipated to be one of the difficulties facing a spiny lobster farming operation.

There is another function that a spiny lobster farm can perform that would be intended to augment natural populations. In such an installation, it would be relatively easy to maintain a small population of spiny lobsters as breeding adults. Chittleborough (1974) describes holding the western rock lobster, *Panulirus cygnus*, from puerulus to reproductive adults. Age at first breeding ranges form 4.9 to 5.7 years. This species bred repetitively in captivity, and since *P. longipes* and *P. argus* are biologically similar, it is reasonable to assume that *P. argus* juveniles reared to adulthood would also breed easily in captivity, especially since captive breeding is not now unusual. The females carrying near- term eggs could be released on the reefs, held in cages on the reefs until the eggs hatch, or the new-hatch phyllosomes could be released to the sea. This could be likened to irrigating the dessert by sneezing with the wind, but female spiny lobsters produce one awful lot of eggs (sometimes more than a million per lobster), and with enough farms and enough gravid females, who knows? Whatever the effect, it would be a good thing for a spiny lobster farm to do.

Once agreements are made with local governments, and the best methods and places for capture of postlarval lobsters are determined, it is time to design and build the lobster grow out farm. A serious attempt at the details of designing a lobster farm is far beyond the scope of this book, but I will mention a few basic considerations. Temperature control is essential. The ideal water temperature would be around 28 °C (82 °F). Sometimes this can be achieved by using a seawater well, directly if the water quality is high, and indirectly (as a heating or cooling element) if it is poor. Electrically powered heating and cooling is far, far too expensive unless the installation is part of a power plant or other source of waste heat, or, possibly, set up as a high tech, closed system facility.

There are two basic designs: an open system where water is drawn from the sea or a shallow well, passed through the facility and back to the sea (or down a discharge well); or a closed system where the water is recycled from the tanks containing the lobsters, through a highly technical filter system, and then back to the grow out tanks. Of course, one could have a combination of these systems—a closed system for the smaller stages and an open system for the final grow out stages when the lobsters are large and better able to handle environmental variation. Foods and feeding, water volumes and exchanges, and space and tank structures are matters that require experimentation. Various food sources such as land snails, earthworms, insect larvae, shrimp waste, and even agricultural products may bring the cost of food for spiny lobster culture to reasonable levels.

Disease may also be a major problem. Lobsters in the wild do not show much incidence of disease, but this may change when they are contained in a farm environment.

Iversen and Beardsley (1976) discuss one disease of crustaceans that has been found in spiny lobster. This is caused by several species of chitinoclastic bacteria that attack through progressive chitinolysis and necrosis of the legs and other areas of the exoskeleton. It is common in crabs that are held for long periods, and it is commonly called shell disease, spot, burned spot, and box burn. A high quality rearing environment is the best defense against disease, but careful use of antibiotics (the right one for each disease) is also helpful.

There are two ways to look at the farming of spiny lobster: as a private, for-profit company and as a nonprofit government-sponsored institution.

Private and non-profit lobster farm possibilities

The most likely path toward establishment of a private sector spiny lobster farm would include extensive research for favorable areas with regard to availability of postlarval lobsters and advantageous environmental conditions, siting under a government umbrella for construction and operation, and access to markets for the product. There may be another way, however, in this day of high tech development. It is possible (maybe not economically feasible, but possible) to establish a grow out facility for spiny lobster in New York, Chicago, Toronto, London, Los Angeles, or Tokyo. A great closed seawater system using large protein skimmers; ozonation; vast settling sumps; automatic water temperature control systems (note that it is a lot less expensive to maintain water temperature in a recirculating system than it is to heat or chill incoming water); state-of-the-art biological, mechanical, and chemical filtration; and denitrifying filters could be built that would provide the environment for grow out of the small lobsters. Such a system may also maintain other types of marine organisms (oysters, clams, soft shell crabs, etc.) for live or very fresh seafood markets. If this type of facility proved to be economically feasible, the only problem would be obtaining the postlarval lobsters. (Sure, I know this is a naive and simplistic approach to a project with horrendously complex biological, engineering, political, legal, and financial problems; but what the heck, it's important to dream about things like this.)

The postlarval lobsters could be obtained with collectors placed near the shoreline in countries that would allow them to be taken from their waters for some form of compensation. It may even be possible to license local residents to set out and work collectors for small lobsters and then sell their catch to the spiny lobster farm. Unlike traps, unworked or lost collectors do not damage the resource, and although they would be a source of coastal debris, they might also provide additional settlement and shelter resources to the lobster populations. Collectors could be constructed of bio-degradable materials so that they would not remain for long in the environment after discard or loss. The small lobsters would be collected and held until they could be air shipped to the grow out facility. If a land based facility is used for holding and shipping, a percentage of the small lobsters could be held for release into natural nearby nursery areas after a few months of growth.

There is another possibility, however, for the acquisition of postlarval lobsters, one that does not necessarily require the participation and regulation of a government agency. There may be oceanic areas in the Caribbean, Gulf of Mexico, and in the Atlantic off the West Indies or the Bahamas where pueruli are present in large numbers and where they may be induced to settle on an artificial substrate presented over deep waters. It would be important for these areas to be relatively near safe harbor. A large barge could be modified or built with open areas midships for placement of properly fouled habitat material that can be manipulated aboard ship to harvest the newly settled pueruli. The barge would drift in oceanic eddies behind islands or in other productive areas during new moons. The pueruli that settle on the artificial habitats would be collected at sea and transported to a land base for packing and shipping to the grow out facility.

Would such a system work? It might. Would it be economically feasible? I doubt it, but under the right conditions, perhaps. Anyway, it's a little food for thought if not yet food for a seafood restaurant.

Spiny lobster farms can also be established in a variety of possible configurations by nonprofit institutions and/or government agencies to exploit a valuable resource currently not utilized, i.e., surplus postlarval lobsters. Such a facility may be more economically feasible when the profit motive is secondary to enhancement of the local economy through provision of jobs and development of local industry.

Farming the environment

This brings us to the last topic on my list for farming spiny lobsters. Up to now we have been discussing farming a natural resource under closely controlled conditions. There is another way to look at it, however, and that is farming the environment to enhance the harvest of a natural resource. Spiny lobster fisheries in many areas depend on environmental enhancement to aid fishery production. This probably does not enhance lobster populations, but it does make it much easier to catch lobsters from the existing population. It is well known that spiny lobsters move extensively by night and seek shelter by day, and this fact has not escaped the notice of fishermen in many local fisheries. If a lone, natural shelter exists in a relatively barren area, where would one expect to find lobsters during the day? And if natural shelter is limited, or absent, in a particular area, what happens if one places an attractive shelter on the sea bottom in the middle of this area?

Lobsters, of course, bunch up in great numbers in these artificial shelters, and one can catch them with much less expenditure of time and effort than hunting them from natural areas. Trap fisheries, of course, are successful in large part because the lobsters that enter the traps are seeking shelter just as much as, if not more than, food. Many lobster fishermen in the Florida Keys used to use traps made of flattened old ice cans and oil drums that served more as artificial habitats rather than the enforced containment of modern wooden and plastic traps.

Davis (1979) described the construction of artificial lobster habitats each built from 9 concrete blocks and placed near a marina just off Elliott Key in southern Biscayne Bay, Florida. A pyramid shape proved to be the most effective of the habitat designs tested. The lobsters in the marina quickly moved to the habitats and used these shelters during their juvenile growth stage of 12 to 18 months.

We found Davis's work very interesting and decided to do a bit of experimentation along those lines ourselves. Beginning in May, 1978, we set out 10 artificial habitats composed of 10 concrete blocks each, in 5 separate areas in 8 to 15 feet of water, offshore of Fat Deer Key in the middle Florida Keys near Marathon. We set the concrete blocks out in one drop of 1 habitat, three drops of 2 habitats, and one drop of 3 habitats. We recorded their locations by ranges on the shoreline so the physical locations of the habitat were not marked, and except for a lucky find, no other lobster divers could fish the habitats.

Lobsters piled into the habitats within a month of placement. One habitat contained 25 lobsters a few weeks after the habitats were set out. We monitored lobster occupation of the habitats every week or two throughout most of the first year and once a month or so during the next few years. The most lobsters recorded in one habitat was 55, and numbers of 20 to 40 lobsters in one habitat were not uncommon. Of course, there were many times when habitats had only one to five lobsters, or were empty. Groupers, moray eels, and small nurse sharks often moved into the block habitats along with the lobsters. Most of the lobsters observed in the habitats were under legal size, especially before the beginning of the lobster fishing season in June, July, and August. The lobsters seemed to increase their movement after the start of the lobster season, and we occasionally found the

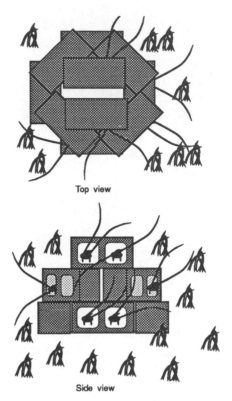

Figure 72. Concrete block habitats occupied by spiny lobsters.

blocks that composed the habitats scattered about the bottom—evidence that lobster divers had found the habitats. Recreational lobster diving was always intense in these near shore areas just after the start of the fishing season, and this activity seemed to keep the lobsters (those that weren't caught) always on the move.

Winter storms also broke down the habitats, and we routinely rebuilt them after winter winds. Sometimes the surge moved the individual concrete blocks 20 to 50 feet away from the original site. A few lobsters were attracted to the blocks even when they were jumbled into a random pile, but when they were placed in a pyramid shape with the hollow interior, the habitats would sometimes be totally

Figure 73. Checking out a concrete block habitat, one of Moe's Motels for spiny lobsters.

Figure 74. Looking down into a rather crowded concrete block habitat. This level of occupation was common during the summer.

filled with lobsters. I found it interesting that when two habitats were close together, only 10 or 15 feet apart, all or all but one or two of the lobsters would be packed into only one of the habitats. One habitat might have 25 lobsters, and the other might contain only 2 or 3 lobsters. All in all, our little experiment mirrored the experiences of shelter fishermen in other areas.

Lobster fishermen in some relatively undeveloped Caribbean fisheries in the Bahamas, Belize, Mexico, and Cuba have learned to make good use of artificial habitats over the last 20 years. These fishermen generally do not have access to large boats and hundreds of traps, and depend greatly on diving and spearing, snaring, gaffing, or netting the lobsters. Their boats are also small and depend on sail or small motors for power, so they must fish areas not far from home. In some of these areas, the use of artificial habitats, termed "casitas", "casas Cubanas", and "sombras", is very extensive. Over 20,000 of these lobster shelters were deployed in the Caribbean off Mexico around 1980 and 1981. Miller (1982, 1983, 1986) has studied and reported on these fisheries, and the following information is taken from his work.

The Mexican casita fishery is located in the Caribbean off the state of Quintana Roo. The casitas were introduced to this area by Cuban fisherman around 1968. The typical lobster shelter (casita) is about 1.5 sq. meters (15 sq. ft.) roughly 4 ft. by 4 ft., perhaps a little larger if light material is used in construction. The basic design of the casita consists of four poles about 15 cm (6 inches) in diameter and 1.5 to 2 m (4 to 6 ft.) in length. Four poles are laid out in a square, two poles on the bottom and two poles on the top, and they are nailed together to form a square frame. The roof is fixed to this frame on top of the two upper poles of the frame, and then two additional upper poles are usually added to give the structure additional support and also to keep the roof still suspended off the bottom if the structure is overturned by storms or dolphins. The structure of the casita is illustrated in Figure 75. When the casita is on the sea bottom, lobsters

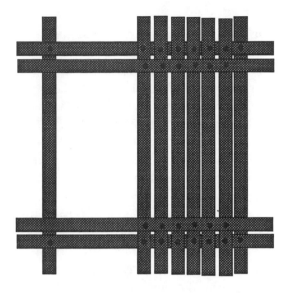

Top view, uncompleted, some roof poles missing

Side view, completed, all roof poles in place

Figure 75. Structure of a log casita, "Casita de Chit". The logs are nailed together as shown in the top view.

can crawl into the 8 to 12 inch space under the roof from the openings on all four sides. This is a simple structure that forms a very effective artificial habitat for spiny lobsters.

The wood used for the poles are trunks of the thatch palm (*Thrinax wendlandiana*). This wood is locally known as "chit". It is a very heavy wood and sinks immediately in salt water. The roof of the casita is made of various materials. An "Entumbado" or "Casita de Chit" is made entirely of poles of chit. The roof is constructed entirely of chit poles placed side by side and nailed to the bottom poles. A "Casita de Tambo" has the basic four pole frame covered by the side of an opened and flattened 55 gallon oil drum. A "Casita de

Asbesto" has a roof of one sheet of corrugated roofing, and a "Casita de Cemento" has a roof of concrete cast about 3 cm thick to the proper dimensions of the frame with nail holes molded into the cast. David Miller (personal communication) reports that the all organic wood casita is most effective at attracting (concentrating) spiny lobsters. This may be because of a more rapid rate of fouling, or perhaps the type of fouling organisms are more to the lobster's liking. There is still much to be learned about the business of a fishery based on artificial shelters.

A typical casita lasts about 3 years, and the fishermen are always reusing parts from old casitas and developing innovations to make the casitas remain functional for longer periods of time. Fishing on these casitas is controlled in two ways. In one area, the fishing grounds is divided into parcels or "campos", and each campo is controlled by a family or individual who constructs, deploys, and harvests from the casitas. In another area, casita construction, deployment, and harvest is controlled by a cooperative, and any member may fish the shelters. There are legal and social problems that have developed along with this shelter fishery. Most fishermen have to guard their shelters against poachers, and frequently when a competing casita is found, fishermen move it to new secret location. The campo or parcel system evolved in part in response to thefts and to settle disputes over casita ownership (Miller, 1982).

According to Miller (1982), the Cuban fishery is made up of cooperatives working separate zones. In fact the fishery is largely regulated by the boundaries of these quadrants. Casitas are the basic structure of the fishery, largely in place of traps and spearing of lobsters from wild areas, although large wire box traps are also used. Cuban fishermen harvest the casitas by placing a seine around the shelter and then tieing a rope to one end of the shelter and bouncing it up and down on the bottom. This drives the lobster from the shelter and into the area surrounded by the seine. The lobster are then herded into the bag of the seine and lifted aboard the boat. This system must be very effective, since the Cuban fishery leads the area in production. Mexican fishermen dive to the casita and capture the lobsters with a short gaff. Gaffing or spearing the lobsters kills them, of course, and the catch must then be processed and iced immediately. Catching them with net or snare allows them to be kept in a live box and transported alive to a processing plant.

A Cuban biologist, R. Cruz, is quoted by Miller (1983) as reporting that shelters and seines are the most productive gear in use. Cruz also reported that habitat construction in nursery areas is planned to increase the survival of postlarvae and juveniles. Artificial habitat fisheries in Belize, the Bahamas, and Florida are far less organized and usually consist of the hidden efforts of individual fishermen. Structures are composed mostly of squashed ice cans and oil drums, although some shelters are made of corrugated roofing, concrete blocks, and other materials that are inexpensive and that will stay in place for at least one fishing season. The locations of these habitats are well-kept secrets of the fishermen who place them in a particular area, and of those who find them and sometimes move them to other areas.

Fishing with artifical habitats was also practiced in Florida in the years prior to 1960 (Smith, 1958). This type of fishing was called "raft fishing". A large, crude wooden raft was constructed, towed to a suitable area, and sunk to the bottom with large rocks placed on top of the raft. After a few weeks, the raft accumulates many lobsters under its shelter, and it is ready for harvest. Netting is placed all around the raft, and the rocks are removed allowing the raft to rise and expose the lobsters underneath. The lobsters are then caught by hand, with bully nets, and by the netting surrounding the site. This type of fishing is no longer legal in Florida.

In the natural world, because of natural predation and instinctive behavior patterns, the presence or absence of natural shelter habitat, assuming an abundant food supply, must have an effect on the size of the lobster population in any particular area. One would surmise that the greater the amount of suitable natural shelter habitat in a particular area, the greater the population of spiny lobsters in that area. It makes sense that an area with a large amount of natural shelter habitat would draw juvenile lobsters from other areas as well as provide for greater survival of the juveniles that settle in that immediate area.

Casitas and other artificial habitats provide a shelter for nomadic lobsters that is superior in many ways to the natural shelters of low rubble, small rocky holes, and natural growths such as sponges, soft corals, and grass flats, especially when heavy natural reef formations are absent or far away. Such artificial shelters may also allow lobster populations to better utilize areas with good food supplies that are remote from natural shelters. Obviously, spiny lobsters that select a casita as a day shelter do not occupy a natural shelter during that time. They may achieve greater protection from natural predators, but are almost sure to succumb to the predator that provided the artificial shelter.

One might also surmise that in an area with a high settlement rate of pueruli and a limited amount of natural juvenile shelter habitat, the presence of numerous protected or lightly fished artificial habitats designed for optimum juvenile lobster shelter characteristics would increase the total lobster population in the area. Providing, of course, that the broad area of deployment produces enough food for the enhanced spiny lobster populations. Given the opportunistic feeding behavior of spiny lobsters and the broad range of food organisms that they consume, most tropical shelf areas could probably support enhanced lobster populations. Availablility of natural food should be a consideration in development of a population enhancement program.

Davis (1979) and Miller (1985) address the ramifications of this idea. Davis' work in Biscayne Bay indicates that juvenile lobsters will inhabit the most desirable shelters present, and if pueruli recruitment into the population is not sufficient, the less desirable habitats will then go unoccupied. As Miller points out, small lobsters are both predators and prey, and the quality and location of their shelter, especially in the early juvenile stages when movement is limited, has much to do with their survival as a prey organism and their success as predators.

The very complex interactions between lobsters and their shelters includes prey and predator relationships, instinctive migratory behaviors, a variety of behavioral interactions between lobsters of different sizes and sex, and reactions to environmental variables such as temperature, food availability, and water movements. Dr. William Herrnkind at Florida State University is working with the problems presented by the early stages of spiny lobster life. He is developing the basic information that will provide the questions and some of the answers in this essential area of lobster biology. What he, and other scientists, learn will help us manage this important multinational resource in the future.

Dr. Herrnkind and Mark Butler of Old Dominion University have recently been working in the Florida Keys on the creation of artifical habitats for newly settled spiny lobster postlarvae and juveniles. The shallow, near-shore algal flats that provide the initial habitat for newly settled spiny lobsters are under stress from siltation caused by dredging, shoreline construction, and constant boat traffic. It is possible that degredation of these habitats may significantly decrease survival of young lobsters that do settle in the Florida Keys. Herrnkind and Butler found that small lobsters can use concrete blocks with three small holes as acceptable postlarval habitat. These artificial postlarval habitats increase the populations in specific areas but cannot substitute for the expanse of natural habitat. Unlike artifical habitats for large juveniles and adults, postlarval habitats such as these concrete blocks do not serve to concentrate stocks from over a broad area into a small area with concentrated shelter capacity. They serve only to increase the potential settlement sites for incoming pueruli. Thus, sites such as these must be very numerous and very widespread to effectively increase the numbers of settling postlarvae.

Because of these considerable ecological and biological complexities, one can't just say, "Hey, increase the amount of shelter habitat in an area, and lobster populations in that area will also increase.", even though it may seem quite logical. One can reasonably predict, however, that in some places at some times, a significant increase in the amount of shelter habitat will result in a quantitative increase in the adult lobster population. As with most issues in this world, we can identify the two extremes.

- In an unfished population, a significant number of artificial habitats would serve to increase the population of spiny lobsters to the point allowed by the rate of settlement, the amount of natural postlarval habitat, and the available food supply. The result is an increase in the numbers of lobsters over that which can be supported by the natural environment (stock enhancement through habitat augmentation).

- In a heavily fished population, a significant number of artificial habitats (casitas and traditional traps) serve to concentrate available stocks into habitats known and exploited by fishermen. The result is a great decrease in the numbers of lobsters that can be supported by the natural environment (overfishing).

It is easy to see that artificial habitats have the potential to increase lobster populations through increasing available habitat and also the potential to decrease populations by concentrating the lobsters into known and easily fished shelter habitats. Although the two extremes are easily identified, it will be difficult to determine that variable center point where stock concentration (with the inherent danger of overfishing) turns to stock enhancement. So far all the action takes place near the overfishing extreme. In most instances, the determining factor on the effect of the habitats on the population would be the intent of their deployment and the management of the fishery. Artificial habitats deployed only to concentrate stocks for harvest will eventually function to decrease and overfish the population, whereas artificial habitats deployed and managed to provide only habitat shelter for developing populations in areas where natural shelter is scarce and food is abundant should serve to increase the lobster population.

In most situations, deployment of artificial habitats would be for the purpose of concentrating the stocks to enhance the fishery. Proper management may also allow the artificial habitats to function part of the time to enhance the population. An artificial habitat that is not maintained may soon, within a year or two, become non-functional because of siltation, breakage, movement, or loss. If fishing the habitat is managed by season or location, the habitat can function solely as a population enhancing shelter during the closed season. When the habitat is again fished, any required renovation of the habitat may be the responsibility of the fishermen. It would probably be possible to use properly designed and deployed artificial habitats to enhance and manage lobster fisheries, but this would require a lot of expensive research and development and a compliant fishery. Such a management/fishery system would probably function best for a small fishery within a limited area, such as a small island with limited shelf area.

Well, if we are going to develop and manage a lobster fishery with artificial habitats, we might as well go all the way. If we can build, deploy, and manage so large a number of artificial habitats that juvenile and adult populations of spiny lobsters are enhanced and the fishery substantially improved, then we can also design, build, deploy, and maintain artificial habitats that increase settlement of pueruli and survival of early stages of juvenile lobsters. (So what if this is 100 years in the future, we can think about it now, can't we?) Large habitat structures designed to attract and nurture the puerulus and early juvenile stages of spiny lobsters would be placed near the surface in areas favorable to settlement. Juvenile habitats would be placed near the postlarval habitats and would be designed to shelter larger juveniles.

The postlarval habitats would be designed to provide maximum survival—the best compromise between high food organism production, lowest possible predation, and attraction of the greatest possible number of settling pueruli. The juvenile habitats would be designed to harbor the small lobsters for several months after they leave the postlarval habitats until they enter the nomadic lifestyle of the larger lobsters on the open bay bottoms. This could be done for a small scale, limited area fishery, or even on a large scale, for a fishery that covers a vast area. It would be a system of well researched, well built, specific purpose artificial reefs—a product of "enviroengineering".

Such a project would be real environmental farming where we would engineer the enhancement of a spiny lobster resource from settlement of the puerulus through harvest of the market sized adult. It would also be very important to provide non-fishable conservation areas for every exploited population so adult lobsters could reproduce naturally in every area and provide larval seed for all populations throughout the central western Atlantic Ocean. As I wrap up this chapter, I hasten to point out that the wild speculations discussed above are just that, wild speculations. The engineering, biological, sociological, political, and economic considerations involved in such developments are beyond current reality—at least they are to me, at this time. Such projects could only be accomplished by intellgent, far sighted human beings. People who put immediate personal profit aside and plan and act for the future of the resource and the fishery. But as that famous philosopher, Fats Domino, once said, "One never knows, do one?"

Chapter Five

THE RECREATIONAL FISHERY
Where, When, and How to Catch Them

"Excuse me, Mr. Moe?... Uh, Mr. Moe?... **HEY MOE** ! Yeah you, the guy squinting into that computer monitor. Sorry to disturb you, but I've got a question for you since you're doing all this research and writing about spiny lobsters. As you know, there's been a lot of talk among fishery managers about what kind of recreational experience most fishermen want who use a particular fishery resource. The fishery managers then try to manage the fishery to keep most of the fishermen happy. This isn't easy since many fishermen have different ideas about what they want out of a fishing experience. Some recreational fishermen are happy with only a few big fish, and others would rather catch a lot of small fish. Some favor long seasons and low bag limits, and others want high bag limits and short seasons. And, of course, there are always the "Garbos", so named by the head boats because they're not happy unless they bring back at least one garbage can full of fish to sell under the table to some restaurant. But "garbos" are really part time commercial fishermen in disguise, not true recreational fishermen. So my question is, what do you, as a recreational lobster diver, consider to be a really good recreational fishing experience?"

That's a good question. Especially when considering the lobster fishery of the Florida Keys, which is perhaps the most intensely fished spiny lobster, *Panulirus argus*, fishery in the whole western central Atlantic /Caribbean region. There are only so many lobsters entering the fishery each year, and they have to supply both an intensive commercial trap fishery and a massive recreational fishery. The border between the commercial and the recreational fishery is sometimes thorny (and sometimes explosive when a commercial fisherman finds a diver with a hand in his trap)! While we're on this subject, I might mention how odd it is that someone who would never stoop so low as to steal a man's wallet, thinks it's alright to take a lobster out of a trap. Actually, there is no difference. If you're going to take a lobster out of a fishermen's trap, you might as well go to his house and steal his children's toys out of the yard, or take the supper off his stove; it's exactly the same thing. But I digress, now to answer your question, I'll describe a good recreational dive for spiny lobster, in my opinion.

It's a calm, cloudless day in mid September. The summer tourists have gone home, and the winter tourists haven't yet arrived. The reefs are quiet, at least during the weekdays. One seldom finds dive knives, snorkels, and swim fins on the bottom these days, even at the popular dive sites. The breeze flows gently, and the water just laps against the side of the boat. You took the afternoon off, and now you're anchored up at a favorite lobster spot, a long point of reef that stretches northward from marker 47 at West Turtle Shoal in Hawks Channel offshore of Fat Deer Key. You know the area very well. A high jumble of fire coral mixed with heads of brain and star coral begins in ten feet of water, extends about 100 yards northward, and then dwindles into deep meadows of turtle grass at a depth of 25 to 30 feet. There are several very large coral heads with spacious cavities under them on this reef that other lobster divers seldom visit and where many lobster often find shelter.

The water is relatively clear on this day, and you can see the outline of the reef stretching down current from your little boat. You're in fairly good shape these days, and you rarely use a SCUBA tank for lobster hunting, especially in less than 20 feet of water. A little extra body fat does require a weight belt to help you get down and stay there for a while, and free diving is a lot more work than tank diving—but free diving does give you a greater over all range, and you don't have to hassle with all the extra gear.

You slip over the side of the little boat into the warm salt water wearing your old holey pair of cotton lobster gloves and carrying only a short steel rod, a "tickle stick", to perhaps persuade a lobster to leave a deep shelter in the reef. The hand net that you usually use to catch lobsters was not in the boat house, and you suspect that one of the kids has lost it. No matter, you only need a few lobster for dinner, and you can catch them by hand.

The hang line over the stern of the boat has a lobster gauge, in case you loose the one that's hooked on your belt, and a hook for a collecting bag. This hook can also hold the scuba tank at the end of the dive, so you don't have to roll into the boat with the tank on your back. This time you're free of heavy tanks and gauges and BC's and wet suits. You're free to roam over hundreds of yards of reef and turtle grass, slipping down to the bottom at any time to investigate anything that catches your eye. At this time of the year, however, you always have to watch for the moon jellies. Some days, when eddies sweep in from the great Florida current that washes past the Keys, the water is alive with great moon jellyfish, *Aurelia aurita*. These translucent blue moons, up to two feet in diameter with clover leaf shaped gonads imbedded in their flesh, drift with the currents and suspend their long stinging tentacles a foot or so beneath the big disk of their body. Although their sting is not as intense and debilitating as that of the Portuguese-man-o-war, a close encounter can end one's desire to dive that day and make sleep difficult to get that night. On a day when the jellies are thick, only 10 to 15 feet apart, then one must use SCUBA just to be able to stay out of the upper ten feet that the jellies claim as their own. Today, thank goodness, the jellies and the Portuguese-man-o-war are few and far between, and you need only to remember to glance upward before ascending from the bottom to the surface.

Over to the west of the reef there's a large sandy area where a huge sting ray usually lays half buried in the sand. Sure enough, he's there today. Head to tail he must be 12 feet long. A big black grouper hangs alongside a coral head. He hasn't seen you yet, because if he had, he wouldn't be there now. The groupers in this area have been hassled by so many spear fishermen that one glimpse of a diver sends them deep into the reef for the rest of the afternoon. But you're not interested in groupers today, and as you peek around the coral head, a quick flip of the grouper's tail sends him deep into the dark recess of the reef. Clouds of French grunts and small mangrove snappers scatter as you swim along the top of the reef, and a pair of coney grouper dart into a deep hole as you pass by. A large male hogfish feeds in the sediments just off the reef. He packs shell hash into his gut and ignores you because you don't have a spear gun today, and he seems to know that. A huge green moray eel smiles at you and then folds and slides its way deep into the reef. A magnificent pair of French angelfish drift along picking casually at reef growths.

The lobsters are gone! There were spinys under every coral head a few weeks ago, and now not a one to be seen. You look way up under one of the biggest coral heads on the reef. This is the one in 15 feet near the offshore edge of the reef formation, and you see the paired antennae of a lobster tucked way up high in a tight little cave under the coral head. A little nudge with the tickle stick back where you figure the tail should be sends a lobster out toward the open space in front of your face. He looks a little small, so you break off and go back up for another breath of air. Free diving is now getting to be as much work as it is fun, so you hang out on the surface over the coral head for a few minutes to see if your encounter with the short lobster has stirred up any of his bigger buddies. After a short wait, a second pair of antennae waves to you from the other side of the coral head. A dive down confirms the presence of a larger lobster, one certainly over the legal size. This one is positioned with his back to an open hole in the rock and all you have to do is keep his attention on your left hand, reach quickly into the hole with your right hand, grasp him firmly around the carapace, and pull him out of the reef. You bring him back to the boat, check his size out with the gauge just to be sure, invite him to dinner, and then toss him into the boat. An easy catch.

Ten dives later you still have only one lobster. There were a few shorts here and there, but nothing worth working for. You're now down about to the point of the reef, the sun is getting low, the water is deeper, and you're a bit tired and about ready to settle for just the one lobster in the boat. There is, however, a large head of boulder coral nearby on the offshore edge of the reef in about 20 feet. You decide to check out this last spot and then go home to half a lobster and a hamburger—Surf and Turf, homestyle.

As you push down into the now dark and murky water toward the big coral head, you notice the tips of a lobster's antennae poking out from under the coral, or maybe two lobsters because they're pretty far apart. You grab the top of the rock ledge and slowly pull down and peek in between the tips of the antennae. There, way, way back in the rear of the cave stands a huge lobster. He must be five pounds and 15 inches long! Now what? The sun is low, it's getting dark on the bottom, you have no handnet, the coral head is 20 feet down and right next to a turtle grass flat. If that lobster shoots off across the grass, he's gone. You've got to get him out of the hole and catch him in one breath. If you break it off to swim up 20 feet for a breath after he's disturbed, he'll surely be marching off into the dark grass when you return.

You check out the situation very carefully with the little time left on this breath. The cave is so deep that you can't reach the lobster's tail with the tickle stick and still be ready to grab him when he comes out. If you just reach in and try to grab him, you'll never get a good grip on the base of his antennae or his carapace, and if he fights back he'll just break off an antenna, shoot out the back door, and disappear into the grass. He could also shoot out another hole while you're head and shoulders into the front of the big cave. Looking over the rear of the coral head, you find a narrow hole, and it seems that you could just reach his tail with your tickle stick and induce him to slowly move out the front door. If he does, then you could swim over the coral head and come down and grab him before he knows what's happening.

It suddenly becomes very important that you take a breath, so you let go and swim upward with hard fast kicks. Twenty feet is a lot deeper now than it was two hours ago. You hang at the surface breathing hard with your heart pounding while you think through this last dive. You won't have much time, 45 to 60 seconds and then you'll have an important appointment back at the surface. After four or five minutes, your heart rate is back to normal, you feel rested, and you're ready to go. You rapidly inhale and exhale about five or six times—a little hyperventilation, not a real good idea. (I certainly advise against it because it can cause dizziness and even fainting, but it does purge carbon dioxide from the blood, and it's the build up of carbon dioxide in the blood, not the lack of oxygen, that creates the involuntary stimulus to breathe.) After hyperventilation you may gain 10 to 15 seconds more bottom time, or so it seems, and if so, this is a situation where that extra time might come in handy.

You take a last mighty breath, flip up your legs and push down toward the dark mass of boulder coral on the bottom. A quick check in the big cave confirms that Oscar has not moved. Evidently he's waiting for the light to wane a little more before starting off on his nightly foraging ramble. You move to the holes at the back of the coral head and gently insert the tickle stick in the narrow hole where Oscar's backside should be. You can't see his tail from the hole, but any disturbance back there should send him out the front. You leave the tickle stick in place and peek around the coral head. Oscar's antennae are slowly moving out the front of the cave. If this was a tank dive, you would be content to wait a bit and let him take his own sweet time getting into the proper position for a good grab at his carapace. But it isn't a tank dive, and you only have 30 seconds of bottom time left.

You move back around the coral head and push the tickle stick further under the head and move it about with vigor to make Oscar move a bit faster. Then you swim over the top of the coral head and look down over the cave entrance. Oscar is almost clear of the cave, and he is a magnificent lobster, bigger than any you've seen this year. If you're going to get him, the time is now. You extend your left hand slowly to a point about a 10 inches in front of his nose and wiggle your fingers. You slowly move your right hand in position over his tail and keep it very still. A lobster responds only to things that move, sometimes moving toward it, but more often backing slowly away from a moving tickle stick or finger and right into a hand net, tail snare, or hand.

Oscar backs up a bit more, and his carapace is directly under your right hand. Your lungs are aching with the demand for another breath, and you have to move now. With one rapid movement, oblivious to the long, sharp thorns on Oscar's carapace and the sharp raking thrusts of the sharp spines on his antennae, you jam your right hand down on his carapace and force him into the bottom while you fight for a firm grip around his huge carapace. Oscar's powerful abdomen flexes and flaps and stirs up the bottom sediments in great clouds as he struggles to get away. His spiny antennae rake across your face and chest and scrape your right arm unmercifully. You know that if you let go to get a better grip, Oscar will be long gone in a second.

You quickly increase the power of your downward kicks and reach your left hand under Oscar's carapace where the needle sharp dactyls on the ends of his ten long legs can dig and scrape into your arm and wrist—but even so, you can then get a two-handed grip on this wildly flapping spiny monster. Just then the soft skin of your shoulder brushes full up against a blade of fire coral. If you had any breath left at that point, it would be lost. The fire coral burns like, well, like fire, but now you have a firm grip on Oscar and can finally head for the surface. You don't bother to look for jellies. If there are any above you, you're going right through them anyway.

Lungs bursting, you break through the surface. The water in your snorkel must go 10 feet into the air as you empty your lungs and greedily take breath after breath of cool, fresh air. Oscar has settled down and isn't flapping wildly anymore. He's just concentrating on digging his dactyls deeply into your wrist and arm and scraping his antennae on anything he can reach. You know that if you try to adjust your grip to avoid the spines, Oscar will break loose and dive into the bramble of reef below.

Could that be the boat—that little dot on the horizon 200 feet up current? With Oscar almost firmly in your grasp, you start on the long swim against the current back to the boat. When you finally get there, you toss Oscar over the side into the boat, and with great relief, grab the hang line to take a well earned rest. You can hear Oscar scraping along the boat bottom as you hang on the line and relieve yourself into the sea. Your favorite tickle stick? The heck with it, let the reef keep it for a week. You know right where it is, and it will stay there until next time. The first scarlet tinge of sunset touches the clouds above as you climb into the boat, start the engine, and head home with dinner crawling around your feet.

Now, in my opinion, that's a good recreational lobster diving experience. The scratches will heal, and the fire coral burn will go away, but Oscar is there on the deck of the little boat, and that makes it all worthwhile, including, of course, a great fresh lobster dinner. Of course, I don't advise **anyone** to dive alone at sunset, or at any time for that matter. A lot of bad things can happen, the motor can break down, one can get bitten by a shark, or attacked by a moray—all these things have happened to me. The shark bite? That's another story, but I was very lucky. When you live next to the sea and work every day down under by the reefs, your familiarity with the underwater realm often beguiles you to push caution to levels less than prudent. A wise man, however, remembers that the sea may often ignore mistakes, little ones or big ones, but it has no capacity to forgive them. What you get away with today, can kill you tomorrow.

The Recreational Lobster Fisherman

A matter of knowledge and attitude

A recreational lobster fisherman enjoys getting outdoors and experiencing the marine environment in the quest for a succulent spiny lobster, *Panulirus argus*. He, or she, uses experience, knowledge, technology, and technique—refinements of the ancient instincts that created the human species—to wrest a bounty from the firm grip of nature. The lobster diver is almost alone in a hostile environment; communication with partners is reduced to hand signs and body gestures, and only diving skills and a knowledge of the marine environment will assure survival and success. The true recreational lobster fishermen invests time, money, and considerable effort to obtain the experience of capturing a lobster on its own turf. Entering a hostile, untamed, and beautiful environment that is out of reach for all but the most adventurous and daring of humans, and finding and ripping a culinary pearl from the bosom of untamed nature is reward enough for most lobster divers. The lobster is only the object of the quest, and it is the quest, not the lobster, that is most important. It is not necessary for the recreational lobster diver to fill the boat with lobsters in order to enjoy the experience.

The commercial fisherman, on the other hand, invests a great deal of time, money, and effort to capture large numbers of spiny lobster. Although the commercial lobster fisherman may also greatly enjoy the fishing experience, his object is not to have fun, but to make a living for himself and his family. Most commercial lobster fishermen enjoy their work, and would rather fish lobster than sell insurance, do brain surgery, deliver mail, teach school, or repair other people's automobiles. Lobstering is hard work, and the hearts of few commercial fishermen burst with joy and song on cold, windy, rainy January mornings when the traps must be pulled with cold, stiff hands onto a rolling, sloppy boat. Even so, to many people, this is a small price to pay for the independent life of a fisherman, working on the open sea in your own boat, being in control of your own work, and doing things how and when you feel they should be done.

A good commercial lobster fisherman and a true recreational lobster diver have little conflict. Each respects the rights, activities, and purposes of the other, and, most important, each has great respect and concern for the natural resource that is the object of their attention. Each knows that only proper management will conserve this intensively fished resource for their own future and their children's future. The lobsters and the fishery suffer most when individuals in either category care nothing for the environment, the resource, and other fishermen. Some of these poor misguided, immature divers must often say to themselves things like:

- "I'm not going back empty handed. I'll just take a few lobsters from this trap."

- "Everybody takes small lobsters. If I don't take it someone else will. I'll just hide them under the seat."

- "I bet I can get this lobster if I break up this coral head."

- "Geeze, I turned over five huge rocks and all the lobsters still got away. Turn the rocks back over where they were? Naw, that's too much work. So what if the sponges and corals die, no one will know I did it."

- "I'll just squirt a little bleach into the reef. That will make those lobsters move out. So what if it kills a coral head or two. I don't give a damn about the reef, I'm just gonna get mine now."

- "Hey, there's a lot of lobsters here. I'll take all fifty and sell them to that little restaurant down the street. No one will know."

- "So what if these lobsters are shorts. I need the money, so I'll ship this load of 500 short lobsters I stole from traps to my cousin in New York. I couldn't care less even if these were the last lobster in the world. I'm going to get all I can for me, now, and to hell with everybody and everything else."

It is very sad, of course, when a few ignorant, selfish, and criminal individuals destroy our environment and the resources that belong to all of us. This is why the Florida Marine Patrol is the lobster's best friend, and the best friend of the honest and knowledgeable commercial fishermen and recreational lobster diver. The Marine Patrol enforces the laws that are written to protect the lobster population from overfishing and to insure that each user group gets a fair share of the resource.

The lobster resource is so stressed and overfished in the Florida Keys, that the recreational and commercial lobster fisheries can continue to exist only through careful management, and this means that all lobster fishermen must have an understanding of, and commitment to, the need for fishery regulations—and this includes a fundamental respect for the environment, the resource, and all others that lawfully use our marine resources.

Enforcement alone cannot save the spiny lobster resource. Fishermen must respect and encourage management efforts, or such efforts will not succeed. Research and education are the keys to wise utilization of the resource by all fishermen, and this is why wise spiny lobster fishermen, recreational and commercial, support the research efforts of national and state marine laboratories, the legislative, management, and enforcement efforts of state and national governments, and all the educational efforts and programs that may come along. Boater and diver ignorance of the delicate reef environment and the laws that protect reef life also contribute to the degradation of the resource and the reef. Education is everyone's responsibility, and it is important to inform others of the laws and proper conduct on the reef whenever possible.

There was a time, even I can almost remember it, when lobsters and fish crowded every hole in the reef, fishermen were relatively few in number, and rules and regulations were sparse. If you caught more than you could use, you sold the excess catch, gave it away, buried it under the orange tree, or (a horror even then) left it on the dock. Even though the real commercial fishermen didn't like it, plenty of people supplemented their income by fishing on weekends or when the weather was nice. If you caught a 100 king mackerel or 100 lobsters, then you had a little extra money for the week, and there was no law against it. It was hard to imagine then that in only a couple of decades there would be so many people and so much pressure on our natural resources that preservation of fish and invertebrate populations would depend on scientific research, laws, quotas, and careful partitioning of the resource. And this is only the beginning. Thousands and thousands of people move to south Florida every year, and this burgeoning population growth stresses the lobster population in many ways, including more recreational pressure and more environmental degradation.

The resource, and the fishing industry, can no longer abide that broad grey area that existed between recreational and commercial fishermen. That hazy divide is, out of great necessity, becoming a sharp line. You either fish for a living or you do not. A recreational lobster fisherman does not exceed the catch limit, does not steal from traps, does not sell lobsters, and does not take shorts. If you do do these things, you aren't a recreational lobster fisherman. You become a poacher, or worse yet, a thief—and no amount of rationalization can change that. In our modern world, it is up to the fishery managers and the fishery biologists, and also the fishermen themselves, to regulate the exploitation of the fishery so that the resource endures and all user groups get a fair share. (Chapter Six provides a lot more information on how the spiny lobster fishery is, and will be, regulated.) Thus old ways must pass, and we must all define our niche in the fishery and abide by it, and protect the fishery from its worst enemy—that little bit of greed that lies within each of us.

It's not easy to find and capture spiny lobster, at least it isn't if you've never done it before or if you aren't familiar with the area. If you don't have much time and you really want results, it pays to go with someone that knows how and where.

Where does one go to find spiny lobster? Well, lobsters are where you find them. Yah, I know this is a "big" help, but it's true. You can go to an area where you're *sure* to find lobsters, hunt all day, and find only one or two or even zip, and then you can stumble over a couple dozen large lobsters when you're least expecting it. As a case in point, in October,

1990, three divers in 65 feet of water off Miami found and caught three spiny lobsters weighing 12, 10, and 8 pounds, as well as two that were only 6 pounds. A storm front with high winds preceded their dive trip by a few days, and the unsettled conditions may have stimulated the huge lobsters to move to relatively shallow water. Lobsters move around a lot, especially when they are frequently disturbed by diving activity. A reef devoid of lobsters this week may harbor dozens of spinys a few days later. Thus, I can't tell you exactly where to find lobsters, but I can tell you where and when to look for them, how to hunt them once you're there, how to catch them when you do find them, and what to do with them after you've caught them.

Where To Find Spiny Lobster

Florida. Spiny lobster can be taken off all Florida coasts, and even off Alabama and Georgia coasts. For all practical purposes, however, spiny lobsters are numerous and accessible in the U.S. only in the waters of the Florida Keys and in the shallow waters of the lower east coast of Florida from the upper Keys northward to about St. Lucie County. Spiny lobsters can be found off Jacksonville and other northeast coast areas, but they are on the deep reefs, 80 feet and more, and they are few and far between. When they are taken, they are usually very large, five pounds or more in weight. The deep offshore patches of "reef" or live bottom areas found off the northeast Florida coast also extend along the Georgia coast. The best known of these live bottom areas off the Georgia coast are the Savannah Snapper Banks and Gray's Reef National Marine Sanctuary. These areas range from about 60 to 150 feet of water. Although winter water temperatures drop to about the lower limit that lobsters can withstand, the sparse populations of large lobsters survive the winters and even breed in late spring and summer. In a study of the spiny lobster population on the Savannah Snapper Banks, Ansley (1983) found the average size lobster was 132 mm (5.28 inches) CL and 1.8 kg (4 lbs) in weight.

Monster lobster. Large spiny lobster are also found in deep water (80 to 150 feet) offshore of the Florida panhandle (Panama City and Pensacola). In these areas (as off the northeast Florida and Georgia coast) it is important to have local help in finding and diving these deep areas. Local dive shops are usually the best starting point for any lobster dive. Spiny lobsters and ridged slipper lobsters (*Scyllarides nodifer*) can also be found in the offshore waters of the central coast of Florida (Tarpon Springs, St. Petersburg, Sarasota, and points south) in depths of 60 to 150 feet, but they are not common, and it takes a lot of looking before productive areas are found. The spiny lobsters from deep Gulf waters are also large, and old. These populations of mature lobsters are slow to recover from fishing pressure, since it may take 10 years or more for a lobster to reach a really large size. These lobsters may also be very important to the reproductive potential of the species, so it is just as well that they are out of the reach of most lobster divers.

Monster lobsters, 13 pounds or more, can be found on the humps of the Florida Middle Grounds. The Florida Middle Grounds are about 125 miles offshore of St. Petersburg/Tarpon Springs and consist of sea mounts that rise to within 60 feet of the surface. This area is large, about 50 square miles, and has always been a major fishing ground for groupers and snappers. Finding and catching by hand one of the great lobsters that live on the Middle Grounds is not a task to take on lightly. Few divers visit this area because of the great distance from shore. One must be a skilled boatman, navigator, and diver to meet these monster lobsters on their own terms on their own reef.

Taking these huge spiny lobsters, however, may be about the worst thing we can do to the lobster populations. Dr. Jim Bohnsack, an evolutionary biologist at the University of Miami, has a theory that we may be actually changing the genetic structure, altering the gene pool, of populations of commercially important fishes. In any species, the maximum size of individuals, the size at first reproduction, and the average size of the individuals in a population are under genetic control. If you want big dogs, just keep breeding the biggest dogs with each other, and eventually all your dogs will be big (Great Danes). Conversely, constantly breeding the smallest dogs results in a population of small dogs (Toy Poodles, for example).

Now even though everyone would like to see a population of numerous, large lobsters on our reefs, our intense fishing activity may be pushing lobster genetics in the opposite direction. Constantly removing all the largest lobsters not only removes the greatest source of eggs, but it also means that most new lobsters come from females that matured at small sizes and did not grow to even the average size of reproductive females in an unfished population. Thus, the evolutionary pressure on both males and females is to reproduce at the smallest possible size; and the genes for long life and reproduction at large size are probably unexpressed, may be neutral or possibly negative to the direction of natural selection, and may even be lost from the population. So if this is true, how can we avoid shrimp sized lobsters a hundred years from now?

Perhaps the best way to maintain natural breeding populations of both fish and lobsters is to establish reproduction reserves or "refugia"—large natural areas spaced at intervals along the coast that are not fished in any way for any species. All species in these areas could grow and reproduce in their natural state. The females of most marine fish and invertebrates produce hundreds of thousands to many millions of eggs over a lifetime, so relatively small reproduction reserve areas could insure adequate egg production for most exploited species. In the long run, this would be cheap insurance for the conservation of our marine resources.

So a deep water dive for monster spiny lobster is possible off almost all Florida coasts, but it is the Florida Keys and the lower east coast where most lobster divers seek their succulent quarry. It is also a good idea in these areas to find a good dive shop and go along on a guided lobster dive, or at least get information on which way to point the boat. During the day, spiny lobsters are almost always found in some type of shelter. This is usually deep in a heavy reef formation, but lobsters are often found singly, or in twos or threes, in small rock holes or under sponges that punctuate relatively flat bottoms of mud, sand, rubble, and grass. It is wise to avoid areas that are heavily frequented by dive boats. For one thing, there probably won't be many lobsters in areas with heavy diver traffic, and for another, these areas don't need the extra stress that a lobster diver may place on that immediate reef environment.

There are three sharply defined series of reefs in the area from West Palm Beach to the Florida Keys. The inshore reef is the weakest, and the third or offshore reef has the most rugged relief. The three reef lines are found at depths of about 45, 75, and 125 feet offshore of West Palm Beach and become more shallow (30, 50, and 80 feet) as they extend southward to the Miami coast (Moe, 1963). Lobsters are found along these reef lines in rocky areas where overhangs and caves provide shelter. Generally, large lobsters are found in deep areas, but they may move inshore due to seasonality and local conditions of wind and weather.

Spiny lobsters are not hard to find in the Florida Keys. Go to the end of almost any dock or the edge of any seawall with a powerful flashlight late at night, and chances are that the light will pick up the twin, bright red, reflections from the eyes of a small lobster wandering nearby. Now I hope you noticed that I didn't say that large, legal sized lobsters were easy to find in the Florida Keys. Small undersized lobsters, "shorts", may be easy to find, but finding large, legal sized lobsters is a whole different story. There are about 200 miles of offshore reefs along the Florida Keys, and lobsters can be found anywhere along the reef line, the patch reefs between the offshore reef line and the shore line, and in the holes and rubble sponge bottoms that punctuate the grassy undersea meadows of shallow Florida Bay and Atlantic waters.

Lobsters found in Florida Bay (Gulf of Mexico) tend to be smaller than those found on the Atlantic side, and a diver will have to handle many more shorts before finding legal size lobsters. I prefer to work the patch reefs on the offshore side of Hawk Channel. The water is usually a little more murky in this area than on the offshore reefs, but there is a lot of reef area, and the recreational lobster diving effort is spread out. There is a greater chance of finding undisturbed lobster dens and more legal size lobster in these areas.

Any user of the natural resources of south Florida should know that on November 16, 1990, President Bush signed Public Law 101-605, and the Florida Keys National Marine Sanctuary was officially created. The entire coral reef tract of south Florida is now a national marine sanctuary that covers 2,600 square miles. The eastern northern boundary of this new sanctuary begins at the northeastern corner of the Biscayne National Monument offshore of Key Biscayne and extends from the 60 foot depth of its offshore edge out to the 300 foot depth contour. The Sanctuary then extends southward and westward along the 300 foot depth contour, including all the reef tract and all the aquatic areas below the high water mark in the Florida Keys, loops around the Dry Tortugas, and extends north and east along the boundary of Florida State waters (three marine leagues or nine nautical miles from the shoreline) up to the boundary of the Everglades National Park. The existing Key Largo and Looe Key National Marine Sanctuaries will be incorporated into the new sanctuary area. Management plans for the natural resources of this new sanctuary are in the early stages of formulation, and it will be a few years before changes, if any, are made in lobster fishery regulations within the new sanctuary.

There are, however, a number of marine State and National parks within this broad south Florida sanctuary area, and some of these have special regulations for the taking of spiny lobster. It is very important to be aware of the location and boundaries of these parks and the lobster fishing regulations that are in force.

The map, Figure 76, shows the approximate locations of these parks and the protected areas where taking any spiny lobster is strictly prohibited. Protected areas are very valuable to populations of spiny lobsters. The protected offshore reefs give them special areas where they can reach maturity and breed; and protected inshore areas give them nursery

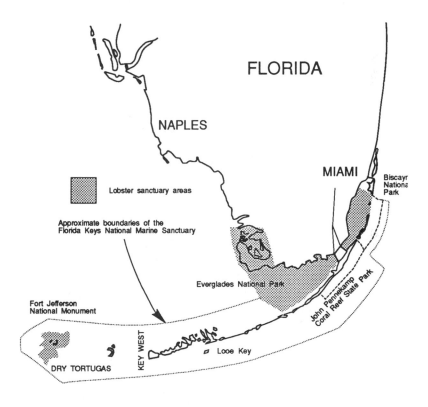

Figure 76. Map of southern Florida and the Florida Keys illustrating the location of south Florida's aquatic parks and lobster sanctuary aeas.

grounds where they can safely pass through the juvenile stages, and then migrate to the offshore reefs and enter the commercial and recreational fishery.

- **Everglades National Park** is located on the tip of the Florida peninsula on the Florida Bay side of the Florida Keys. No lobstering of any type, commercial or recreational, or possession of lobsters is allowed in this park. It covers a large part of Florida Bay and provides a very important nursery ground for spiny lobster, shrimp, crabs, and many species of marine fish. More information may be had from the Everglades Park Service (305) 247-6211.

- **Biscayne National Monument,** including the Biscayne Bay—Card Sound Lobster Sanctuary, is located in Biscayne Bay just north of John Pennekamp State Park. No lobstering of any type is allowed in the Lobster Sanctuary portion of the Park. The Lobster Sanctuary extends from the northern edge of Matheson Hammock Park east to the tip of Cape Florida (Key Biscayne). It extends south from the tip of Key Biscayne to Soldier Key and along the eastern edges of Soldier Key, the Ragged Keys, Boca Chita Key, Sands Key, Elliott Key, Old Rhodes Key, Swan Key, Palo Alto Key, and Angelfish Key to the southern edge of Pumpkin Creek. The boundary then extends along the southern edge of Pumpkin Creek northward into Card Sound to the high water line of Key Largo, then southward along the high water line of the east coast of Key Largo through Card Sound and Little Card Sound to the Card Sound Bridge. From the Card sound bridge the Sanctuary boundary extends northward along the high water mark of Little Card Sound, Card Sound, and Biscayne Bay and back to the northern boundary of Matheson Hammock Park. In other words, don't take lobsters from Biscayne Bay south of Key Biscayne or from Card Sound and Little Card Sound. Lobsters taken on the offshore reefs outside of the Sanctuary may be transported through the Sanctuary as long as no one dives from the boat while the boat is in the Sanctuary. More information may be had from the Biscayne Bay Park Service (305) 247-2044.

- **Key Largo National Marine Sanctuary** is located offshore of John Pennekamp State Park. Lobsters may be taken from all areas of this park in accordance with Federal law (see Appendix B). More information can be had from the Key Largo National Marine Sanctuary (305) 451-1644.

- **John Pennekamp State Park** is located on the Atlantic side of Key Largo and extends from the southern boundary of Biscayne National Park southward to the northern edge of Rodriguez Key. The eastern boundary of this park meets with the western boundary of Key Largo National Marine Sanctuary. Lobsters may be taken from all areas of this park in accordance with Florida law (see Appendix A). More information can be had from the John Pennekamp Park office (305) 451-1202.

- **Looe Key National Marine Sanctuary** is located on the offshore reefs off Big Pine Key in the lower Florida Keys. It is named after the HMS *Looe*, a British ship that ran aground on the high coral growths in 1744. The Sanctuary covers about 5.32 square nautical miles in a parallelogram shape with marker 24 near the center. The core area is marked on each corner with a yellow buoy. Lobsters may be taken from this Sanctuary in accordance with Federal law, except in the marked core area of the reef. This core area contains remarkable growths of coral, and to preserve the coral growth, no user impact is permitted in this core area. No lobsters may be taken by any means from this central core area. About 54 mooring buoys are provided throughout the Sanctuary to prevent anchor damage to coral and sponge growth. Lobsters do leave the core area at night to forage on rubble areas around the reef, and they are subject to capture from traps set in this area (Lyons, 1991). A larger core area is needed if this is to be a complete lobster refuge. More information can be had from Looe Key National Marine Sanctuary (305) 872-4039.

- **Fort Jefferson National Monument** at the Dry Tortugas islands is located about 70 miles west of Key West and about 90 miles southwest of Naples, Florida and covers an area of about 100 square miles. Lobstering is not permitted within the boundaries of the Monument. More information can be had from the Everglades National Park office (305) 247-6211.

Finding legal size spiny lobsters in the Florida Keys is not as easy as it used to be. It takes a lot more dive time than it used to, and it really helps to be very familiar with local marine areas. Lobster antennae no longer poke out from every reef. There are still places, however, in the Bahamas and the Caribbean, where lobster populations are still relatively unexploited, and large mature spiny lobster inhabit most reef structures.

Bahamas. The Commonwealth of the Bahamas covers 5,380 square miles, includes 700 inhabited islands, and about 2,400 uninhabited islands and islets. The total area occupied by the Bahama Banks covers over 50,000 square miles. Coral and rock reefs are found off almost all coasts. The Bahamas are spiny lobster country. Of course, the reef areas near cities and towns suffer some pretty intense lobster diving, but there are remote areas that harbor lightly fished lobster populations composed of large, mature individuals. Note that visitors to the Bahamas can not fish lobsters commercially, but one can take enough lobsters for a dinner or two (6 lobster bag limit). Spiny lobsters can be taken in the Bahamas with a Hawaiian sling (more on this in the section on how to catch lobsters), but there are prohibited areas. One can not spear lobster or fish within a mile of the coast of New Providence or within a mile of the southern coast of Freeport, Grand Bahama, or within 200 yards of the coast at low water mark on any other Family Island.

The Bahamas National Trust has also established regulations that make Bahamian National Parks havens for marine life. No fishing, conching, crawfishing, or the taking of any live plant, animal, coral, or any creature whatsoever is allowed. Sea life is the great treasure of the Bahamas, and these parks are the replenishment areas for this treasure. The Exuma Cays Land and Sea Park has been closed to all fishing since 1985. Be sure to be aware of local fishing laws when planning to take lobster in the Bahamas or in any Caribbean country. Otherwise a very uncomfortable and expensive situation could develop. For example, if one does take lobster from a Bahamian National Park, one can be fined $500.00 and suffer confiscation of all boats, vessels, aircraft, and equipment. As they say, "A word to the wise is sufficient."

Other countries (including British Dependencies and US Territories)—Belize, Bermuda, Brazil, Cayman Islands, Costa Rica, Cuba, Dominican Republic, Grenada, Haiti, Honduras, Martinique, Mexico, Montserrat, Netherlands Antilles (Curacao, Bonaire, Aruba), Nicaragua, Panama, US Commonwealth of Puerto Rico, St. Kitts/Nevis, Turks and Caicos, U.S. and British Virgin Islands, Venezuela, and other small Caribbean islands—have fisheries for spiny lobster and to a greater or lesser extent, support recreational diving for lobster. Chapter 6 has more information on the lobster fisheries of some of the Caribbean countries. Be sure to check local rules and regulations before taking lobster or any other marine organisms.

When to Fish for Spiny Lobster

Spiny lobster are found in reef environments year round, but they can be taken only during a specified fishing season in most countries. There may be exceptions in areas with very small populations where there is no commercial and only a very small recreational fishery; but no matter where you are, never just assume that there are no seasonality regulations. **Always** check for, and abide by, current fishery regulations for all marine activities in every place you dive. (See Appendix A for a reprint of the Florida laws, statutes, and regulations on the recreational and commercial spiny lobster fisheries.)

The main reason for a closed season on spiny lobsters is to protect the lobster population during the breeding season. Just protecting females with eggs is not enough during the period of most active breeding. Eliminating fishing stress from the population enhances breeding activity and protects eggless females that will soon spawn eggs. Although spiny lobsters can breed year round, most breeding occurs during late spring and early summer, especially in areas with cool winter temperatures.

The lobster season in Florida extends from August 6 through March 31. Properly licensed commercial fishermen and recreational fisherman may take lobsters during this season (Note: a recreational lobster diver must have a salt water fishing license with a lobster stamp, obtainable at many retail fishing supply outlets). There is also a two day sport season for recreational lobster fishermen on the last full weekend prior to August 1 of each year. This Saturday and Sunday sport season gives recreational lobster fishermen a chance to catch six lobsters on each day of the sport season.

The **closed** season for spiny lobster in the Bahamas extends from April 1 through July 31.

How to Catch Spiny Lobster

Spiny lobsters can be taken from above or below the water. There are a number of other ways to catch lobsters without diving, such as bully nets, cast nets, hoop nets, traps, seines, trawls, and even hook and line. Some of these methods such as gill nets, seines, and grains (a type of spear) were used many years ago in the early days of the spiny lobster fishery, and are only of historical interest. The chapter on the commercial fishery includes a brief history of the commercial lobster fishery. I might mention that it is a rare event to catch a lobster on a hook and line. The lobster has to have a chance to chew on the bait without intervention from fish, and the hook has to get caught somewhere among the mouth parts of the lobster firmly enough to keep the lobster on the line while the line is retrieved. More likely is the snatching or foul hooking of a lobster while it explores a baited hook. Not a common occurrence, but it has happened.

Divers use a variety of methods and equipment including hand capture, tickle sticks, hand nets, tail snares, mop heads (not recommended, in fact I don't know anyone who has actually used a mop head to entangle and capture spiny lobster) and, **only in the Bahamas**, Hawaiian slings and pole spears. The main methods recreational fishermen use for catching spiny lobster in the Florida Keys are bully netting and diving.

Some recreational fishermen did get commercial licenses (a $50 fee, now $100) for a few traps and ran perhaps 10 to 20 traps just to get lobsters for family and friends, but this sort of trapping is not common. Note that the 1991-1992 season is the last year that a recreational fisherman who holds a saltwater products license can run a small line of traps, and **only if he already holds a crawfish trap number,** since no new numbers are being issued. The latest Florida laws on the spiny lobster fishery (see Appendix A, Laws of Florida, Ch. 91-154) will allow a person holding a recreational saltwater fishing license to use up to three crawfish traps. Under this new law, effective July 1, 1992, three recreational trap tags at a fee of 50 cents per tag may be issued to a recreational lobster fisherman along with a trap number that is issued at no charge. This trap number must be attached to the trap and the buoy.

A few lobster are also taken once in while in shrimp trawls. These are usually sorted out and taken by the crew or eaten on board the trawler. Once in a while shrimpers used to come across a massive lobster walk—lobsters migrating in the fall by the thousands, moving across the bay bottom in long lines headed for the offshore reefs. When that happened, the shrimpers quickly forgot about shrimp and begin to trawl their nets back and forth through the area where the lobsters were walking. If it was a big walk, and the boat was in the right place, a shrimper could get "well" in couple of nights of lobster trawling. Recreational lobster fishermen, however, don't use trawl nets. And now it is against the law to directly harvest spiny lobsters with any net or trawl (hand net excepted). A shrimper can still catch lobster, but the amount of whole weight bycatch of spiny lobster must be less than 5% of the total weight of all species lawfully in possession of the commercial trawler.

Cast nets

Not so long ago, back in the days before the advent of modern skin and SCUBA diving equipment, few people ventured into the underwater realm of reefs and lobsters. Lobsters were also quite numerous and could be found in abundance under bridges and docks. The clarity of water and abundance of lobsters in those days made fishing for lobster with a cast net a productive method. A cast net is a circular net, usually 8 to 20 feet in diameter (4 to 10 feet in radius) with a weighted line around the circumference of the net, small lines (brails) that extend from the circumference line around the bottom of the net to the center and then extend through a small hole in the center and tie onto a heavy metal swivel. A long heavy line ties onto the swivel and is used to retrieve the net after it is thrown. Small cast nets are now used to catch bait fish and larger nets are used for mullet and other fin fish. The fisherman throws the net out over the water with a swinging motion that causes the net to rotate in the air and open up in a large circle before it hits the water. The weighted line around the circumference of the net causes the net to sink quickly and trap any fish that may have been under the net. Pulling the net back to the surface with the line attached to the brails pulls the edge of the net along the bottom to the center, and traps the fish within the net. Lobster can easily crawl out from under a cast net on rough bottom, or the net can be pulled over the lobster if the lobster does not swim up off the bottom and into the net; thus cast nets are not an efficient method for capturing lobster, especially in these days when lobsters are relatively small and scarce.

Hoop nets

A hoop net, also called a pull net or lift net, is a large round net built on a rigid circular frame, a hoop. The hoop may be 3 to 8 feet in diameter, but most are 6 feet. A bridle is attached to the hoop at several points, and a line attached to the bridle serves to raise and lower the net in a horizontal position. The mesh of the net is one to two inches, and the net is not taut but sags a bit in the middle. A bait is tied to the center of the net, and the net is lowered off a bridge, dock, or anchored boat in an area with little or no current. Lobsters are attracted to the bait and crawl on the net to get to the bait. If the fishermen can see the net, it is retrieved when one or two lobster are observed on the net. When the net can not be observed, it is retrieved after a period of time, 15 to 30 minutes or even a couple of hours, with the hope that a few lobster will have found the bait.

The net must be pulled to the surface with a strong, steady pull to keep the lobsters from crawling out of the net. Large, heavy hoop nets can be used in deep water and buoyed like traps, but pulled to the surface every few hours. The South African lobster fishery used such nets as the principal gear in past years. Like the cast net, this method was more useful in days long gone when lobster were big and numerous, and people were few and far between. Hoop nets are still used from time to time in different areas, but they are not very efficient, since the fisherman must wait for the lobster to find the net rather then bring the net to the lobster.

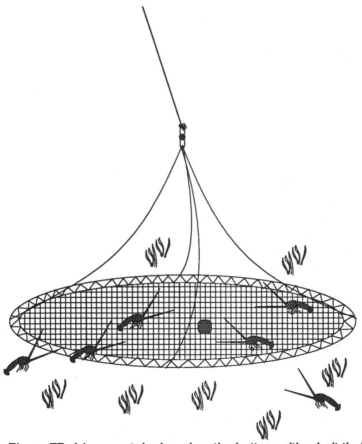

Figure 77. A hoop net deployed on the bottom with a bait tied to the center. Lobsters move toward the bait.

Bully nets

Bully nets came into wide use in the Florida Keys in the early 1920's. Seines dragged over the grass flats were no longer productive because, even at that time, fishing pressure had reduced lobster populations. Bully netting was then, and still is, a very efficient method of collecting lobsters without diving. There are serious limitations, however. Bully netting must be done at night, the water must be calm and clear, and 10 to 15 feet is about the deepest depth that most bully net fishermen can fish. Bully netting is done at night because lobsters wander the shallow flats and rubble areas at night to forage for food. They spend the day hiding in holes and under ledges and are not easily accessible to bully netters during the daylight hours. The rocky banks along canals and the shallows on the edge of mangrove stands are areas popular with bully netters.

A bully netter's equipment consists of a small, shallow draft boat that can be pushed with a pole, or a small trolling motor, along the edges of canals and over shallow flats; an underwater light that hangs over the side and lights up the bottom over broad areas; a strong, hand held spotlight; a good pair of gloves; a lobster measuring gauge; mosquito repellent; a hand net; a good eye; a quick hand; and, of course, a bully net.

A bully net consists of a round net about 18 inches in diameter on the end of a long, sturdy pole. The net has a mesh of 1 to 2 inches and is about 2 feet deep. The hoop extends out at a right angle to the bottom of the pole. The end (center) of the net has a line attached that the bully netter holds to keep the net extended vertically along the pole and out of the way of the bottom growths (Figure 78). When a lobster is sighted, the bully netter attains a stable position over the lobster and quickly places the hoop around the lobster. The tension on the net line is relaxed to allow the net to partially collapse on the lobster encircled by the hoop.

Figure 78. Barb holds a bully net and shows how the end of the net is held off the bottom with cord attached to the center of the net.

The lobster should, at this point, try to escape and shoot over the hoop and into the net. The netter then scoops up the net in the opposite direction of the lobster's flight and brings the net and lobster aboard the boat. If the lobster does not shoot off into the net, then the netter must scoop the lobster off the bottom and into the net. The risk of losing the lobster at this point is great, especially on rocky bottom, because the hoop often goes over instead of under the lobster, and as soon as one edge of the hoop rises a little off the bottom, the lobster may shoot out from under the net. If the lobster refuses to swim up into the net, one can sometimes wiggle the net around and stimulate him to make his move. This is usually about the time that the boat slowly moves away from the pole, and the netter is then suspended between the boat and pole, and unless some fast foot work is accomplished, the netter may join the lobster in its natural element.

A bully netter may use just a hand-held spotlight, but this is not very efficient, and many lobsters are lost because of lack of light. It is an easy matter to rig up a 12 volt underwater light that will illuminate the entire bottom area around the boat. Such a lighting set up consists of a 12 volt car battery, a couple of sturdy electrical clamps attached to about 10 feet of sturdy outdoor electrical cord, a 60 watt 12 volt bulb, a rubber outdoor light socket, a 4 foot length of 1½ or 2 inch vinyl tubing, a cage for the bulb to protect it from rocks and boat bottoms, and a tube of silicone sealer.

The electrical cord is passed through the vinyl tubing and wired to the rubber socket. Electrical tape secures the wiring and the rubber socket is fitted and sealed into the vinyl tubing with the silicone sealer. The bulb is screwed into the rubber socket, and silicone sealer is used to waterproof the area where the bulb joins the socket. The cage is attached to the socket, and the light is ready for use after the silicone sealer cures, about 24 hours. Figure 79 illustrates a completed underwater light.

Figure 79. A typical underwater light apparatus for bully netting. The light is deployed over the side of a small aluminum boat.

The light is attached to the bow of the boat and hangs about two feet under the water. If it is too high in the water, the boat will shade too much area, if it is too low, it may drag on the bottom. The light should be turned on and off only after it is under water. The bulb heats up when it is lit above the water, and if thrust under water when hot, it is likely to burst.

Measuring spiny lobster. The lobster must be measured immediately when brought aboard and released if the the three inch gauge can be slipped over the carapace. Place the front inner edge of the gauge over the ledge between the horns and bring the back edge of the gauge down to the rear edge of the top part of the carapace. If the back edge of the gauge slips over the rear edge of the carapace, the lobster is under legal size and must be returned unharmed to the

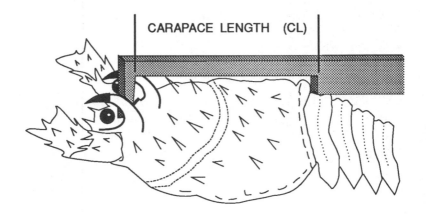

CARAPACE LENGTH   (CL)

Figure 80. The carapace of a spiny lobster with the "yes-no" measuring gauge applied. The gauge fits over the ledge between the horns and extends back to the posterior edge of the carapace. **If the rear of the gauge slips over the back edge of the cara-pace, as in the above illustration, the lobster is a short and must be released.**

water. Figure 80 illustrates the placement of the gauge on the lobster. This is very important because the Marine Patrol Officer who stops you to measure the lobster will do it right, and if that gauge slips over the back edge of the carapace, you're in trouble, and a little laugh and the comment, "Oh, so that's how you measure them." will not get you out of it.

A bully netter can go alone and be quite successful if he or she is experienced, but two or even three people stand a better chance of finding and catching lobster on a bully net expedition. Don Goldberg, a veteran bully netter, says "Take the teen-agers, they can spot lobster much better than us old folks." The usual sequence of events consists of moving the boat slowly along the edge of a canal or over a grass flat. The netter in the bow of the boat and the driver at the rear both watch for the twin red gleams that signal the location of a roving lobster. Although the reflections from the eyes are usually the first thing seen, one must also watch for the carapace and broad uplifted tail of a lobster moving away from the light. When a lobster is spotted, the helmsman steers the boat into proper position for the netter, and the netter captures and delivers the lobster to the boat for measuring and, hopefully, storage in the catch bucket. Great care must be taken in removing the lobster from the net, for if it is a short, it must be released, and any injury such as lost legs or antennae will decrease growth rates and lower its chance for survival. Do not separate the tail from the head of the lobster until you are back at the dock and begin to clean the catch. This is against fishery regulations, and the Marine Patrol officer will not look kindly at finding "wrung" or headless lobster tails in the boat.

If a bully netter works alone, he usually poles the boat along rather than using the motor. He uses the opposite end of the bully net pole and then flips it over to use the net when a lobster is spotted. In the old days, bully netters worked during the day and used two poles. One had the net attached and the other had a long stiff wire about two feet long extending out at a right angle from the end of the pole.

This probe or tickle pole was used to tease lobster out from under a ledge. The bully netters used a glass bottom bucket to get a good view of the bottom, and when they saw the antennae of lobsters sticking out from a reef or from under a ledge, the wire probe on the pole was used to disturb the lobsters and get them to move out of the reef onto the open bottom where they could be captured by the bully net. Commercial bully netters often pour a little fish oil on the water to "slick down" the surface and make the lobster easier to see when a light wind ruffles the water. Although a few fishermen still make a living with a bully net, it is no longer a conventional method of commercial lobster fishing. Many recreational fishermen, however, bully net lobsters at the start of the season when lobsters are more plentiful, the weather is warm, and the water is calm and clear.

Diving for Spiny Lobster

The 1950's were fantastic years for skin and SCUBA divers. Mass production of diving equipment began in earnest in the 50's, and a new world opened up for those who wanted to venture beneath the sea. This was bad news for spiny lobsters, however, for now a lobster fisherman could easily visit the reefs and net, spear, grab, and snare lobsters in their own element. And they did. No area of the reef is now too deep, too murky, or too far away for a serious lobster diver. Florida Keys lobsters suffer hundreds of thousands of traps and an ever growing legion of recreational lobster divers. Under these conditions, actually finding legal size lobsters to catch is one of the most difficult tasks of the modern lobster diver.

Finding spiny lobsters

Generally, one has to cover a lot of bottom area to find lobsters. In deeper water, 20 feet or more, perhaps the best way to find lobsters is to find a fairly large patch reef, one with large coral heads around the edges of the reef. Begin at one end and work your way all around the edges of the reef looking carefully under all the large coral heads and into the caves and crevices of the reef structure. Although lobsters are also found in the shallower center of patch reefs, they are more likely to den in the heavy structure around the edge of the reef. They do frequently move to the center of a patch reef if there are deep cracks in the rocks or pathways through the coral that lead toward the reef center. Such reef structure is more common in the Bahamas.

In the middle of the day, lobsters are usually deep into shelter and are often completely hidden to the diver who just swims over their den. This is the time that a good look under ledges and coral heads pays off. Late in the day, as they anticipate their nightly foraging rounds, they move near the den entranceway, and their antennae can be more easily observed from a few feet above the den. At this time it is better to cruise the patch reef more rapidly looking just for antennae extending out from under a sheltered area. The more area covered, the greater the chances of finding a pod of lobsters. Spiny lobsters are gregarious, and if you find one, there are probably four or five or perhaps even a dozen more tucked away in the same general reef area. Finding one lobster, even a short, is good reason for spending some time looking carefully at nearby reef formations.

Coral protection. It is difficult to avoid touching the coral when hunting and catching lobster on the reef, but it is very important to avoid touching live coral whenever possible. One light touch will probably not seriously affect a coral head, but any damage to the coral polyps, including removal of the thin coat of protective mucus on the live coral head, invites infection from bacteria and algae—and this infection can spread and destroy or seriously damage a large, ancient coral head. Never use a coral head or other coral growth to stand on or to push off toward the surface. Never anchor the boat on live coral or allow the boat or SCUBA gear to bump against a shallow reef structure. Always check the placement of the anchor at the start of the dive. Move it away from any live coral if necessary and make sure that it is well set. Also, avoid running the boat over shallow grass flats and cutting a swath through the grass. Not only is this very hard on the boat propeller, but erosion of the grass flat can start in the path cut by the prop. It's **very** important for the future of Florida's coral reef habitat to keep these points in mind as you work the reefs and flats looking for spiny lobster.

All spiny lobster are not on the reefs. They scatter over all types of bottom during their nightly foraging and may hole up in any shelter during the day. There are extensive shallow bottoms, 6 to about 12 feet, throughout the Keys where lobster may be found if a diver is lucky enough to stumble over them. The limestone base of the geological platform of the Florida keys is filled with holes and cracks that appear and disappear from year to year. Storms, siltation, current changes, and the activity of groupers, snappers, lobsters, octopus, and other animals fill and clear these small holes from time to time. There are also very small reef areas where the base rock protrudes up from a sand or grass bottom, and areas where currents have created a grassy ledge by cutting the sand out from under the edge of a grass bed. There are also stretches of hard rubble bottom overgrown with big sponges and gorgonians. These are all areas where spiny lobster are likely to be found. Suitable shelter is scarce in such areas, however, and lobster are seldom found in the high densities that occur in some reef formations. One has to cover a lot of bottom area to find these small lobster shelters. One of the best ways is to tow a diver slowly behind the boat. The diver looks for lobster antennae and suitable natural bottom structure and drops off the tow line to investigate likely areas. A lot of bottom can be covered in this manner, but diver and boat operator must be very careful to avoid mistakes that can result in injury. Be sure to fly the diver down flag if you do tow a diver.

Catching spiny lobster

A good lobster diver has two important goals:

- 1. Capturing a legal size lobster and keeping it secure throughout the dive. (Letting a lobster escape, especially after a lengthy and difficult capture, is extremely frustrating.)

- 2. Avoiding any injury to the lobster during capture. If the lobster is a short, it should be released without injury, and if it is legal, it should not be injured so that it can survive if the capture attempt fails or if the lobster later escapes.

Reaching out and wildly grabbing at a spiny lobster to try to catch it before it escapes is the sign of a real novice. Rapid movement is the best way to spook a lobster into flight, and grabbing an antenna or a handful of legs is a sure way to injure the lobster and lose it as well. The first thing the lobster does is break off the captured appendage, and the next thing is does is either disappear into the deepest recess of the reef or shoot off out of sight. Some experienced lobster divers prefer to hand catch lobster because they feel that they can catch most lobsters more quickly, and they have less gear to carry around on a dive. A pair of good gloves is essential for any lobster diver. Heavy cotton garden gloves with little plastic anti-slip dots work well, but the lobster spines sometimes get caught in the fabric and make the lobster hard to release. Plastic coated or plastic impregnated gloves are sturdy, last a long time, give a good grip on the lobster, and are not as likely to get caught up in the spines. Leather gloves give good protection against spines but tend to get stiff and hard after one or two trips.

Most divers use a tickle stick to move the lobster into a position where it can be grabbed by hand either around the carapace or at the very base of the antennae. Grabbing a lobster, especially a large lobster, by the tail is not recommended. The sharp points on the edge of the abdomen can give one's fingers a sharp pinch when the lobster flexes its tail. Even experienced lobster divers often injure lobsters during hand capture, however, and this alone is a strong argument for net or tail snare capture.

A tickle stick, Figure 81, is practically essential for catching spiny lobster in the reefs. The typical tickle stick is made of aluminum or fiberglass and is two to four feet in length. It usually has a bend of about 45 degrees at the far end and wrist or belt loop at the near end. It can be made of other materials, of course, but make sure that isn't so buoyant that it floats. If it is too light, it will just drift away when you put it down to bag a lobster. Spiny lobster usually respond to touch by moving away from the point of contact. Inserting the tickle stick into the reef behind the lobster and gently nudging it from behind or on the side usually causes the lobster to move forward out of the reef structure.

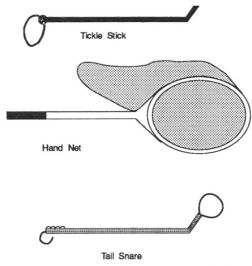

Figure 81. Tools used by Florida recreational divers in the capture of spiny lobsters.

Note that this implement is called a "tickle" stick. It is **not** called a poke, punch, prod, penetrate, stab, spear, pry, or wallop stick. Violent activity with the tickle stick has quite the opposite effect on a lobster. It will either retreat deep into the reef or go flying out the back door and disappear. Careful and gentle manipulation of the tickle stick moves the lobster slowly into hand net range or into a position where a tail snare can be slipped over the tail. Note that a tickle stick must have no sharp points or hooks that can injure a lobster.

I prefer to use a good hand net and a tickle stick to capture spiny lobster. The hand net is placed in position just outside the den, and the tickle stick is used to move the lobster out of the den and into the net. It is important to hold the net very still while the lobster is moving toward the net, for then he doesn't recognize the net for what it is, and he will often move right into it. A net made of heavy monofilament line is almost transparent in the water and is very effective. The net can also be quickly placed over the lobster when it moves out into an open area. Once the lobster is in the net, it will try to escape by swimming rapidly. This is the point where many lobster manage to escape from the hand net by quickly reversing direction. Keep the frame of the net tight to the bottom until the lobster can be securely grabbed (by the carapace) from outside the net. Then reach into the net with the other hand, grasp the lobster securely about the carapace, and very carefully remove it from the net. Measure the lobster with the gauge and then place it into your lobster bag if it is of legal size. Never just assume it is legal, for things appear larger under water than they actually are.

Many divers prefer to use tail snares to capture lobster (Figure 81). This device consists of a hollow pole 3 to 4 feet long, a wire that extends the length of the pole, loops out into a noose, and then doubles back through the pole to the divers hand. The wire noose loop is protected by a plastic sheath so that it will not cut the lobster in half or otherwise injure it when the noose is cinched tightly around the lobster's tail. Tail snares also usually have a one way catch on the pull wire so that once the noose is securely drawn up around the lobster's tail, the struggles of the lobster will not loosen the noose and allow escape. There are now several types of tail snares available at dive shops. The trick to using a tail snare is to slip the noose over the tail of the lobster without making it move away. Avoid getting a leg tucked in the noose, for the lobster will surely break it off when the snare is cinched. It takes a steady hand and patience, but once the lobster is snared, it seldom gets away. Use of a tail snare also keeps sharp legs and spiny antennae away from a diver's hands and arms, holds the lobster tight for measurement, and makes undersize bugs easy to release.

Only in the Bahamas is it permissible to take spiny lobsters with a pole spear or Hawaiian sling. No spear device with a trigger may be used, and no underwater breathing apparatus (SCUBA) may be used in the taking of lobsters. An air compressor (hookah) may be used by commercial harvesters if a $10.00 permit is obtained, but it can only be used in a water depth range of 30 to 60 feet and only from August 1 through March 31 of each year. Although lobsters may be speared, the laws against use of a triggered spear device and SCUBA gear give the lobster an even chance. It isn't easy to free dive more than 20 feet or so, find and sink a spear into a lobster hidden in a reef, and then get back to the surface with both spear and lobster—but when you're good at this, you can get a lot of lobster in a day of diving. In fact, almost all lobster commercially taken in the Bahamas are taken by spear, since this method is very efficient, especially since use of an air compressor is now allowed between 30 and 60 feet, and requires much less capital outlay than trapping. If the laws against the use of SCUBA to take lobster are effective, then the Bahamian lobster resource is protected, since this places an effective depth limit on the lobster fishery. Lobsters deeper than 60 feet are relatively safe from capture, and this insures a reservoir of breeding lobster.

One must be very sure that a lobster is legal size before spearing it, because a speared lobster is a dead lobster. It doesn't matter if it's undersized or if it gets off the spear and dives deep into the reef where it can't be found. It's still a dead lobster. Once the spear penetrates the hard shell (exoskeleton) and the membranes under the shell, the lobster usually cannot repair the damage and soon bleeds to death. If you do spear lobster in the Bahamas, be sure your aim is true and only go for those you are sure are legal size. A pole spear with a three pronged tip works well on lobster since the three prongs spread out through the lobster and usually hold it securely until you can get a hand around the carapace and hold it on the spear. A pole spear can also be operated with one hand more easily than a Hawaiian sling.

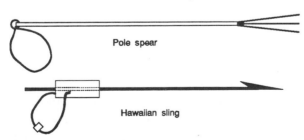

Figure 82. A typical pole spear and Hawaiian sling used to take spiny lobster only in the Bahamas.

If one is experienced, however, a Hawaiian sling is very good since once the spear goes through the center of the lobster, it isn't going to get off the spear. It's also possible to take several lobsters on one dive on the same spear, stacking them up on the shaft three or four deep. However, if the spear is not aimed true, and hits the lobster near the edge of the shell, the lobster may break off and be lost. **Note that the legal size of lobster in Bahamas is a 3 ⅜ inch CL, not the 3 inch CL of Florida law.** A lobster gauge made for Florida lobster will take undersized lobster in the Bahamas. The legal size of lobsters in Puerto Rico is a 3.5 inch CL. Note that there is a bag limit of 6 lobsters per person in the Bahamas

Always put the lobster into your bag tail first. Not only do lobsters swim backward, but they can also use their spiny antennae very effectively to foil your efforts to stick them head first into a bag; and as soon as you relax your grip when they are halfway into the bag, they shoot out backwards and swim off with a distressed diver in hot pursuit. And, if the diver forgets to close his bag securely in his haste to chase after the fleeing escapee, and the three lobsters he already had in the bag also escape, then he is a very, very, distressed lobster diver. He may even say a bad word or two. To avoid such frustration, put the lobster into the bag tail first, then it will swim straight down into the bag when it is released. There are several commercially made lobster bags that have a protected entrance that allows one to push a lobster into the bag without actually opening the bag. This is a good feature, because as soon as you open a regular mesh bag to stuff another lobster into it, the ones you have already put in the bag often come flying out to freedom. So there you are, with one lobster out of the bag and long gone, another half out and flapping like crazy as you try hard to keep it in the bag with one hand and a knee, and the big one in your other hand is clawing at your wrist and flapping so hard that you're rising up off the bottom. Underwater photography, incidently, is a great hobby, and much less stressful than lobster hunting.

Boating in Florida

If you lobster dive, you almost have to go boating, and if you go boating, even if you don't operate the boat yourself, there are some things you should know. Boating in Florida is regulated by the United States Coast Guard and the Florida Marine Patrol. If anything, operating a boat is more complex than operating an automobile, and if anything goes wrong, a boater is subject to drowning and exposure, and quick rescue is not a sure thing—hazards that are seldom encountered on land. Ignorance is always dangerous and more so on a boat. If you are new to boating, take a safe boating course, and take a trip with an experienced boat operator before venturing out on the ocean with family and friends.

It is very important to observe the rules for safe boating, for unsafe boaters can not only lose their lives, they can be cited and may be subject to hefty fines. Civil penalties up to $500 can be imposed by the Coast Guard for failure to comply with numbering requirements on the boat, failure to carry proper equipment, and failure to report a boating accident. A civil penalty of up to $5,000 can be imposed for failure to comply with the unified inland Rules of the Road (Inland Navigation Rules Act of 1980). Grossly negligent operation of a boat can subject the boat operator to a fine of $1,000, imprisonment of not more than one year, or both. Some of the things that are considered as grossly negligent operation are operating a motor boat in swimming areas, operating a boat while under the influence of alcohol or drugs (**strictly enforced**), excessive speed in the vicinity of other boats, in manatee areas, or in dangerous waters, hazardous water skiing, and riding on the bow, seatback, gunwale, and transom of the boat. Boating regulations exist to guard the safety of the boating public, including those who endanger themselves as well as other boaters. Coast Guard and Marine Patrol officers are understanding to novice boaters, but still firm in the enforcement of boating regulations.

The Coast Guard and Marine Patrol can require a boat operator to immediately correct an unsafe or especially hazardous condition and even order the boat to return to the dock to correct the deficiency. The Coast Guard classifies boats as Class A (less then 16 feet), Class 1 (16 to less than 26 feet), Class 2 (26 to less than 40 feet), and Class 3 (40 to not more than 65 feet). **Note that there is now (summer 1991) a new federal user fee on pleasure craft over 16 feet long. The fee ranges from $25 to $100 depending on length class. Failure to obtain this federal permit for pleasure boats can result in fines up to $5,000.** The equipment regulations for each class are a little different. Larger boats (Class 1, 2, and 3) are required to carry more fire extinguishers, have an extra throwable Type IV Personal Flotation Device (PFD), and have whistles and bells audible for at least a mile. It is important to check the boat before leaving the dock to make sure it is seaworthy. This is especially important if you rent or borrow a boat. Of course, make sure there is enough fuel, the motor runs properly, and that the boat doesn't leak. After that, check the things that the Coast Guard and Marine Patrol will check if they happen to stop the boat on the water. The following list includes most of the conditions that can return a large or small boat to the dock.

1. Insufficient number of Personal Flotation Devices.

There must be one Coast Guard Approved Type I, II, III, or IV PFD for each person on board, diving, or being towed by water skis. PFD include approved life vests, cushions, life rings, and other devices.

2. Insufficient fire fighting devices.

At least one B-1 type approved hand portable fire extinguisher. (Not required on outboard motorboats less than 26 feet in length and not carrying passengers for hire if fuel tanks are not permanently installed and if flammable vapors cannot be trapped in compartments. Even though a small outboard with portable gas tanks isn't required to carry a fire extinguisher a wise boater does so, for it could come in very handy under some circumstances.)

3. Overloaded condition.

Most boats have a U.S. Coast Guard Capacity Information Plate mounted on the hull. This plate tells you how many persons and how much weight the boat can safely carry. If there is no capacity plate you can determine the number of 150 pound people the boat can safely carry (in good weather) by multiplying the length times the width of the boat and dividing by 15. For example a boat 16 feet long and 5 feet wide (16 times 5 equals 80, divided by 15, equals 5.3) can safely carry 5 people according to this formula.

4. Improper navigation light display.

At night, all boats must display navigation lights. A small motor boat, under 26 feet long, must display a white stern light visible for 2 miles and a red light (port) on the left side of the bow and a green light (starboard) on the right side of the bow. Row boats must have a white light that can be displayed in sufficient time to prevent a collision.

5. Fuel leakage.
Make sure all fuel lines are tight and do not drip gas.

6. Fuel in the bilges.
Always check and vent the bilge in larger boats in case of fuel leakage before starting the engines.

7. Improper ventilation.
At least two ventilator ducts fitted with cowls or their equivalents for the purpose of properly and efficiently ventilating the bilges of every engine and fuel tank compartment of boats using gasoline or other fuels having a flash-point of 110 °F or less are required. Make sure that the vents are not inadvertently covered over with misplaced items of equipment or clothing.

8. Improper backfire flame control.

One approved backfire flame arrestor must be installed on each carburetor of all gasoline engines except outboards.

9. Manifestly unsafe voyage.

If you give the officer a hard time and refuse to comply with directions, or you and/or your boat is really messed up, the officer can cite unsafe use of the boat and order the termination of the voyage.

Other boating tips

Make sure that a good anchor is aboard, one large enough to hold the boat in a swift current, and that the anchor line is at least three to nine times the maximum depth of the water where you intend to anchor. The deeper the water, the longer the necessary anchor line.

A flare kit is very important to carry along in case the motor dies and no other boats come along before sunset. A flare sent up every 20 minutes or so after full dark will alert someone that you are in distress and indicate your location.

Bring along enough fresh water to last each person a couple of days, just in case, and have something that can create shade just in case the boat is stranded during the day.

Bring along a first aid kit, one never knows.

Be very careful with oil and gas. A cupful of gasoline has the explosive power of 16 sticks of dynamite. Oil on a boat deck is a slippery invitation to a serious fall. Wash off all oil and gas spills immediately. Sloppy maintenance and carelessness is the major cause of marine accidents.

Be sure there is enough fuel on board to take you out and back with an ample safety factor for contingencies. (One can walk to a gas station on land, but swimming five miles with an empty gas can is not recommended.)

Always remember to put the drain plug in place before launching a boat off a trailer.

Always give the right-of-way to sailboats, boats limited in turning ability, boats restricted to channel water depth, and boats occupied in commercial fishing or trolling fishing lines. Give right-of-way to boats ahead and to the right of you. Always pass oncoming boats on the right. Keep the red channel buoys to your right when you return to port and to your left when heading out. (Red, Right, Returning)

Florida State waters extend three nautical miles out from the shore on the Atlantic side of the Keys and nine miles out from shore on the Gulf of Mexico side of the Keys. U.S. Federal waters extend from the end of Florida jurisdiction out 200 miles. Note that this change in jurisdiction does not change boating laws and safety regulations.

The refuse act of 1989 prohibits the throwing, discharging, or depositing of any refuse matter of any kind (including trash, garbage, oil, and any other liquid pollutants into the waters of the United States. The Federal Water Pollution Control Act prohibits the discharge of oil or hazardous substances into waters within 200 miles of the coast. Many types of plastic trash remain in the marine environment for years and even decades. Plastic bags can be eaten by sea turtles, plastic six pack rings can snare birds and fish, nylon netting and fishing line can entangle fish, birds, turtles, and marine mammals, and small bits of styrofoam and other plastics can be eaten by fish and other animals and block digestive tracts. Trash doesn't just disappear when it's tossed overboard, it accumulates in the marine environment and causes problems for many years.

In other words, take responsibility for the marine environment. If you take it out, bring it back! If you observe any polluting discharges from land base or ship it should be immediately reported to the nearest Coast Guard Station or call the toll free number 1-800-424-8802. Violations of Florida marine fishery laws should be reported to the State Resource Alert toll-free number 1-800-342-1821 (1-800-DIAL

FMP). See Appendix C for a list of phone numbers important to Florida divers and fishermen.

Boaters in the Florida Keys soon learn to "read the
water" and experienced boaters seldom run aground, even
in unfamiliar territory. Brown water ahead signals very shallow water, white water contains a lot of sediment and might
be very shallow, green water is usually deep enough for a
shallow draft boat, and blue water is clear sailing. A sudden
change from choppy to smooth water is also a sign of shallow water. Running aground can be dangerous and costly. If
the tide is rapidly running out, the boat might be stuck till
the next high tide. If you do go aground, don't run the motor
in the grass bed. Not only can the prop and motor be damaged, but the grass bed is also scarred and injured. Raise the
motor and pull or push the boat to deep water.

Diving

Diving is a skill and a science all its own. It is a dangerous activity even if you know what you're doing. If you
don't know how to properly use SCUBA gear, and you have
never had a dive course, and you think you can dive anyway—then you can probably also sky dive without a para-
chute. This book is not a dive manual. If you want to use
SCUBA gear to dive for spiny lobster, the first thing is to
become a properly certified SCUBA diver. Then you'll know
to never hold your breath when ascending to the surface on
a compressed air dive, no matter what the circumstance, and
what to do when a lobster shoots out from a den and knocks
off your dive mask. There are a few things to keep in mind,
however, that are special to Florida lobster diving.

Always fly the diver down flag when a diver is in the
water. The minimum size of the flag is 12 by 12 inches
(commercial lobster divers must have a flag or symbol that
is 16 by 20 inches), and it should be flown at least 3 feet
above the surface. The divers flag must be flown even if the
diver does not have a boat and enters the water from the
shore. In this case the flag flies from a buoy that the diver

pulls along behind. Boaters must stay at least 300 feet from a dive flag and must always operate a boat with extreme caution in areas near dive flags. Watch carefully for diver bubbles and stay as far away from diving activity as possible. When diving in crowded areas, always try to ascend and descend in the vicinity of the dive flag. Avoid swimming at or near the surface in areas frequented by divers and boats, especially during the two day sport lobster season.

Diver Down Flag
(white and red)

Alpha Flag
(white and blue)

Figure 83. The diver down and the Alpha flag .

Florida law states that the diver down flag must be displayed whenever there is a diver or snorkeler in the water. A federal law states that the "Alpha" flag must be displayed whenever divers are operating from the boat. The Alpha flag is a world wide signal used by boats engaged in diving operations to signal that the boat cannot maneuver. However, according to the federal law, a diver involved in a accident when the alpha flag is not displayed has no legal rights or recourse against the negligent action of other boaters. Although the "diver down" flag is widely recognized as a diver caution signal, it does not provide the same legal protection as does the Alpha flag. Divers may even receive a citation if the Alpha flag is not displayed. The Alpha flag is more important to commercial diving activity than to recreational diving, but a prudent diver would display both flags.

Spiny Lobster Rules and Regulations

The complete text of the current Florida Laws, Statutes, and Adminstrative Codes on spiny lobster, including the 1991 amendments to the Florida Statutes, Chapter 370.14 (Laws of Florida Ch. 91-154), are reproduced in Appendix A, and the Federal regulations pertaining to Florida are included in Appendix B. Please be aware that these regulations may change from year to year and current regulations may not be exactly as they appear in these appendices. Although regulations from different countries are similar, there are significant differences (legal size and legal methods of capture, for example) between countries, and one should always check the local regulations before taking spiny lobster. For convenience, the rules and regulations pertinent to recreational lobster divers in Florida and the Bahamas are summarized below.

Florida

A recreational harvester must possess a valid saltwater fishing license with a crawfish stamp. One can then take spiny lobsters under the laws regulating the recreational fishery.

Possession of a Florida Department of Natural Resources saltwater-products license ($50) and a Lobster Permit ($100) (these fees include the increase provided for in the 1991 F.S. amendments) allows one to take more than the recreational limit of 6 lobster per person or 24 per boat, and also allows the fisherman to sell the catch if the lobsters were harvested in State waters. One is then a commercial harvester rather than a recreational lobster fisherman. At this point, however, this is simply historical information since no new crawfish licenses or trap numbers have been issued since 1988, nor will be issued until 1993. And, on August 1, 1993, Florida spiny lobster become a "restricted species" (see Chapter 6). In essence, all this new legislation means that one cannot become a commercial spiny lobster fisherman unless one holds a valid crawfish trap number or license and a saltwater products license, meets the requirements to fish for a restricted species, and purchases whatever number of trap certificates one can that are available on the open trap certificate market.

The minimum size of possession for any spiny lobster is a 3 inch carapace length. If the tail is **legally** separated from the carapace it must be 5½ inches not including any protruding muscle tissue. The carapace length is measured as described in Figure 80. (Every year the Marine Patrol makes about 150 to 200 arrests in just Broward and Dade Counties, and many more in Monroe County, for the taking of short lobster during the two day sport season. Never assume that "The Man" isn't going to check your catch.)

Spiny lobsters taken from Florida waters shall remain in whole condition at all times while on or below the water. Separation of the head (carapace) and tail (abdomen) is prohibited on or below Florida waters, although separation is permited in Federal waters (EEZ) with a special permit.

No person shall harvest or attempt to harvest spiny lobster by diving unless he or she possesses, **while in the water**, a measuring device (a lobster gauge) capable of measuring the carapace length (CL) of a spiny lobster while in the water.

The bag limit for spiny lobster in Florida waters during the regular season is no more than 6 per recreational harvester per day or 24 per boat, whichever is greater. This means that if you go out in a boat during the regular season with one to three divers, the total number of lobsters that can be taken is 24 (different regulations are in effect during the two day sport season, see below). Four or more licensed divers, however, can take up to 6 lobsters per diver. Five licensed divers in one boat, for example, can take up to 30 lobsters. Note that a lobster diver without a boat who enters the water from the shore can take only 6 lobster per day.

Note that the bag limit for spiny lobster in Federal waters (EEZ) is only 6 per person per day. Two divers in a boat over three miles from shore on the Atlantic side of the Florida Keys may have only 12 legal lobster in the boat, **not 24**, as is allowed in Florida waters during the regular season.

The bag limit during the two day sport season is 6 per recreational harvester per day. No recreational harvester may possess more than 6 spiny lobster on or off the State waters on the first day. No recreational harvester may possess more than 12 spiny lobsters on the second day once the harvester has landed and left State waters.

The spiny lobster season extends from August 6 through March 31 of each year.

A two day sport season for recreational harvesting occurs on the last full weekend prior to August 1 each year.

The harvest or possession of egg bearing females is prohibited. All egg bearing spiny lobsters must be returned to the water unharmed. Stripping or otherwise removing the eggs from an egg bearing female is strictly prohibited.

No person shall harvest spiny lobster by diving at night (from 1 hour after official sunset until 1 hour before official sunrise) in excess of the bag limit prescribed in Rule 46-24.004. (In other words, you can't take 6 lobster before midnight and 6 more lobster after midnight by diving.)

The harvest of spiny lobster by any net or trawl, other than a landing or dip net, bully net, or hoop net, is prohibited.

No person shall harvest or attempt to harvest spiny lobster using any device which will or could puncture, penetrate, or crush the exoskeleton (shell) or the flesh of the lobster.

Except by special permission, granted by the Division of Law Enforcement of the Department of Natural Resources, no person may pull or work traps other then those owned and licensed by the commercial harvester himself.

The harvest or possession of egg bearing slipper lobsters is prohibited. All egg bearing slipper lobsters must be returned to the water unharmed. Stripping or otherwise removing the eggs from egg bearing slipper lobster is strictly prohibited.

It is illegal to place any drugs or poisons (including bleach or any other chemical substance used to drive lobster from the reef) in marine waters except by permit from the Florida Department of Natural Resources.

It is unlawful to take, kill, molest, disturb, harass, mutilate, destroy, cause to be destroyed, sell, offer for sale, or transfer any marine turtle or marine turtle egg.

It is unlawful to take or harvest any queen conch from the land or waters or to possess or transport any queen conch in Florida waters.

It is unlawful to take, possess, or destroy sea fans, hard corals, or fire corals from Florida reefs.

Legal size stone crab claws (2¾ inch claws) may be taken in season between October 15 and May 15, but the live crab must be released. No spears, grains, grabs, hooks, or other devices that can puncture, crush, or injure the crab are allowed. Claws may not be taken from egg bearing females.

There are many other rules and regulations that pertain to activities above and below Florida waters that the diver and boater should know about, but the above laws are those that are most important to lobster divers. Check with the Florida Marine Patrol before taking any marine life to be sure that the activity you plan is legal and will not harm the resources or the environment.

Bahamas

Foreign vessels intending to engage in sport fishing must have a permit. Permits are available through Customs Officers at the port of entry or by writing to the Department of Fisheries, Ministry of Agriculture, Trade & Industry, Post Office Box N3028, Nassau, Bahamas. Information is also available from the Bahamas Tourist Office in Coral Gables, FL , 1-800-327-7678. The cost of a sport fishing permit is $10, or $50 annually. There are restrictions under this permit.

Fishing gear is restricted to hook and line unless otherwise authorized. Only six lines are allowed in the water at one time unless otherwise authorized. (If more than 6 lines are allowed, the cost of the permit is $7,000 annually.)

The bag limit for kingfish, dolphin, and wahoo is a maximum combined total of six fish per person on the vessel, comprising any combination of these species.

Vessel bag limits for other marine products are 20 lbs. of scalefish, 10 conch, and six crawfish per person at any time. The possession of turtle is prohibited. The above amounts may be exported by the vessel upon leaving the Bahamas.

No person shall have in his possession, or use for fishing, dogwood or other poisonous wood or bark, quicklime, household bleach, or any other noxious or poisonous substance.

No person shall use any spearfishing apparatus to fish within one mile of the coast at low water mark of New Providence; or within one mile of the southern coast at low water mark of Freeport, Grand Bahama; or within two hundred yards of the coast at low water mark of any other Family Island.

No person shall uproot, destroy, or without written permission of the Minister, take or sell any hard or soft coral.

No person shall construct any artificial reef within the exclusive fishery zone except with the written permission of the Minister.

The annual closed season for crawfish extends from April 1 to July 31 (inclusive). No person may have live or dead spiny lobster in his possession during the closed season or have in his possession on board a vessel a trap or device designed for crawfish trapping, or set a trap on or below the surface of the sea for purpose of trapping crawfish.

The person in charge of a vessel engaged in fishing for crawfish must ensure that the vessel carries a measuring gauge for determining the legal size (3⅜ inches CL) of any crawfish taken.

No person shall take, have in his possession, or sell any crawfish which measures less than three and three-eighths inches from the base of the horns to the end of the jacket (Carapace Length) or which, if the tail is severed, has a tail measurement of less than six inches, not including any protruding muscle tissue.

No vessel shall be used in crawfish trapping unless the operator has obtained a permit from the Minister authorizing the vessel to be used for trapping.

No person shall take, have in his possession, or sell any egg-bearing crawfish; clip or otherwise remove the eggs from an egg-bearing crawfish; have in his possession or sell any crawfish from which eggs have been removed.

No person may sell or export crawfish for commercial purposes without a commercial license. Shipments of crawfish for export must be submitted to a fisheries inspector and the export duty must be paid.

The Catch: Care, Cleaning, and Cooking

Suppose you found a tuna salad sandwich that had been sitting on the deck of the boat for four hours on an August day. Would you eat it? I would hope not. On the other hand, would you eat a spiny lobster that had been laying dead in the bottom of the boat for three hours in the August sun? I hope this little analogy puts things in their proper perspective. Unless the catch is taken care of properly, the succulent, gustatory reward that derives from the expense, time, and effort invested in a lobster trip is either lost or greatly degraded. If it's worth catching, keeping, and eating, then it's certainly worth taking proper care of the catch between sea bottom and table top.

Keep the spiny lobsters you catch alive as long as possible. The best lobster dinners are the ones where the lobsters are killed at cleaning and then cooked immediately. Fresh caught lobsters can be kept alive in a 24 to 50 quart cooler half filled with salt water if the water is changed often. The container must be shaded and be given partial or complete water changes about every 30 minutes. Two or three lobsters kept in the sun in an open topped, half filled bucket will not last long. A dead lobster in warm bucket of sea water quickly becomes a bacterial stew. Another way to keep spiny lobster in clean, fresh condition, especially if they must be kept on board more than a few hours, is to put them on ice. Place the lobster in a cooler half full of ice while still alive, and they quickly cool down and keep very well for the entire trip. Although few of us worry about how, and if, lobsters and fish suffer when they are caught and allowed to slowly die on the deck of a hot boat, it is something to consider. If a legal lobster cannot be kept alive in cool, well oxygenated water, it should be killed quickly and humanely.

Remember, lobster can not be tailed or cleaned while the boat is on open water. Lobsters have to remain whole, for possible inspection and measurement, until the boat returns to shore. The time for cleaning is after the boat is docked.

There are many ways to clean and prepare spiny lobster. Usually, the tail is the only part of the lobster that is saved for cooking. Two exceptions are use of the whole, split lobster for preparing various stuffed lobster recipes and, in the event that a really large lobster is being prepared, saving and recovering the meat in the antennae and legs. It isn't worth the trouble to recover meat from the antennae or legs unless the lobster is more than three or four pounds. When the lobster is five or six pounds, there is considerable meat in these areas that can be recovered. The easiest way to get it is to boil the legs and antennae, and then strip the meat for use in salads or pieced meat dishes. The liquid can be strained and saved for use as "stock" in many lobster dishes.

When a whole, split lobster is required for a stuffed lobster recipe, remove the legs and antennae, trim the spines, and split the lobster lengthwise through carapace and tail. The intestinal tract that runs through the center of the tail is then exposed for removal. The gills, stomach, gonads, and other organs in the head section are also removed, and this hollowed out area is where the stuffing is placed. A crab meat stuffing complements the lobster very well, but many other stuffing recipes can be used.

The quickest, easiest, and simplest way to remove the tail to prepare it for cooking is illustrated in the accompanying photographs, Figures 84 through 91. The split tail that results from this method is called the "butterfly lobster tail", and it makes an excellent preparation for broiling or grilling a fresh lobster tail. Tails can also be frozen after cleaning and will keep about six months in a freezer if well protected. Leave the meat in the shell when freezing as this protects the flesh. Never refreeze lobster that has thawed; cook it and use it right away. It is best to thaw lobster completely, preferably in the refrigerator overnight, before cooking, to prevent over or under cooking of various sections of the meat. Lobster may be refrozen after cooking, but the quality of the meat declines with refreezing and with extended time in the freezer.

Figure 84. An afternoon catch of lobster, grouper, and hogfish from the shallow waters offshore of the middle Keys.

Figure 85. Although it isn't absolutely necessary, running a knife between the tail and carapace severs the tail muscle that extends up under the carapace, makes the tail easier to remove, and assures that all the tail muscle is removed with the tail.

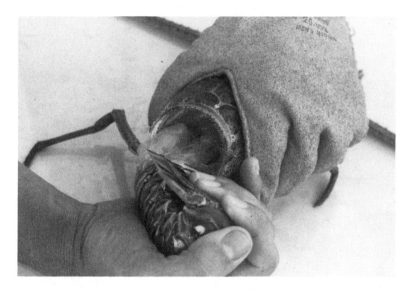

Figure 86. Twist the tail and pull to separate it from the head.

Figure 87. Snap off about 4 or 5 inches from the end of an antenna.

Figure 88. Insert the large end of the broken piece of antenna into the vent under the tail fan and gently push it about 2 inches up into the intestinal tract.

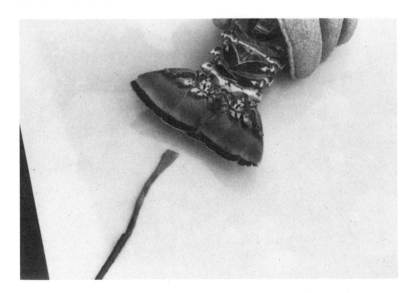

Figure 89. Twist the piece of antenna a half to a full turn and smoothly draw it from the lobster tail. The intestinal tract, and its contents, will be easily removed from the tail.

Figure 90. Cut lengthwise through the dorsal surface of the lobster tail with a sharp, large bladed knife. Do not cut through the ventral (bottom) section of the shell.

Figure 91. The finished butterfly cut lobster tail. Spread each half of the tail outward until the bottom of the shell snaps open and the tail remains spread apart.

Lobster tail is also often broiled as "piggyback lobster tail" in many restaurants. To prepare this cut, the top shell of the tail is cut along the center from the front down to the tail fan. The tail meat is freed from the shell except where it is attached at the end of the tail and is lifted out of the shell through the slit and rested on top of the shell. The tail meat is cut about half way down to allow it to spread out and cover most of the shell.

A "fancut lobster tail" is prepared by completely cutting out the bottom (ventral surface) of the shell of the tail, then spreading the shell apart a bit, but leaving the meat attached to the top shell. Lobster tails cut this way can be broiled, but are usually deep fried or boiled.

Lobster is low in fat, 1.5%, and moderately low in calories, 125 c in 3.5 ounces of uncooked meat. The shells of uncooked lobster tails are greenish to brownish with yellow spots, and the meat is soft and translucent. Uncooked lobster tails usually run from 4 ounces to 1 pound each, and a one pound lobster will usually yield about ⅓ cup of cooked, flaked, meat. The shells of boiled lobster tails are orange to red in color, and the meat is firm and white. Lobster can be boiled, steamed (poached), broiled, grilled, or deep fried. Remove cooked lobster from the shell by separating the meat from the shell at the tail with a fork and then pulling the meat outward and forward. The tail meat will usually separate cleanly from the shell when using this method on boiled or broiled lobster.

Broiled

Broiling is perhaps the most popular way of preparing fresh lobster tail. It is our favorite. Split the tail in the butterfly fashion; rinse, pat dry, then squeeze some lemon or key lime juice on the flesh. If you have time to let them marinate for a few hours, you can use more juice and also add crushed garlic, a few drops of hot sauce, or what ever seasonings you like. When you are ready to eat, place the tail on the broiler—**shell side up** toward the heat and about 5 inches below the heating element. A large tail should be a little further from the heat to avoid burning. Broil until the shell turns reddish, approximately 5 minutes. Then turn the tail over, drizzle with a little melted butter and any other seasoning you wish (garlic, key lime), and continue to broil until the buttered flesh begins to brown in spots—maybe just a few minutes or perhaps up to 10 minutes for a really large tail but be careful not to overcook. When some of the little points of flesh that extend upward begin to get very dark brown, it's time to pull the tails from under the broiler. I personally don't think a broiled lobster needs anything else—well perhaps a small individual cup of melted butter (with crushed garlic or key lime juice if you wish) for dipping each bite. If you're cutting down on fat, you can make a "dipping broth" from strained and boiled down lobster stock with lemon juice, and just a small amount of butter for flavor. You could even substitute one of the new products on the market that keep the butter flavor but not the fat. Then maybe you can have a piece of key lime pie for dessert.

Grilled

Lobsters can be grilled with delicious results. Marinate the tails for a few hours if you have time before cooking. Some people prefer to brush the split butterfly tail with melted butter, place it shell side down on a moderately hot grill for 8 to 10 minutes, turn it over, brush it again with butter and cook for another 5 to 10 minutes. Others prefer to package the lobster tail in heavy aluminum foil with butter and perhaps seasonings (lemon, orange peel, ginger, garlic, garlic salt, onion, cognac, pepper, or even sweet and sour sauce, alone or in various combinations), place the foil package shell side down for 10 to 20 minutes depending on the size of the tail and the heat of the grill. Then unwrap the tail and cook it on the grill flesh side down for 3 to 5 minutes or until the meat browns a bit. This produces a more moist, softer meat than open grilling. Serve hot with melted butter and lemon.

Boiled

Live, thawed frozen, whole, and tailed lobster are often boiled. This is the most common method of preparing lobster when it is intended for a dish other than a basic broiled lobster. Lobster should be cooked only once, with the possible exception of boiled lobster pieces that will be used in soups, chowders, pasta sauces, or casseroles. Twice cooked lobster and overcooked lobster becomes tough, rubbery, and dry, so if a second cooking is intended, boil the lobster only 4 or 5 minutes and then finish the cooking in the prepared dish.

Bring to a boil enough water to completely cover all the tails you plan to cook. Salt and lemon or lime juice or slices can be added to the water for flavor. When the water is boiling, add the tails (with shells still on), return to boil, and then turn the heat down and simmer for about 10 minutes—maybe longer for a large lobster or less for small tails—at least until the shell turns red. Drain the lobsters (save the liquid for stock) and rinse with cold water

Now the boiled lobster can be served warm with lemon and melted butter or with a sauce (seafood, cocktail, barbecue, sweet and sour). Or, it is ready to be used in pot pie, tetrazzini, casserole, bisque, etc. or chilled for use in a salad.

Steamed

Steaming is another way to prepare lobster since it does not saturate the meat with water and keeps the meat soft and moist as well. Set a rack above a couple of inches of vigorously boiling water in a deep pot and cover the pot well. Steam the lobster about 10 minutes for one pound tails, up to 20 or 25 minutes for tails that run two pounds or more. Steamed lobster is eaten as is boiled lobster, although it is a little more delicate.

Fried

Deep Fried Lobster (from Bonnie Hunt)

Cut off the flared end of the tail, run a sharp pointed knife around inside of tail and remove meat in one piece. Cut meat into 4 to 6 chunks. Dip in any batter suitable for deep frying (especially the beer batter recipe below). Drain excess and fry in hot oil. Cook 2 minutes or until golden brown. Serve with garlic butter. Allow at least one tail per person.

Beer Batter (from Bonnie Hunt)

1 ½ cups all purpose flour
1 ½ cups beer (cold, warm, or flat)
Mix flour and beer. Let stand 3 hours (this is the secret) add salt and pepper just before frying.

Baked

Baked Lobster Tails (from Bonnie Hunt)

Split tails lengthwise. Marinate for 2 to 4 hours in a mixture of salad oil, crushed garlic cloves, parsley flakes, a few drops of hot sauce, and a little lemon juice. When ready to bake, line a square pan with foil. Sprinkle each tail with garlic powder, dot with butter, and pour remaining marinade over the tails. Cover lightly with foil and bake 45 minutes at 350°. Serve with garlic butter.

Baked lobster with crabmeat stuffing

Split the whole lobster lengthwise. Remove the intestinal tract from the tail; clean out the gills, stomach, and other organs from the head. Rinse well. Preheat the oven to 400°. Place the stuffing (recipe on next page) in the body cavity and also spread it over the tail. If desired, drizzle with butter and sprinkle with paprika. Place on a baking pan and bake for 15 to 20 minutes or until lightly browned.

Crabmeat Stuffing (6 servings)

1 pound of crabmeat (fresh, frozen, or canned)
½ cup of chopped onions
⅓ cup of chopped celery
⅓ cup of chopped green and/or red pepper
2 cloves of garlic, minced
¼ cup of melted butter, margarine, or cooking oil
2 cups bread crumbs
2 eggs, beaten
1 tablespoon chopped parsley
½ teaspoon salt
(½ teaspoon pepper and/or a few drops of Tabasco can be added if desired)

Cook the onion, celery, peppers and garlic in butter until soft, but not brown. Mix all ingredients well and stuff the lobster. Bake as above.

Cheese Stuffing (2 servings)

1 ½ cups of soft bread crumbs
½ cup of grated cheddar cheese (or jalapeno?)
¼ cup chopped parsley
2 tablespoons melted butter or margarine
2 tablespoons chopped green onion

Mix all ingredients well and stuff lobster. Sprinkle with slivered almonds and/or paprika. Bake 15 to 20 minutes in a 400° oven or until golden brown.

Lobster Bisque

2 tablespoons butter, 2 tablespoons flour, 1½ cups stock (or broth or water), 1 can tomato soup, 1 can evaporated milk, 1 teaspoon minced dried onion, "leftover lobster" cut into small pieces.

Melt butter, stir in flour, slowly add stock, soup, onion, and milk. Cook stirring constantly. A few minutes before serving add the cooked lobster. Heat until lobster is hot, but don't boil.

Lobster Pie (from Janice Goldberg)
Ingredients:Pastry shells and pastry for top crust
3 cups cooked lobster meat cut into bite sized pieces
6 tablespoons butter
6 tablespoons flour
2 ¼ cups milk
¼ to ½ cup dry sherry
7 drops worcester sauce
salt and pepper

3 green onions minced (about ¼ cup)
8 oz canned sliced mushrooms drained
2 tablespoons butter

In a 3 quart saucepan, melt butter and mix in flour. Slowly add milk, stirring constantly to keep mixture smooth. Cook over medium heat, stirring until mixture comes to a boil and thickens. Add sherry, worcester sauce, salt, and pepper. Simmer 2 minutes. In another pan, saute green onions and mushroom in butter until onions are tender. Add to sauce mixture. Gently stir lobster into sauce mixture.

Put mixture into individual pastry shells and put pastry on top (like pot pies). Bake at 450° until light brown and shells are done—about 10 to 15 minutes. serves 6

Kedgeree of Lobster
1 cup of raw rice—cooked to yield approx. 3 cups
4 tablespoons butter melted in casserole dish
Mix in a casserole dish:
the cooked rice
2 cups cooked lobster—cut into small bite sized pieces
3 boiled eggs chopped
¼ pound boiled ham—cut into small pieces
½ cup half and half
salt and paprika
Sprinkle top with cheese (optional)
Bake 350° for about 30 minutes

Lobster Pot (from Bonnie Hunt)

This is a great recipe for a crowd. It is so easy and everything is in one pot.

Ingredients: red new potatoes, fresh corn on the cob, keilbasa, onion, Old Bay Seasoning®, salt & pepper, lobster, and shrimp (optional). The amounts depend on how many people—two potatoes, one corn, one tail, etc. per person.

Place 4 quarts of water into a large stock pot. Add 1 teaspoon salt and ¼ teaspoon pepper, at least 1 tablespoon of Old Bay Seasoning®, 2 sliced onions, and the potatoes. Cook about 10 minutes, then add corn (whole or broken in half), 2 lbs kielbasa (or more) cut into pieces, and whole lobster tails. Bring to boil and cook 15 minutes or until done. Shrimp can be added during last 10 minutes.   Dish out with a slotted spoon or tongs. Broth can be used for dipping.

Lobster Pasta Salad

This is another one that gets adjusted by how many people it needs to feed, what you have available, and how much dressing you like in your salad.

Ingredients:

pasta : sea shells (or twists, elbows, etc) cooked, drained, and cooled.

vegetables: choose which ever ones you like or have on hand—any combination—chopped onion, celery, red or green pepper, snow peas, frozen peas (put them in a strainer and run hot water over to thaw them fast), shredded carrot, water chestnuts, jicima, broccoli, radish, tomatoes, any raw or leftover vegetable.

meat: lobster cut in small pieces (can also add cooked shrimp, chicken, ham, or boiled egg).

dressing: a combination of mayonnaise and a red bottled dressing gives a nice pink color to the salad. Mayonnaise and Kraft® Catalina dressing is a good combination. Pritikin® Ranch dressing and a "no fat" mayo gives a nice barbecue flavor. Mix everything together and chill.

Mounting Lobster for Show and Tell

Yes, you can eat your lobster and have it too. If you get a very large spiny lobster and want to keep it as a trophy, or even if you just want a regular size lobster as an unusual display, the thing to do is to preserve and mount the lobster. A lobster can be preserved and mounted on a display board or even mounted on a dried sponge, or in a sea shell display, or in any other manner you wish.

There are several methods for mounting lobster, all involve the use of formalin. Formalin is a 37% solution of formaldehyde gas, but when it comes to preserving lobster that will be dried, it is better to go with a 10 to 20% solution of formalin. Formalin can be purchased at some drugstores or at janitorial supply houses. If a drugstore doesn't carry it, they will sometimes order it for you. Be very careful with formalin. It is a very poisonous and noxious substance and should not be left where children can reach it.

The most unsatisfactory, but easiest, method for mounting lobster is to submerge the entire lobster in 15% or 20% formalin for a week or two, take it out, position the legs and antennae as desired, and let it dry in a cool, dry place for a couple of months (someplace where the formaldehyde fumes will not get into living areas). Then give it a couple of good coats of polyurethane varnish or clear fiberglass resin. Such mounts won't last very long, tend to accumulate bugs because all the preserved meat is still in the lobster, and often go off color.

A better method is to first separate the head and tail of the lobster. Then remove as much of the internal organs from the head as possible, cut the under side of the tail shell lengthwise along the center down to the beginning of the tail fan, and remove the meat by loosening it from the end of the tail and pulling it forward. If you want to mount just any old lobster, find one that is almost ready to molt because then it is easy to separate the old hard shell on the outside from the new soft shell that is forming on the inside. If the lobster is quite large, then separate the legs and the antennae from the head section also and remove the meat from these areas as well. Soak the de-meated exoskeleton in 15% formalin for a few days, remove it and let it dry thoroughly, spray the inside with polyurethane varnish, re-attach the parts with super glue and/or wire. Mount the lobster on a nice wooden plaque, and then give both the plaque and the mounted lobster two or three coats of polyurethane varnish or clear fiberglass resin.

The best mounts, however, take more time and care to prepare. First separate the parts (head, tail, antennae, and legs) and strip all the meat possible from every part. Then, with a small brush paint the entire inside of each piece with either straight formalin or a high percentage formalin solution (50 to 80%). The color of the mount remains more natural for a longer time if the formalin is not applied to the outer shell. Then, after drying well for a week or so, mix up some plaster of paris and carefully fill each section. Avoid air pockets in the plaster. After the plaster is hard, carefully re-assemble the lobster with wire and glue, mount it on a plaque or whatever, and give it a two or three coats of a good polyurethane varnish. Clear fiberglass resin makes a strong hard coat and gives the mount excellent protection, but it does not look as natural as a polyurethane finish and may separate from the shell after time.

Chapter Six

THE COMMERCIAL FISHERY
Balancing Effort and Conservation

The commercial fishery for Caribbean spiny lobster is about 100 years old. In most areas, including Florida and the Bahamas, it has developed from small, local bait fisheries to one of the most valuable international fisheries in the western central Atlantic. The history and economics of the spiny lobster fishery reflect the rich history of the tropical Atlantic/Caribbean region—and in the future, this fishery will reflect, and perhaps stimulate, the development of international relationships formed around the conservation of common marine resources.

At one time, not so many years ago, fishermen were few and spiny lobsters, fish, and other marine animals were so plentiful that there was no need for regulation and no thought that fishery regulation would ever be necessary. In fact, only a little over a hundred years ago Professor T. H. Huxley, a very respected biologist of that time, stated:

"I believe, then, that the cod fishery, the herring fishery, the pilchard fishery, the mackerel fishery, and probably all the great sea fisheries are inexhaustible; that is to say, that nothing we do seriously affects the number of fish. And any attempt to regulate these fisheries, seems, consequently, from the nature of the case, to be useless."

Professor Huxley, of course, could not foresee electricity, internal combustion engines, plastics, pollution, high technology fisheries, the incredible explosion of human populations—and the effect of all these factors on oceanic natural resources. In the last 50 years we have proved that the "inexhaustible resources" of the sea are anything but infinite and boundless, and our industrial development has put most of them on the brink of disaster.

The long and extensively traveled larval stage of the spiny lobster provides a recruitment buffer for heavily fished spiny lobster populations such as that of the Florida Keys, thus the real peril that faces the spiny lobster resource is not fully apparent to the Florida Keys fishery. Jones et al. (1985) estimates that the Keys spiny lobster populations are fished to a reproductive potential that is reduced by at least 88% from that of an unfished population. The legal size of 3 inches (76 mm) carapace length (CL) is below that required to maintain a population of reproductively active adults; and without the annual influx of lobster larvae from relatively unfished areas, the Keys population would not be able to sustain itself. The intensity of the fishery is increasing in the Caribbean and western central Atlantic, and there is great concern among fishery biologists for the entire resource at a regional and international level. Now in the early 1990's marine scientists are saying:

"Presumably if these distant reservoir stocks are harvested at similar high levels as in Florida and before reproductive maturity, a population crash would result." (Richards and Bohnsack, 1990).

Not only must we make laws that protect the resource, but of even greater importance, we must each abide by those laws, else the resource is lost to all. And when, in the not too distant future, all or most of the spiny lobster populations in the western central Atlantic are fully exploited—then all the fisheries, including that of the Florida Keys, will depend on management through cooperative regulation for the very survival of this common resource.

The Tragedy

The root of most of the problems that modern fisheries face, especially the spiny lobster fishery of the Florida Keys, can be found in the phrase "The Tragedy of the Commons" coined by Garrett Hardin in a 1968 article in Science magazine (Hardin, 1968). The basic tenet of this theory is that unrestricted freedom to use a resource always results in the destruction of that resource, or in Hardin's words:

> "Freedom in a commons brings ruin to all."

A commons is an unregulated resource that is open to everyone, such as an unfenced cattle range, a pasture in a public square, a vast herd of wild buffalo, a flight of passenger pigeons—and an unregulated fishery. Hardin uses the example of herdsmen exploiting a common pasture to illustrate the inevitability of overexploitation of an open-access resource, but let's look at it from the viewpoint of the spiny lobster population in the Florida Keys.

In the beginning, there were far more lobster than any fisherman could catch or could want. It wasn't until the nineteen forties and fifties that the demand for lobsters stimulated the beginning of the modern trap fishery, and lobster fishermen began to run strings of 100 traps or more. According to the theory of the commons, each fisherman wants to increase or at least maintain a steady rate of production from his effort in the fishery. As the fishery reaches the maximum rate of total possible production, however, and effort begins to exceed the available catch, the fisherman notices that his rate of production is declining. Now let's give a unit of ten traps the arbitrary catch value of "1". If the fisherman, we'll call him Bob, adds ten traps to his trap line two things happen.

- A. He increases his yield from the fishery by a value of very close to "1". The yield from his participation in the fishery has increased significantly, because he receives all of the increased yield from this additional ten-trap unit of effort.

- B. The enhanced yield that Bob enjoys, however, has decreased the yield of all the ten-trap units in the fishery. This total catch decline of "1" is shared by all the traps in the fishery, thus the drop in yield to each of the ten-trap units that Bob runs is only a very, very small fraction of "1". Bob notices only the increased yield from the addition of his new ten traps and not the small reduction in yield to all the ten-trap units, including his, in the fishery.

The result, of course, is that Bob, and every other rational, ambitious fisherman, continues to add traps to the limit of his ability, to first increase, and then to just maintain his yield from the fishery. There is no motivation to reduce effort and every motivation to increase effort. Without regulation, including limitation of effort, the overfished population collapses and the fishery and the fishermen are ruined. This is the tragedy that without natural or artificial controls, is an inevitable result of the freedom of the commons.

Johnson and Stein (1986) have developed a laboratory exercise based on a computer model of a commercial fishery that demonstrates the inevitability of over-exploitation of an open-access resource. Students were divided into fishing teams or crews and could control the yield from their fishing activity in a hypothetical, unregulated competitive fishery. Once the fishing crews developed an effective fishing strategy, the fishery always crashed. The program is an effective tool for teaching students about exploitation and management of open-access fisheries.

Were it not for the great reproductive potential of spiny lobsters and, most important, the long lived and greatly dispersed larval stage that provides recruitment to the Keys from other areas, the spiny lobster fishery in the Florida Keys would probably have collapsed quite some time ago. In fact, a model developed by the Gulf of Mexico and the South Atlantic Fishery Management Councils indicates that 40% of the current number of traps now active in the fishery could produce the maximum sustainable yield of the fishery. The 60% additional traps is the result of a fierce battle between the commercial fishermen to increase their individual share of the resource at the expense of all the other fishermen and the resource itself. Although the participants in the battle are gentle people that help each other and try to work together for the good of the fishery, the ferocity of the battle is very intense at the level of the resource. Just ask a Florida spiny lobster.

Florida

To understand the current condition of the Florida spiny lobster resource, one must know something of how the fishery developed. Labisky et al. (1980) prepared a good historical perspective of the Florida lobster fishery for an American Fisheries Society publication on spiny lobster, and the reader is referred to that paper for more detailed historical information.

A little history

"A species of prawns, (shrimps) growing to a weight of five pounds apiece, live in great numbers in the holes of coral rocks, on the mangrove islands: these shrimps are by West-Indians improperly called lobsters, although they have not the two claws, as lobsters: they are beautifully spotted with red, yellow, blue, green, grey, and a little black; but they all change into one red colour by boiling...."

These words, penned in 1772 by William Gerard De Brahm, Surveyor General of the British Colony of East Florida, are among the first written about the Caribbean spiny lobster. Although the relationship of the spiny lobster to the northern lobster was well known by naturalists in the 18th and 19th centuries, it was not that clear to the casual observer, and the spiny lobster was often referred to as a giant shrimp, prawn, crayfish, or crawfish, with emphasis on the word "giant". They were often eaten by Indians and settlers in these early years, but were not highly prized as people food, even in Key West, until the mid 1920's. This may have been because they were so plentiful that anyone could have crayfish for dinner whenever one wished, and that they were far more valuable as bait for finfish than as food for people. Spiny lobsters sold for only 2 cents a pound in 1895, and they sold for about $1.00 a dozen in Key West in the early 1920's. At that time, however, four dozen lobster used as bait could bring a fisherman $40.00 to $50.00 worth of finfish.

The status and abundance of spiny lobsters in the early years of the 20th century is apparent in the words of Ralph D. Paine (Paine, 1987) who writes in a 1903 article of being marooned in Florida on No Name Key with two companions and about 40 Cubans after the Spanish American War battle of Rio San Juan.

"Men are not altogether lovely when they face a possible struggle for existence in close quarters. We three tent-mates began to hunt the giant crayfish of the Florida coast. Lashing the cleaning-rods of our rifles to the ends of wooden harpoons, we waded through the shallows, and speared our prey, crustaceans that averaged as much as a lobster in weight and size. Boiled in salt water, with green bananas as a side dish, the menu was filling, but not various."

This occurred only a little over 90 years ago. It's hard to believe that one could ever wade the shallows of the lower Keys and, with wooden spears, take enough three to 5 pound lobsters to feed forty men for over two weeks in mid winter. The spiny lobster population of the Florida Keys must have been a bit different then from what it is now.

The population centers in southeast Florida during the 1800's were Key West, Indian Key, and Miami. The other keys were uninhabited or very sparsely settled. Lack of access except by boat, scarcity of fresh water, hoards of vicious mosquitoes, and fear of frequent hurricanes limited settlement of the Keys until the Florida East Coast Railway (FEC) was built by Henry Morrison Flagler. The railway was started in 1904 and completed in 1912. It changed the Keys forever by providing easy access for transportation of people, supplies, and produce to and from Key West and all the Keys between Key West and Homestead.

The early commercial fishery for spiny lobsters that developed in the Keys during the last quarter of the 19th century was a bait fishery. Spiny lobsters are excellent bait for large snapper and grouper, and although lobsters were also fished locally for food, the fishery was primarily a bait industry. The fishery was not regulated, of course, and lobsters were taken with cast nets, gill nets, haul seines, and spears. Lobsters were so numerous then that gill nets and seines pulled over the grass flats were very effective when lobsters were foraging out over the flats.

The late 1800's and early 1900's were economically difficult for Key West. The sponge industry suffered from overfishing, and when the sponge blight hit in 1879, the industry moved to better fishing grounds off Tarpon Springs. The cigar industry suffered from labor disputes and also moved to the Tampa area. Cuba and the United States suffered strained relations and Cuba, the major market for Key West fish, imposed such a severe duty on the import of fresh fish in 1868 that the finfish industry, and its supportive lobster bait fishery, languished on into the early years of the 20th century without a strong market. According to Schroeder (1924), the estimated annual catch of lobster in Key West in 1910 was about 350,000 pounds, 40% was exported, 40% was consumed locally, and 20% was used as bait.

The coming of the railroad in 1912, however, brought new life to the fishing industry. Although lobsters were still

Flagler, incidently, did not build his railway just to reach Key West. It was Cuba and a trade link to Panama and South America that was the real goal and inspiration of the FEC. Flagler believed that Cuba was destined to become an economically powerful country and that his railroad could be linked with Cuba by large ferries that would carry entire trains between Key West and Cuba. After all, The Ann Arbor Railroad carried twenty six freight cars on ferries over 112 miles of water on the Great Lakes, and so Flagler was convinced that a railroad/ferry link between Key West and Havana would open rail travel all the way from New York to Cuba.

The ferries to Cuba never developed, but the railroad ran from Key West to Homestead for 23 years until the great hurricane of 1935 dealt it the final economic blow. Although the rails were ruined beyond economically feasible repair, the bridges were still sound and became the foundation of the Overseas Highway that was completed and opened for traffic on March 29, 1938. The original seven mile bridge south of Marathon was completed in 1911. The bridge foundations that Flagler built lasted until the new bridges were completed in 1982. Traffic vibrations so weakened the foundations of the old bridges, that new bridges at a cost of 200 million dollars were built in the late 1970's. Now, less than 10 years later, the new bridges are suffering serious decay. The steel rebar that runs deep in the concrete and supports the bridge is rusting, expanding, and splitting open the concrete pillars just above water level. Many millions of dollars in maintenance will be required over the next 50 years.

The foundations of the old bridge are still standing, resisting corrosion and hurricanes eighty years after they were built. Flagler had his friend Andrew Carnegie roll out a special batch of steel for his bridge reenforcement that still resists rust in the corrosive atmosphere of the Florida Keys. The formula for the concrete that Flagler used was lost after the bridges were built and could not be duplicated for the new bridges. One important component was known, however, New Jersey granite rocks. Cost conscious modern bridge builders opted for Florida limerock instead. The Overseas Highway is one of the wonders of south Florida, and it will be there for a long, long time, but it will be expensive.

mainly sought as bait, it was now possible to ship them direct to northern hotels and restaurants. Lobster were first shipped alive in barrels with sponge clippings and ice, but this method proved costly and spoilage was high. Tails were soon precooked and shipped on ice, and although this method was more labor intensive, a better product was delivered. The lobster fishery was firmly established by the early 1920's, and the fishing grounds were expanding from the shallow waters immediately around Key West to a 25 mile area that included the shallow southern shores of the lower Keys and the shallow reefs east and west of Key West. According to Crawford and De Smidt (1922) the geographical extent of the fishery was limited mostly by the range of the small, shallow draft sail and motor boats that comprised the lobster fishing fleet. Motorized boats had greater range, but were still severely limited by the vagaries of weather.

By the mid 1920's, lobsters were getting less abundant on the shallow water fishing grounds, and use of seines and spears gave way to bully nets. About 50% of the catch was now taken with bully nets. Wire fish traps, measuring 36 by 24 by 20 inches became the second most used method of taking lobsters, and fishermen discovered that traps could be fished in deep water and during spells of bad weather, both of which severely limited the bully netters. The lobster fishery in the Keys did not expand much during the 1920's and 1930's. Key West went through turbulent economic times, the great depression cut the northern retail demand for the luxury of lobster off at the knees, and the destruction of the railroad by the great hurricane of 1935 disrupted the flow of products and supplies to and from Key West and all the Keys. The price of lobster remained at 5 to 8 cents a pound from the early 1920's to the early 40's, and production averaged only about 500,000 pounds of lobster per year during that time.

The 1940's were a period of growth and change for the Keys and the lobster fishery. Production rose from a low of about 400,000 pounds in 1940 to about 4,000,000 pounds in the closing years of the decade (Labisky et al., 1980). The U.S. Navy revitalized Key West in the 40's with a naval base that boosted the population and a pipeline from Homestead that brought a reliable supply of fresh water to all the Keys. This pipeline served all the Keys until it was replaced by a new, larger capacity pipeline in 1982.

The wooden slat trap was introduced into the Keys fishery in about 1940 and soon became the dominant fishing gear for spiny lobsters in Florida. The fishery also expanded up the Florida coast to Palm Beach and westward to the Dry Tortugas during this decade. Bully nets were still used by commercial fisherman, especially those that did not or could not invest in large vessels and the expenses of running trap lines. Ice can traps and raft fishing was also practiced, but no other method of fishing spiny lobster could beat the wooden slat-trap for consistent efficiency and economy.

The traps were still pulled by hand, however, and this limited the depth and number of traps that could be worked. Traps were baited with fish heads and canned pet food or just left unbaited with the availability of shelter as the only attractant for lobsters. The shallow waters of Florida Bay were fished by bully netters, but a few trap lines were also set in the bay. Trappers found that they could not use fish heads as bait in the bay because fish heads attracted stone crabs that attacked the lobsters as soon as they finished off the fish heads. The ability to deep freeze lobster tails also developed in the 40's, and this greatly expanded the demand for spiny lobsters. The fishery began to get very serious about production.

The population of the Keys doubled in the 1950's. Navy men based in Key West retired and decided to stay in the salubrious Florida Keys and supplement their pension by fishing lobster. The number of boats in the fishery more than doubled during this decade rising from 102 in 1952 to 254 in 1959. The number of traps tripled, however, increasing from about 17,000 in 1951 to 52,000 in 1959. The demand for lobsters also increased the price from 18 cents per pound in

1950 to 30 cents per pound in 1959. Production, or at least records of production, varied considerably from year to year in the 1940's and 50's (Labisky et al., 1980). The 1940's closed with annual yields of about 3.5 to almost 5 millon pounds, but the yield for 1950 was only about 1.5 million pounds. Production remained in the area of two to three million pounds per year during the 1950's except for 1957 when production jumped to about four million pounds.

Wooden slat traps were the most used commercial gear during the 1950's, but ice can traps and gasoline drum traps, raft fishing (see Chapter 4), wire traps, hoop nets, bully netting, grains (a type of spear), and spears were also used in the commercial fishery (Smith, 1958). Habitat type traps were made from gasoline drums and ice cans (the large metal tanks used by ice houses to freeze water into blocks of ice, hence the term ice cans). The open end of the metal 55 gallon drum or ice can was crushed down to limit access to holes of only 4 to 8 inches across. A few holes were also usually punched in the back of the drum, or can, to allow water to drain from the drum during recovery and harvest. These traps were deployed with or without buoys in shallow water and harvested every two weeks or so by pulling the drum upright into the boat and removing the lobsters. Lobsters were able to enter and leave these habitat traps at will, thus there was no critical need to visit the traps at frequent intervals.

Commercial spearing of lobsters was discouraged because fishermen believed that fluids released from an escaped, speared lobster induced other lobsters to leave the area. The practice of wringing tails at sea and discarding the heads was also believed to drive other lobsters from the fishing area.

Three small, new developments in the great pursuit for spiny lobster occurred during the 1950's. Although each in itself did not seem to be of earthshaking significance at the time, together they foreshadowed the future of the Keys lobster fishery. In the mid 1950's, the new science and sport of skin and SCUBA diving hit the world, and especially the Keys. Divers with good dive masks, powerful swim fins, and SCUBA began to explore the waters of the Florida Keys and found that lobster were sitting ducks for a diver with a spear gun. Spearing lobster was not illegal at that time, and many a diver became a commercial lobster fisherman. More important than the brief duration of the commercial lobster spearfisherman, however, was the birth of the recreational lobster diving industry. Once established, the recreational lobster diving industry became a very important source of revenue to south Florida and a serious competitor with the commercial fisherman for a dwindling resource. Recreational divers now take an estimated 10% of the total lobster harvest in the Florida Keys.

The second important development was the use of a gypsy head powered by a takeoff from the main boat engine, or by a small gasoline motor, to haul the traps on board the boat. This made life a lot easier for the crew of lobster boats, for the traps no longer had to be hauled by hand from the sea bottom 20 to 50 feet below the boat. This meant that boats could haul more traps per day from deeper water than ever before, and thus could fish further and deeper and produce more lobster with less human effort. By the mid 1960's, no serious lobster fisherman pulled traps by hand anymore. Hydraulic systems for trap pulling were absolutely essential to the fishery.

Third, and perhaps most important to the future of the resource, lobster fishermen began to leave two or three short lobsters in the traps returned to the sea. After all, they could not benefit from the short lobster by legal sale, and the shorts would just be lost if they let them go; so by leaving them in the trap, they thought, the lobster might just molt before the trap was pulled again and then be of legal size on the next pull, and, as an added bonus, they might also attract other legal sized lobsters to the trap. The fishermen had no motivation to release the shorts and every motivation to keep them in the trap. Thus, the deep water trap fishery, the use of shorts as attractants in traps, and recreational lobster diving all began as the 50's drew to a close.

It turned out that use of shorts in the traps increased catches significantly, and soon every fisherman used shorts whenever possible as well as the standard cowhide bait (Trap baiting experiments showed that traps baited with short lobsters caught approximately three times more lobster than any other baiting method (Heatwole et al., 1988.)). The use of fish heads as baits declined over the years because they were messy and awkward to transport to the traps, messy in the traps, attracted stone crabs and other predators, and smelled to high heaven when the traps were pulled. Small cans of cheap cat food became, and still are, a major bait. A few stabs with an ice pick before the can is placed in the bait compartment and the trap is baited for a week. In the mid 1960's, salted cowhide became the bait of choice, along with shorts when available, because it lasted longer, was less expensive, attracted lobster but not stone crabs, and could be easily stored. The use of salted cowhide as bait was instrumental in opening the vast fishing grounds of Florida Bay to the lobster fishery. Although lobsters were smaller in Florida Bay, there were a lot of them. There were also a lot of stone crabs as well, and when a stone crab went into a trap after a fish head, it made short work of any lobsters that were also in the trap. Through the use of cowhide, fishermen could catch spiny lobster without attracting stone crabs, and that made the difference in operating a profitable trap line in the Bay.

The 1960's were turbulent times for Florida, the nation, and the lobster fishery. The upper limit of the production potential of the fishery was starting to be probed at the same time that product demand and growth of the fishery was entering an explosive phase. The value of lobster climbed from about 40 cents per pound in 1960 to about 70 cents per pound in 1969. The number of boats in the fishery doubled from 221 in 1960 to 440 in 1969, and the number of traps in the fishery increased from about 74 thousand in 1960 to about 165 thousand in 1969. Production climbed from the 3 million pound per year range in the early 60's to 7.5 million pounds in 1969. The average number of traps per vessel was less than 100 in the early 1950's, rose to about 200 traps per vessel at the end of the 50's, and this average was almost 400 traps per vessel by the end of 1969.

As lobster fishermen prospered, the old wooden boats of the 50's and early 60's were replaced by large, sleek, 30 to 55 foot fiberglass boats built expressly for lobster fishing with powerful diesel engines, large fuel tanks for great range, lots of space for piles of traps, and big fish boxes that could keep lots of lobster on ice during many days of fishing. Many of the 300,000 Cubans that fled from the government of Fidel Castro obtained U.S. Government loans through the Cuban Alien Act and bought boats to do what they already knew how to do, and that was to fish lobster in Bahamian waters.

The high demand for lobster and the new technology in boats and equipment pushed the lobster fishery from its base in Key West and Miami out over the Bahama banks and down into the Caribbean. By 1967, only 43% of the lobsters landed in Florida came from Florida's waters; almost all the rest came from Bahamian waters. The sovereign zone of the Bahamas extended offshore only three miles during the 60's, and American and Cuban lobster fishermen took full advantage of this by working much of the vast, shallow Bahamian Banks. The Bahamian Government extended the sovereign fishing zone from 3 miles out to 12 miles in 1969, and many of the large lobster boats, now with freezer capacity, moved their operations down to the Caribbean. At the end of the 60's, lobster fishermen knew their trade well and had the boats and equipment to range through the Bahamas and into waters off Mexico, through the Caribbean, and along the coast of Central and South America.

The 1970's and 1980's were years marked by conflict in the lobster fishery. Conflicts between new commercial fishermen and old commercial fishermen, legitimate commercial fishermen and poachers and trap robbers, commercial fishermen and the economic temptations of drug smuggling, commercial fishermen and recreational fishermen, resource users and environmentalists, and increasing governmental regulation and the old ways, were, and still are, plaguing the lobster industry. Although the limits of production for the Florida grounds were reached in the late 60's, extension of the fishing effort to the Bahamas, and also to other areas, allowed the fishery to continue to expand. Florida landings rose from about 7.5 million pounds in 1969 to a high of about 11 million pounds in 1972 through 1974.

The Bahamian government shut the door on American lobster fishermen in 1975 when it completely closed the waters of its continental shelf to foreign fishermen and enforced the laws against poaching. About 260 Florida based lobster fishermen lost their fishing grounds and had to either work the Florida grounds or find another way of life. Florida lobster landings dropped from almost 11 million pounds in 1974 back down to 7.5 millon pounds in 1975. Most countries enacted laws in the mid 1970's, including the United States, that extended their seaward boundaries to 200 miles and established protective and exclusive regulations on the fisheries within this limit.

For the most part, Florida lobster fishermen have had to return to their roots and do battle for their fair share of a limited resource, the Florida spiny lobster. Reported annual production of spiny lobster in Florida has remained reasonably constant at 5 to 6 million pounds per year. Only in 1979 did landings rise above 7 million pounds. The number of traps, however, has increased from about 500,000 in 1975 to about 850,000 (or more) in 1990. The number of traps a commercial harvester can now legally employ in Florida waters is 2,000, and although this is an awful lot of traps, many fishermen are at or above this limit. Federal law has no restriction on trap numbers in Federal waters, so some fishermen still fish 5,000 traps or more.

If there is such a thing as a sharp line between the "good ole days" and this modern era of strife and anxiety, it was surely drawn in 1976. That was the year that Congress enacted the Magnuson Fishery Conservation and Management Act of 1976 (Public Law 94-265), usually referred to as simply the FCMA. The Act created the Fishery Conservation Zone (FCZ) and extended the territorial limits of the United States to 200 nautical miles offshore, except where modified to accommodate international boundaries. The FCZ was later redefined by Presidential Proclamation 5030, dated March 10, 1983, as the Exclusive Economic Zone (EEZ).

The National Marine Fisheries Service (NMFS) was charged with the exclusive management of fisheries seaward of state jurisdiction, including specific fishery stocks and habitat. Eight Regional Fishery Management Councils were established to prepare fishery management plans for each fishery in accordance with national standards and objectives specified in the Act. The South Atlantic Fishery Management Council and the Gulf of Mexico Fishery Management Council were formed; engaged in a brief squabble to determine where the boundary was between the Atlantic and the Gulf of Mexico, and who had jurisdiction in the Keys; decided on joint management for Keys resources in most instances; and proceeded to work on fishery management plans for spiny lobsters and other marine natural resources.

The fishery councils are comprised of individuals who represent state and federal research and management agencies and individuals representing private fishery and public and private environmental interests. For commercial spiny lobster fishermen, it was the classic double edged sword. They had much more regulation immediately facing them, but they also had an unprecedented opportunity to voice their concerns and opinions and to participate directly in the process of actually creating the necessary regulations.

To be a commercial lobster fisherman now meant that you not only had to know how to navigate a boat, fix a diesel engine, build a trap, out guess a lobster, and work 14 hours a day; you also had to know about maximum sustainable yield (MSY), optimum yield (OY), fishery management plans (FMPs), fishery management councils (FMCS), scientific and statistical committees (S&S), advisory panels (AP), environmental impact statements (EIS), regulatory analyses (RA), regulatory impact review (RIR), Regulatory Flexibility Act (RFA), initial regulatory flexibility analysis (IRFA), exclusive economic zone (EEZ), expected domestic annual harvest (EDAH), total allowable catch (TAC), total allowable level of foreign fishing (TALFF), and even fishery biology concepts like recruitment overfishing, growth overfishing, unit stocks, age and growth rates, natural mortality, immigration, fishery mortality, reproductive strategies, eggs per recruit, and yield per recruit analyses. It used to be that if you overheard two commercial fishermen at lunch you could identify their occupation by the color and homily of their language. Now you have listen hard just to determine if two rocket scientists from NASA are lunching at the next table or if they're just two plain and ordinary commercial fishermen.

Current practice

The commercial fishing grounds for Florida spiny lobster extends from about Palm Beach in the north, southward, and then west around to the Dry Tortugas. There is little commercial lobster activity, however, north of Broward County. These lobster grounds include Florida Bay between Everglades National Park and the passages between the Keys out into the Atlantic to the offshore reef lines. The areas near the channels between the Keys are favored since lobsters must move through these areas in their migration from the bay to the reefs. Most of the Florida spiny lobster fishing grounds are now part of the new Florida Keys National Marine Sanctuary. See Chapter 5 for more information on South Florida parks and lobster sanctuaries.

The spiny lobster fishing season extends from August 6 to March 31 of each year. There is a rush to get the traps in the water by August 1, five days before the opening of the season to give them "soak" time and allow them to begin catching lobster. For all practical purposes, the season is over by the end of January. About 85% of the annual catch is on the dock by the end of December, and 93% has been taken by the end of January. Some fishermen pull all their traps and stop fishing in January and February, or they may fish just a few productive trap lines until the end of the season.

Wood slat traps no larger than 3 by 2 by 2 feet baited with salted cowhide and populated with two or three short lobster are the primary gear used by the commercial fishery in south Florida. Short lobster are taken in traps that are set at the beginning and throughout the fishing season. Some fishermen may actually fish a trapline or two in nursery areas where they know there are few legal lobsters, just to get shorts to add to other trap lines. Shorts are now transported in live wells, with at least 0.75 gallons of water in the system for each short lobster. No more than 50 short lobsters or 1 per trap, whichever is greater, may be aboard the boat at any time. Federal regulations also require live wells and 0.75 gallons per lobster but allow 100 per boat in the EEZ. Short lobster not only attract larger lobster to the trap, but they also keep the trap clean of marine growths, a factor that many fishermen feel is almost as important as attracting larger lobster. In Bermuda, traps are baited with fish racks, salted cowhide, and even pieces of broken porcelain are used to attract lobsters (Burnett-Herkes et al., 1989).

Cypress is the preferred wood for traps because it has a slight negative buoyancy, and cypress heart wood is resistent to attack by marine boring organisms. Florida cypress is increasingly hard to find, and wood is often imported from out of state or even from overseas. Pressure treated pine is becoming more common in trap construction (Craig, 1974). Two slabs of concrete are poured into the base of the trap after construction to weight the trap so that it stays in place through storm and wave surge and so that it falls to the sea floor with bottom side down when dropped off the boat. Fishermen try not to drop traps on reef sites because not

Figure 92. The Florida wood slat lobster trap with line and buoy rig.

Figure 93. The wood slat trap with top access panel removed to show the structure of the central throat.

Figure 94. Lobster traps are piled in out-of-the-way places throughout the Florida Keys during the closed season.

Figure 95. Lobster traps piled high on a commercial lobster boat as the boat moves out to deploy the traps.

only can traps break up live coral, but traps on reefs do not catch as well as traps on sand or grass. Lobsters have little incentive to enter traps that are on reef areas because there are so many natural shelters.

Traps have traditionally been dipped in oil to extend the life of the trap in salt water, and most traps so treated have a work life of two to five years. Oil dipping of traps was banned as of July 31, 1990 and oil dipped traps will be completely phased out of the fishery by July 31, 1995. Lobster fishermen are currently dipping traps in a water based, black paint to darken the trap and make it more effective in attracting lobsters. Each trap or trap trotline is buoyed with a polypropylene line and, usually, a styrofoam buoy. Most fishermen place a lead weight on the line 6 to 10 feet below the buoy to keep the line from floating on the surface, thereby reducing buoy loss from passing boats running over the line. Fishermen that do not use a weighted line loose many traps due to buoy loss from boats. A small float is often attached to the line about 15 to 20 inches below the buoy. This lets the buoy float freely on the end of the line and makes it easier to catch the buoy with a boat hook.

Each styrofoam buoy is painted with the color combination assigned to the commercial harvester's current lobster license and must have the fisherman's license number or trap number permanently affixed on the buoy in numbers at least two inches high. The accompanying photographs illustrate the traps and trap pulling gear now in use by most commercial harvesters.

Traps are usually pulled every two or three days at the start of the season, and the time between pulls may extend to two weeks if fishing is slow and/or a boat is running a large number of traps. The traps are pulled aboard the vessel by catching the buoy line with a hook on the end of a pole, bringing the line on board and wrapping it around a rotating drum powered by either the boat's engine or a separate, small gasoline engine. The trap is pulled quickly up through the water and onto a stainless steel frame that tips up into a

Figure 96. A trap pulling platform in the down position waiting for the trap to be pulled aboard.

Figure 97. The trap platform in the up, or horizontal, position after the trap has been pulled. The trap can be worked on the platform or pulled onto the work table nearby.

horizontal position as the trap hits the back of the frame. The trap may be moved to a separate table or worked right on the pull frame. The top is removed from the trap, the legal lobsters removed, one or two short lobsters are left in the trap, and excess shorts are removed and held for other traps. The top is replaced, and the trap is dropped overboard. A good crew can pull a trap about every five minutes and work about 100 traps per day.

The commercial lobster fleet is composed of shallow draft boats, mostly of fiberglass construction, 16 to 55 feet long. The lobster boats in the lower Keys tend to be larger and make trips of several days duration. Some fishermen work together very closely and synchronize their trips so that one boat is always in a particular area and can watch all the trap lines in that area for poachers. These large boats now fish up to 2000 traps per boat. Lobster boats in the upper Keys are generally smaller than those in the lower Keys, and each boat usually returns to the dock each day. These fishermen seldom fish more than 1000 traps per boat; most fish around 500 traps.

Commercial harvest by diving is still an important part of commercial lobster fishing, especially during the early part of the lobster season. Commercial divers usually use SCUBA, although some use hookah and some free dive in shallow areas. They work the channels between the Keys where lobsters are often found in abundance during the early part of the season. The tidal flows are often fast and strong in the narrow channels, and these currents have cut many deep ledges and holes in the channel banks and bottoms where lobsters find temporary refuge. The divers must time their dives for the slack period between tidal flows and, under the right conditions, a good lobster diver can harvest many lobsters from the cuts. Commercial divers also work the shallow Florida Bay areas south of Everglades National Park and also the reef areas on the Atlantic side of the Keys.

It doesn't take a crystal ball to see what will happen to the Florida spiny lobster fishery in the future. One way or another, the combined fishing pressure on Florida spiny lobster by commercial and recreational fishermen will continue to expand. The recreational fishery will continue to grow and will demand a larger share of the available lobster harvest. Recreational lobster divers spend a lot of money in the Keys on their lobster hunts, and there is, and there will be, considerable political pressure to attract and satisfy this growing recreational market. The commercial fishery is beset by economic pressure on the individual fishermen to increase their catch (more traps) on one hand, and, on the other hand, political and management pressure to reduce effort (fewer traps). There were 1,800 lobster permits issued by the State of Florida in 1975 and 4,100 issued in 1986. It is quite clear that the commercial fishery cannot expand any further, and that reduction in effort and protection of under-size lobster is essential to the continued economic existence of the commercial fishery (fewer fishermen with higher production per trap and per vessel)—and to the continuance of Florida spiny lobster as a valuable natural resource. The many biological, economic, and sociological problems that face this fishery can only be solved by sound management implemented through effective regulation. Now, in the early 1990's, new laws and regulations are creating great changes in the Florida spiny lobster fishery.

The Florida fisherman even has to battle the economics of imported lobster products. The Florida fishery supplies only a small fraction of the average world catch of 401.74 million pounds of all species of lobster (Williams, 1986). Brazil alone now produces 5,280 metric tons (11,627,120 pounds) of *Panulirus argus* and 2,256 metric tons (4,972,224 pounds) of *P. laevicauda* (Fonteles-Filho, 1990). The United States imports lobster products from all over the world and this often causes problems in identification of lobster tails. Williams (1986) developed a key to the worlds lobsters based on just the tails so it is possible for commercial and enforcement interests to identify lobsters when only the tail is available.

Current problems

There are great difficulties in the lobster fishery that must be resolved during the 1990's. Most of the 1980's were spent identifying the problems and accumulating the scientific information necessary to define and evaluate these problems. The time has come to use this knowledge to begin to build a sound and sustainable lobster fishery. The major problems in the fishery, as defined by fishery biologists, fishery managers, and fishermen are discussed below.

Perhaps the greatest problem is the extraordinary number of traps in the Florida fishery. There are an estimated 850,000 to 1,000,000 traps now deployed in the lobster fishery. The best estimate of actual traps used in the fishery is about 856,000. The number of traps claimed for licenses is about 1,500,000. At best estimate, fewer than 300,000 traps, perhaps only 200,000, are needed to capture all available lobsters from the Florida grounds each year. This gross excess of traps, termed overcapitalization of fishing capacity, is the root of almost all the other problems in the fishery.

The mortality of short lobsters in the fishery is also a huge problem. Short lobsters are lost to the fishery though illegal harvest, damage from recreational fishermen, and maintenance as "attractors" in traps until they either die or escape the trap. Those who catch and sell short lobsters are stealing from their future, their children's future, and the future of the fishery. The loss of these short lobsters is estimated to cost the fishery between 63% to 83% of its potential future yield (Amendment 2, Fishery Management Plan, GMFMC and SAFMC, 1989). Another estimate by the Florida Marine Fisheries Commission (April 1990) estimates that the increased yield to the fishery by eliminating the use of shorts would be over 50 percent. The more traps in the fishery, the greater the number of short lobsters that live out their lives in traps. Basically, the ferocious battle of the traps robs the fishery of its future.

The lobster trap fishery is not a clean industry. Lobster traps, as they are now constructed and fished, create petroleum and debris pollution on land and in the sea. While the piles of traps scattered through the Keys during the closed season may provide a sort of "fishing village charm" to seaside areas, there are aspects of the trap fishery that are not charming. Abandoned traps on land and in the sea may be just unsightly, but the petroleum pollution from the traps is damaging to the environment. Wooden traps were soaked in oil each year to extend the life of the traps by protecting the wood from marine boring organisms. An estimated 0.5 to 0.75 gallons of oil is absorbed by each trap. This means that approximately 250,000 to 500,000 gallons of used, discarded crankcase oil or bunker C crude oil and other petroleum products were introduced into the marine environment of the Florida Keys each year. And this does not include the oil that was spilled on the ground during years of soaking traps that has, or will eventually, wind up in the surface runoff water, ground water, and shallow marine waters near the Keys. This practice has now ended.

Oil soaked traps will be phased out of the fishery by July 31, 1995, and traps are no longer dipped in oil; but wood, trap line, buoy, and concrete debris can only be reduced by trap reduction. A black, water-based paint is now used to darken the wooden traps to make them more attractive to lobsters, but this treatment probably does not offer much protection to the trap from wood boring organisms. This practice may not do much to beautify the trap dipping sites, but it should not be as harmful to the general environment as oil dipping.

A saturated salt solution (heavy brine) has been found to protect wooden lobster traps (DeAlteris et al., 1988). A 30 second dip in a saturated brine solution effectively killed all shipworms, *Teredo* and *Xylophaga*, that had invaded wooden traps. The brine dip does not prevent shipworms from invading the trap wood, but does kill all worms that are present. The dip must be repeated every 60 days to effectively protect the the trap. A lobster fisherman would have to carry a brine dip tank aboard the boat for periodic trap treatment, but this does seem to be a workable alternative to the oil dip; especially when the quantity of traps that must be protected is reduced to a third of the current number.

A trap that has lost its buoy is called a "ghost trap". It is given this name because no one knows it's there, no one harvests it, and no one removes it at the end of the season. It just keeps on catching lobsters, and lobsters keep on dying in it until the wood in the trap eventually decays and the trap falls apart. A new trap that looses its buoy to a passing boat may "ghost fish" for three years. Again, the more traps in the fishery, the greater the number of ghost traps.

The actual amount of spiny lobster taken from the Florida grounds is unknown. Only the lobster sold to wholesale fish houses are directly recorded and reported as landings of spiny lobster. Although this is our best scientific data and must be used to manage the fishery, other unrecorded landings of lobster have to be taken into consideration. Some fishermen now have their own freezing facilities, and some of the catch is sold directly to customers or to trucking firms without passing through the wholesale fish houses, and is not recorded in the landings. The illegal harvest of short lobster is also unrecorded. The recreational harvest is unrecorded and is estimated to be about 10% of the commercial harvest, but it is not possible to accurately measure the total recreational harvest. The accuracy of the recorded catch is also compromised by the addition of some short lobsters and some lobsters taken in foreign waters.

The source of the juvenile lobsters that settle in the Keys is still unknown. Although most lobster biologists believe that the postlarval spiny lobsters that settle in the Keys originate primarily from the Caribbean Sea, and that variations in annual oceanic current patterns and other factors probably cause annual variations in the source of post larval lobster recruits, there is no clear evidence for any specific pattern of recruitment from any particular area or areas. The Florida fishery can be managed without knowing specifically where the recruits come from, but this is a very unsettling loose end to fishery biologists and managers. Powers et al. (1990), in an excellent overview of modern techniques for genetic and molecular analyses of the identity of fishery stocks, states that comparisions of isozymes and mitochondrial DNA (mtDNA) are very useful in detecting variations within species. Hardwick (1987) used isozyme analysis on populations of the scyllarid lobster, *Scyllarides nodifer*, in the western Gulf of Mexico and concluded that the populations of ridged slipper lobsters in this area are all one unit stock. In a properly designed and executed study, similar techniques could provide great insight into the origin of the various populations of Caribbean spiny lobsters that support the great fisheries of the western central Atlantic.

The long term future of the Florida lobster fishery probably depends on the management of many other fisheries, and not solely on our own management efforts. However, unless we manage the Florida fishery to provide for an adequate reproductive potential, we may find ourselves in the untenable position of asking other countries to manage their fisheries so that, through dependence on the reproductive potential of the stocks of other countries, we will be able to continue to harvest our stocks to the nub.

Assuring an adequate reproductive potential in Florida lobster stocks may come down to a future choice between establishment of sizable "reproductive reservations" or "refugia" where no lobster fishing of any kind is allowed, or raising the minimum legal size to a 3.5 or even 3.7 inch CL to allow for at least one spawn per female before harvest. Assuring a reproductive potential in Florida stocks should be a very important part of all future management strategies. Waugh (1981) made an insightful statement concerning the future exploitation of the Caribbean spiny lobster.

"There is an acute need for fisheries development and management throughout the Caribbean, Central and South America. Overfishing, pollution and inefficient use of natural resources in these regions often occur without the people or government being able to recognize and fully appreciate the consequences."

There is no western central Atlantic lobster fishery to which Waugh's statement does not have some application. If the basic unit stock of Caribbean spiny lobster includes most major lobster populations in the western central Atlantic, which current evidence certainly indicates, then the future of all these spiny lobster fisheries is inextricably linked. In other words, if we look at the unit stock of Caribbean spiny lobsters as one large bank account, then there are many, many people that are authorized to make withdrawals—the "Tragedy of the Commons" on an international scale! If the principal in this "bank account" is not protected by all fisheries, unlimited withdrawals will eventually bankrupt the account.

The same oceanic currents that bring larval lobsters to the Florida Keys also bring poisonous pesticides from agricultural runoff in Cuba and South America. Even airborne dust from African wind storms brings pesticides. Chlorinated hydrocarbon pesticides banned in the United States for 20 years (Heptachlor and Chlordane) are still in use in other countries and freely enter the oceanic environment. These poisons are picked up by tiny zooplankters and are then concentrated in the tissues of the hard and soft corals that feed on them. University of Miami researcher Peter Glynn found levels of these pesticides in Florida soft corals as much as 25 times greater than what is allowed in U.S. seafood and from 100 to 10,000 times greater than levels found in Australian Great Barrier Reef corals in 1978. The threat to the coral reef environment of the Florida Keys, the Bahamas, and the Caribbean is potentially very great. The spiny lobster fishery is only a small fraction of the aquatic resources that can suffer severe future negative impacts from pesticide pollution.

There are many other problems and points of conflict in the Florida fishery in addition to those mentioned above. Some of these are the problem of "blowouts" in the grass flats where abandoned traps have aided the destruction of the grasses in a small circle around the trap, various conflicts between resource users and environmentalists, differences between state and federal regulations, use of plastic traps, capture of other species in addition to lobsters, limited entry to the fishery, reduction of trap numbers, preservation of traps, the trap certificate program, restricted species status for spiny lobster, conflicts between commercial and recreational fishermen (there is strong opposition to the two-day recreational sport season), conflicts between recreational fishermen and environmentalists, activities of poachers and thieves, and many more local and general concerns.

These problems are currently being addressed through the research, legislation, and management efforts of the Florida Marine Fisheries Commission, the South Atlantic and Gulf of Mexico Fishery Councils, the Florida Department of Natural Resources Marine Research Institute, and the fishermen themselves through their professional organization, The Organized Fishermen of Florida. Legislation in this fishery is now very complex because of the many conflicts of interest within the fishery and the intensity of the fishing effort. Most of these problems have been with the fishery for almost 20 years and have been the subject of extensive scientific research, reams of anecdotal and empirical information, intense political activity, and expansive debate between the commercial fishery, the recreational fishery, environmental interests, fishery scientists, and regulatory agencies. It has not been possible to obtain consensus on what must be done and when it must be done. Progress has been made, however, and recent Florida legislation will help solve many of these problems. To understand the direction of the fishery, we need to look at the history of spiny lobster legislation and review a little fishery science.

History of legislation

The first Act regulating the lobster fishery was passed in 1919, Fla. Laws 1919, Ch. 7909 (Prochaska and Baarda, 1975). This act established a three month closed season extending from March 1 to June 1. Lobsters taken for bait purposes, research, or propagation, however, were excluded. The Act was amended in 1921, Fla. Laws 1921, Ch. 8591, to extend the closed season from March 21 to June 21. The closed season was changed several times over the years. It was extended in 1929, Fla. Laws 1929, Ch. 13618, to a four month period from March 21 to July 21. It was changed again in 1953, Fla. Laws 1953, Ch. 28145, from April 15 to August 15; and again in 1955, Fla. Laws 1955, Ch. 29896 to its current interval, March 31 to August 1.

The 1965 act, Fla. Laws 1965, Ch. 65-53, included a provision allowing a trap "soak" period of five days before the start of the season to allow the trap to begin to attract bottom growths and mellow a bit before the start of the season, and five days after the end of the season to allow for trap removal. The first size restriction was enacted in 1929, Fla. Laws 1929, Ch. 13618, with the minimum size set at one pound. The minimum size was changed in 1953, Fla. Laws 1953, Ch. 28145, to a lobster with a tail length of 6 inches. In 1965, Fla. Laws 1965, Ch. 65-53, more extensive legislation defined the minimum size by tail and carapace measurement, a tail length of 5½ inches and a carapace length of 3 inches, which has not changed into the 1990's. This law also specified the type of gear that could be used in the commercial fishery. The dimensions of the wood slat trap were set at 3 by 2 by 2 feet and allowed for 1 inch, 16 gauge poultry wire to be used on the sides, but not the top or bottom of the trap, to protect it from sharks and turtles. It also allowed up to 20 traps to be attached to a trot line and required that the trap buoy carry the permit number.

The 1965 legislation also prohibited capture of egg-bearing females and the stripping of eggs from egg-bearing female lobsters. In 1969, Fla. Laws 1969, Ch. 69-228, allowed a 6 inch tail when the head and tail were separated before landing under a special permit. In 1971, a $50.00 fee was imposed on obtaining a permit to fish lobster in commercial quantities. The permit was required before an individual could possess more than 24 lobster. After this fee was required, the number of permits issued dropped from 2,719 in 1969-70 to only 961 in 1970-71 (Simmons, 1980). In 1988 the Florida legislature created a cap on trap numbers based on the active number of traps in the 1987-1988 fiscal year. The number of lobster permits in 1988 was 4,840.

Current legislation

After 1976, the power of Florida legislation covered only the dock and state waters, a distance of 3 nautical miles from shore into the Atlantic and 3 marine leagues (9 miles) from shore on the Gulf of Mexico side. The Magnuson Fishery Conservation and Management Act of 1976 (MFCMA or FCMA), Public Law 94-265, gave responsibility to Regional Fishery Management Councils to manage fisheries in the FCZ, the Fishery Conservation Zone that extends from state waters out to the limits of territorial waters, 200 miles from shore. (Presidential Proclamation 5030, March 10, 1983, termed Federal waters the Exclusive Economic Zone (EEZ)). The South Atlantic and Gulf of Mexico Fishery Management Councils began to jointly prepare a Fishery Management Plan (FMP) for spiny lobsters in the FCZ (now the EEZ). This management plan was completed in April, 1981. There have been three amendments to this plan, dated February 1987, July 1989, and November 1990. The most recent regulations, dated July 2, 1990 are included in Appendix B. As one might imagine, it would be difficult to live with two separate sets of regulations for a single fishery, one for state waters and one for the EEZ, areas with only a thin, imaginary line between them. Therefore, regulatory agencies work together to formulate regulations that are compatible.

The federal fishery councils proved to be effective agencies in the formulation of fishery regulations. They provided an essential interface between government legislative bodies, user groups, lobbyists, and scientists. Legislators could depend on the fishery councils for information and recommendations that were based on the best available scientific data that had been analyzed, debated, and scrutinized by all user groups in great detail, and on which the public itself had had the opportunity to evaluate and provide comment. Although political influence can still be applied at the actual legislative level, the recommendations of the councils are based on seven national standards that provide for consistency in fishery plan development. There are seven standards for management measures.

- 1. Be designed to prevent overfishing and to achieve optimum yield on a continuing basis.

- 2. Be based on the best scientific information available.

- 3. To the extent practicable, manage an individual stock of fish as a unit throughout its range.

- 4. Be fair and equitable to all fishermen.

- 5. Promote efficiency in the use of fishery resources.

- 6. Allow for variations among, and contingencies in, fisheries, fishery resources, and catches.

- 7. Minimize costs and avoid unnecessary duplication.

A fishery management plan (FMP) is developed by the staff of the Fishery Management Councils and requires information from the various disciplines of biology, fishery science, sociology, biometrics, ecology, and economics. The modern goal of management is not to take every last pound from the fishery that the fishery can give without collapsing (maximum sustained yield or MSY), but to evaluate all the pressures on the fishery, including the human factors that impact user groups, and develop a fishery yield that best meets the needs of all user groups as well as sustaining the biological health of the resource (optimum yield or OY).

This is a long and difficult process and requires the input of Scientific and Statistical Committees (SSC) (scientists and experts from various disciplines that help draft the management plan) and Advisory Panels (AP) (representatives from user groups and other informed individuals that provide insight and comment on the plan) to help formulate the first drafts of the management plan. An Environmental Impact Statement (EIS) and a Regulatory Analysis are also required to assess the impact of the plan on the environment, regulatory agencies, and affected fishermen. Finally, public hearings are held within the area affected by the plan, and the public is encouraged to provide ideas and information on how the plan will work and how it will affect them. The plan is modified to include all pertinent information and is forwarded to the Secretary of Commerce for approval and implementation.

In 1980, the Florida Legislature created the Saltwater Fisheries and Advisory Council to study all aspects of Florida's saltwater fisheries and to develop a comprehensive saltwater fishery conservation and management policy for Florida territorial saltwaters. After two years of study, one of the major recommendations of the Council was a proposal to create a Marine Fisheries Commission to increase management flexibility, introduce public response to proposed management, and to ensure that no single user group could dominate a resource through political or economic pressure. The Florida Legislature created the Marine Fisheries Commission in July, 1983 (Laws of Florida, Ch 83-134; Florida Statutes, Ch 370.026) as an independent agency within the Florida Department of Natural Resources. The new Marine Fisheries Commission was given full rulemaking authority over marine life, with the exception of endangered species, and subject to final approval by the Governor and Cabinet.

The area of authority of the Commission extends over gear specifications, prohibited gear, bag limits, size limits, species that may not be sold, protected species, closed areas, quality control codes, seasons, and special considerations relating to egg-bearing females and oyster and clam relaying. The Florida Marine Commission operates under State standards similar to the National Standards of the Federal Fishery Councils.

Thus, the rules that now regulate the Florida lobster fishery are developed by the Florida Marine Fisheries Commission for State waters and jointly by the Gulf of Mexico and South Atlantic Fishery Councils for federal waters. Great effort is made to insure that the rules are the same for state and federal waters, but timing in rule development and enactment is not always synchronous. In the case of the spiny lobster fishery, the Federal fishery councils follow the lead of the Florida Marine Fisheries Commission since most of the fishery is within Florida waters, and federal regulations usually reflect Florida law.

Things were a lot simpler back in the 1960's when I was Senior Fisheries Biologist for the Florida State Board of Conservation Marine Laboratory (now the Florida Marine Research Institute). The fishery biologists made their recommendations, the fishing industry made theirs, the politicians fought it out, and the resulting regulations may, or may not, have actually benefited the resource. The modern regulatory system makes a lot more sense, and all the user groups and our resources are much better off. The Florida Marine Fisheries Commission sunsets in 1993 (this means that it is dissolved unless the Legislature re-establishes it). Let's hope that the Florida Legislature of 1993 has the wisdom to continue the Commission, for Florida's marine resources need this important interface between the resource users, fishery scientists, politicians, and Federal regulations.

The most recent legislation (see Appendix A) is a result of all regulatory and user groups working together to solve the problems. This legislation was a long time in formation and represents the best compromise possible between divergent environmental, scientific, and vested interests. However, before I discuss how the problems in this fishery are being addressed, we need to understand some of the basics of fishery science and fishery management.

Fishery Science

A modern fisheries scientist has to be a statistician, an ecologist, a sociologist, and an economist as well as a biologist. The modern science of fisheries is as much concerned with the well being of the environment, the fishermen, and the fishing communities as with the biology of the stocks. The well being of the fishery stock is, of course, the foundation of the discipline, for without the fish stock, there is no fishery. Fishery regulations are promulgated to protect and conserve the present and future fish stocks—but these regulations also have a great effect on fishing communities, and when regulations are developed, modern fisheries science takes into consideration how they will effect the environment, the fishing industry, and the community. The industry and public input into the process of developing fishery regulations has created a need for the layman to become familiar with the concepts and language of fishery science.

What do you do if you attend a fishery meeting for the first time and the fellow sitting next to you says; "Look, if they don't put the OY a lot lower than the MSY, then the yield per recruit in the EEZ will be too low, and then the TAC is going to be too high in three years, and growth overfishing is going to be the result. What do you think?" If you think fast, you'll probably put your notebook over your lap and say; "Gee, my fly is open, I'll be back in a minute." and then get up and go find another seat. Perhaps another day you may have a ready answer or have an opinion of your own, but for now the important thing is to learn what's it all about.

I don't have space in this book to write an introductory text on fishery biology, and I really don't have to do so. There is a book available from Florida Sea Grant College that presents the basic concepts of fishery biology in an easy to understand manner (Bortone, 1986). The title is Fisheries Biology for Everyone written by Dr. Steve Bortone and is available for $3.00 from the Sea Grant Extension Office in

Gainesville, Florida. I will, however, define the most common terms below that one needs to know just to understand the basics of a spiny lobster or other resource fishery plan.

Fishery Management Plan (FMP)

A document of information and management measures developed by a fishery council to direct the management of a specific fishery.

Unit Stock

The unit stock is the population of fish (lobsters in this case) that form a reproducing, self replicating fishery stock. In the classic sense, a population of temperate fishes that all migrate to one area to spawn at the same time each year is a unit stock. There may be several unit stocks in one broad oceanic area, but each unit stock is a separate reproductive entity, and the fishery for each stock is managed separately since each is a distinct unit. Thus, a unit stock is a biological population that can be managed as a single unit. In the case of the spiny lobster of the western central Atlantic, the unit stock, or stocks, have not been defined because of the complex distribution of the long lived larval stage. The chances are, however, that the unit stock of western central Atlantic *Panulirus argus* includes all the major populations in this broad area, and, if so, management as a unit stock will be very difficult.

A unit stock is a very valuable thing. Think of it as next years "seed corn" or the principal of a savings account.

Maximum Sustainable Yield (MSY)

The maximum sustainable yield of a fishery is the total amount of fish that can be taken from the unit stock year after year. If the MSY is exceeded, the unit stock itself declines. If the total MSY is taken from the fishery, it's sort of like taking all the interest from a savings account, but leaving the principal intact. The amount of fish taken from a fishery that is required to sustain the MSY may change a bit each year depending on things like environmental conditions, annual reproductive success, recruitment success, and intensity of fishing pressure—just as interest rates on a saving account may change from year to year. Thus the amount of fish that can be taken from a well understood, well monitored, and tightly managed fishery may change from year to year.

The federal fishery councils have estimated the MSY for the Florida lobster grounds at 12.7 million pounds per year. This figure is based on the total recorded catch, the estimated total unrecorded catch from both commercial and recreational activity, the losses due to fishing practices (use of short lobsters in traps), and the potential increased yield of a larger legal carapace length, in the range of 3.4 to 3.7 inches CL. The total unrecorded catch is estimated to be 5.9 million pounds. The MSY at the current 3.0 inch legal carapace size is 12.0 million pounds. In other words, if we stop the illegal harvest of shorts, stop using shorts in traps, raise the minimum size of a legal lobster to 3.5 inches CL or a little more, then it should be possible to harvest almost 13 million pounds of lobster a year without overfishing the resource. Assuming that recruitment levels remain constant, of course.

Optimum Yield (OY)

The optimum yield is based on the MSY, but also includes ecological, social, and economic factors. It can't exceed the MSY, but it can be considerably less depending on things like a year of very poor recruitment, changes in fishing gear, changes in user groups, the price and product demand in the fishery, and many other tangible and intangible factors. So even if the MSY of a fishery doesn't change, the OY might change. Just as one may decide to take a little more or a little less of the interest earned on a savings account, depending on economic conditions during the year. The official definition of OY is as follows.

The OY of a fishery is the amount of fish:

- **A.** which will provide the greatest overall benefit to the Nation, with particular reference to food production and recreational opportunities; and

- **B.** which is prescribed as such on the basis of the maximum sustainable yield from such fishery as modified by any relevant economic, social, or ecological factors.

This is the current federal OY statement for the Florida spiny lobster fishery.

"OY is all spiny lobster with carapace or tail lengths equal to or larger than the minimum legal lengths that are harvested legally under the provisions of the FMP. OY is estimated at 9.5 million pounds."

The spiny lobster OY is based on a size limit rather than numbers of individuals or pounds taken (as it is for all species with a minimum legal size), and consists of all the legal sized lobsters in the stock. Thus OY is managed by changing the size limit rather than limiting the catch. Management of spiny lobster is by yield per recruit rather than by surplus production models. The current OY of 9.5 million pounds includes all reported and unreported harvest and represents all available lobster in a very stressed fishery. The EDAH (Expected Domestic Annual Harvest) is currently set at 9.5 million pounds and the TALFF (Total Allowable Level of Foreign Fishing) is set at 0.0 pounds.

Recruitment
New individuals are added to fishery populations each year as post larvae or juveniles. These individuals are "recruited" into the fishery population when they reach the smallest harvestable size. Strong reproductive success usu-

ally means high recruitment levels in the fishery year class formed from that reproductive effort, but not necessarily. Negative environmental conditions may not allow many larvae and/or juveniles to survive and may negate the results of high reproductive activity. Conversely, good environmental conditions may turn a year of average reproductive activity into a banner year for recruitment. A well managed fishery monitors annual recruitment and mathematically models the strength of each year class in the fishery. In a well managed fishery, the industry has some idea of what production will be like in coming years and can plan accordingly.

Growth Overfishing

A well managed fishery harvests just the right numbers of fish at just the right size to produce the maximum return to the fishery without diminishing the unit stock. If the fish are allowed to grow too big, there is too much loss due to natural mortality before the fish are caught, and if the fish are not allowed to grow large enough before they are caught, then the fishery looses the increased growth that a longer growing period would provide. A fishery stock suffers from growth overfishing when the reproductive capacity of the stock is not diminished, but the fish are harvested before they reach the point of optimum harvest size. This is sort of like taking all the interest from your savings account every month instead of letting it accrue and compound over a whole year. You don't get all the interest you could, but you don't dip into the principal either.

The maximum yield per recruit for the spiny lobster fishery occurs at a carapace length of between 3.4 to 3.7 inches. The current minimum size of 3.0 inch CL results in a yield at least 20% below the maximum yield per recruit, and the spiny lobster fishery is growth overfished at this time.

Recruitment Overfishing

A fishery stock suffers from recruitment overfishing when the fish are harvested to the point that the unit stock is so reduced that reproduction cannot replace mortality. First, the reproductive capacity of the unit stock is significantly reduced because of fishing mortality. Then, as fishing continues, the unit stock continues to decline because the reproductive rate of the remaining adults is not adequate to replace losses from the population, the population crashes, and the fishery is soon ruined. Not only is all the interest being removed from the savings account, but the principal is also being depleted, and the account is soon empty. A fishery stock that suffers only from growth overfishing can quickly rebound when the excess mortality is eliminated (as shown by recovery of stocks of North Sea plaice after WWII); but one that has suffered severe recruitment overfishing continues on a downward spiral, and may never recover even after fishing pressure is relieved.

The Florida spiny lobster stock does not presently suffer from recruitment overfishing because recruitment, as evidenced by relatively stable production, has been constant. Fishing pressure has, however, severely reduced the reproductive capacity of the Florida spiny lobster population. It is down to an estimated 12% of an unfished population (Jones et al., 1985). The Florida population has not experienced reproductive overfishing, only because it is probably part of a much larger unit stock that ranges over the whole western central Atlantic, including the Caribbean Sea and the Gulf of Mexico. However, as Waugh (1981) points out:

"The greatest danger facing the more developed spiny lobster fisheries is recruitment overfishing."

In most western central Atlantic spiny lobster populations, there is no evidence of a stock/recruitment relationship; that is, the abundance, or absence, of berried females in a population has no effect on the annual numbers of recruits to that population. This may be true in current Florida,

Bahamian, and Caribbean spiny lobster populations but not in other heavily fished, but more geographically restricted, lobster populations in other areas of the world.

Waugh (1981) quotes studies on *Panulirus cygnus*, the western Australian rock lobster, that compare the abundance of spawning females and the settlement of puerulus post larvae for the years 1969-78. These studies show that there is a definite relationship between the abundance of spawning females in the stock and subsequent settlement of post larvae in this population. Thus, the absence of indications of recruitment overfishing in the current Florida population of spiny lobster is no guarantee that this will not occur at some future time.

Mortality: Fishing (F), Natural (M), and Total (Z)

Fish and lobster, like all other creatures, die. Annual addition of individuals to the population (recruitment) must equal or exceed the annual loss of individuals (mortality) or the population is eventually extinguished. Even though fish and lobsters can die from many causes—predators, disease, old age, pollution, stress, starvation, and fishing—fishery managers lump all mortality into two categories: fishing mortality and natural mortality. Fishing mortality is the death of all individuals that are taken in the fishery or whose death is caused by the fishery. Natural mortality is the death of all individuals from causes other than fishing. Total mortality is the sum of natural and fishing mortality. Like recruitment, mortality in a population occurs continuously and can be expressed in mathematical terms.

Fishery Studies

There are a number of research tools that fishery scientists use to determine things like natural and fishing mortality, relative abundance, absolute abundance, and recruitment. Some of these methods are acoustic surveys (effective on oceanic stocks of pelagic fishes), visual surveys (effective on reef animals), fishing surveys, tagging studies (effective for migration and fishing mortality estimates), egg, larval, and juvenile surveys, age and growth studies, year class analysis, and of course, complete life history studies. All of these methods contribute data that is analyzed and used in developing fishery management plans.

A fishery scientist uses mathematical equations to analyze the interaction of many factors and find out what various rates of fishing mortality will do to the fishery stocks and the fishery. A fishery scientist needs to know as accurately as possible the size of the unit stock, fishing mortality, natural mortality, total mortality, the yield per recruit, growth rate, reproductive strategy, and the catch per unit effort to be able to monitor and manage the fishery.

Fishing Effort (Fishing Pressure)

The act of fishing, actually catching fish or lobster by whatever method, is fishing effort, and this exerts fishing pressure on the resource and causes fishing mortality. The amount of fishing effort on the resource can be measured in various ways. The total amount of fish or lobster caught is one measure of fishing effort. The number of boats engaged in the fishery, the number of fishermen, and the amount of fish taken by day, week, or month, by area, and by different types of fishing gear are other methods of effort measure. All contribute to an understanding of the fishery and its effect on the unit stock. Management of a fishery usually includes some method of controlling fishing effort. Closed seasons, limited entry, control of net and mesh size, and trap number limits are all methods of managing fishing effort.

Catch Per Unit Effort (CPUE)

Catch per unit effort is a very important effort measurement because it provides a rapid indication of what is happening to the fishery. With the proper landings data, catch per unit effort can be monitored as the fishing season is in progress, and the effect of the fishery on the resource can be assessed immediately. The definition of a unit of effort depends on the methods used in the fishery. It may be the amount of time that a trawl net of a particular type and size is pulled, the number of times a purse net is set, the number of traps in use (as in the lobster fishery), the number of lines in the water, a creel census, the number of fisherman days (useful when measuring individual effort such as a spear fishery for lobster), or any other measure of effort that makes sense for a particular fishery. The average yield for each unit of effort is a measure of the effectiveness of the methods and the gear and, over time, indicates the status of the resource. Catch per unit effort can also be used in regulation of the fishery as it may be the definition of effort that is used to regulate the total effort on the fishery.

Quotas

Quotas are often set for heavily fished stocks. This is a way of limiting effort and of allocating the resource among user groups. A bag limit is a sort of quota on recreational fishermen. A fishery may be able to sustain only so much fishing effort in one year depending on the size of the fishable stock, and a quota may be imposed to define the Total Allowable Catch (TAC). The fishery is then closed when the catch quota is reached, whenever that might occur during the season.

Limited Entry

Limited entry is a very controversial, but effective way of controlling effort in a fishery. It greatly improves the effectiveness of control and regulation in a fishery, but direct fishery regulation (a minimum size limit in the case of the lobster fishery) is still the core of effective management. Limited entry is defined in many different ways depending on the biology and sociology of the fishery, but basically it limits effort by controlling the number of participants or effort units in the fishery. There are three basic methods of limiting entry into a fishery: *license limitation, stock certificates*, and *entry barriers* (Austin, 1989). License limitations allow for only a limited number of licenses for that fishery. The licenses can be bought and sold so that anyone may participate in the fishery, but participation depends on availability of a license. Stock certificates refer directly to the fishery stock and divide the total allowable catch (TAC) into units that represent quotas for individual fishermen or boats. Entry barriers may permit participation in the fishery to only residents of certain areas; or a particular level of economic investment or professional background may be required; or only those that have historically participated in the fishery at a certain level of effort may be allowed to continue in the fishery; or only a certain number of gear elements may be allowed to fish—all are various forms of limited entry. The methods vary, but the sore point in this type of effort control is the exclusion or difficult entry of those who legitimately wish to enter the fishery. Because of the possibility of a form of limited entry being applied to the Florida lobster fishery, the federal fishery councils published a notice of a control date (January 15, 1986) for entry into the fishery (51 FR 5713). The notice announced that anyone entering the commercial fishery after that date may not be assured of future access if a system that limits participants is implemented. Austin (1989) presents a detailed discussion of limited entry.

The Florida Legislature also passed on F. S. 370.14 (2) in 1988 that provided for a moratorium on issuance of new trap permits from July 1, 1988 through July 1, 1991 while the state and the lobster industry evaluate the structure of a limited access system. The statute limits issuance of permit numbers to those held in the 1987/88 season. The permits are transferable and permits not renewed each year may be reissued. This restriction has been extended through the 1991-1992 season. The trap certificate program (Laws of Florida, 91-154) became law on May 29, 1991, and its provisions will take effect on July 1, 1991. Although the trap certificate program and the restricted species designation limits access to the fishery, prospective commercial lobster fisher-

men can enter the fishery after meeting certain requirements.

Yield Per Recruit (YPR)

There are two basic approaches to determine the proper
yield from a fishery: the surplus production model and
yield per recruit. The surplus production modeling approach describes the actual yield of the fishery. It uses population growth curves and catch data, and assumes that the
catch per unit effort can accurately determine population
size. The catch and effort data are used to develop a yield
curve from which MSY can be calculated. To be accurate,
this method requires at least 10 years of accurate historical
data on a fishery, including commercial and recreational
effort and landings, and this is seldom available, especially
when the unit stock of the fishery covers a broad geographical area. The best surplus yield model (Fox, 1970) applied to
the Florida spiny lobster fishery indicates an MSY of 5.8
million pounds that can be taken by about 206,000 traps.

The spiny lobster fishery is managed on a yield per
recruit (YPR) basis. This is an analytical method of mathematically predicting the potential yield of the fishery according to growth patterns of individuals rather than
growth patterns of populations. It does not allow calculation
of total landings, but it does allow an estimate of relative
yield from a fishery under various regulations and effort. To
be successful, this method of management demands that
recruitment in the fishery be constant (Cushing, 1981), and
this is the case in the Florida spiny lobster fishery. It is not
necessary to know the total catch and the catch per unit
effort (CPUE) to estimate the yield. The required information is an estimate of natural mortality and the age of the fish
or lobster at various sizes. YPR in the lobster fishery should
be viewed with caution, however, because estimates of natural mortality in the lobster population are not precise. This
parameter is very important because slight changes in the
natural mortality estimate can make large changes in the

predicted size at maximum yield. The lobster fishery YPR model is accurate enough to show that a larger minimum size will increase the yield per recruit, but it does not reliably predict the exact size at maximum yield or the exact amount of an increase in yield due to an increase in minimum size. As an equation, the yield per recruit (YPR) is equal to the yield divided by recruits. When recruitment is constant, YPR changes only when the yield changes.

The strengths of the yield per recruit method of fishery yield prediction are that the analysis can be made quickly without waiting for the accumulation of years of data and the relative yield of a fishery under various regulations can be easily estimated. According to the YPR analysis of the federal fishery council's management plan, the maximum yield of the lobster fishery would be achieved at a minimum size of 3.4 inches (87 mm) to 3.7 inches (95 mm) CL with 39% of the current fishing effort.

With the yield per recruit method, the yield of the spiny lobster fishery can be managed by controlling the minimum legal size of the lobsters. Historically, and currently, the demands of the fishery have kept the yield at least 20% below the maximum possible yield per recruit of the Florida spiny lobster stock. Fortunately, the biology of spiny lobster is such that it can withstand considerable exploitation. As long as recruitment to the Florida stock holds steady, growth overfishing is more detrimental to the Florida fishery than to the Florida lobster population. Over time, and with understanding, the Florida fishery can be managed to control growth overfishing, increase yield, decrease effort, and provide for an adequate reproductive potential in the Florida stock.

Eggs Per Recruit (EPR)

The Eggs Per Recruit ratio is a method of defining overfishing. According to Amendment 3, November, 1990, of the federal council's fishery management plan for spiny lobster,

"Overfishing exists when the eggs per recruit ratio of the exploited population to the unexploited population is reduced below five percent, **and** recruitment of small lobsters into the fishery has declined for three consecutive fishing years. Overfishing will be avoided when the eggs per recruit ratio of exploited to unexploited populations is maintained above five percent."

The average number of eggs produced over its lifetime by a lobster recruited to the fishery is defined as eggs per recruit. At present, the eggs per recruit of exploited populations is only 18.24% of that of populations in unexploited areas (the Tortugas Sanctuary area) (Gregory et al., 1982). Since recruitment has not apparently diminished, however, Florida lobster stocks are not overfished according to this definition.

Saltwater Products License (SPL)

The State of Florida requires that every person, firm, or corporation which sells, offers for sale, barters, or exchanges for merchandise any saltwater products with certain gear or equipment as specified by law, must have a valid Saltwater Products License. The license must be in the possession of the license holder or aboard the vessel and shall be subject to inspection at any time that harvesting activities for which the license is required are being conducted. The cost of an annual SPL is $50.00 when issued in the name of an individual, $100.00 when issued to a valid boat registration number. Nonresidents of Florida must pay a $200.00 annual fee for an SPL issued in the name of an individual and $400.00 if the license is issued to a vessel. Just holding an SPL, however, does not make one a commercial lobster fisherman.

All Florida commercial lobster fishermen must have an SPL, of course, **and** a crawfish permit (trap number). The cost of a crawfish trap number is $100; but according to the Laws of Florida 91-154 (see Appendix A) no crawfish trap numbers except those that were active during the 1990-1991 fiscal year shall be renewed or reissued. The spiny lobster, *Panulirus argus*, will become a restricted species on August

1, 1993, and a commercial lobster fisherman will then have to meet additional requirements as well. In addition, a commercial spiny lobster fisherman who fishes in the EEZ must have a seasonal vessel permit. A sworn statement certifying that at least 10% of earned income was derived from commercial fishing during the calendar year preceding the application is required (along with other information and a permit application fee of $26) for issuance of this permit (see Federal Regulations, Appendix B).

Restricted Species Designation (RSD)

Obtaining a Saltwater Products License allows a serious recreational fisherman to exceed bag limits by allowing the fisherman to become, in fact, a part time commercial fisherman (Note that a crawfish trap number must also be obtained, which are no longer being issued, if the fisherman wishes to use traps).

There are some species of marine fish and invertebrates for which it is not in the best interests of the resource or the fishery to allow an excessive recreational harvest. Thus the Florida Legislature (Florida Statues, Ch. 370.01, 1987), has provided the Marine Fisheries Commission with the authority to designate any particular species of saltwater product as a Restricted Species. The authority to designate a species as restricted is entirely at the discretion of the Florida Marine Fisheries Commission and depends on the current condition of the resource and the fishery.

This designation was established to allow the MFC to more closely control harvest of a particular resource by drawing a strong line between commercial and recreational harvesters. It does not prevent a recreational fishermen from catching a restricted species, or a commercial fisherman from making a living from fishing a species as he has done in the past—but it does restrict all recreational fisherman to the legal bag limit, and it is a type of limited entry since it requires a commercial fisherman to have a history of commercial fishing (see Restricted Species Endorsement) before a restricted species can be fished commercially. Once a species is designated as a restricted species, a commercial fisherman must have a Restricted Species Endorsement before he can commercially catch and sell that species.

According to the Florida Adminstrative Code, Chapter 46-24, 1990, spiny lobster, *Panulirus argus*, will become a restricted species on August 1, 1993. Other species that are now designated as restricted are king mackerel, Spanish mackerel, spotted seatrout, black drum, snappers (14 species), grouper (14 species), black mullet, amberjack, and many species (aquarium fish and invertebrates) in the marine life fishery.

Restricted Species Endorsement (RSE)

A commercial fisherman must have a Restricted Species Endorsement on the Saltwater Products License in order to sell to a licensed wholesale dealer those species that the State has designated, by law or rule, as restricted species. Not just any commercial fisherman can qualify to fish for restricted species. The RSE is issued only to those persons, firms, or corporations certifying that over 25% of their income, or $5,000.00, whichever is less, is attributable to the sale of saltwater products under a SPL of Florida or a similar license from another state. This income must apply to at least 1 year out of the last 3 years. The income referred to in this law can come from work, employment, entrepreneurship, pensions, retirement benefits, and Social Security benefits. In other words, to be legally able to commercially fish for a restricted species, one must have made at least $5,000 or 25% of his or her total income from commercial fishing in at least one of the last three years. This income must be proven by a copy of the Federal Income tax return, including Form 1099 attachments, verifying income earned from the sale of saltwater products, crew share statements verifying income earned from the sale of saltwater products, or a certified public accountant's notarized statement attesting to qualifying source and amount of income. New legislation, a 1991 amendment to Florida Statutes, 370.06, allows a person age 62 or over who documents that at least $2,500 of income is attributable to the sale of saltwater product to obtain a Restricted Species Endorsement. This amendment also provides for issuance of a permanent RSE to a person age 70 or older who has had a saltwater products license for at least 3 of the last 5 years.

At first glance, one might think that one can't begin fishing for a restricted species unless one has already been fishing for a restricted species, a classic catch 22. This isn't exactly true. One can become a commercial fisherman and fish for species that are not restricted for a year, and if income is high enough from commercial fishing, one can then qualify for a RSE; or one can work as crew on a commercial fishing boat for a year, and if income is high enough, then be able to qualify for a RSE. In other words, one must pay one's dues as a commercial fisherman before being awarded the privilege of commercially fishing for a restricted species. Although it is a form of limited entry, anyone can qualify for an RSE if he or she is willing to work for a year in a commercial fishery in some capacity other than directly fishing a restricted species. This insures that only experienced, serious commercial fishermen enter fisheries where stocks are stressed and tight control over the fishery is required for proper management of the resource.

A federal commercial permit is now required for commercial lobster fishermen working in federal waters, the Exclusive Economic Zone (EEZ). This permit was established to distinguish between commercial and recreational fishermen in federal waters. To be eligible for a federal commercial permit, the fisherman must derive at least 10% of his or her income from commercial fishing during the calendar year preceding his or her last application.

Solving the Problems

Everyone—the commercial and recreational fishermen, the fishery scientists, the fishery mangers, and the legislators—know about the problems in the lobster fishery. How to solve these problems, however, is another matter. A serious effort has been made in current Florida law to resolve these problems in the best interests of the resource and all the user groups. The text of the Florida Adminstrative Code, Chapter 46-24, Florida Statutes 370.14, and the Laws of Florida, Ch 91-154 (a 1991 amendment to F. S. 370.14 on spiny lobster) are reproduced in Appendix A, and a compilation of the Federal regulations are reproduced in Appendix B, to provide access to the most recent rules and legislation.

As mentioned above, the greatest problem in the fishery is overcapitalization—the excessive number of traps in the fishery. The second greatest problem is the mortality of short lobster due to trap confinement and illegal harvest. These are not easy problems to solve because there are no solutions that are warmly embraced by all interested parties. Everyone agrees that the number of traps and short mortality must be reduced, but how to reduce these is a matter of fierce debate. The Florida Marine Fisheries Commission and the Florida Legislature is very serious about reduction of fishing effort and short mortality. Legislation passed in 1991 (Appendix A) should help resolve these problems.

The 1991-1992 season, however, will be very hard on lobsters. The number of traps will probably be at an all time high because commercial lobster fishermen will run all the traps they can to compete with other commercial fishermen and recreational divers for a now very limited resource. Things will get better for the lobsters in the 1992-1993 season when the number of traps will be limited to 750,000. Spiny lobsters will not become a restricted species until August 1, 1993, so recreational divers who already hold a lobster permit ($100) and an SPL ($50) will be able to exceed the bag limit for the two seasons before the RSD goes into effect.

When the Restricted Species Designation is in place, recreational lobster divers will be allowed to pursue their sport, but will not be able to exceed whatever bag limits are in place at that time. The RSD will provide a larger share of the resource for the commercial fishery, and limit commercial fishing activity to serious commercial fishermen. About 931 (47% of commercial lobster fisherman with SPLs in the 1987-88 year) would qualify for a restricted species endorsement for spiny lobster.

The commercial fishery, although generally benefiting from the restricted species status, is also being forced to get its house in order by all this recent legislation. The problem of oil dipped traps was one of the first major problems to be addressed. The Marine Fisheries Commission banned the use of oil dipped traps after August 1, 1993, (FAC 46-24.006 (a)), but the legislature changed that ruling in F.S. 376.07 (3). The law now states that beginning August, 1995, no wood slat trap that has been dipped in or treated with any oil product shall be used to harvest lobster. This gives the industry four fishing seasons to phase out all oil soaked traps. The practice of soaking traps in oil was banned as of July 31, 1990. Fisherman are now dipping traps in a black, water based paint to darken the traps.

The Marine Fisheries Commission also attempted to prohibit the possession of undersized spiny lobster for the purpose of luring, decoying, or otherwise attracting noncaptive spiny lobster (Florida Adminstative Code 46-24.003, (4)) and stated that an escape gap of 2⅛ inches wide and 20 inches long must be built into the trap at the narrow end opposite the buoy line (FAC 46-24.006 (1) (d)). The escape gap must be unobstructed and will allow the escape of undersized lobster from the trap. Research with escape gaps, (Hunt and Lyons, 1985; Frazel, 1986) has shown that 97 to 99% of undersized lobsters escape from traps with a 2⅛ inch escape gap. Interestingly, in a number of studies in spiny lobster fisheries around the world, traps equipped with appropriately designed escape gaps catch more legal

Figure 98. A 2⅛ inch escape gap built into a standard Florida wood slat trap. The gap is placed near the bottom on the opposite side of the pull line.

sized lobster than traps without escape gaps (Bowen, 1963; Ritchie, 1966; Bain, 1967). The accompanying photograph (Figure 98) illustrates an escape gap built into a lobster trap.

Another method of eliminating shorts from being taken in the fishery is to require that grid sorters be used aboard lobster boats. A grid sorter is a 3 by 5 foot tray or box with a bottom composed of stainless steel bars placed 2 inches (50 mm) apart, or any other dimension required by law. A chute runs from the bottom of the grid sorter box overboard to the sea. The lobster are emptied from the trap into the grid sorter, and undersized lobster are automatically returned to the ocean. Only the lobster that remain on top of the grid can be retained by the fishermen. Grid sorters have been required on South African rock lobster boats since 1973 (Waugh, 1981). **If necessary,** a combination of escape gaps, grid sorters, stringent enforceable regulations against use and/or sale of undersized lobster, and effective control of recreational fishing effort could adequately protect the lobster resource.

Many commercial fishermen feel that a prohibition on using short lobsters as attractors and mandating the use of escape gaps will cut the fishery off at the knees. They feel that the use of shorts as attractors is now essential to making a living as a commercial lobster fisherman. There was an "out", however, for the commercial fishermen that was made part of the MFC regulations. FAC, Ch. 46-24001 (5) states that it is the goal of the Commission to reduce the mortality of undersize lobster in the fishery, and that the ban on the use of shorts as attractants and the requirement for an escape gap in traps are intended to accomplish this goal. It also states, however, that the Commission is willing to consider the **elimination of these measures** prior to their implementation on August 1, 1993, if an effort reduction program is adopted by the Legislature and successfully implemented by the Commission for the fishery.

Thus, there was a strong motivation for the commercial fishery to come together with the fishery managers and develop and implement an effective program for effort reduction. This may now be in place with the adoption of the 1991 amendment to the Florida Statutes (Appendix A, Laws of Florida, Ch. 91-154) providing for the trap certificate program. This amendment repeals the elimination of use of short lobsters as attractants and the implementation of escape gaps in traps until at least April 1, 1998. After that date, the Marine Fisheries Commission may reintroduce these measures if effort reduction in the fishery does not succeed in reducing the number of traps and mortality of short lobsters to acceptable levels. The feeling is that if effort (trap numbers) can be reduced to reasonable levels, then it **may** be possible to live with the amount of short mortality produced by the greatly reduced number of traps. Also, the great reduction in trap number and increased restrictions on harvest (Restricted Species Designation) should make it easier to detect and control illegal harvest of short lobsters, and trap reduction should also greatly reduce the need for use of short lobsters as attractors in traps.

There are many ways to reduce effort in the lobster fishery. The trick is finding one that everyone can live with and that does the job. Dr. Michael Orbach, a fisheries anthropologist at East Carolina University, was contacted in 1985 by the Gulf of Mexico and South Atlantic Fishery Councils and the National Marine Fisheries Service (NMFS), and was asked to look into the problem of effort reduction in the Florida lobster fishery. Dr. Orbach worked with the commercial fishermen through the Organized Fishermen of Florida (OFF) and fishery managers and administrators from 1986 through 1990 identifying problems and developing and evaluating alternatives for effort limitation. An extensive series of workshop meetings were held throughout the lobster fishery to discuss current practice and explore ways of effort reduction that would cause the least amount of displacement in the fishery and maintain the flexibility of current and future lobster fishermen to work the fishery at whatever level they wish. Dr. Orbach established five basic standards necessary in an effort reduction program.

1. An accurate system of documenting the actual number of traps used in the fishery.

2. An equitable way to distribute use among fishermen.

3. An efficient method to allow fishermen to adjust their fishing operations.

4. A clear mechanism to reduce the total number of traps in the fishery, while maintaining or increasing overall catch levels.

5. Mechanisms to ensure fair and equitable establishment and administration of the system, including monitoring of the effects of the system and proper enforcement.

With these five standards as a guide, the industry workshops established and evaluated six possible methods of effort reduction.

1. Restricted species endorsement. This was considered only from the standpoint of trap reduction, and although it would be relatively easy to implement and enforce, it alone would not achieve a significant reduction in trap numbers. It would also cause some fishermen to leave the fishery.

2. Trap Certificate System. This system ranked high in both trap reduction and fishermen flexibility, but would be costly to implement and enforce.

3. Extend the present moratorium. This would be easy to implement and enforce, but would not immediately begin effort reduction, and serious social and economic effects might occur in the fishery when significant effort did retire from the fishery.

4. Direct license limitation. This would be costly to implement and administer, and a program strong enough to actually reduce trap numbers would limit flexibility and cause severe social and economic effects. It would also require that some current fishermen leave the fishery.

5. Individual cap on traps at 1000. This program would also be costly to implement and enforce and probably would not result in a significant reduction in trap number.

6. Individual cap on traps at 250. Although this would result in reduction of trap numbers, it would also be costly to implement and enforce, severely limit fishermen flexibility, and cause severe social and economic effects.

It was determined that the Transferable Trap Certificate program would be the most effective way to reduce effort, maintain catch at current production levels, and cause the least limitations in fishermen flexibility. The basic elements of this program, as adopted, are presented on the next page. Also, the text of Florida Law 91-154, the amendment on the trap certificate program, is presented in Appendix A.

Trap tags. Each trap must have a durable plastic tag attached with the trap owners identification number printed on the tag. A per tag fee covers administrative costs and the tags will be issued in a different color each year. There are provisions for tag replacement due to in-season loss, and the tags apply to both state and federal waters.

Transferable trap certificates. Initially, trap certificates shall be issued to bona fide commercial lobster fishermen on the basis of actual trap count and historical usage. One certificate is the authorization to use one trap in the lobster fishery. Trap certificates can be bought and sold between commercial lobster fishermen, including a transfer fee to cover the cost of administration. The number of certificates an individual fisherman or business entity can directly or indirectly control is limited to 1.5% of total available certificates in any license year to prevent monopolistic control.

Trap reduction. An optimum number for the total number of traps in the fishery will be determined. The initial issuance of certificates will reflect the actual number of traps now used in the fishery, however, a specific yearly percentage for reduction of existing traps (not to exceed 10% per year) will be established, and each fisherman will surrender the agreed upon percentage of certificates each year until the optimum number of traps in the fishery is reached. The total effect of this trap reduction rate on the fishery will be closely monitored, and the commission may resume, terminate, or even reverse the schedule as is deemed necessary.

Administration. The Florida Marine Fisheries Commission is to be responsible for overall policies including setting the target number for traps in the fishery, establishing the annual percentage rate for trap reduction, and development of monitoring parameters. The Department of Natural Resources will issue trap tags (trap certificates) and record trap certificate transfers. A Trap Certificate Technical Advisory and Appeals Board will be established to hear all claims, and handle issues that might develop in the initiation of the trap certificate system. This body will be composed of certificate holders from all geographical areas of the fishery and include representatives from various participant levels in the fishery. Two board members will hold between 100 and 750 certificates, three will hold between 750 and 2,000, and two will hold over 2,000 certificates.

The trap certificate program will allow for a controlled, systematic, across the board reduction in trap numbers that will affect each fisherman equally according to the extent of each fisherman's participation in the fishery. More accurate records will be available on the total number of traps in the fishery, and enforcement of regulations will be easier due to the reduced number of traps and increased accountability from trap tags. The value of individual trap certificates will probably increase as the total number of certificates declines, and the cost of entering the fishery will also increase. Although fishermen who qualify for a restricted species endorsement will still have flexibility as far as entering the fishery and determining their level of participation, their degree of flexibility will depend on affordablity and availability of trap certificates. As a case in point, a rock lobster license in western Australia went for about $20,000 in 1962 ten years after limited entry began. The value of the same license in 1985 had risen to $450,000 (Phillips and Brown, 1989). Fishermen entering this fishery now have to carry huge loans in addition to equipment expenses. Poaching and trap theft may increase as the number of traps decreases and the yield per trap increases.

Although not without problems, the trap certificate program seems to be the best plan for gaining management control of the biological, economical, and sociological problems in the lobster fishery, and it is generally favored above other possibilities by all concerned parties. Decisions made over the next few years are crucial to the future of the Florida spiny lobster fishery. **Whatever the short term impact on the recreational and commercial fisheries, decisions based on insuring the future health of the resource are the right decisions.**

Slipper Lobster in Florida

Catches of slipper lobster, the common name used in Florida Law for the Scyllarid lobster of the species *Scyllarides nodifer*, and the Spanish slipper lobster, *Scyllarides aequinoctialis*, have historically been a bycatch of the spiny lobster and shrimp trawl fisheries. A few found their way to conventional markets, but most were consumed by fishermen or marketed locally. The Spanish lobster, *S. aequinoctialis*, is still a relatively rare bycatch in lobster traps, but the situation has changed in recent years for the ridged slipper lobster, *S. nodifer*. A significant part time fishery for ridged slipper lobster has developed off the Florida west coast during the 1980's. This fishery is also described in Chapter 3 in the species account for *S. nodifer*. The yield for this fishery has remained at a little less than 100,000 pounds per year. There is no season or size limit on this species. The only state and federal regulation is the prohibition of taking egg-bearing females and a prohibition on stripping the eggs from egg-bearing females.

There is concern for the resource as the fishery continues, since the season of the fishery coincides with the spawning season of *S. nodifer* (April through August), and as much as 45% of the females taken in the trawl fishery are egg-bearing. Unlike the spiny lobster with a broad, reproductive reservoir that extends over much of the western central Atlantic, ridged slipper lobster are basically restricted to the Gulf of Mexico, and reproductive overfishing could occur quickly. The distribution, taxonomy, and biology of *S. nodifer* in the Gulf of Mexico was studied in detail by Lyons (1970). Hardwick (1987) performed statistical analyses of isozyme bands of ridged slipper lobster from different areas in the Gulf of Mexico (Pensacola, Apalachicola, and the Florida Keys), and supports the assumption that there is only a single unit stock of *S. nodifer* in the northern and eastern Gulf of Mexico.

Hardwick (1987) collected detailed information on the fishery for ridged slipper lobster in the Gulf of Mexico off Apalachicola, the "Big Bend Area" of Florida. Some shrimp trawlers working this area for lobsters caught over 5,000 ridged slipper lobsters in trips of three to five days, an average of about 500 lobsters are taken during each night of trawling. The fishery is conducted by shrimp trawlers during the off season for shrimp. The fishing grounds consists of primarily two "hang-free" corridors where a modified shrimp trawl can be dragged with a minimum of hang ups and net damage. Even in these areas, however, the trawls sustain damage on the rough, rocky bottom. The width of these corridors is estimated at about five widths of the trawl (175 meters), and the total area of these two corridors is estimated at 0.078 square kilometers, an estimated 0.017% of the entire area of the ridged slipper lobster grounds.

Based on estimations of the size of the trawlable areas that are fished, the average catch, and the size of the area occupied by the entire population, Hardwick (1987) calculates that the size of the slipper lobster population in the Big Bend area is 6.14 million lobsters. He also calculates the estimated MSY of the fishery as 319.6 kg per square km. The actual yield of the fishery is 17.5 kg per km; thus the efficiency of the fishery is only 5.4%. These figures are, of course, very tentative since very little fishery data and biological information is available.

The same two tracks are trawled night after night, and the yield remains fairly constant at about 500 lobsters per night. Interestingly, the second and third trawls over the same area each night usually produce more lobster than the first trawl. The trawls are pulled for about 20 to 30 minutes, and the boat then makes another trawl over the same corridor. Hardwick presents several possible explanations for the increased catches on the second and third trawls:

1. The trawls may catch only a few of the lobsters that are present on the first trawl. It is possible that many lobsters swim out of the way or are buried on the first pass of the trawl and are taken on the next pass.

2. The trawl efficiency may be high, and lobsters are moving into the disturbed area between passes. Doubtful because SCUBA observations indicate that concentrations of lobsters in areas away from the corridors are not that high.

3. The second and third trawls are actually on different tracks within the corridor. Quite possible since the corridors are actually 5 to 10 trawl widths wide, and the nets continue to fill with rocks and debris from the bottom that would have been removed previously had the same exact track been followed.

4. The activity of the trawl disturbs hidden and buried lobster and causes them to move into open areas between trawls.

The apparent size of the total lobster grounds, the nature of the bottom topography, and the limitations of a trawl fishery in these areas indicate that only 1.2 % of the slipper lobster population is taken from this area each year. Thus it would seem that a trap fishery and/or discovery of other hang-free corridors are economic opportunities in a developing fishery. The ridged slipper lobster population is, however, a fragile resource. Because of the limited area of the fishing grounds, and a reproductive area restricted to the Gulf of Mexico, development of an intensive, uncontrolled fishery has a potential for rapid overfishing of the resource.

If a trap fishery is developed, the standard spiny lobster trap used in the Florida Keys will not be effective. Ridged and Spanish slipper lobsters have a very different morphology, behavior, and ecology than spiny lobsters. Although they occasionally get into the standard lobster trap, climbing up on top of a trap and entering a vertical shaft does not fit their lifestyle. They do not have the mobility and climbing ability of spiny lobsters. In 1979-80, I worked with a group in the Florida Keys (T. A. Herbert & Associates, Inc.,

Tallahassee, FL) on a National Science Foundation Grant to develop a trap that would be effective on both slipper and spiny lobsters. It was an interesting project, and we developed a lobster trap design that was extremely effective in capturing all three species in our experimental population of lobsters. This work was described in detail in National Fishermen, November 1983 (Anonymous, 1983).

Eight different trap designs were tested. One design, Figure 99, far outperformed all other trap designs. It captured over 60% of all the lobsters taken (82% of the spiny lobsters and 58% of the slipper lobsters) in the first phase (seven weeks) of the experiment. The trap is a modified den-type trap, a design that allows lobsters to leave the trap, but does make it difficult for them to do so. Thus it will not kill lobsters, even if it becomes a ghost trap, but it does contain them while the trap is being pulled. The den trap was constructed from standard wooden trap lath and measured 6 inches high, 24 inches wide, and 48 inches long. A single funnel entrance built into one end of the trap made it easy for lobsters to enter, but a bit difficult to exit.

The key feature in this design was that the top and sides, except the end with the funnel, was covered by a relatively inexpensive, very tough, very durable, cross laminated 4 mil black polyethylene sheet material. Ordinary black polyethylene sheeting will not work as it is too fragile. The black covering made the interior of the trap very dark and helped to simulate a natural, low reef ledge habitat. If such a trap were put into wide use, a plastic sheeting trap cover would not be acceptable, of course, because lost plastic sheeting would create bottom debris. Other methods of darking and enclosing the trap could be developed. For example, a trap of this design could be built entirely of plastic, perhaps even recycled plastic.

The lobsters were difficult to remove from the trap, and later designs were built 8 inches high instead of 6 inches high. Lobsters were easier to remove from the higher traps, but they did not catch as well as the low traps. A removable door (access panel) is built into the bottom or top of the trap to allow harvest of the lobsters. A biodegradable panel is not needed in this design since lobsters will eventually leave the trap. In fact, leaving the den trap and returning to it the next morning may function to bring other lobsters to the trap. (Perhaps this is why, in areas with a high availability of lobsters, spiny lobster traps with escape gaps have higher catch rates than traditional traps that retain short lobsters.)

This type of trap may function well for slipper lobsters in areas similar to the Big Bend area where there are populations of slipper lobsters that cannot be taken with trawls. Traps that retain lobsters until they die should not be used in deep or murky waters where it is difficult, at best, to recover lost traps. In fact, use of a den-type trap design, even in the spiny lobster fishery, would eliminate the problems of ghost traps and short mortality, and although the catch per trap might decline, at least until total effort is reduced, elimination of short mortality and ghost trapping would be immediately accomplished. Use of this type of trap design might even increase catch per trap under certain conditions since it is more attractive and easier for the lobster to enter than the standard lobster trap.

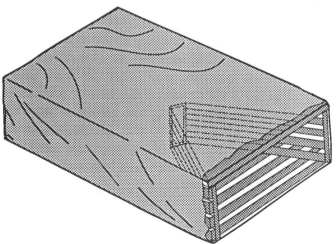

Figure 99. A den trap design for slipper and spiny lobsters.

Bahamas

The Bahamas encompass a vast, shallow marine environment rich in natural resources. The spiny lobster population is one of the most valuable of these resources. The total area of the Bahamas covers almost 60,000 square miles and consists of a chain of 29 islands and countless cays and rock outcroppings. These islands extend 760 nautical miles over 7 degrees of latitude from northwest to southeast. The Bahama Banks are made up of 16 shallow plateaus, including the northern Little Bahama Banks and the southern Great Bahama Banks.

The bottom biotopes can be classified as reef, rock, vegetated, and unvegetated (Smith and van Nierop, 1986). Reef areas are dominated by massive corals in the genera *Acropora*, *Montastrea*, *Diploria*, and *Meandrina* and include fringing, barrier, and patch reef formations. Reefs make up only a little over 2% of the total area of both bank areas. Rock areas consist of a limestone rock substrate variously covered by thin sediments and colonized by soft corals, sponges, small hard corals, various invertebrates, and macroalgae, notably attached *Sargassum*. Rock areas cover about 22% of the Little Bahama Banks and 12% of the Great Bahama Banks. Vegetated bottoms cover about 60% of the bottom area of both major banks and consist mostly of turtle grass, *Thalassia*. Shoal grass, *Halodule*, and manatee grass, *Syringodium*, are also present and may be locally abundant. Many macroalgae are also present throughout the grass beds. Unvegetated bottoms consist of barren sediments of calcareous rubble and sand that are unstable and shift and move with the currents. Although coral and plant life cannot survive on these shifting sediments, many echinoderms and mollusks live in, on, and around these shifting sediment bottoms. Spiny lobsters are found on all these biotopes, but adults are most concentrated on the reef areas. Post larval and juvenile lobsters are primarily found in shallow grass beds and rocky, alga-covered rubble areas.

The history of the Bahamian lobster fishery is similar to the Florida Keys lobster fishery in many ways. An internal Bahamian government report (Thompson, 1980) on the spiny lobster fishery of the Bahamas is the most comprehensive document available on the Bahamian lobster fishery. The early days of the Bahamian fishery were also local bait fisheries centered around population centers. These small, local fisheries expanded as lobsters became one of the most important food fisheries in the Bahamas. Export of spiny lobsters began in the 1930's, and as the sponge fishery declined, the lobster fishery gained in importance. In the early days, before the export market really developed in the mid 40's, Bahamian fishermen fished the shallow waters with two-pronged spears attached to wooden shafts. Bully netting with a bully net, tickler, and glass bottomed bucket (see Chapter 5 for more information on the techniques of bully netting) quickly became the method of choice. Spiny lobsters were so abundant in those days that some older fishermen remember taking over 500 in a half-day's work.

As a rule, Bahamian fishermen did not engage in lobster trapping. Successful trapping required a large number of traps, a large vessel, an expertise in trap fishing, and a large capital investment—resources that few Bahamian fishermen could acquire. In the early 1960's, refrigeration became more available, and lobster buyers began accepting lobster tails rather than whole lobsters. Lobster fishermen began to dive and spear lobsters. The high production and low overhead of spearfishing soon displaced the bully net, and spearfishing quickly became, and still is, the primary method of lobster capture by Bahamian fishermen. Spearfishing accounts for over 80 percent of the lobster now taken in the Bahamas.

A great deal of trap fishing occurred in the Bahamas, however, during the 1960's and early 70's. The Bahamian fishermen worked the shallow waters near population centers, and U.S. and Cuban fishermen on large trap boats worked the more remote areas of the Banks, primarily

Mackie Bank, South Andros, Guinchos Cay, Cay Lobos, and Cochinos Bank on the Great Bahama Banks, north of Grand Bahama Island on the Little Bahama Banks, and the Cay Sal Bank. From 1966 to 1974 the estimated catch from U.S. boats on the Bahama Banks equaled and often exceeded the annual Bahamian catch by up to three million pounds (Thompson, 1980).

Foreign fishermen also used spearfishing methods to take lobsters and employed the use of illegal SCUBA and hookah gear to extend the depth range and efficiency of spearfishing operations. The use of lobster traps in Bahamian waters was illegal from 1963 to 1973, a measure established to help catch the poachers who used traps almost exclusively during that time. Bahamians may now trap lobsters under a special permit. Although only a relatively few trap permits have been requested and issued in the past, the number of trap permits has increased in recent years.

Spanish Wells is one of the major centers of the Bahamian lobster fishery. Popov (1989) described the methods of the modern Bahamian lobster fishery. Mother ships operating out of Spanish Wells have a freezer capacity of up to 30,000 pounds of lobster tails. Some commercial lobster boats are over 85 feet long and carry a fleet of 6 to 9, 15 foot outboard boats with 40 to 50 horsepower engines. These fast outboards carry a crew of two or three spearfishermen and range far and wide over the reef systems, returning to the mother ship with their catch each evening. The lobsters are processed at sea, the heads discarded in areas remote from the fishing grounds, and the tails dipped in a sodium bisulphite solution to prevent the flesh from blackening before freezing. Fishing trips may last from two to five weeks depending on the weather, fishing success, and the season. In other areas of the Bahamas, day trips on small boats are the rule. Most of the catch is exported to the U.S. through West Palm Beach and Miami and then distributed throughout the country.

In shallow areas, spearfishermen free dive to the reefs, but in deeper areas, over 15 feet or so, a hookah rig with a hose of up to 150 feet long is used to extend the divers bottom time and depth capability. One man usually stays in the boat to tend the gas compressor that runs the hookah and to watch for promising reef habitat. When the diver slips over the side of the boat, he carries a Hawaiian sling and 4 to 6 spears about four or five feet long . He uses one spear to impale up to ten lobster and may stack lobsters on all his spears on one dive if he finds a good spot.

Fishermen in Abaco and Spanish Wells have started to put out artificial habitats in the manner of Cuban and Mexican fishermen (see Chapter 4) to concentrate lobster and increase fishing efficiency. Work is now underway at the Caribbean Marine Research Center at Lee Stocking Island in the Exuma Cays on the efficacy of artificial habitats in stock enhancement of spiny lobster. It is illegal to build artificial habitats in the Bahamas without a government permit. Lobster fishing is a lucrative occupation in the Bahamas these days. Lobsters in 1989 brought $7.50 a pound to the fishermen, and some boats can harvest up to 25,000 pounds in trips of only a few weeks. One boat from Spanish Wells brought in a record catch of 42,000 pounds in the second trip of the 1988-89 season—a catch worth well over $300,000.

There is a dark side to the current fishery practices of Bahamian commercial fishermen. The combination of spearfishing and use of compressors and hookah gear are a very efficient method of fishing lobster. The inevitable increase in fishing pressure on Bahamian lobster populations as the fishery grows, in itself casts a shadow on the future of the fishery. And when this basic technique is combined with the sickening, horribly destructive practice of bleaching the reefs to drive lobster out of deep crevices, then this shadow is dark indeed. Although completely illegal, morally reprehensible, and a criminal act against the fishery and the irreplaceable coral reefs of the Bahamas—the practice of bleaching the reef is widespread in the Bahamian fishery.

Once a diver begins to take lobster from a reef formation, many lobsters crawl deep into the reef to seek sanctuary from the intruder with the spear. These lobster are inaccessible to the diver and assure that not all the lobster are taken from the reef. The diver, however, concerned only with the immediate profit of the current trip, has learned that if he squirts household bleach, a poisonous chlorine solution, deep into the reef—the lobsters quickly leave the deep crevices and escape from the burning chlorine into open areas where they can be speared. Not only is every lobster then taken from that reef, but corals, other invertebrates, and algae are killed as well, and the reef, and its ability to support life, dies a little or a lot. The continuous use of bleach will eventually destroy the reefs. One has only to look at the decaying coral reefs of the Philippines to see the results of destructive fishing practices.

The Bahamian Government has long recognized the destructive effects of bleaching and has always outlawed this and other detrimental fishing practices, but enforcement over thousands of square miles of ocean is a difficult matter. The coral reefs of the Bahamas are the wealth, the pride, and the heritage of the Bahamian people and must not be degraded and destroyed for the short term profit of a few individuals. Let us hope that Bahamian fishermen can be persuaded through education, and their love for the unique and beautiful natural resources of their country, to discontinue this harmful practice and convince others to do likewise.

The use of hookah has greatly increased the occupational hazards of the Bahamian lobster fisherman. The use of hookah gear for lobster diving was completely illegal for many years, but the ban could not be enforced and was, and is, ignored by many Bahamian fishermen. It is now legal to use hookah for lobster diving, but only though acquisition of a special permit to do so. Many fishermen do not bother to obtain a permit and, much worse, do not obtain proper training in use of compressed air in diving operations. The dangers of nitrogen saturation of the blood leading to de-compression sickness (the bends) and air embolisms (lung distensions) are unknown or not understood by many novice divers. Every year, some Bahamian lobster divers are rushed to facilities in Miami for decompression treatment. The Bahamian Department of Fisheries has long recognized that lobster divers are at risk, has stressed the need for diver education, and has required this education through the permit process.

The Bahama Banks cover a vast area. The potential lobster grounds are considerably larger than the Florida grounds, and the vast expanses of turtle grass flats provide extensive nursery habitat for juvenile lobsters. It is difficult to estimate the potential yield of spiny lobsters from Bahamian waters, and figures for maximum sustainable yield (MSY) and optimum yield (OY) are nebulous. Catch data and unit of effort data is scarce and approximate for the Bahamas, as with most spiny lobster fisheries. Smith (1946) estimated that the potential yield of lobsters from the Bahamas was probably about 3,000,000 pounds. Thompson (1980) cites estimates of the potential yield, assuming proper minimum size and protection of egg carrying females, at about 10,000,000 pounds per year, and reports catch estimates of lobsters from Bahamian waters during the 60's and early 70's of 2 to 10 million pounds. All of these catch estimates, including the highest for 1972 and 73 of over 10 million pounds, include both the U.S. and Bahamian catch of lobsters in Bahamian waters. Current Bahamian landings from the Bahamas Department of Fisheries 1989 Annual Report show increasing production from 10,120,839 lbs. in 1987 to 13,625,897 in 1989 (tail weight converted to whole weight) (Ron Thompson, personal communication).

In areas like the Bahamas, it is usually more meaningful to estimate the standing stock and/or the potential yield in terms of the amount of lobsters that are present or can be harvested per unit of bottom area. Once this figure is known, the potential harvest from the entire area can be estimated. Mean standing crops of about 50 pounds of lobster per acre of reef area is the generally recorded stock figure. Unfortunately, there is little standardization of methods or measures in the literature. Lobster quantities are reported as numbers of individuals, pounds of whole lobster, pounds of tails, metric tons, tons, and kilograms; units of area are reported in square miles, hectares, and square kilometers. Comparisons of the actual and/or estimated potential yield of spiny lobsters between different areas and different studies is difficult, at best, because of these variations in units of measure. Basic methods, study designs, and data analysis also differ greatly, however, and these fundamental differences lead one to be apprehensive of the value of direct comparisons.

According to Thompson (1980), in 1976 the Little Bahama Bank produced an average of 358 pounds of lobster per square mile, and the Great Bahama Bank produced an average of 75 pounds of lobster per square mile. Thompson points out that a yield of 359 pounds per square mile for both banks would produce a total of 16 million pounds of lobster per year from Bahamian waters, and that this may even be a low figure for potential yield since production in Jamaican waters is around 660 pounds per square mile. Waugh (1981) discusses density of lobster population in numbers of lobsters per hectare (ha) (a hectare is a metric unit of area equal to 100 ares, which is 10,000 square meters or 2.471 acres). In Waugh's 1981 study, he found densities of 84, 744, and 1,230 lobsters/ha in the three years, 1976, 77, and 78, on the northern shore of Grand Bahama Island and 328 and 766 lobsters/ha in two years, 1977 and 78, on the southern shore—a grand average of about 630 lobsters/ha. Waugh points out that this is considerably higher than other studies have reported in the Virgin Islands and Tortugas, 15 to 65 lobsters/ha.

Smith and van Nierop (1986) conducted a visual census of the Little and Great Bahama Banks as part of a UNDP/FAO Fisheries Development Project in the Bahamas.

They estimated the standing stock and potential yield of spiny lobster on these Banks in kilograms per square kilometer, kg/km^2. According to the estimates of Smith and van Nierop (1986) based on actual count and size estimates of lobsters on various types of bottoms at randomly selected stations on both Bank areas, the Little Bahama Banks have a mean lobster density of 420 kg/km^2, and the Great Bahama Banks have a mean lobster density of 287 kg/km2. For comparison, landings in Florida indicate that the Florida grounds have a mean lobster density of over 371 kg/km^2. The results of Smith and van Nierop's survey indicate that landings of spiny lobster from the Little Bahamas Bank are 30% of the estimated annual potential yield, and landings from the Great Bahamas Bank are only 10% of the estimated annual potential yield.

If these estimates are reasonably accurate, the Bahamian lobster fishery has ample room to expand, and given the inevitable future increase in the human population of the Bahamas and in worldwide demand for the succulent spiny lobster, the Bahamian lobster fishery will expand to fit the resource, as did the Florida fishery. With proper management and knowlegable fishermen, the Bahamian fishery will develop into an extremely valuable fishery that respects and protects the resource and enjoys a stable optimum annual yield. The alternative is a dying fishery that destroys the

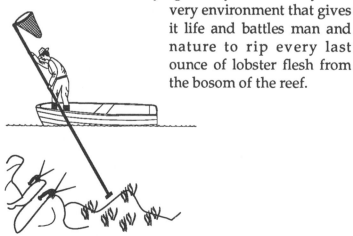

very environment that gives it life and battles man and nature to rip every last ounce of lobster flesh from the bosom of the reef.

Puerto Rico and the US Virgin Islands

The territorial seas of the United States Commonwealth of Puerto Rico and the Territory of the United States Virgin Islands form a single Fishery Conservation Zone (FCZ). This fishery zone includes the southern end of the Greater Antilles island chain and borders The Dominican Republic and Navided Bank on the west and the British Virgin Islands and the Leeward Islands of the West Indies on the east. State waters extend from the shoreline to 3 miles offshore and are not under federal jurisdiction.

There is a commercial and recreational fishery for spiny lobsters in Puerto Rican and U.S. Virgin Island waters. The annual harvest in the early 1980's for the entire region was estimated at 582,000 to 830,000 pounds. The intensity of the fishery was such that fishermen began taking smaller lobster to sustain their established yield from the fishery, and there were conflicts between commercial, recreational, and non-consumptive users. It is estimated that 21.3% (328 sq. miles) of the Puerto Rican shelf area is lobster habitat, the St. Thomas-St. John shelf has 10% lobster habitat (47.5 sq. miles), and the St. Croix shelf has 25% lobster habitat (25 sq. miles). The maximum sustainable yield of the this area was estimated at 610,000 pounds/year for Puerto Rico, 116,900 pounds/year for St. Thomas-St. John, and 102,400 pounds/year for St. Croix. The minimum size for an optimum yield in the range of 582,000 to 830,000 pounds/year was set at a 3.5 inch CL. The entire harvest is consumed locally, and lobsters are also imported to fulfill market demand. The main commercial fishing gear in the early 1980's was mostly wire fish traps and a few wooden and iron wire lobster traps. Recreational and commercial divers use tail snares and illegal spears and gaffs. Harvest of egg-bearing females is illegal as is use of explosives, chemicals, and hooks in taking lobsters. Recreational catch data is not recorded, but is estimated to be about 10% of the catch in Puerto Rico and 6 to 52% of the catch in Virgin Island waters.

Caribbean Lobster Fisheries

There are other important spiny lobster fisheries in the western central Atlantic. Many of these fisheries, such as those of Cuba, Bermuda, Puerto Rico, Mexico, Jamaica, and many of the island nations with small continental shelf areas, are now well established and may be approaching maximum levels of exploitation. The lobster fisheries around relatively small islands with limited continental shelf resources are mainly bycatch from Antillian wire-trap finfish fisheries and cannot be managed as a fisheries separate from the wire-trap finfishery. The demand for spiny lobsters in the hotels and restaurants of new and old Caribbean resorts, and the money to be made from the export of lobsters from far out islands to the population and tourist centers of the Caribbean has greatly expanded the lobster fisheries of the region in the last couple of decades. A few of these fisheries are mentioned below to provide some information on the general nature of small Caribbean lobster fisheries.

The lobster fishery of the **Turks & Caicos Islands** of the British West Indies are now overexploited and in need of management (Simon, 1983). The MSY of this fishery was estimated by Simon (1983) to be 606,732 pounds. The major problems in the fishery were poaching by foreign vessels and overfishing of the resource.

The lobster fishery of the **Grenadines** in the windward islands of the Lesser Antilles was described by Adams (1977). The fishery was not developed until the 1950's, after a large market for lobster developed in Martinique. Up to that time, large lobsters could be found in shallow water under every rock and ledge. Dozens of lobsters could be collected in just a few hours. In 1974, the lobster catch was about 100,000 pounds per year, and about 150 men were employed in the fishery. About half the catch was used in the Grenadines and half exported to other markets. The fishermen dove for lobsters, but used a wire tail snare instead of a spear. This was necessary because refrigeration and ice were scarce and the lobsters had to be kept alive in wire cages for several days to a week or so before transport to market. SCUBA gear was just coming into use in the Grenadine fishery in the mid 70's. Even at that time the need for fishery management was apparent and fishermen were ranging far afield to find lobster and resenting the development of management measures.

The **Jamaica** spiny lobster fishery has been studied by Munro (1974), Aiken (1977), and Haughton and Shaul (1989). The fishing grounds include the south Jamaica Shelf, a broad area that sustains fairly heavy fishing pressure; the north and the southeast and southwest shelf areas that are narrow and sustain very heavy fishing pressure from small vessels; and the rather distant Pedro Bank that sustains lighter fishing pressure. The fishery in the 70's was primarily a trap fishery. Spiny lobster were harvested at small sizes on the Jamaica Banks, and this caused concern for the fishery. Aiken (1977) proposed that an initial minimum size of 2¾ inch CL (70 mm) be set and then raised every two years until a minimum size of 3⅜ inch CL (85 mm) was reached. Haughton and Shaul (1989) report that the fishery exported about 1.5 million dollars in lobsters to the U.S. in 1986. The Antillean wire Z traps that were in almost exclusive use in the 70's are still in use by artisanal fishermen, but wooden lobster traps are now used to fish exclusively for lobster by larger boats. These large boats now fish 1,500 to 2,000 traps on the Pedro Bank. The lobsters taken in the Antillean wire traps are marketed whole and alive, while the lobster taken in wooden traps are processed aboard the boat, and are landed as tails, dipped in sodium bisulphate, and kept under refrigeration.

The spiny lobster fishery of **Antigua and Barbuda** was investigated by Peacock (1974). At the time of that study in 1973, the landings of spiny lobster had been declining at a rate of about 15% per year. This is a small scale fishery composed of three sectors. A small inshore fishery takes place in lagoon and near shore areas. The catch is consumed locally. A diving fishery was composed of about 10 to 15 full time fishermen that dive the reefs and use tail snares to catch live lobsters. This catch, amounting to about 25,000 pounds per year, was exported live to Puerto Rico. The trap fishery occurs on the offshore banks to the west and between the islands at depths of 50 to 150 feet. A fleet of 38, 25 to 40 foot, diesel powered sloops composed the trap fishery. Unbaited, wire Antillean fish traps were used to catch both fish and lobster, with fish being the most important catch. Use of other types of traps for lobsters have not been successful. About 110,000 pounds of lobsters were exported per year from this fishery at that time.

Peacock found that post larvae settled on mangrove roots near shore, particularly in the mouth of the large lagoon on Barbuda throughout the year, with highest settlement during the months of May to October. Peacock postulated that the peak settlement during two relatively short periods in summer, each about a weeks duration, was a result of large water masses carrying late stage larvae passing by Antigua. Analysis of modal length data indicated that lobsters migrated from the inshore areas toward the offshore reefs, leaving in April through June and arriving on the offshore reefs in December through February. The lagoons harbored large numbers of small lobsters and apparently served as nursery areas for the population. Peacock recommended that fishing in the lagoon areas be reduced as much as possible.

The spiny lobster management program of **St. Kitts/Nevis** was discussed by Wilkin et al. (1986). St. Kitts/Nevis are located in the windward islands of the

Lesser Antilles north of Guadeloupe and west of the Virgin Islands. The lobster fishery was made up of about a third of the 238 boats in the fishery. Although the fishery was traditionally an Antillean trap fishery, there has been a move to spearfishing using SCUBA diving equipment. The annual catch was estimated at about 65,000 pounds, and this was also the estimated MSY of the fishery. Overfishing was likely at that time since fishermen were complaining that lobsters were scarce, and SCUBA divers were going to deeper waters to find lobster. This increased the risk to divers because few were properly trained in SCUBA diving techniques. Fishermen also disregarded fishery regulations and captured undersized lobsters and egg carrying females. The government of St. Kitts/Nevis was concerned about the developing problems in the lobster fishery and began a program to obtain data on the fishery and develop proper management of the fishery. A legal minimum size of a 95 mm CL (3.75 inches) was proposed that would allow for at least one reproductive season for the female lobsters. Education of the fishermen and the public as to the need for fishery management was considered very important.

South American Lobster Fisheries

According to Fonteles-Filho (1990), the **Brazilian** lobster fishery began in 1955 and was concentrated on the northeastern and eastern shelf areas. It is the second largest warmwater lobster fishery in the world. The fishing fleet was composed of wooden rafts and sailing canoes until the 1960's and then fishermen began to use motorized craft. Large, modern boats with freezer capacity that can make trips of up to 60 days duration are now common in the fishery. The large motorized boats fish with traps, and the smaller sail powered boats fish gill nets, which are illegal, but the regulation is difficult to enforce. They operate from the port of Fortaleza, and about 80% of the Brazilian lobster catch is landed at this port.

The Brazilian catch is made up of the Caribbean spiny lobster, *Panulirus argus*, average landings of 5,280 metric tons per year from 1965 to 1987; and the smoothtail lobster, *Panulirus laevicauda*, average landings of 2,256 metric tons in the same period. Landings reported for the period March through November, 1987, were 3869 tons of *P. argus* and 5356 tons of *P. laevicauda*. Recruitment into the fishery is about 50 million individuals of each species, and this provides a virtual population of about 31 million lobsters. About 18.5 million are taken by the fishery. The landings in the fishery have been in decline since 1982 despite discovery of new grounds and a three-fold increase in the size of the total fishing area. A four month closed season has been established, December through March, to protect the fishery, and a minimum tail size of 13 cm (5.1 inches) for *P. argus* and 10.6 cm (4.2 inches) for *P. laevicauda* was also enacted. Slipper lobsters are also taken and are common in Brazilian markets and restaurants.

The lobster fishery of **Venezuela** is centered on the island of Los Roques in the southern Caribbean. It was a trap fishery in the 1960's and early 70's and was suffering a decline in landings over the decade of the 60's. Landings decreased from 140 tons in 1962-63 to about 100 tons in 1969-70. The catch per trap dropped from 17 to 9 kg, and it was estimated that the maximum sustainable yield could be realized with 50 to 60% of the 13,000 traps in the fishery at that time (Griffiths and Simpson, 1973).

Brazil's lobster fishery is one of the most developed in South America, but other countries—French Guiana, Suriname, Guyana, Venezuela, and Columbia—also have offshore lobster grounds and developed or developing lobster fisheries. The Central American countries with Caribbean coasts, Panama, Costa Rica, Nicaragua, Honduras, Belize, Mexico, and to some extent Guatemala, also have lobster fisheries. The Caribbean continental shelf off southern Honduras and Nicaragua is broad and leads to the Rosalind Bank and other relatively shallow banks in the western Caribbean that can be fished for spiny lobster. The Pedro Bank south of Jamaica is a large, shallow, central Caribbean bank that has been fished for lobster by Jamaican fishermen for many years, although less intensively than the south Jamaican bank. And then, of course, there are the many island nations that lie on the eastern and northern rim of the Caribbean Sea. Most of these support low technology fisheries that are growing and expanding every year as the demand for lobster to satisfy the tourist industry and export markets also grows. Integrated, or at least interactive, management of all the lobster fisheries in the western central Atlantic, the Caribbean, and the Gulf will eventually become essential.

The state of the resource and the management of spiny lobster fisheries in the broad area of the Caribbean, the Bahamas, and Florida has been discussed by Cato and Prochaska (1980) and Caddy (1989). These papers, and Beardsley et al. (1975) and the Fishery Management Plans for Florida and Puerto Rico, discuss the kind of data and information that is necessary for the proper management of the various Caribbean spiny lobster fisheries. Waugh and Goodwin (1986) present examples of a data sheet and data analysis from a project designed to collect essential data on Caribbean spiny lobster fisheries. This data sheet illustrates the type of data fishery managers need to adequately understand and manage a spiny lobster fishery. Despite the high economic and social value of Caribbean spiny lobster fisheries, there is relatively little funding available for research. For now, the one thing that all fishery managers and scientists stress as being of utmost importance is accurate fishery data. The need for information, fishery statistics on the catch and the fishery, as they now exist in every fishery, is crucial to the future management of all the fisheries.

References

Hundreds of scientific papers and popular articles have been written about the fisheries and biology of spiny lobsters. Many of these papers are buried deep in the archives of specialized libraries where only professional marine biologists and advanced students have easy access to them. The references listed below identify the source of most of the information presented in this book and allow those with a further interest in lobsters to find the original scientific papers. Sims (1966) and Kanciruk and Herrnkind (1976), both listed below, are extensive bibliographies and are very helpful references to the older worldwide literature on spiny lobsters.

ABELE, L.G. and W. KIM. 1986. An Illustrated Guide to the Marine Decapod Crustaceans of Florida. Parts I & II. State of Florida Dept. of Environmental Reg., Fla. State Univ., Tech. Series. 8(1): 760 p.

ADAMS, J.E. 1972. The lobster fishing industry of Mt. Pleasant, Bequia Island, West Indies. Proc. Gulf and Caribbean Fish. Instut. 1971. 24: 126-133.

ADAMS, J.E. 1977. Spiny lobster fishing in the Grenadines. Sea Frontiers. 23(6): 322-330.

ADEY, W.H. and K. LOVELAND. 1991. Dynamic Aquaria: Building Living Ecosystems. Academic Press. Harcourt Brace Jovanovich, San Diego, CA. USA. 704 pp.

AIKEN, D.E. 1980. Molting and growth. *in:* The Biology and Management of of Lobsters. Editors, J. S. Cobb and B.F. Phillips., Vol. I. Physiology and behavior: pp 91-163. Acad. Press, N.Y.: 463 p.

AIKEN, K.A. 1977. Jamaica spiny lobster investigations. *in* Symposium on progress in marine research in the Caribbean and adjacent regions. FAO Fish. Rept. No. 200: 11-22.

ALMOG-SHTAYER, G. 1988. Behavioral-ecological aspect of Mediterranean lobsters in the past and of the slipper lobster, *Scyllarides latus* in the present. M.A. Thesis, University of Haifa, Israel (in Hebrew): 165 p.

ANONYMOUS. 1983. A look at lobsters. National Fisherman, November 1983. *64* (7):64-71.

ANSLEY, H.L.H. 1983. Chapter IV. Identification and quantification of spiny lobster *Panulirus argus* (Latreille), populations on the Georgia outer continental shelf, 1979-1981. *in* Studies and assessment of Georgia's marine fisheries resources 1977-1981. Completion Report. Ga. Dept. Nat. Res., Coast. Res. Div. 456-494.

AUSTIN, C.B. 1989. How to measure the potential advantages of limited entry. Proc. Gulf and Caribbean Fish. Inst., 1986. *39:* 12-22.

AUSTIN, H.M. 1972. Notes on the distribution of phyllosoma of the spiny lobster, *Panulirus* ssp., in the Gulf of Mexico. Proc. Nat. Shellfish Assoc. *62:* 25-30.

BAIN, J. 1967. Investigations into the effectiveness of escape gaps in crayfish traps. New Zealand Marine Department. Fish. Tech. Report. No 17. 18p.

BAISRE, J.A. and M.E. RUIZ de QUEVEDO. 1964. Sobre los estudios larvales de la langosta comun, *Panulirus argus*, Contr. Inst. nat. Pesca Cuba *19:* 1-37.

BAISRE, J.A. and M.E. RUIZ de QUEVEDO. 1982. Two phyllosomalarvae of *Panulirus laevicauda* (Latreille, 1817) (Decapoda, Palinuridae) from the Caribbean Sea with a discussion about larval groups within the genus. Crustaceana. *43:* 147-153.

BARDACH, J.E, J.H. RYTHER, and W.O. McLARNEY. 1972. Aquaculture: The farming and husbandry of freshwater and marine organisms. John Wiley & Sons. New York, NY. USA. 868 p.

BATHAM, E.J. 1967. The first three larval stages and feeding behaviour of phyllosoma of the New Zealand Palinurid crayfish *Jasus edwardii* (Hutton 1875). Trans. Royal Soc. New Zealand. *9*(6): 53-64.

BEARDSLEY, G.L. 1973. Studies of the tropical Atlantic spiny lobster, *Panulirus guttatus* (Latreille). 1. Notes on distribution, size, sex ratios and commercial potential along the southeast coast of Florida. Univ. Miami Sea Grant Program.

BEARDSLEY, G.L., T.J. COSTELLO, G.E. DAVIS, A.C. JONES, and D.C. SIMMINS. 1975. The Florida spiny lobster fishery: a white paper. Florida Sci. *38* (3): 144-149.

BERG, C.J. JR., J.B. MITTON and K.S. ORR. 1986. Genetic analyses of the queen conch, *Strombus gigas*, 1. Preliminary implications for fishery management. Proc. Gulf and Caribbean Fish. Instit. *37*: 112-118.

BILL, R.G. and W.F. HERRNKIND. 1976. Drag reduction by formation movement in spiny lobsters. Science. *193:* 1146-1148.

BORTONE, S.A. 1986. Fisheries Biology for Everyone. Sea Grant Extension Bulletin, SG EB-11. Florida Sea Grant, Gainesville, Fl. 169 p.

BOWEN, B.K. 1963. Effectiveness of escape gaps in crayfish pots. Western Australia Fisheries Dept. Report II. 13 p.

BRADY, J. 1991. Florida's flaming reef lobster. Skin Diver. *40* (1): 34-40.

BROWER, K. 1981. Life by night in a desert sea. National Geographic. *160* (6): 834-847.

BUESA MAS, R.J. 1970. Migraciones de la langosta (*Panulirus argus*). Mar y Pesca *60* :22-27. Translated from Spanish by P. Aulkand, Nat. Mar. Fish. Serv., Foreign Fish. Transl. 11403, 10p.

BURNETT-HERKES, J., B. LUCKHURST and J. WARD. 1989. Management of Antillean trap fisheries—Bermuda's Experience. Proc. Gulf and Caribbean Fish. Inst., 1986, *39*: 5-11.

BURUKOVSKII, R.N. 1982. Key to shrimps and lobsters. Oxonian Press Pvt. Ltd., New Delhi. 164 p.

CADDY, J.F. 1989. A personal perspective on future cooperative research on lobsters: The International Lobster Recruitment Workshop Held in St. Andrews, N.B. Pro. Gulf and Caribbean Fish. Inst., 1986. *39*: 302-317.

CAILLOUET, Jr., C.W., G.L. BEARDSLEY, G.L. and N. CHITTY. 1971. Notes on size, sex ratio, and spawning of the spiny lobster, *Panulirus guttatus* (Latreille), near Miami Beach, Florida. Bull. Mar. Sci. *21* (4): 944-951.

CALINSKI, M.D. 1981. Natural behavior and recruitment of postlarval spiny lobsters, *Panulirus argus*, in the lower West Indies. *in* Proceedings of a Workshop on Florida Spiny Lobster Research and Management. W. Lyons, Editor. Fla. Dept. Nat. Resour., Marine Research Laboratory. p 5.

CALINSKI, M. D. and W. G. LYONS. 1983. Swimming behavior of the puerulus of the spiny lobster *Panulirus argus* (Latreille, 1804) (Crustacea: Palinuridae. Jour. Crustacean Bio. *3* (3); 329-335.

CARIBBEAN FISHERY MANAGEMENT COUNCIL. 1981. Environmental Impact Statement/Fishery Management Plan and Regulatory Impact Review for the Spiny Lobster Fishery of Puerto Rico and the U.S. Virgin Islands. July, 1981: 43 p.

CATO, J.C. and F.J. PROCHASKA. 1980. Economic Management Concepts in Small Scale Spiny Lobster Fisheries. Proc. Gulf and Caribbean Fish. Inst., 1980. *33*: 301-321.

CHACE, F.A. and W.H. DUMONT. 1949. Spiny lobsters identification, world distribution and U.S. trade. Comm. Fish. Rev. *11* (5): 1-12.

CHITTLEBOROUGH, R.G. 1974. Western rock lobster reared to maturity. Aust. Journal Mar. Freshwater Res. *25:* 221-225.

CHITTY, N. 1973. Aspects of the reproductive biology of the spiny lobster, *Panulirus guttatus* (Latreille). MS Thesis, Univ. of Miami.

CLINE, G.B. and C.W. HARDWICK, Jr. 1986. Habitraps: a new type of trap for Scyllarid and other lobsters. Pro. Ala. Acad. Sci. *56* (3): 77.

COBB, J.S. and B.F. PHILLIPS (editors). 1980. The Biology and Management of Lobsters. Vol. I. Physiology and Behavior. Acad. Press, N.Y., 463 p. Vol. II. Ecology and Management. Acad. Press, N.Y.: 390 p.

COLIN, P.L. 1978. Caribbean Reef Invertebrates and Plants. T.F.H. Publications, Inc., Neptune City, N.J.: 512 p.

CRAIG, A.K. 1974. New developments in the S.E. Florida spiny lobster fishery. Gulf and Carib. Fish. Inst. *26*: 131-143.

CRAWFORD, D.R. and W.J.J. de SMIDT. 1922. The spiny lobster, *Panulirus argus* of southern Florida, its natural history and utilization. Fish. Bull., U.S. *38*: 281-310.

CREASER, E.P. 1950. Repetition of egg-laying and the number of eggs of the Bermuda spiny loster. Proc. Gulf Carib. Fish. Inst. 2: 30-31.

CUSHING, D.H. 1981. Fisheries Biology, A Study in Population Dynamics. Second Edition. University of Wisconsin Press, Madison, WI, USA: 295 p.

DAVIS, G.E. 1979. Management recommendations for juvenile spiny lobsters, *Panulirus argus*, in Biscayne National Monument, Florida. U.S. Nat. Park Serv., S. Fla. Res. Cent. Manage. Rep. M-350: 32 p.

DAVIS, G.E. 1980. Juvenile spiny lobster management. Fisheries 5 (4): 57-59.

DAVIS, G.E. 1981. Effects of injuries on spiny lobster, *Panulirus argus*, and implications for fishery management. Fish. Bull. U.S. 78: 979-984.

DAVIS, G.E. and J.W. DODRILL. 1980. Marine parks and sanctuaries for spiny lobster fisheries management. Proc. Gulf and Carib. Fish. Inst. *32*: 194-207.

DAVIS, G.E. and J.W. DODRILL. 1989. Recreational fishery and population dynamics of spiny lobsters, *Panulirus argus*, in Florida Bay, Everglades National Park, 1977-1980. Bull. Mar. Sci. 44(1): 78-88.

DAWSON, C.E. 1949. Florida crawfish research. Proc. Gulf and Carib. Fish. Inst. *1*: 21-28.

DeALTERIS, J.R., R. BULLOCK and W. ROMEY. 1988. Brine dip for lobster traps. Jour. Shellfish Res. 7: 445-451.

de GRAAF, F. 1982. Marine Tropical Aquarium Guide, (English translation, Dr. Joseph Spiekerman). T.F.H. Publications, Inc., Neptune City, NJ, USA: 284 p.

DEBELIUS, H. 1984. Armoured Knights of the Sea. English version, Alfred Kernen Verlag, distributed in the U.S. by Quality Marine, Los Angeles, CA.: 120 p.

DEES, L.T. 1968. Spiny lobsters. U.S. Dept. Interior. Fish and Wild-life Service. Fish. Leaf. 523: 7 p.

DEXTER, D.M. 1972. Molting and growth in laboratory reared phyllosomes of the California spiny lobster, *Panulirus interruptus*. Calif. Fish and Game. *58*(2): 107-115.

FARMER, M.W. 1983. Large scale dispersal and recruitment of phyllosoma larvae (Palinuridae, *Panulirus*). unpublished manuscript: 13 p.

FARMER, M.W. and C.J. BERG, JR. 1989. Circulation around islands, gene flow, and fisheries management. Pro. Gulf and Caribbean Fish. Inst., 1986. *39*: 318-330.

FARMER, M.W., J. WARD and B.E. LUCKHURST. 1989. Development of spiny lobster (*Panulirus argus*) phyllosoma larvae in the plankton near Bermuda. Pro. Gulf and Caribbean Fish. Inst., 1986. *39*: 289-301.

FILHO, J.F. 1970. On the occurrence of *Enoplometopus antillensis* Lutken, 1865 (Decapoda, Nephropidae) on the Brazilian coast. Crustaceana. *18* (1): 55-59.

FONTELES-FILHO, A.A. 1990. The fishery for spiny lobsters in Brazil. The Lobster Newsletter, J. S. Cobb and J. Pringle, Ed. *3*(1): 8-9.

FOX, W.W., Jr. 1970. An exponential surplus-yield model for optimizing exploited fish populations. Trans. Amer. Fish. Soc. *99*(1): 80-88.

FRAZEL, D.W. 1986. The effect of escape gaps on capture of the spiny lobster, *Panulirus argus* (Latreille), with notes on the impact of escape gaps on behavior. Masters Thesis, Nova University, Oceanographic Center, Dania, FL.

GEORGE, R.W. and A.R. MAIN. 1967. The evolution of spiny lobsters (Palinuridae): A study of evolution in the marine environment. Evolution. *21*: 803-820.

GLAHOLT, R.D. 1990. Social behavior and habitat use of captive juvenile spiny lobster, *Panulirus argus* (Latreille 1804) (Decapoda, Palinuridae). Crustaceana. *58*(2): 200-205.

GREGORY, D.R. and R.F. LABISKY. 1981. Ovigerous setae as an indicator of reproductive maturity in the spiny lobster, *Panulirus argus* (Latreille). Northeast Gulf Sci. *4* (2): 109-113.

GREGORY, D.R. and R.F. LABISKY. 1986. Movements of the spiny lobster *Panulirus argus* in south Florida. Canad. Jour. Fish. and Aquatic Sci. *43* (11): 2228-2234.

GREGORY, D.R., R.F. LABISKY and C.L. COMBS. 1982. Reproductive dynamics of the spiny lobster *Panulirus argus* in south Florida. Trans. Amer. Fish. Soc. *111* (5):575-584.

GRIFFITHS, R.C. and J.G. SIMPSON. 1973. The present status of the exploitation and evaluation of the fishery resources of Venezula. Proc. of the Gulf and Caribbean Fish. Instit., Nov. 1972. *25*: 129-155.

GULF OF MEXICO AND SOUTH ATLANTIC FISHERY MANAGEMENT COUNCILS. 1981. Fishery Management Plan Environmental Impact Statement and Regulatory Impact Review for Spiny Lobster in the Gulf of Mexico and South Atlantic. April 1981.

   Amendment Number 1 to Spiny Lobster Fishery Management Plan, February, 1987
   Amendment Number 2 to Spiny Lobster Fishery Management Plan, July, 1989.
   Amendment Number 3 to Spiny Lobster Fishery Management Plan, November, 1990.

HARDIN, G. 1968. The tragedy of the commons. Science, *162:* 1243-1248.

HARDWICK, JR., C.W. 1987. Biochemical, biological, and morphometric data on the slipper lobster, *Scyllarides nodifer*, from the Eastern Gulf of Mexico. A Dissertation. The University of Alabama at Birmingham: 135 p.

HAUGHTON, M. and W. SHAUL. 1989. Estimation of growth parameters for the spiny lobster (*Panulirus argus*) in Jamacian Waters. Pro. Gulf and Caribbean Fish. Inst., 1986. *39*: 279-288.

HEATWOLE, D.W., J. HUNT and F.S. KENNEDY, JR. 1988. Catch efficiencies of live lobster decoys and other attractants in the Florida spiny lobster fishery. Fla. Dept. Nat. Res., Fla. Marine Res. Pub. No. 44: 15 p.

HERRNKIND, W.F. 1969. Queing behavior of spiny lobsters. Science *164* (3886): 1425-1427.

HERRNKIND, W.F. 1980. Chap. 7. Spiny Lobsters: Patterns of Movement. *in:* The Biology and Management of of Lobsters. Editors, J. S. Cobb and B.F. Phillips., Vol. I. Physiology and behavior: pp 349-407. Acad. Press, N.Y.: 463 p.

HERRNKIND, W.F. 1985. Evolution and Mechanisms of Mass Single-file Migration in Spiny Lobster: synopsis. *in* Migration: Mechanisms and adaptive significance, M. A. Rankin (editor) Contributions in Marine Science Supplement, *27*: 197-211.

HERRNKIND, W.F. and M.J. BUTLER, IV. 1986. Factors regulating postlarval settlement and juvenile microhabitat use by spiny lobsters *Panulirus argus*. Mar. Ecol. Prog. Ser. *34*: 23-30.

HERRNKIND, W.F. and P. KANCIRUK. 1978. Mass Migration of Spiny Lobster, *Panulirus argus* (Crustacea: Palinuridae: Synopsis and Orientation. *in* Animal Migration, Navigation and Homing. Ed. K. Schmidt-Koenig and W.T. Keeton. Springer-Verlag, N.Y., USA: 430-439.

HERRNKIND, W.F., P. KANCIRUK, J.HALUSKY, and R. Mc-LEAN. 1973. Descriptive characterization of mass autumnal migrations of spiny lobster, *Panulirus argus*. Proc. Gulf and Caribbean Fish. Instit. November, 1972. *25*: 79-98.

HERRNKIND, W.F. and R.N. LIPCIUS. 1989. Habitat use and population biology of Bahamian spiny lobster. Pro. Gulf and Caribbean Inst., 1986. *39*: 265-278.

HERRNKIND, W.F. and M.X. REDIG. 1975. Preliminary study of establishment of den residency by spiny lobster, *Panulirus argus*, at Grand Bahama Island. Hydro-Lab Jour. *3*: 96-101.

HERRNKIND, W.F., J.A. VANDERWALKER and L. BARR. 1975. Population dynamics, ecology and behavior of spiny lobsters, *Panulirus argus*, of St. John, U.S.V.I.: (IV) Habitation, patterns of movement and general behavior. Relults of the Tektite Program. Bull. Nat. Hist. Muse. of Los Angeles Co. *20*:31-45.

HOLTHUIS, L.B. 1946. The decapod macrura of the Snellius Expedition, I. The Stenopodidae, Nephropsidae, Scyllaridae, and Palinuridae. Biol. Res. Snellius Expd. XIV.

HOLTHUIS, L.B. 1959. The crustacea decapoda of Suriname (Dutch Guiana). Zool. Verh., Leiden No. 44: 1.219.

HOLTHUIS, L.B. 1960. Preliminary descriptions of one new genus, 12 new species and 3 new subspecies of the scyllarid lobsters (Crustacea Decapoda Macrura). Proc. Biol. Soc. Wash., 73: 147-154.

HOLTHUIS, L.B. 1961. The taxonomic status of *Panulirus echinatus* Smith, 1989 (Cecapoda Macrura, Palinuridae). Crustaceana, 2(3): 223-227.

HOLTHUIS, L.B. 1969. A new species of shovel-nose lobster, *Scyllarus planorbis*, from the southwestern Caribbean and northern South America. Bull. Mar. Sci. 19 (1): 149-158.

HOLTHUIS, L.B. 1974. The lobsters of the superfamily Nephropidea of the Atlantic Ocean (Crustacea: Decapoda). Bull. Mar. Sci. 24 (4): 723-884.

HOLTHUIS, L.B. 1983. Notes on the genus *Enoplometopus*, with descriptions of a new subgenus and two new species (Crustacea Decapoda, Axidae). Zool. Meded. Rijksmus. Natuur. Hist. Leiden 56 (22): 281-298.

HUGHES, J.T. 1973. Aquaculture: Lobsters. Sea Scope. Fall. 1973: p 1,6, and 7.

HUGHES, J.T. and G.T. MATTHIESSEN. 1962. Observations on the biology of the the American lobster, *Homarus americanus*. Liminology and Oceanography, 7(3): 414-421.

HUNT, J.H. 1981. The effect of fishery practices on the Florida Keys spiny lobster population. *in* Proceedings of a Workshop on Florida Spiny Lobster Research and Management. W. Lyons, Editor. Fla. Dept. Nat. Resour., Marine Research Laboratory: p 21.

HUNT, J.H. and W.G. LYONS. 1985. Comparisons of catch rate and size frequency of spiny lobsters, *Panulirus argus*, captured in standard traps and traps with escape gaps. Unpublished Manuscript, Fl. Dept. Nat. Resources, Fl. Marine Research Inst., St. Petersburg, FL.

HUNT, J.H. and W.G. LYONS. 1986. Factors affecting growth and maturation of spiny lobsters, *Panulirus argus*, in the Florida Keys. Canad. Jour. Fish. and Aquatic Sci. *43* (11): 2243-2247.

HUNT, J.H., W.G. LYONS and F.S. KENNEDY, Jr. 1986. Effects of exposure and confinement on spiny lobsters, *Panulirus argus*, used as attractants in the Florida trap fishery. Fish. Bull. *84* (1): 69-76.

IGARASHI, M.A., J. KITTAKA, and E. KAWAHARA. 1990. Phyllosoma culture with inoculation of marine bacteria. Nippon Suisan Gakkaishi. *56*(11): 1781-1786.

INGLE, R.M. and R. WITHHAM. 1968. Biological considerations in spiny lobster culture. Proc. Gulf and Caribbean Fish Inst., November 1968. 22: 158-162.

INOUE, M. 1981. Special Rep. Kanagawa Pref. Fish. Exp. St. *1*: 1-91.

INOUE, M. and M. NONAKA. 1963. Notes on cultured larvae of the Japanese spiny lobster, *Panulirus japonicus* (von Siebold). Bull. Jap. Soc. Sci. Fish. *29* (3): 211-218.

ITO, M. 1990. The complete larval development of the Scyllarid lobster, *Scyllarus demani* Holthuis 1946 (Decapoda, Scyllaridae) in the laboratory. Crustaceana. *58*(2): 144-167.

IVERSON, E.S. and G.L. BEARDSLEY. 1976. Shell disease in Crustaceans indigenous to South Florida. Prog. Fish-Cult. *38* (4): 195-196.

JOHNSON, B.L. and R.A. STEIN. 1986. Competition for open-access resources: A class exercise that demonstrates the tragedy of the commons. Fisheries *11*(3): 2-6.

JOHNSON, M.W. 1956. The larval development of the California spiny lobster, *Panulirus interruptus* (Randall), with notes on *Panulirus gracilis*. Proc. Galif. Acad. Sci., Ser 4, *26*(1): 1-19.

JOHNSON, M.W. 1971. The palinurid and scyllarid lobster larvae of the tropical eastern Pacific and their distribution as related to the prevailing hydrography. Bull. Scripps Inst. Ocean. *19*: 36 p.

JONES, A.C, S.A. BERKELEY, J.A. BOHNSACK, S.A. BORTONE, D.K. CAMP, G.H. DARCY, J.C. DAVIS, K.D. HADDAD, M.Y. HEDGEPETH, E.W. IRBY, Jr, W.C. JAAP, F.S. KENNEDY, Jr., W.G. LYONS, E.L. NAKAMURA, T.H. PERKINS, J.K. REED, K.A. STEIDINGER, J.T. TILMANT, and R.O. WILLIAMS. 1985. Ocean habitat and fishery resources of Florida. *in* Florida Aquatic Habitat and Fishery Resources, W. Seaman, Jr., Editor. Fla. Chap. Amer. Fish. Soc.: 437-542. (available from: Florida AFS, 207 West Carroll Street, Kissimmee, FL 32741)

KANCIRUK, P. 1980. Ecology of Juvenile and Aadult Palinuridae (SpinyLlobsters). *in* J.S. Cobb and B.F. Phillips (editors), The Biology and Management of Lobsters. Vol. II, Ecology and Management. p. 59-96. Acad. Press, N.Y.: 390 p.

KANCIRUK, P. and W. HERRNKIND. 1976. Autumnal reproduction in *Panulirus argus* at Bimini, Bahamas. Bull. Mar. Sci. *26*(4): 417-432.

KANCIRUK, P. and W. HERRNKIND, Editors. 1976. An indexed bibliobraphy of the spiny lobsters, Family Palinuridae. Fla. Sea Grant Prog. Report No. 8: 101 p.

KANCIRUK, P. and W. HERRNKIND. 1978. Mass migration of spiny lobster, *Panulirus argus* (Crustacea: Palinuridae): Behavior and Environmental Correlates. Bull. Mar. Sci., *28*(4): 601-623.

KENNEDY, F.S. Jr. 1981. Catch rates of lobster traps baited with shorts, with notes on effects of confinement. *in* Proceedings of a Workshop on Florida Spiny Lobster Research and Management. W. Lyons, Editor. Fla. Dept. Nat. Resour., Marine Research Laboratory. p. 20.

KENSLER, C.G. 1970. The potential of lobster culture. The American Fish Farmer. *1*(11): 8-12, 27.

KITTAKA, J. and K. KIMURA. 1989. Culture of the Japanese spiny lobster *Panulirus japonicus* from egg to juvenile stage. Nippon Suisan Gakkaishi. *55* (6): 963-970.

LABISKY, R., GREGORY, D. Jr. and J.A. CONTI. 1980. Florida's spiny lobster fishery: an historical perspective. Fisheries *5* (4): 28-36.

LELLIS, W. 1990. Early studies on spiny lobster mariculture. The Crustacean Nutrition Newsletter. 6(1): p 70.

LELLIS, W. 1991. Spiny Lobster: A mariculture candidate for the Caribbean? World Aquaculture. 22(1): 60-63.

LELLIS, W.A. and J.A. RUSSELL. 1990. Effect of temperature on survival, growth and feed intake of postlarval spiny lobsters, *Panulirus argus*. Aquaculture. *90*: 1-9.

LEWIS, J.B. 1951. The phylosoma larvae of the spiny lobster, *Panulirus argus*. Bull. Mar. Sci. *1* (2): 89-103.

LEWIS, J.B., H.B. MOORE and W. BABIS. 1952. The post-larval stages of the spiny lobster, *Panulirus argus*. Bull. Mar. Sci. 2 (1): 324-337.

LIPCIUS, R.N. and W.F. HERRNKIND. 1982. Molt cycle alterations in behavior, feeding and diel rhythms of a decapod crustacean, the spiny lobster, *Panulirus argus*. Marine Biology. 68: 241-252.

LIPCIUS, R.N. and W.F. HERRNKIND. 1985. Photoperiodic regulation and daily timing of spiny lobster mating behavior. J. Exp. Mar. Bio. Ecol. *89*: 191-204.

LIPCIUS, R.N., M.L. EDWARDS, W.F. HERRNKIND and S.A. WATERMAN. 1983. *In situ* mating behavior of the spiny lobster, *Panulirus argus*. Jour. Crust. Bio. 3 (2): 217-222.

LITTLE, E.J. 1977. Observations on recruitment of postlarval spiny lobsters, *Panulirus argus*, to the South Florida Coast. Fla. Marine Res. Pub., No. *29*: 35 p.

LITTLE, E.J. and G.R. MILANO. 1980. Techinques to monitor recruitment of postlarval spiny lobster, *Panulirus argus*, to the Florida Keys. Fla. Marine Res. Pub., No. *37*: 16 p.

LYONS, W.G. 1970. Scyllarid lobsters (Crustacea, Decopoda). Mem. Hourglass Cruises. *1* (4): 1-74.

LYONS, W. G. 1980 a. The postlarval stage of scyllaridean lobsters. Fisheries 5 (4): 47-49.

LYONS, W.G. 1980 b. Possible sources of Florida's spiny lobster population. Proc. Gulf Caribb. Fish. Inst. *33*: 253-266.

LYONS, W.G. 1986. Problems and perspectives regarding recruitment of spiny lobsters, *Panulirus argus*, to the south Florida fishery. Canad. Jor. of Fish. and Aquatic Sci. *43* (11): 2999-2106.

LYONS, W.G. 1991. A history of activities by the Florida marine research institute in the Florida Keys and contiguous waters of Monroe County. *in* Marine Resource Issues and Reseach in the Florida Keys. report from Division of Marine Resources, Florida Deptartment of Natural Resources. May 1991: 6-23.

LYONS, W.G. and F.S. KENNEDY, Jr. 1981. Effects of harvest techniques on sublegal spiny lobsters and on subsequent fishery yield. Gulf and Carib. Fish. Inst. *33*: 290-300.

LYONS, W.G., D.G. BARBER, S.M. FOSTER, F.S. KENNEDY, Jr. and G.R. MILANO. 1981. The spiny lobster, *Panulirus argus*, in the middle and upper Florida Keys: Population structure, seasonal dynamics and reproduction. Fla. Mar. Res. Publ., No. *38*: 38 p.

MANNING, R.B. 1978. FAO species identification sheets for fishery purposes. Western central Atlantic [W. Fischer, editor], (Fishing area 31). Vol. 6, Crustaceans, molluscs, and sea turtles; Nephropidae, Palinuridae, Scyllaridae, Synaxidae.

MANNING, R.B. and D.K. CAMP. 1989. Additional records for an Atlantic reef lobster, *Enoplometopus antillensis* Lutken, 1865 (Crustacea, Decapoda, Enoplometopidae). Proc. Biol. Soc. Wash. *102* (2): 411-417.

MARGULIS, L. and K.V. SCHWARTZ. 1988. Five Kingdoms. W.H. Freeman and Company, NY, U.S.A.: 376p.

MARX, J.M. and W.F. HERRNKIND. 1985 a. Macroalgae (Rhodophyta: *Laurencia* spp.) as habitat for young juvenile spiny lobsters, *Panulirus argus*. Bull. Mar. Sci. *36* (3): 423-431.

MARX, J.M. and W.F. HERRNKIND. 1985 b. Factors regulating microhabitat use by young juvenile spiny lobsters, *Panulirus argus*: food and shelter. Jour. Crust. Bio. *5* (4): 650-657.

MARX, J.M. and W.F. HERRNKIND. 1986. Species profiles: life histories and environmental requirements of coastal fishes and invertebrates (south Florida) Spiny Lobster. Fish and Wildlife Service, Bio. Rep. *82* (11.61): 1-22.

MENZIES, R.A. 1981. Biochemical population genetics and the spiny lobster larval recruitment problem: an update. Pro. Gulf and Carib. Fish. Inst. *33*: 230-243.

MENZIES, R.A. and J.M. KERRIGAN. 1979. Implications of spiny lobster recruitment patterns of the Caribbean — A biochemical genetic approach. Pro. Gulf and Carib. Fish. Inst. *31*: 164-178.

MENZIES, R.A. and J.M. KERRIGAN. 1980. The larval recruitment problem of the spiny lobster. Fisheries *5* (4): 42-46.

MILLER, D.L. 1982. Construction of shallow water habitats to increase lobster production in Mexico. Proc. Gulf and Caribb. Fish Inst. *34*: 168-179.

MILLER, D.L. 1983. Shallow water mariculture of spiny lobster (*Panulirus argus*) in the western Atlantic. *Proceedings* International Conference on warm-water aquaculture - Crustacea B.Y.U. Hawaii, Feb. 1983.

MILLER, D.L. 1986. Spiny lobster (*Panulirus argus*) fisheries and artificial habitats: Increasing the yields by merely concentrating stocks? Manuscript Copy. Intended for Canadian Journal of Fisheries and Aquatic Sciences.

MILLER , G.C. and D.L. SUTHERLAND. 1978. Behavior of the Florida spiny lobster, *Panulirus argus*, to baited Florida and and prototype traps. in R.E. Warner, Editor, Spiny lobster research review: proceedings of a conference held December 16, 1976, in Key West, Florida. Florida Sea Grant Tech. Pap. No. 4: 15-20.

MOE, M.A. JR. 1963. A survey of offshore fishing in Florida. Fla. St. Bd. Conserv. Prof. Pap. Ser. *4*: 117 p.

MOE, M.A. Jr. 1982. The Marine Aquarium Handbook: Beginner to Breeder. Green Turtle Publications, Plantation, FL, USA: 170 p.

MOE, M.A. Jr. 1989 The Marine Aquarium Reference: Systems and Invertebrates. Green Turtle Publications, Plantation, FL, USA: 510 p.

MOORE, D.R. 1962. Notes on the distribution of the spiny lobster *Panulirus* in Florida and the Gulf of Mexico. Crustaceana, 3(4): 318-319.

MUNRO, J.L. 1974. The biology, ecology, exploitation and management of Caribbean reef fishes. Pt. VI The biology, ecology and bionomics of Caribbean reef fishes: crustaceans (spiny lobsters and crabs). Res. Dep. Univ. West Indies Zool. Dept., Kingston, Jamaica, 3: 1-57.

NONADA, M., Y. OSHIMA and R. HIRANO. 1958. Culture and ecdysis of spiny lobster at phyllosoma stage. Aquaculture. 5(3): 13-15.

OPRESKO, L., D. OPRESKO, R. THOMAS and G. VOSS. 1973. Guide to the lobsters and lobster-like animals of Florida, the Gulf of Mexico, and the Caribbean region. Sea Grant Field Guide Series, Univ. of Miami. 1: 44 p.

OXENFORD, H.A. and W. HUNTE. 1986. Migration of the dolphin (*Coryphaena hippurus*) and its implications for fisheries mangement in the Western Central Atlantic. Proc. Gulf and Caribbean Fish. Instit. November 1984. 37: 95-111.

PAINE, R.D. 1987. On No-Name Key, Marooned with a Crew of Filibusters (1903). *in* Tales of Old Florida. F. Oppel and T. Meisel, editors. Castle, Secaucus, NJ, USA: 417-427.

PAIVA, M. and R.S. da COSTA. 1968. Comportamento biologica da lagosta, *Panulirus laevicauda* (Latreille). Arq. Est. Biol. Mar. Univ. Fed. Ceara. 8(1): 1-6.

PEACOCK, N.A. 1974. A study of the spiny lobster fishery of Antigua and Barbuda. Proc. Gulf and Caribbean Fish. Instit. November 1973. 26: 117-130.

PHILLIPS, B.F. 1975. The effects of water currents and intensity of moonlight on catches of the puerulus larval stages of the western rock lobster. CSIRO Aust. Div. Fish Oceanogr. Rep. No. 63: 9 p.

PHILLIPS, B.F. 1985. Aquaculture potential for rock lobsters in Australia. Australian Fisheries, June, 1985: p. 2-7.

PHILLIPS, B.F. and R.S. BROWN. 1989. The west Australian rock lobster fishery: research for management. *in* Marine Invertebrate Fisheries: Their Assessment and Management. J.F. Caddy, ed., John Wiley & Sons, NY, USA: 159-181.

PHILLIPS, B.F., J.S. COBB and R.W. GEORGE. 1980. General Biology. *in:* The Biology and Management of Lobsters. Editors, J. S. Cobb and B.F. Phillips., Vol. I. Physiology and behavior: pp 1-82. Acad. Press, N.Y.: 463 p.

PHILLIPS, B.F. and D.L. MACMILLAN. 1987. Antennal receptors in puerulus and postpuerulus states of the rock lobster, *Panulirus cygnus* (Decapoda: Palinuridae) and their potential role in puerulus navigation. Jour. Crust. Bio. 7 (1): 122-135.

PHILLIPS, B.F. and A.N. SASTRY. 1980. Larval Ecology. *in:* The Biology and Management of of Lobsters. Editors, J. S. Cobb and B.F. Phillips., Vol. II. Ecology and Management: pp 11-57. Acad. Press, N.Y.: 390 p.

PHILLIPS, R.B., G.R. MORGAN and C.M. AUSTIN. 1980. Synopsis of biological data on the western rock lobster, *Panulirus cygnus* George, 1962. FAO Fish. Synop. 1289: 64 p.

POLLOCK, D.E. 1973. Growth of juvenile rock lobster, *Jasus lalandii*. Sea Fisheries Branch Investigational Report, No. *106:* 1-16.

POPOV, N. 1989. Crawfishing in the Bahamas. Sea Frontiers. *35*(4): 222-230.

POWERS, D. A., F.W. ALLENDORF and T. CHEN. 1990. Application of Molecular Techniques to the Study of Marine Recruitment Problems. *in* Large Marine Ecosystems: patterns, processes and yields. S. Sherman, L.M. Alexander and B.D. Gold, Editors. AAAS, Washington, D.C.: 104-121.

PROCHASKA, F.J. and J.R. BAARDA. 1975. Florida's Fisheries Management: Their Development, Adminstration, and Current Status. Florida Agricultural Experiment Station Bulletin No. 768. Univ. of Florida: 64 p.

PROCHASKA, F.J. and J.C. CATO. 1980. Economic considerations in the management of the Florida spiny lobster fishery. Fisheries 5 (4): 53-56.

PROVENZANO, JR., A.J. 1968. Recent experiments on the laboratory rearing of tropical lobster larvae. Gulf and Carib. Fish. Inst. *21*: 152-157.

QUACKENBUSH, L.S. and W.F. HERRNKIND. 1983. Regulation of the molt cycle of the spiny lobster, *Panulirus argus,*: effect of photoperiod. Comp. Biochem. & Phy. 76A: 259-263.

RICHARDS, W.J. and J.A. BOHNSACK. 1990. The Caribbean Sea: A large marine ecosystem in crisis. *in* Large Marine Ecosystems: patterns, processes and yields. S. Sherman, L.M. Alexander and B.D. Gold, Editors. AAAS, Washington, D.C.: 44-53.

RICHARDS, W.J. and T. POTTHOFF. 1980. Distribution and seasonal occurrence of larval pelagic stages of spiny lobsters (Palinuridae, *Panulirus*) in the western tropical Atlantic. Proc. 33rd Ann. Gulf Carib. Fish. Inst., San Jose, Costa Rica: 244-252.

RITCHIE, L.D. 1966. Crayfish pot escapement gap survey. November 1965-January 1966. New Zealand Marine Department. Tech. Fish. Report. No. 14. 12 p.

ROBERTSON, P.B. 1968 a. The larval development of some western Atlantic lobsters of the family Scyllaridae. Dissertation. Univ. of Miami., Coral Gables, Florida, USA.

ROBERTSON, P.B. 1968 b. The complete larval development of the sand lobster, *Scyllarus americanus* (Smith), (Decapoda, Scyllaridae) in the laboratory, with notes on larvae from the plankton. Bull. Mar. Sci. *18* (2): 294-342.

ROBERTSON, P.B. 1969. Biological investigations of the deep sea. 49. Phyllosoma larvae of a palinurid lobster, *Justitia longimana* (H. Milne Edwards), from the western Atlantic. Bull. Mar. Sci. *19* (4): 922-944.

ROBERTSON, P.B. 1971. The larvae and postlarva of the scyllarid lobster *Scyllarus depressus* (Smith). Bul. Mar. Sci. *21* (4): 841-865.

ROE, R. B. 1966. Potentially commercial nephropsids from the western Atlantic. Trans. Amer. Fish. Soc. *95* (1): 92-98.

RUDLOW, A. and E.J. LITTLE, Jr. 1981. Light responses of postlarval spiny lobsters, *Panulirus argus*. *in* Proceedings of a Workshop on Florida Spiny Lobster Research and Management. W. Lyons, Editor. Fla. Dept. Nat. Res., Marine Res. Lab.: p. 4.

de SAINT LAURENT, M. 1988. Enoplometopoidea, nouvelle superfamille de Crustaces Decapodes Astacidea.—Compte Rendu Hebdomedaire des Seances de l'Academie des Sciences, Paris, Zoologie 3(307): 59-62.

SCHMIDT, J. 1925. The breeding places of the eel. Annual Report, The Smithsonian Institution. 1924. Pub. 2795: 279-317.

SCHROEDER, W.C. 1924. Fisheries of Key West and the clam industry of southern Florida. Appendix XII to the Report of the United States Commissioner of Fisheries for 1923. Bureau of Fisheries Document 962. US Gov. Printing Office, Washington, D.C.

SERFLING, S.A. and R.F. FORD. 1975. Laboratory culture of juvenile stages of the California spiny lobster *Panulirus interruptus* (Randall) at elevated temperatures. Aquaculture, 6 (1975): 377-387.

SHIPP, R.L. and T.S. HOPKINS. 1978. Physical and biological observations of the northern rim of the De Soto Canyon made from a research submersible. Northeast Gulf Science 2 (2): 113-121.

SIMMONS, D.C. 1980. Review of the Florida spiny lobster resource. Fisheries 5 (4): 37-41.

SIMON, H. 1983. Management alternatives for the spiny lobster (Panulirus argus) fishery of the Turks and Caicos, B.W.I. Masters Thesis. State Univesity of New York, Stony Brook. 96 p.

SIMS, H.W. 1965. The phyllosoma larvae of *Parribacus*. Quart. Jour. Fla. Acad. Sci. *28* (2): 142-172.

SIMS, H.W. 1966. The phyllosoma larvae of the spiny lobster *Palinurellus gundlachi* von Martens (Decopoda, Palinuridae). Crustaceana *11* (2): 205-215.

SIMS, H.W. 1966. An annotated bibliography of the spiny lobsters. Fla. St. Bd. of Cons. (DNR). Tech. Ser. No. *48*: 84 p.

SIMS, H.W. and R.M. INGLE. 1967. Caribbean recruitment of Florida's spiny lobster population. Q. J. Fla. Acad. Sci. *29* (3): 207-242.

SMITH, F.G.W. 1946. Report on the Bahamian crawfish industry. Unpublished report to the Bahamas Government.

SMITH, F.G.W. 1958. The spiny lobster industry of Florida. Fla. Bd. Cons., Educational Series No. *1*: 36 p.

SMITH, G.B. and M. van NIEROP. 1986. Abundance and potential yield of spiny lobster (*Panulirus argus*) on the Little and Great Bahama Banks. Bull. Mar. Sci. *39* (3): 646-656.

SPOTTE, S. 1970. Fish and Invertebrate Culture: Water Management in Closed Systems. John Wiley & Sons. NY, USA: 145 pp.

SPOTTE. S. 1979. Seawater Aquariums, The Captive Environment. John Wiley & Sons. NY, USA: 413 pp.

STERRER, W. (editor) 1986. Marine Fauna and Flora of Bermuda. John Wiley & Sons, Inc., New York, NY, USA: 742 pp.

SUTCLIFFE, W.H., Jr. 1952. Some observations on the breeding and migration of the Bermuda spiny lobster, *Panulirus argus*. Gulf. Carib. Fish. Inst. *4*: 64-69.

SUTCLIFFE, W.H., Jr. 1953. Notes on the biology of a spiny lobster, *Panulirus guttatus*, in Bermuda. Ecology *34* (4): 794-796.

SWEAT, D.E. 1968. Growth and tagging studies on *Panulirus argus* (Latreille) in the Florida Keys. Fla. Bd. Cons. (DNR) Mar. Res. Lab., Tech. Ser. No. *57*: 30 p.

TAMM, G.R. 1980. Spiny lobster culture: an alternative to natural stock assessment. Fisheries *5* (4): 59-62.

TAMURA, T. 1970. Marine Aquaculture. Translation through the National Technical Information Service. National Science Foundation, Washington, D.C., USA: 1000 + p.

TAYLOR, H. 1984. The Lobster: its life cycle. Pisces Book Co., Inc., NY, USA: 96 p.

THIEL, A. 1988. The Marine Fish and Invert Reef Aquarium. Aardvark Press. Bridgeport, CT, USA: 278 p.

THIEL, A. 1989. Advanced Reef Keeping I. Aardvark Press. Bridgeport, CT, USA: 440 p.

THOMPSON, R.W. 1980. The spiny lobster fishery of the Bahamas. Report from Department of Fisheries, Minstry of Agriculture, Fisheries and Local Government, Nassau, Bahamas: 51 p.

TRAVIS, D.F. 1954. The molting cycle of the spiny lobster, *Panulirus argus* Latreille. I. Molting and growth in laboratory-maintained individuals. Biol. Bull. *107*: 433-450.

VERMEER, G.K. 1987. Effects of air exposure on desiccation rate, hemolymph chemistry, and escape behavior of the spiny lobster, *Panulirus argus*. Fish. Bull. *85* (1): 45-51.

VOSS, G.L. 1980. Seashore life of Florida and the Caribbean. Banyan Books, Inc., Miami, FL, USA: 199 p.

WALTON, A.S. and W.F. HERRNKIND. 1977. Hydrodynamic orientation of spiny lobster, *Panulirus argus* (Crustacea: Palinuridae): wave surge and unidirectional currents. Pro. Annual Northeastern Mtg. Animal Behavior Soc. 1977 Plenary Papers. Memorial Univ. of New Foundland. Marine Sci. Res. Lab, Tech. Report No. *20*: 184-211.

WARD, J. 1989. Patterns of settlement of spiny lobster (*Panulirus argus*) postlarvae at Bermuda. Pro. Gulf and Caribbean Fish. Inst., 1986. *39*: 255-264.

WARNER, R.E., C.L. COMBS and D.R. GREGORY, Jr. 1977. Biological studies of the spiny lobster, *Panulirus argus* (Decapoda, Palinuridae) in South Florida. Proc. Gulf and Carib. Fish. Inst. *29*: 166-183.

WAUGH, G.T. 1980. Population dynamics of juvenile spiny lobster, *Panulirus argus*, near Grand Bahama Island. MS Thesis, Univ. Miami, Coral Gables, FL: 195 p.

WAUGH, G.T. 1981. Management of juvenile spiny lobster (*Panulirus argus*) based on estimated biological parameters from Grand Bahama Island, Bahamas. Proc. Gulf and Caribbean Fish Inst. 1980. *33*: 271-289.

WAUGH, G.T. and M.H. GOODWIN. 1986. Implementation of a Caribbean regional spiny lobster management program. Proc. Gulf and Caribbean Fish. Instit. November 1984. *37*: 119-122.

WAUGH, G.T. and H.R.H. WAUGH. 1977. An economical method of trap fishing for spiny lobster, *Panulirus argus*, in the Bahamas. Proc. Culf Carib. Fish. Inst. *29*: 160-165.

WILLIAMS, A.B. 1984. Shrimps, Lobsters, and Crabs of the Atlantic Coast of the Eastern United States. Maine to Florida. Smithsonian Institution Press, Washington, D.C., USA: 550 p.

WILLIAMS, A.B. 1986. Lobsters—Identification, World Distribution, and U.S. Trade. Mar. Fish. Rev. *48* (2): 36 p.

WILLIAMS, A.B. 1989. Lobsters of the World - An Illustrated Guide. Osprey Books, Huntington, NY, U.S.A.: 180 p.

WILKIN, R.M., M.H. GOODWIN and G.T. WAUGH. 1986. Spiny lobster management program in St. Kitts/Nevis. Proc. Gulf and Caribbean Fish. Instit. November 1984. *37*: 87-90.

WITHAM, R., R.M. INGLE and H.W. SIMS, JR. 1964. Notes on postlarvae of *Panulirus argus*. Quart. Jour. Fla. Acad. Sci. *27*(4): 289-297.

WITHAM, R., R.M. INGLE and E.A. JOYCE, JR. 1968. Physiological and ecological studies of *Panulirus argus* from the St. Lucie Estuary. Fla. Bd. of Cons. (DNR) Mar. Res. Lab., Tech. Ser. *53*: 31 p.

WOLFE, S.H. and B.E. FELGENHAUER. 1991. Mouthparts and foregut ontogeny in larval, postlarval, and juvenile spiny lobster, *Panulirus argus* Latreille (Decapoda, Palinuridae). Zoologica Scripta, *20*(1): 57-75.

YAMAKAWA, T., NISHIMURA, M., MATSUDA, H., TSUJIGADO, A., and N. KAMIYA. 1989. Complete larval rearing of the Japanese spiny lobster, *Panulirus japonicus*. Nippon suisan Gakkaishi *55*(4): 745.

ZUBOY, J.R., A.C. JONES and T.J. COSTELLO. 1980. Lobster fishery management under the fishery conservation and management act. Fisheries *5* (4): 50-52.

Appendix A

Florida Laws, Statutes, and Adminstrative Codes

The set of volumes known as the Laws of Florida contain legislation enacted by the Florida Legislature. All bills passed by the Legislature are published every year as the Laws of Florida. Laws of a continuing and permanent nature are codified in the Florida Statutes every odd numbered year, with a supplement issued in even numbered years. Chapter 46 of the Florida Adminstrative Code is created by the Florida Marine Fisheries Commission under the powers granted to it by the State Legislature. The Law Enforcement Division of the Department of Natural Resources (Marine Patrol) is charged with enforcement of Florida Laws, Statutes, and Adminstrative Code and Federal Laws that apply to their jurisdiction. Note that the Laws, Statutes, and Codes that apply to active fisheries change often as the Legislature and regulatory agencies strive to best manage the fishery.

The documents in Appendix A are up to date as of summer, 1991. They are presented here only as an unofficial guide to Florida regulations. Please consult proper authorities for current and official information on Florida lobster laws and rules. Recent changes in the laws that I consider important and interesting are printed in bold type. The 1991 Florida Legislature made substantial changes in the laws governing the spiny lobster fishery, particularly pertaining to the establishment of a trap certificate program. These admendments to the Florida Statutes 370.142 (Laws of Florida, Ch. 91-154) are included at the end of Appendix A.

FLORIDA ADMINSTRATIVE CODE , CHAPTER 46-24
SPINY LOBSTER (CRAWFISH) AND SLIPPER LOBSTER

46-24.001 Purpose and Intent.-

(1) The primary purpose and intent of this chapter are to protect and conserve Florida's spiny lobster resources, assure the continuing health and abundance of those resources, and to provide for optimum sustained benefits and use from the resources for all the people of the state.

(2) It is the intent of this chapter to repeal and replace Chapter 29299, Special Acts of Florida, 1953, a special act relating to gear authorized to be used in the waters of Monroe County.

(3) It is also the intent of this chapter to prohibit the molestation of eggbearing slipper lobster.

(4) Beginning August 1,1993, **spiny lobster shall be designated as a restricted species** pursuant to Section 370.01(20), Florida Statutes.

(5) It is the goal of the Commission to substantially reduce the mortality of undersize spiny lobster in the fishery. **The prospective prohibition on the use of such lobsters as attractants and the escape gap requirements are intended to achieve this goal. If, prior to the effective date of these measures, an effort reduction program is adopted by the Legislature and successfully implemented by the Commission for the fishery, The Commission intends to give primary consideration to the elimination of these measures prior to their effective date.** It is further the intent of the Commission to require that Commission staff, prior to July 1,1992, prepare a resport assessing the progress made toward adoption and implementation of an effort reduction program.

Specific Authority.- 370.027, F.S., Section 8 of Chapter 83-134, Laws of Florida, as amended by Section 2 of Chapter 84-121 and Section 1 of Chapter 85-163, Laws of Florida. Law Implemented 370.025, 370.027, 370.14, F.S., Section 8 of Chapter 83-134, Laws of Florida, as amended by Section 2 of Chapter 84-121 and Section 1 of Chapter 85-163, Laws of Florida.

History. - New 7-2-87, Amended 7-2-90.

46-24.002 Definitions.—

As used in this rule chapter:

(1) "Bully net means a circular frame attached at right angles to the end of a pole and supporting a conical bag of webbing. The webbing is usually held up by means of a cord which is released when the net is dropped over a lobster.

(2) "Commercial harvester" means a person who holds a valid crawfish license or trap number and a valid saltwater products license issued by the Department of Natural Resources. Beginning August 1,1993, "commercial harvester" shall mean a person who holds a valid crawfish license or trap number and a valid saltwater products license with a restricted species endorsement issued by the Department of Natural Resources.

(3) "Diving" means swimming at or below the surface of the water.

(4) "Harvest" means the catching or taking of spiny lobster by any means whatsoever, followed by a reduction of such spiny lobster to possession. Spiny lobster that are caught but immediately returned to the water free, alive and unharmed are not harvested. In addition, temporary possession of a spiny lobster for the purpose of measuring it to determine compliance with the minimum size requirements of this chapter shall not constitute harvesting of such lobster, provided that it is measured immediately after taking, and immediately returned to the water free, alive and unharmed if undersized.

(5) "Hoop net" means a frame, circular or otherwise, supporting a shallow bag of webbing and suspended by a line and bridles. The net is baited and lowered to the ocean bottom, to be raised rapidly at a later time to prevent the escape of lobster.

(6) "Land" when used in connection with the harvest of a spiny lobster, means the physical act of bringing the harvested lobster ashore.

(7) "Oil product" means any new, used, or waste liquid hydrocarbon mixture originally derived or refined from petroleum, natural gas, or coal, or any new, used, or waste liquified animal or vegetable fat.

(8) "Person" means any natural person, firm, entity or corporation.

(9) "Recreational harvester" means any person other than a commercial harvester.

(10) "Slipper lobster," also known as Spanish, sand, shovelnose, and bulldozer lobster, means any crustacean of the species *Scyllarides nodifer*, or any part thereof.

(11) "Spiny lobster" or "crawfish" means any crustacean of the species *Panulirus argus*, or any part thereof.

Specific Authority.— 370.027, F.S., Section 8 of Chapter 83-134, Laws of Florida, as amended by Section 2 of Chapter 84-121 and Section 1 of Chapter 85-163, Laws of Florida. Law Implemented 370.025, 370.027, 370.14, F.S., Section 8 of Chapter 83-134, Laws of Florida, as amended by Section 2 of Chapter 84-121 and Section 1 of Chapter 85-163, Laws of Florida.

History.— New 7-2-87, Amended 7-2-90.

46-24.003 Minimum Size Limits.—

(1) No person shall harvest or possess any spiny lobster with a carapace measurement of 3 inches or less or, if the tail is separated from the body, a tail measurement less than 5 1/2 inches not including any protruding muscle tissue, except as may be provided in subsection (3) of this rule.

(2) The carapace (head, body, or front section) measurement shall be determined by beginning at the anteriormost edge (front) of the groove between the horns directly above the eyes, then proceeding along the middorsal line (middle of the back) to the rear edge of the top part of the carapace, excluding any translucent membrane. The tail (segmented portion) shall be measured lengthwise along the top middorsal line (middle of the back) of the entire tail until the rearmost extremity is reached; provided, the tail measurement shall be conducted with the tail in a flat straight position with the tip of the tail closed.

(3) Until April 1,1993, the holder of a valid crawfish license or trap number and a valid saltwater products license issued by the Department of Natural Resources may harvest and possess, while on the water, **undersized spiny lobster not exceeding 50 per boat or 1 per trap aboard each boat, whichever is greater,** if used for luring, decoying, or otherwise attracting noncaptive spiny lobster into traps. Such undersized spiny lobster shall be kept alive, while in possession, in a shaded continuously circulating live well with pump capacity to totally replace the water at least every 8 minutes and large enough to provide at least 3/4 gallon of seawater per lobster. All undersized lobster so maintained shall be released to the water alive and unharmed immediately upon leaving the trap lines and prior to 1 hour after official sunset.

(4) **Beginning August 1, 1993, the possession of undersized spiny lobster for the purpose of luring, decoying, or otherwise attracting noncaptive spiny lobster is prohibited.**

(5) Spiny lobster harvested in Florida waters shall remain in a whole condition at all times while on or below the waters of the state and the practice of wringing or separating the tail (segmented portion) from the body (carapace and head) section is prohibited on state waters. Possession of spiny lobster tails that have been wrung or separated, on or below the waters of the state, is prohibited, unless the spiny lobster are being imported pursuant to Rule 46-24.0045 or were harvested outside the waters of the state and the wringing or

separation was pursuant to a federal permit allowing such wringing or separation. In the latter case, the federal permit shall be present and accompany any wrung or separated spiny lobster tails while possessed on or below the waters of the state.

(6) No person shall harvest or attempt to harvest spiny lobster by diving unless he possesses, while in the water, a measuring device capable of being used to perform the carapace measurement described in subsection (2). Each measurement performed by such a person shall occur in the water.

Specific Authority.—370.027, F.S., Section 8 of Chapter 83-134, Laws of Florida, as amended by Section 2 of Chapter 84-121 and Section 1 of Chapter 85-163, Laws of Florida. Law Implemented: 370.025, 370.027, 370.14, F.S., Section 8 of Chapter 83-134, Laws of Florida, as amended by Section 2 of Chapter 84-121 and Section 1 of Chapter 85-163, Laws of Florida. **History.**—New 7-2-87, Amended 7-2-90.

46-24.004 Bag Limit.—

(1) Except as provided in subsection (2) and (3), the harvest from state waters, or possession while on or below such water, of more than 6 spiny lobster per recreational harvester per day or 24 spiny lobster per boat, whichever is greater, is prohibited.

(2) During the first day of the two day sport season specified in Rule 46-24.005, no recreational harvester shall possess more than 6 spiny lobster, whether on or off the water of the state. During the second day of the two-day sport season, no recreational harvester shall possess more than 12 spiny lobster, once such harvester has landed and departed the state waters.

(3) No person shall harvest or possess, while on or below the water, more spiny lobster than the limit established in subsection (1), unless he is engaged in the lawful importation of spiny lobster pursuant to Rule 46-24.0045 or he possesses a current valid crawfish license or trap number issued pursuant to Section 370.14(3)(b), Florida Statutes, and a current valid saltwater products license. Additionally, beginning on August 1, 1993, such person shall also have a restricted species endorsement on his saltwater products license to exceed the limit established in subsection (1) pursuant to this subsection.

Specific Authority.—370.02, F.S., Section 8 of Chapter 83-134, Laws of Florida, as amended by section 2 of Chapter 84-121 and Section 1 of Chapter 85-163, Laws of Florida. Law Implemented 370.025, 370.027, 370.14, F.S., Section 8 of Chapter 83-134, Laws of Florida, as amended by Section 2 of Chapter 84-121 and Section 1 of Chapter 85-163, Laws of Florida.

History.— New 7-2-87, Amended 7-2-90.

46-24.0045 Importation of Spiny Lobster During Open Season; Documentation Requirements.—

During the open season specified in Rule 46-24.005(1), a person may possess wrung spiny lobster tails or possess spiny lobster in excess of the bag limit specified in Rule 46-24. 004(1), while on state waters, if such person is also in possession of appropriate receipt(s), bill(s) of sale, or bill(s) of lading to show that the spiny lobster were purchased in a foreign country and are entering the state in international commerce. Failure to maintain such documentation or to promptly produce same at the request of any duly authorized law enforcement officer shall constitute prima facie evidence that such spiny lobster were harvested in Florida waters.

Specific Authority.- 370.027(2), F.S. Law Implemented: 370.025, 370.027, F.S.

History. - New 7-2-90

46-24.005 Seasons.—

(1) Except as provided in subsection (2) of this rule, the season for harvest of spiny lobster in state waters shall be August 6 of each year through March 31 of the following year. No person shall harvest, attempt to harvest, or have in his possession, regardless of where taken, any spiny lobster during the closed season of April 1 through August 5 of each

year, except pursuant to subsection (2), for storage and distribution by lawfully possessed inventory stocks as provided by Section 370.141, Florida Statutes, or by special permit issued by the Department of Natural Resources.

(2) There shall be a sport season for recreational harvesters of spiny lobster, which season shall occur on the last full weekend prior to August 1 each year.

(3) Commercial harvesters of spiny lobster may bait and place their traps in the water beginning on August 1 of each year. Harvest or sale of spiny lobster from such traps during the "soak" period prior to the beginning of the season is prohibited.

(4) All traps used for harvest of spiny lobster shall be removed from state waters by April 5 of each year. All spiny lobster taken from traps after the close of the season on March 31 shall be returned to the water free, alive and unharmed. The division of Law Enforcement of the Department of Natural Resources may grant an extension for the retrieval of traps up to a maximum of 10 days after the expiration of the 5-day retrieval period, or a total of up to 15 days after the close of the spiny lobster season, upon the following conditions:

(a) A commercial harvester or his lawfully designated agent shall request, in writing, permission for an extension of the period for retrieval of traps. The request shall specify the commercial harvester's name and license or trap number, the approximate number of traps and their location, the identity of the boat to be used for trap retrieval, the boat owner's name, the period of additional time needed for trap retrieval, and the reasons for the request.

(b) On the day that trap removal begins, and on each subsequent day that it continues, the Division of Law Enforcement shall be advised in person or by telephone of the remaining trap locations and landing site.

(c) Reasons for granting an extension shall be limited to hazardous weather (small craft warnings, at a minimum), medical emergencies that make it impossible for the commercial harvester to operate a boat, or equipment breakdown.

(d) Nothing in this subsection shall authorize the harvest, landing or sale of any spiny lobster during the closed season.

(5) Except as provided in subsections (3) and (4) of this rule for trap soaking and retrieval periods, no person shall transport on the water, fish with, set, or place any spiny lobster trap or part thereof during the closed season. Any such trap remaining in the water or abandoned during the closed season (following any extension for retrieval as provided in subsection (4) and prior to the soak period authorized in subsection (3)) is declared to be a public nuisance and shall be disposed of in the manner approved by the Division of Law Enforcement of the Department of Natural Resources. This provision shall be in addition to any penalty imposed by law.

Specific Authority.— 370.027, F.S., Section 8 of Chapter 83-134, Laws of Florida, as amended by Section 2 of Chapter 84-121 and Section 1 of Chapter 85-163, Laws of Florida. Law Implemented 370.025, 370.027, 370.14, F.S., Section 8 of Chapter 83-134, Laws of Florida, as amended by Section 2 of Chapter 84-121 and Section 1 of Chapter 85-163, Laws of Florida.

History.— New 7-2-87, Amended 7-2-90.

46-24.0055 Exportation During Closed Season By Mariculture Operations; Conditions.—

Notwithstanding the provisions of Rule 46-24.005, beginning on April 1 and continuing through August 5 of each year, a licensed or lawfully allowed mariculture operation may possess and ship live spiny lobster to customers and for consumption outside the State of Florida, if each of the following conditions are met:

(1) Each such spiny lobster shall have been either harvested from Florida or adjacent federal (EEZ) waters legally during the open season or cultivated entirely within the facility

of the operation. This rule shall not be construed to allow the harvest of spiny lobster from Florida or adjacent federal (EEZ) waters during the closed season.

(2) Each such spiny lobster shall meet the minimum size requirements of Rule 46-24.003 (1). No undersize lobster shall be shipped pursuant to this rule.

(3) Each such spiny lobster shall be indelibly marked to identify the operation or have securely attached thereto a tag bearing such identification. Any marking or tagging system used shall be approved prior to the beginning of the closed season by the Division of Law Enforcement of the Department of Natural Resources.

(4) Each mariculture operation possessing live spiny lobster for exportation pursuant to this rule shall, prior to April 1 each year, report to the Division of Law Enforcement of the Department of Natural Resources the quantity of such live lobster in inventory, in pounds and in numbers of individuals, and the location of the operation. On the 1st and 15th day of each month during the closed season, the operation shall report to the division the quantity of live spiny lobster shipped out-of-state pursuant to this rule, in pounds and in numbers of individuals, and also the quantity of lobsters, in like terms, remaining in inventory. Copies of all documentation provided by the U. S. Department of Commerce covering any shipments made during the reporting period shall be provided with these bimonthly reports.

(5) At least 48 hours prior to beginning harvest of such spiny lobster from the operation's facility for marking or tagging and packing for shipment, the operator shall notify the Division of Law Enforcement of the Department of Natural Resources of the time. date, and location of such activity, the specific mode of transportation to be used for the shipment, and the point of destination out-of-state.

(6) A Marine Patrol officer shall be present at all times to monitor the harvest, marking or tagging, and packing of any live spiny lobster for shipment during the closed season.

(7) By August 20 of each year the operator shall report to the Division of Law Enforcement of the Department of Natural Resources the quantity of live spiny lobster shipped out-of-state during the entire closed season pursuant to this rule, in pounds and in terms of numbers of individuals, and also the quantity of lobsters, in like terms, remaining in inventory.

Specific Authority.— 370.027(2), F.S. Law Implemented: 370.025, 370.027, F.S. **History.**—New 7-2-90.

46-24.006 Gear: Traps, Buoys, Identification Requirements, Prohibited Devices.—

(1) No commercial harvester shall harvest lobster by any means other than by diving, by the use of a bully net or hoop net, or by the use of trap as specified in this subsection. No person shall, in state waters, fish with, set, place, or cause to be fished with, set, or placed, any trap except those described below:

(a) Wood slat traps no larger in dimension than 3 feet, by 2 feet, by 2 feet, or the volume equivalent. Such traps may be reinforced with wire mesh no heavier than 9 gauge, which shall only be affixed to the vertical surfaces of such traps. **Beginning on August 1, 1993, no wood slat trap shall be used to harvest lobster, which trap has been dipped in or treated with any oil products.**

(b) Until April 1,1993, plastic traps no larger in dimension than 3 feet, by 2 feet, by 2 feet, or the volume equivalent, with an untreated wood slat top panel.

(c) Traps not meeting the requirements of paragraph (a) or (b), which traps shall only be fished, set, or placed pursuant to a special activity permit issued by the Department of Natural Resources. Each such trap shall have a degradable panel or mechanism to assure that if lost or not retrieved, the trap will not continue to fish for spiny lobster for an extended period of time.

(d) Beginning on August 1,1993, all traps shall have an escape gap or opening near the bottom of the trap at the narrowest end opposite the buoy line, which escape gap or opening shall be rectangular, 2 1/8 inches wide and 20 inches long. For other traps used pursuant to special activity permit as allowed in paragraph (c), the Department of Natural Resources shall, as a condition of the permit, require a comparable escape gap or opening to be built into each such trap to allow the escape of undersize spiny lobster. No person shall obstruct, cause to be obstructed, or alter any escape gap required by this subsection in any manner so as to render the escape gap nonfunctioning or ineffective in allowing the escape of undersize spiny lobster.

(2) A buoy or time release buoy shall be attached to each spiny lobster trap or at each end of a trap trotline and shall be of sufficient strength and buoyancy to float and of such color, hue, and brilliancy as to be easily distinguished, seen, and located.

(3) Each trap and buoy used to harvest spiny lobster shall have the commercial harvester's current crawfish license or trap number permanently affixed in legible figures. On each buoy, the affixed number shall be at least 2 inches high. The buoy color and license or trap number shall also be permanently and conspicuously displayed on the boat used for setting traps and buoys, in the manner prescribed by the Department of Natural Resources, so as to be readily identifiable from the air and water.

(4) Except as provided herein, no numbers shall be used to identify traps or buoys other than the commercial harvester's current crawfish license or trap numbers or numbers designating federal permits. Ownership of spiny lobster traps may be transferred to other persons, so long as the following conditions are met:

(a) The person acquiring ownership of such traps shall notify the Division of Law Enforcement or the Department of Natural Resources within five days of acquiring ownership as to the number of traps purchased, the vendor, and the license or trap number currently displayed on the traps, and shall request issuance of a crawfish license or trap number if the person does not possess same.

(b) Buoys shall be renumbered and recolored at the first pulling of traps.

(c) The new license or trap number shall be permanently attached to the traps prior to their being set at the beginning of the next open season.

(d) The new owner shall retain a valid bill of sale.

(5) Each commercial harvester who harvests spiny lobster by diving shall permanently and conspicuously display on the boat used in such diving a "divers-down flag" symbol on an identification placard, which symbol shall have dimensions no less than 16 inches by 20 inches. The term "divers-down flag" shall have the meaning ascribed in Section 861.065(3), Florida Statutes. The commercial harvester's current crawfish license or trap number shall be permanently affixed to the diagonal stripe on the placard in legible figures to provide ready identification from the air and water.

(6) Permission to pull or work traps belonging to another, during the regular season, may be granted by the Division of Law Enforcement or the Department of Natural Resources. Such permission shall be granted by the Division only upon receipt of a written statement signed by the commercial harvester detailing license or trap number and buoy colors. Additionally, the commercial harvester shall list the license or trap number, buoy colors, and audit numbers of the commercial harvester and general locations of the pulling activity of the boat engaged in pulling or working the traps. Permission to pull traps in this manner shall be obtained daily; however, extension of permission may be obtained by telephone for up to a maximum of 5 days.

(7) No person shall harvest or attempt to harvest spiny lobster using any device which will or could puncture, penetrate, or crush the exoskeleton (shell) or the flesh of the lobster, and the use of such devices as part of, or in conjunction with, any trap is also prohibited.

(8) No commercial harvester shall fish with, set, place, or cause to be fished with, set, or placed, more than 2,000 spiny lobster traps. The number of spiny lobster traps fished with, set, or placed from a single boat shall be limited to no more than 2,000 such traps. These prohibitions shall not apply if a commercial harvester is given permission to pull or work traps belonging to another such harvester pursuant to subsection (6) of this rule.

Specific Authority. - 370.027, F.S., Section 8 of Chapter 83-134, Laws of Florida, as amended by Section 2 of Chapter 84-121 and Section 1 of Chapter 85-163, Laws of Florida. Law Implemented 370.025, 370.027, 370.14, F.S., Section 8 of Chapter 83-134, Laws of Florida, as amended by Section 2 of Chapter 84-121 and Section 1 of Chapter 85-163. Laws of Florida.

History.—New 7-2-87, Amended 7-2-90.

46-24.007 Other Prohibitions.—

(1) The harvest or possession of eggbearing spiny lobster is prohibited. Eggbearing spiny lobster found in traps shall be immediately returned to the water free, alive and unharmed. The practice of stripping or otherwise molesting eggbearing spiny lobster in order to remove the eggs is prohibited and the possession of spiny lobster or spiny lobster tails from which eggs, swimmerettes, or pleopods have been removed or stripped is prohibited.

(2) Spiny lobster traps may be worked during daylight hours only, and the pulling of traps from 1 hour after official sunset until 1 hour before official sunrise is prohibited.

(3) No spiny lobster traps shall be set, placed or caused to be set or placed at, on, or below the waters of the state within 100 feet of the intracoastal waterway or within 100 feet of any bridge or sea wall.

(4) No person shall harvest spiny lobster by diving at night (from 1 hour after official sunset until 1 hour before official sunrise) in excess of the bag limit prescribed in Rule 46-24.004.

(5) The directed harvest of spiny lobster by the use of any net or trawl other than a landing or dip net, bully net, or hoop net is prohibited. Spiny lobster harvested by the use of any net or trawl as an incidental bycatch of other target species lawfully harvested shall not be deemed to be unlawfully harvested in violation of this subsection if the combined whole weight of all spiny lobster so harvested does not exceed 5% of the total whole weight of all species lawfully in possession of the harvester at any time. For purposes of this subsection the term "net or trawl" shall not include any hand held net.

Specific Authority.- 370.027, F.S., Section 8 of Chapter 83-134, Laws of Florida, as amended by Section 2 of Chapter 84-121 and Section 1 of Chapter 85-163, Laws of Florida. Law Implemented: 370.025, 370.027, 370.14, F.S. Section 8 of Chapter 83-134, Laws of Florida, as amended by Section 2 of Chapter 84-121 and Section 1 of Chapter 85-163, Laws of Florida.

History.- New 7-2-87, Amended 7-2-90.

46-24.008 Slipper Lobster; Prohibitions Relating to Eggbearing Slipper Lobster.—

The harvest or possession of eggbearing slipper lobster is prohibited. Eggbearing slipper lobster found in traps shall be immediately returned to the water free, alive and unharmed. The practice of stripping or otherwise molesting eggbearing slipper lobster in order to remove the eggs is prohibited and the possession of slipper lobster tails from which eggs swimmerettes or pleopods have been removed or stripped is prohibited.

Specific Authority.— 370.027, F.S.Law Implemented: 370.025, 370.027(2),F.S.

History.—New 7-2-87, Amended 7-2-90.

Florida Statutes, Chapter 370, 1989
370.14 Crawfish; regulation.-

(1) It is the intent of the Legislature to maintain the crawfish industry for the economy of the state and to conserve the stocks supplying this industry. The provisions of this act regulating the taking of saltwater crawfish are for the purposes of ensuring and maintaining the highest possible production of saltwater crawfish.

(2) Each trap, can, drum, and similar device used for taking or attempting to take crawfish must have a trap number permanently attached to the device and the buoy This trap number may be issued by the Division of Law Enforcement upon the receipt of application by the owner of the traps, cans, drums, buoys, or similar devices and accompanied by the payment of a fee of $50. The design of the applications and of the trap number shall be determined by the division. However, effective July 1,1988, and until July 1, 1991, no crawfish trap numbers issued pursuant to this section except those numbers that were active during the 1987-1988 fiscal year shall be renewed or reissued. No new trap numbers shall be issued during this period. In 1988, persons holding a trap number that was active in the 1987-1988 fiscal year or an immediate family member of that person or a person to whom a trap number was transferred in writing by the holder of the active trap number, must request renewal of the number before December 31, 1988. In subsequent years and until July 1,1991, trap number holders or members of their immediate family or a person to whom the trap number was transferred in writing must request renewal of the number prior to June 30. If a person holding an active trap number or a member of the person's immediate family or a person to whom the trap number was transferred in writing does not request renewal of the number before the applicable date as specified above, the department may reissue the number to another applicant in the order of the receipt of the application for a trap number. Any trap, drum, can, buoy, or similar device used in the taking or in attempting to take crawfish, other than a device with trap number attached as prescribed in this subsection, shall be seized and destroyed by the division. The proceeds of the fees imposed by this subsection shall be used by the Department of Natural Resources for the purposes of enforcing the provisions of this subsection through aerial and other surveillance and trap retrieval. The Department of Natural Resources is authorized to promulgate rules and regulations to carry out the intent of this section.

(3) The crawfish license must be on board the boat, and both the license and the harvested crawfish shall be subject to inspection at all times. Only one license shall be issued for each boat. The crawfish license number must be prominently displayed above the topmost portion of the boat so as to be easily and readily identified.

(4) It is a felony of the third degree, punishable as provided in s. 775.082 or s. 775.083, for any person willfully to molest any crawfish traps, lines, or buoys belonging to another without permission of the licenseholder.

(5) Any crawfish licenseholder, upon selling licensed crawfish traps, shall furnish the division notice of such sale of all or part of his interest within 15 days thereof. Any holder of said license shall also notify the division within 15 days if his address no longer conforms to the address appearing on the license and shall, as a part of such notification furnish the division with his new address.

(6) Upon the arrest and conviction for violation of any of the crawfish regulations or laws, the licenseholder must show just cause why his license should not be suspended or permanently revoked.

(7) A person who takes more than 24 crawfish per boat or 6 crawfish per person, whichever is greater, within any 24-hour period by any method other than with traps, cans,

drums, or similar devices must also pay a fee of $50 and obtain a trap number to be displayed on his boat.

(8)(a) By a special permit granted by the Division of Law Enforcement, a Florida licensed seafood dealer may lawfully import, process, and package saltwater crawfish or uncooked tails of the species *Panulirus argus* during the closed season. However, crawfish landed under special permit shall not be sold in the state.

(b) The licensed seafood dealer importing any such crawfish under the permit shall, 12 hours prior to the time the seagoing vessel or airplane delivering such imported crawfish enters the state, notify the Division of Law Enforcement as to the seagoing vessel's name or the airplane's registration number and its captain, location, and point of destination.

(c) At the time the crawfish cargo is delivered to the permitholder's place of business, the crawfish cargo shall be weighed in the presence of the marine patrol officer, and a signed receipt of such quantity in pounds shall be furnished to said officer, which receipt shall be filed by the marine patrol officer with the Division of Law Enforcement.

(d) Within 48 hours from the time the receipt is given to the marine patrol officer, the permitholder shall submit to the Division of Law Enforcement, on forms provided by the division, a sworn report of the quantity in pounds of the saltwater crawfish received, which report shall include the location of said crawfish and a sworn statement that said crawfish were taken at least 50 miles from Florida's shoreline. The landing of crawfish or crawfish tails from which the eggs, swimmerettes, or pleopods have been removed; the falsification of information as to area from which crawfish were obtained; or the failure to file the report called for in this section shall be grounds to revoke the permit.

(e) Each permitholder shall keep throughout the period of the closed season copies of the bill of sale or invoices covering each transaction involving crawfish imported under this permit. Such invoices and bills shall be kept available at all times for inspection by the division.

(9)(a) A Florida licensed seafood dealer may obtain a special permit to import, process, and package uncooked tails of saltwater crawfish upon the payment of the sum of $100 to the Division of Law Enforcement.

(b) A special permit must be obtained by any airplane or seagoing vessel other than a common carrier used to transport saltwater crawfish or crawfish tails for purchase by licensed seafood dealers for purposes as provided herein upon the payment of $50.

(c) All special permits issued under this subsection are nontransferable.

(10) No common carrier or employee of said carrier may carry, knowingly receive for carriage, or permit the carriage of any crawfish of the species *Panulirus argus*, regardless of where taken, during the closed season, except of the species *Panulirus argus* lawfully imported from a foreign country for reshipment outside of the territorial limits of the state under U.S. Customs bond or in accordance with paragraph (8)(a).

(11)(a) In addition to licenses required by s. 370.0605, any person that takes and possesses any crawfish for recreational purposes from any waters of the state must have a crawfish stamp affixed to the license issued pursuant to s. 370.0605. The cost of each crawfish stamp shall be $2. Each crawfish stamp issued pursuant to this section shall be valid only during the times established by law for the taking of crawfish.

(b) The intent of paragraph (a) is to expand research and management to increase crawfish populations in the state without detracting from other programs. Moneys generated from crawfish stamps shall be used exclusively for programs to benefit crawfish populations.

(12) The department may conduct competitions to periodically select a designer of the crawfish stamp. Also, the department may enhance revenues from the sale of crawfish stamps by issuing special editions for stamp collectors and other such special purposes.

History. - s.2, ch. 28145, 1953; s 1, ch . 29896, 1955; s. 1, ch . 65-53; s. 1, ch. 65-251; ss. 25, 35, ch . 69-106; s. 1, ch. 69-228; s. 1, ch. 70-140; s. 1, ch . 70-162; s. 1, ch 70-369; ss. 292, 293, ch. 71-136; s. 1, ch. 72-76; s. 1, ch 72-250; s. 1, ch. 73-45; s. 1, ch. 73-211; s. 2, ch .74-220; s. 1, ch. 76-107; s. 110, ch. 77-104; ss 3,4,5,6,7,ch. 77-142; s. l, ch. 77-174; s. 8, ch. 83-134; s. 2, ch. 84-121; s. 1, ch. 85-163; ss. 16, 17, ch. 85-234; s. 11, ch. 86-240; s. 3, ch. 87-116; s. 3, ch. 87-120; s. 1, ch. 88-369; ss. 5, 12, ch. 89-98; s. 4, ch. 89-270.

Note. - Repealed effective July 1, 1986, by s. 8, ch. 83-134, as amended by s. 2, ch. 84-121, and by s. 1, ch. 85-163, which further provides that if the Governor and Cabinet have not adopted appropriate rules by July 1, 1986, this section shall remain in force until such rules are effective. Section 9, ch. 83-134, provides that, prior to the adoption of rules amending, readopting, or repealing those provisions set forth in s. 8, the Marine Fisheries Commission shall hold a public hearing thereon, and no such amendment, readoption, or repeal shall be acted upon until it has been determined, based upon appropriate findings of fact, that such action will not adversely affect the resource.

370.141 Crawfish and stone crab; reports by dealers during closed season required.—

(1) Within 3 days after the commencement of the closed season for the taking of saltwater crawfish and stone crabs, each and every seafood dealer, either retail or wholesale, of the state shall submit to the Division of Marine Resources on forms provided by the division, a sworn report of the quantity, in pounds, of frozen saltwater crawfish and stone crabs, frozen crawfish tails, and frozen crawfish and stone crabmeat in his (its) name or possession at the beginning of the aforementioned closed season. This report shall state the location of and describe each as to the number of pounds of frozen crawfish and stone crabs, frozen crawfish tails, and frozen crawfish and stone crabmeat. Any reports postmarked later than midnight of the 3rd day after the commencement of the closed season may not be accepted by the Division, and the frozen stocks or crawfish and stone crabs reported therein may be seized by the division.

(2) Whenever any dealer fails to submit a report as described above or should any dealer report a greater or lesser amount of frozen crawfish or stone crabs, frozen crawfish tails or frozen crawfish or stone crabmeat than is actually in his (its) possession or name, said dealer is and shall be considered in violation of the provisions of ss. 370.13 and 370.14, and the division may seize the entire supply of unreported or falsely reported frozen crawfish and stone crabs, tails or meat and shall carry same before the court for disposal as provided for under s. 370.061.

(3) Each and every dealer having reported stocks of frozen crawfish and stone crabs as aforesaid may sell or offer for sale such stocks of frozen crawfish or frozen stone crabs; however, such dealer shall submit an additional report on the 1 st and 15 th day of each month during the duration of the closed season on forms supplied by the division. Each dealer shall state on this report the number of pounds sold during the report period and the pounds remaining on hand. In every case the amount of frozen crawfish and stone crabs sold and the amount remaining on hand shall total to equal the amount reported on hand in the last submitted report. Reports postmarked later than midnight of the 2nd and 16th of each month during the duration of the closed season may not be accepted by the division. Whenever any dealer fails to submit the semimonthly supplementary report as described above the division may impound said dealer's entire stock of frozen crawfish and stone crabs for the remainder of the closed season.

(4) Each and every seafood dealer shall at all times during the closed season make his stocks of frozen crawfish and stone crabs, frozen crawfish tails or frozen crawfish and stone crabmeat available for inspection by the division.

(5) Each dealer in frozen crawfish of stone crabs, frozen crawfish tails or frozen crawfish and stone crabmeat shall keep throughout the period of the closed season copies of

the bill of sale or invoice covering each transaction involving frozen crawfish and stone crabs, tails or meats excepting only retail sale directly to the consumer. Such invoices and bills shall be kept available at all times for inspection by the division.

History— ss. 1, 2, 3, 4, 5, 6, ch. 57-386; ss. 25, 35, ch. 69-106; s. 294, ch. 71-136; s. 1, ch. 76-27; s. 16, ch. 85-234.

370.143 Retrieval of lobster and stone crab traps during closed season; department authority; fees.—

(1) The Department of Natural Resources is authorized to implement a trap retrieval program for retrieval of lobster and stone crab traps remaining in the water during the closed season for each species. The department is authorized to contract with outside agents for the program operation.

(2) A retrieval fee of $10 per trap retrieved shall be assessed trap owners. Traps recovered under this program shall become the property of the Department or its contract agent and shall be either destroyed or resold to the original owner. Revenue from retrieval fees shall be deposited in the Motorboat Revolving Trust Fund and used for operation of the trap retrieval program.

(3) Payment of the assessed retrieval fee shall be required prior to renewal of the trap owner's trap number as a condition of number renewal. Retrieval fees assessed under this program shall stand in lieu of other penalties imposed for such trap violations.

(4) In the event of a major natural disaster, such as hurricane or major storm causing massive trap losses, the department shall waive the trap retrieval fee.

History.— s. 4, ch. 87-116; s. 4, ch. 87-120.

1990 Supplement to Florida Statues 1989

S. 376.071 (3)

After July 31, 1990, no lobster trap or traps to be deposited into waters of the state shall be impregnated with a petroleum product that may released from such trap or traps. After July 31, 1995, no person shall deposit into the waters of the state any lobster trap or traps that have been impregnated with a petroleum product that may be released from such trap or traps into the waters of the state.

The following amendment to the Florida Statutes (Laws of Florida, 91-154) dealing with the spiny lobster fishery became law on May 29, 1991. It substantially changes spiny lobster law, and provides for a trap certificate program with the intent of reducing total fishing effort on the Florida spiny lobster population.

Laws of Florida, Ch. 91-154Amendment to the Florida statutes 370.14, Crawfish regulation. Florida Legislature, 1991.

Section 1. Section 370.142, Florida Statutes, 1990 Supplement, is amended to read: (Substantial rewording of section. See S. 370.142, F.S., 1990 Supp., for present text.)

370.142 Spiny lobster trap certificate program.—
(1) INTENT.— Due to rapid growth, the spiny lobster fishery is experiencing increased congestion and conflict on the water, excessive mortality of undersized lobsters, a declining yield per trap, and public concern over petroleum and debris pollution from existing traps. In an effort to solve these and related problems, the Legislature intends to develop pursuant to the provisions of this section a spiny lobster trap certificate program, the principal goal of which is to stabilize the fishery by reducing the total number of traps, which should increase the yield per trap and therefore maintain or increase overall catch levels. The legislature seeks to preserve as much flexibility in the program as possible for the fishery's various constituents and ensure that any reduction in total trap numbers will be proportioned equally on a percentage basis among all users of traps in the fishery.
(2) TRANSFERABLE TRAP CERTIFICATES; TRAP TAGS; FEES; PENALTIES.
— The Department of Natural Resources shall establish a trap certificate program for the spiny lobster fishery of this state and shall be responsible for its administration and enforcement as follows:
(a) Transferable trap certificates.— Effective July 1, 1992, each holder of a saltwater products license who uses traps for taking or attempting to take spiny lobsters shall be required to have a certificate on record for each trap possessed or used therefore, except as otherwise provided in this section.
1. The department shall initially allot such certificates to each licenseholder with a current crawfish trap number who uses traps. The number of such certificates allotted to each such licenseholder shall be based on the trap/catch coefficient established pursuant to trip ticket records generated under the provisions of s. 370.06(2) (a) over a 3-year base period ending June 30, 1991. The trap/catch coefficient shall be calculated by dividing the sum of the highest reported single license-year landings up to a maximum of 30,000 pounds for each such licenseholder during the base period by 700,000. Each such licenseholder shall then be allotted the number of certificates derived by dividing his highest reported single license-year landings up to a maximum of 30,000 pounds during the base period by the trap/catch coefficient. Nevertheless, no licenseholder with a current crawfish trap number shall be allotted fewer than 10 certificates. However, certificates may only be issued to individuals; therefore, all licenseholders other than individual licenseholders shall designate the individual or individuals to whom their certificates will be allotted and the number thereof to each, if more than one. After initial issuance, trap certificates are transferable on a market basis and may be transferred from one licenseholder to another for

a fair market value agreed upon between the transferor and transferee. Each such transfer shall, within 72 hours thereof, be recorded on a notarized form provided for that purpose by the department and hand delivered or sent by certified mail, return receipt requested, to the department for recordkeeping purposes. In addition, in order to cover the added administrative costs of the program and to recover an equitable natural resource rent for the people of the state, a transfer fee of $2 per certificate transferred shall be assessed against the purchasing licenseholder and sent by money order or cashier's check with the certificate transfer form. Also, in addition to the transfer fee, a surcharge of 25 percent of the fair market value given to the transferor shall be assessed the first time a certificate is transferred outside the transferor's immediate family. No transfer of a certificate shall be effective until the department receives the notarized transfer form and the transfer fee, including the surcharge, is paid. No sooner than April 1, 1994, the Governor and Cabinet may direct the department to establish by rule an amount of equitable rent per trap certificate that shall be recovered as partial compensation to the state for the enhanced access to its natural resources. In determining whether to establish such a rent and, if so, the amount thereof, the Governor and Cabinet shall consider the amount of revenues annually generated by certificate fees, transfer fees, surcharges, trap license fees, and sales taxes, the demonstrated fair market value of transferred certificates, and the continued economic viability of the commercial lobster industry. The proceeds of equitable rent recovered shall be deposited in the Marine Biological Research Trust Fund and used by the department for research, management, and protection of the spiny lobster fishery and habitat.

2. No person, firm, corporation, or other business entity may control, directly or indirectly, more than 1.5 percent of the total available certificates in any license year.

3. The department shall maintain records of all certificates and their transfers and shall annually provide each licenseholder with a statement of certificates held.

4. Beginning January 1, 1992, for purposes of early implementation, but applicable to the 1992-1993 season and thereafter, the number of trap tags issued annually to each licenseholder shall not exceed the number of certificates held by the licenseholder at the time of issuance, and such tags and a statement of certificates held shall be issued simultaneously.

(b) Trap tags.— Each trap used to take or attempt to take spiny lobsters in state waters or adjacent federal waters shall, in addition to the crawfish trap number required by s. 370.14(2), have affixed thereto an annual trap tag issued by the department. Each such tag shall be made of durable plastic or similar material and shall, beginning with those tags issued for the 1992-1993 season, have stamped thereon the owner's license number. To facilitate enforcement and recordkeeping, such tags shall be issued each year in a color different from that of each of the previous 4 years. A fee of 15 cents per tag shall be assessed until certificates are allotted, and until 1995, an annual fee of 50 cents per certificate shall be assessed, and thereafter until 1998, an annual fee of 75 cents per certificate shall be assessed upon issuance in order to recover administrative costs of the tags and the certificate program. Beginning 1998, the annual certificate fee shall be $1 per certificate. Replacement tags for lost or damaged tags may be obtained as provided by rule of the department.

(c) Recreational trap tags. — **Effective July 1, 1992, a person holding a recreational saltwater fishing license may use up to three crawfish traps.** Recreational trap tags may be issued by the department to a person holding a recreational saltwater fishing license at a fee of 50 cent per tag. It is unlawful for any person to fish with or possess on the water any recreational crawfish trap unless the trap has a valid trap tag properly attached to it. The traps must have a trap number permanently attached to the trap and the buoy. The trap number may be issued by the department at no charge. A person holding a recreational saltwater fishing license who is using the traps must comply with the rules of the department and the Marine Fisheries Commission for people holding recreational saltwater fishing licenses and using up to three crawfish traps. The traps are not subject to the trap reduction schedule provided by this section unless the commission determines that the number of traps issued under this subsection is detrimental to the goals and effectiveness of the overall trap reduction program. The number of traps allowed under this provision does not affect the number of tags authorized under s. 370.14(3).

(d) Prohibitions; penalties. —

1. Effective July 1, 1991, it shall be unlawful for a person to possess or use a spiny lobster trap in or on state waters or adjacent federal waters without having affixed thereto the trap tag required by this section.

2. Effective July 1, 1992, it shall be unlawful for a person to have or use spiny lobster trap tags without having the necessary number of certificates on record as required by this section.

3. Unless otherwise provided in this section, a commercial harvester, as defined by chapter 46-24.002(1), F.A.C., who violates the provision of this section, or the provision of chapter 46-24, F.A.C., shall be punished as follows:

a. If the first violation is for violation of subparagraph 1. or subparagraph 2., the department shall assess a civil penalty of up to $1,000 and the crawfish trap number issued pursuant to s. 370.14(2) or (7) may be suspended for the remainder of the current license year. For all other first violations, the department shall assess a civil penalty of up $500.

b. For a second violation of subparagraph 1. or subparagraph 2. which occurs within 24 months of any previous such violation, the department shall assess a civil penalty of up to $2,000 and the crawfish trap number issued pursuant to s. 370.14(2) or (7) may be suspended for the remainder of the current license year.

c. For a third violation of subparagraph 1. or subparagraph 2. which occurs within 36 months of any previous two such violations, the department shall assess a civil penalty of up to $5,000 and may suspend the crawfish trap number issued pursuant to s. 370.14(2) or (7) for a period of up to 24 months. The department may also require the licenseholder to show just cause why his crawfish trap number should not be revoked.

d. Any person assessed a civil penalty pursuant to this section shall within 30 calendar days after notification:

(I) Pay the civil penalty to the department; or

(II) Request an administrative hearing pursuant to the provision of s. 120.60.

e. The department shall suspend the crawfish trap number issued pursuant to s. 370.14(2) or (7) for any person failing to comply with the provisions of sub-subparagraph d.

4. a. It is unlawful for any person to make, alter, forge, counterfeit, or reproduce a spiny lobster trap tag or certificate.

b. It is unlawful for any person to knowingly have in his possession a forged, counterfeit, or imitation spiny lobster trap tag or certificate.

c. It is unlawful for any person to barter, trade, sell, supply, agree to supply, aid in supplying, or give away a spiny lobster trap tag or certificate or to conspire to barter, trade, sell, supply, aid in supplying, or give away a spiny lobster trap tag or certificate unless such action is duly authorized by the department as provided in this chapter or in the rules of the department.

5. a. Any person who violates the provisions of subparagraph 4., or any person who engages in the commercial harvest, trapping, or possession of spiny lobster without a crawfish trap number as required by s. 370.14(2) or (7) or during any period while such crawfish trap number is under suspension or revocation, commits a felony of the third degree, punishable as provided in s. 775.082, s. 775.083, or s. 775.084.

b. In addition to any penalty imposed pursuant to sub-subparagraph a., the department shall levy a fine of up to twice the amount of the appropriate surcharge to be paid on the fair market value of the transferred certificates on any person who violates the provisions of sub-subparagraph 4.c.

6. Any certificates for which the annual certificate fee is not paid for a period of 3 years shall be considered abandoned and shall revert to the department. During any period of trap reduction, any certificates reverting to the department shall become permanently unavailable and be considered in that amount to be reduced during the next license-year period. Otherwise, any certificates that revert to the department are to be reallotted in such a manner as provided by the department.

7. The proceeds of all civil penalties collected pursuant to subparagraph 3. shall be deposited into the Marine Biological Research Trust Fund.

8. All traps shall be removed from the water during any period of suspension or revocation.

(e) No vested rights. — The trap certificate program shall not create vested rights in licenseholders whatsoever and may be altered or terminated as necessary to protect the spiny lobster resource, the participants in the fishery, or the public interest.

(3) TRAP REDUCTION.— **The objective of the overall trap certificate program is to reduce the number of traps used in the spiny lobster fishery to the lowest amount that will maintain or increase overall catch levels, promote economic efficiency in the fishery, and conserve natural resources.** Therefore, the Marine Fisheries Commission shall set an overall trap reduction goal based on maintaining or maximizing sustained harvest from the spiny lobster fishery. To reach that goal, the commission shall, by July 1, 1992, set an annual trap reduction schedule not to exceed 10 percent per year, applicable to all certificateholders until the overall trap reduction goal is reached. All certificateholders shall have their certificate holdings reduced by the same percentage of certificates each year according to the trap reduction schedule. The department shall then issue the number of trap tags authorized by the commission, as requested, and a revised statement of certificates held. Certificateholders may maintain or increase their total number of certificates held by purchasing available certificates from within the authorized total. The commission shall provide for an annual evaluation of the trap reduction process and shall suspend the annual percentage reductions for any period deemed necessary by the commission in order to assess the impact of the trap reduction schedule on the fishery. The commission may then, by rule, resume terminate, or reverse the schedule as it deems necessary to protect the spiny lobster resource and the participants in the fishery.

(4) TRAP CERTIFICATE TECHNICAL ADVISORY AND APPEALS BOARD.—
There is hereby established the Trap Certificate Technical Advisory and Appeals Board. Such board shall consider and advise the department on disputes and other problems arising from the implementation of spiny lobster trap certificate program. The board may also provide information to the department on the operation of the trap certificate program.

(a) The board shall consist of the executive director of the department or his designee and nine other members appointed by the executive director, after determination of the initial certificate allotments by the department, according to the following criteria:

1. All appointed members shall be certificateholders, but two shall be holders of fewer than 100 certificates, two shall be holders of at least 100 but no more than 750 certificates, three shall be holders of more than 750 but not more than 2,000 certificates, and two shall be holders of more than 2,000 certificates.

2. At least one member each shall come from Broward, Dade and Palm Beach Counties; and five members shall come from the various regions of the Florida Keys.

3. At least one appointed member shall be a person of Hispanic origin capable of speaking English and Spanish.

(b) The term of each appointed member shall be for 4 years, and any vacancy shall be filled for the balance of the unexpired term with a person of the qualifications necessary to maintain the requirement of paragraph (a). However, of the initial appointees, three shall serve for terms of 4 years, two shall serve for terms of 3 years, two shall serve for terms of 2 years, and two shall serve for terms of 1 year. There shall be no limitation on successive appointments to the board.

(c) The executive director of the department or his designee shall serve as a member and shall call the organizational meeting of the board. The board shall annually elect a chair and a vice chair. There shall be no limitation on successive terms that may be served by a chair or vice chair. The board shall meet at the call of its chair, at the request of a majority of its membership, at the request of the department, or at such times as may be prescribed by its rules. A majority of the board shall constitute a quorum, and official action of the board shall require a majority vote of the total membership of the board.

(d) By January 1, 1992, the board shall adopt procedural rules pursuant to s. 120.53.

(e) Members of the board shall be reimbursed for per diem and travel expenses as provided in s. 112.061.

(f) Upon reaching a decision on any dispute or problem brought before it, the board shall submit such decision to the executive director of the department for final approval. If such decision involves the allotment of available certificates, the executive director of the department may allot such certificates accordingly. However, the executive director of the department may alter or disapprove any decision of the board, with notice thereof given in writing to the board and to each party in the dispute explaining the reasons for disapproval.

(g) In addition to those certificates allotted pursuant to the provisions of subparagraph (2)(a)1., up to 50,000 certificates may be allotted by the board to settle disputes or other problems arising from implementation of the trap certificate program during the 1992-1993 and 1993-1994 license years. Any certificates not allotted by March 31, 1994 become permanently unavailable and shall be considered as part of the 1994-1995 reduction schedule.

(h) On and after July 1, 1994, the board shall no longer consider and advise the department on disputes and other problems arising from implementation of the trap certificate program nor allot any certificates with respect thereto.

(5) DISPOSITION OF FEES AND SURCHARGES. —

(a) Transfer fees and surcharges collected pursuant to paragraph (2)(a) shall be deposited as follows:

1. The first dollar of each certificate transfer fee collected shall be deposited in the Motorboat Revolving Trust Fund for the purposes of administering the trap certificate program.

2. The remainder of all certificate transfer fees and surcharges collected shall be deposited as follows:

a. At least 25 percent of the fees and surcharges collected shall be deposited in the Marine Biological Research Trust Fund for research and monitoring of the spiny lobster fishery.

b. At least 15 percent of the fees and surcharges collected shall be deposited in the Marine Fisheries Commission Trust Fund to be used for the purposes of this section.

c. The remainder of such fees and surcharges shall be deposited in the Motorboat Revolving Trust Fund to be used by the department for administration, enforcement, and public education activities in support of the purposes of this section and s. 370.013.

(b) Annual trap certificate fees and recreational tag fees collected pursuant to paragraphs (2)(b) and (c) shall be deposited as follows:

1. No more than 70 percent shall be deposited in the Motorboat Revolving Trust Fund to be used by the department for administrative and public education activities in support of the purposes of this section.

2. No less than 30 percent shall be deposited in the Marine Biological Research Trust Fund for research and monitoring of the spiny lobster fishery.

Section 2. Effective June 1, 1991, subsections (2) and (7) of section 370.14, Florida statues 1990 Supplement, are amended to read:

(CODING: words stricken are deletions from existing law; words underlined are additions.)

370.14 Crawfish; regulation.—

(2)(a) Each trap, ~~can, drum and similar device~~ used for taking or attempting to take crawfish must have a trap number permanently attached to the trap ~~device~~ and the buoy. This trap number may be issued by the Division of Law Enforcement upon the receipt of application by the owner of the traps, ~~cans, drums, buoys or similar devices~~ and accompanied by the payment of a fee of $100 ~~$50~~. The design of the applications and of the trap number shall be determined by the division. However, effective July 1,1988, and until July 1, 1992, ~~1991~~, no crawfish trap numbers issued pursuant to this section except those numbers that were active during the 1990-1991 ~~1987-1988~~ fiscal year shall be renewed or reissued. No new trap numbers shall be issued during this period. ~~In 1988, persons holding a trap number that was active in the 1987-1988 fiscal year or an immediate family member of that person or a person to whom a trap number was transferred in writing by the holder of the active trap number, must request renewal of the number before December 31, 1988. In subsequent years and~~ Until July 1, 1992, ~~1991~~, trap number holders or members of their immediate family or a person to whom the trap number was transferred in writing must request renewal of the number prior to June 30 of each year. If a person holding an active trap number or a member of the person's immediate family or a person to whom the trap number was transferred in writing does not request renewal of the number before the applicable date as specified above, the department may reissue the number to another applicant in the order of the receipt of the application for a trap number. Any trap, ~~drum, can, buoy,~~ or ~~similar~~ device used in ~~the~~ taking or ~~in~~ attempting to take crawfish, other than a trap ~~device~~ with the trap number attached as prescribed in this paragraph ~~subsection~~, shall be seized and destroyed by the division. The proceeds of the fees imposed by this paragraph ~~subsection~~ shall be deposited and used as provided in paragraph (b) ~~used by the Department of Natural Resources for the purposes of enforcing the provisions of this subsection through aerial and other surveillance and trap retrieval~~. The Department of Natural Resources is authorized to promulgate rules and regulations to carry out the intent of this section.

(b) Fees collected pursuant to paragraph (a) shall be deposited as follows:

1. Fifty percent of the fees collected shall be deposited in the Motorboat Revolving Trust Fund for use in enforcing the provisions of paragraph (a) through aerial and other surveillance and trap retrieval.

2. Fifty percent of the fees collected shall be deposited as provided in s. 370.142(5)(a)2.

(7) A person who takes more ~~than 24~~ crawfish per boat or ~~6 crawfish~~ per person than that number set therefor by rule of the Marine Fisheries Commission for recreational harvesters, ~~whichever is greater,~~ within any 24-hour period by any method other than with traps, ~~cans, drums,~~ or similar devices must also pay a fee of $100 ~~$50~~ and obtain a trap number to be displayed on his boat.

Section 3. (1) The Department of Natural Resources may adopt rules to implement the provisions of s. 370.142, Florida Statutes, 1990 supplement, as amended by this act, relating to the spiny lobster trap certificate program.

(2) This section shall take effect upon this act becoming a law.

Section 4. Subsection (4) of section 370.142, Florida Statutes, as created by this act, is repealed on October 1, 2001, and the Trap Certificate Technical Advisory and Appeals Board shall be reviewed by the Legislature pursuant to s. 11.611, Florida Statutes.

Section 5. For the purposes of chapter 46-24.001(5), F.A.C., passage of this act and the authority for subsequent rulemaking constitutes successful implementation of an effort reduction program for the spiny lobster fishery. Therefore, effective July 1, 1993, chapter 46-24.006(1)(d), chapter 46-24.003(4), and that portion of chapter 46-24.003(3), F.A.C. regarding an effective date in conflict herewith are hereby repealed. However, after April 1, 1998, the Marine Fisheries Commission is not precluded from initiating rulemaking proceedings utilizing any of the concepts or measures addressed in those respective chapters.

Section 6. (1) There is hereby appropriated from the Motorboat Revolving Trust Fund to the Division of Law Enforcement of the Department of Natural Resources the sum of $235,182 for fiscal year 1991-1992, and five Career Service positions are authorized for the department, to carry out the spiny lobster trap certificate program.

(2) There is hereby appropriated from the Marine Fisheries Commission Trust Fund to the Marine Fisheries Commission the sum of $20,000 for fiscal year 1991-1992 for expenses incurred pursuant to this act.

Appendix B

Federal Regulations

Federal regulations pertain to the waters of the Exclusive Economic Zone (EEZ), the area between Florida territorial waters to 200 miles offshore. Florida's territorial waters extend from the coast to three nautical miles offshore of Florida's Atlantic coast and nine nautical miles (three marine leagues) offshore of Florida's Gulf of Mexico coast. Federal fishery regulations for the spiny lobster fishery reflect Florida regulations and should soon incorporate recent changes in Florida laws.

MARCH 29, 1991

NOTE: THE FOLLOWING IS AN UNOFFICIAL COMPILATION OF FEDERAL REGULATIONS PREPARED IN THE SOUTHEAST REGIONAL OFFICE OF THE NATIONAL MARINE FISHERIES SERVICE FOR THE INFORMATION AND CONVENIENCE OF INTERESTED PERSONS. IT DOES NOT INCLUDE CHANGES TO THESE REGULATIONS THAT MAY HAVE OCCURRED AFTER THE DATE INDICATED ABOVE.

DEPARTMENT OF COMMERCE
National Oceanic and Atmospheric Administration
National Marine Fisheries Service (NMFS)
50 CFR Part 640
PART 640 — SPINY LOBSTER FISHERY OF THE GULF OF MEXICO AND SOUTH ATLANTIC

Subpart A - General Provisions
Sec.
640.1 Purpose and scope.
640.2 Definitions.
640.3 Relation to other laws.
640.4 Permits.
640.5 Recordkeeping and reporting. (Reserved)
640.6 Gear and vessel identification.

640.7 Prohibitions.
640.8 Facilitation of enforcement.
640.9 Penalties.
Subpart B - Management Measures
640.20 Seasons.
640.21 Harvest limitations.
640.22 Size limitations.
640.23 Gear limitations.
640.24 Authorized activities.
Authority: 16 U.S.C. 1801 et seq.

Subpart A - General Provisions
§640.1 Purpose and scope.
The purpose of this part is to implement the Fishery Management Plan for the Spiny Lobster Fishery of the Gulf of Mexico and South Atlantic developed by the South Atlantic and Gulf of Mexico Fishery Management Councils under the Magnuson Act. The regulations in this part govern fishing for spiny lobster and slipper (Spanish) lobster by vessels of the United States within the EEZ in the Atlantic Ocean and Gulf of Mexico along the coast of the South Atlantic States from the Virginia/North Carolina border south and through the Gulf of Mexico.

§640.2 Definitions.
In addition to the definitions in the Magnuson Act and in §620.2 of this chapter, the terms used in this part have the following meanings:

Carapace length means a head-length measurement taken from the orbital notch inside the orbital spine, in a line parallel to the lateral rostral sulcus, to the posterior margin of the cephalothorax (Figure 1).

Commercial fishing means any fishing or fishing activities which result in the harvest of any marine or freshwater organisms, one or more of which (or parts thereof) is sold, traded, or bartered.

Degradable panel means a panel constructed of wood, cotton, or other material that will degrade at the same rate as a wooden trap.

Live well means a shaded container used for holding live lobsters aboard a vessel in which aerated seawater is continuously circulated from the sea. Circulation of seawater at a rate that replaces the water at least every 8 minutes meets the requirement for aeration.

Management area means that area of the EEZ adjacent to the territorial sea off the coasts of the States adjacent to the Gulf of Mexico and off the Atlantic Coast south of the Virginia-North Carolina border.

Recreational fishing means fishing or fishing activities which result in the harvest of fish, none of which (or parts thereof) is sold, traded, or bartered.

Regional Director means the Regional Director, NMFS, Southeast Region, Duval Building, 9450 Koger Boulevard, St. Petersburg, FL 33702; telephone 813-893-3141, or his designee.

Slipper (spanish) lobster means the species *Scyllarides nodifer*.

Spiny lobster means the species *Panulirus argus*.

Tail length means the measurement, with the tail in a straight, flat position, from the anterior end of the exoskeleton ("shell") of the first abdominal (tail) segment to the tip of the closed tail.

Trip means a fishing trip, regardless of number of days duration, that begins with departure from a dock, berth, beach, seawall, or ramp and that terminates with return to a dock, berth, beach, seawall, or ramp.

§640.3 Relation to other laws

(a) The relation of this part to other laws is set forth in §620.3 of this chapter and paragraph (b) of this section.

(b) The regulations in this part apply within the boundaries of any national park, monument, or marine sanctuary in the Gulf of Mexico and South Atlantic EEZ.

§640.4 Permits.

(a) Applicability. (1) To sell a spiny lobster in or from the EEZ, or to be exempt from the daily catch and possession limit of spiny lobster in or from the EEZ specified in §640.21 (c) (1) (i), an owner or operator of a vessel must obtain a seasonal vessel permit.

(2) To possess a separated spiny lobster tail in or from the EEZ aboard a vessel, the owner or operator of that vessel must obtain a tail-separation permit. A tail-separation permit will not be issued to an owner or operator who does not qualify for a seasonal vessel permit.

(3) An owner or operator of a vessel that has legally harvested spiny lobsters in the waters of a foreign nation and possesses spiny lobsters or separated tails In the EEZ incidental to such foreign harvesting is exempt from the permit requirements of paragraphs (a)(l) and (2) of this section provided a proper bill of lading or other proof of lawful harvest in the waters of a foreign nation accompanies such lobsters or tails.

(4) For a corporation or partnership to be eligible for a seasonal vessel permit specified in paragraph (a) (1) of this section, the earned income qualification specified in paragraph (b) (2) (viii) of this section must be met by, and the statement required by that paragraph must be submitted by, a shareholder or officer of the corporation, a general partner of the partnership or the vessel operator.

(b) Application for permit.

(1) An application for a seasonal vessel or tail-separation permit must be submitted and signed by the owner or operator of the vessel. The application must be submitted to the Regional Director at least 60 days prior to the date on which the applicant desires to have the permit made effective.

(2) A permit applicant must provide the following information:

(i) A copy of the vessel's U.S. Coast Guard certificate of documentation or state registration certificate;

(ii) The vessel's name, official number, length, home port, and engine horsepower;

(iii) Name, mailing address including zip code, telephone number, and Florida saltwater products license number, if applicable, of the owner of the vessel;

(iv) Name, mailing address including zip code, telephone number, and Florida saltwater products license number, if applicable, of the applicant, if other than the owner;

(v) Social security number and date of birth of the applicant and the owner;

(vi) Approximate live well capacity in gallons;

(vii) Any other information concerning vessel and gear characteristics required by the Regional Director;

(viii) A sworn statement by the applicant certifying that at least 10 percent of his or her earned income was derived from commercial fishing during the calendar year preceding the application;

(ix) Proof of certification, as required by paragraph (b)(3) of this section; and

(x) If a tail-separation permit is desired, a sworn statement by the applicant certifying that his fishing activity —

(A) Is routinely conducted in the EEZ on trips of 48 hours or more; and

(B) Necessitates the separation of carapace and tail to maintain a quality product.

(3) The Regional Director may require the applicant to provide documentation supporting the sworn statement under paragraph (b)(2)(viii) of this section before a permit is issued or to substantiate why such a permit should not be denied, revoked, or otherwise sanctioned under paragraph (g) of this section.

(4) Any change in the information specified in paragraph (b)(2) of this section must be submitted in writing to the Regional Director by the permit holder within 30 days of any such change. The permit is void if any change in the information is not reported.

(c) Fees. A fee of $26 will be charged for each permit application submitted under paragraph (b) of this section. The appropriate fee must accompany each permit application.

(d) Issuance.

(1) Except-as provided in Subpart D of 15 CFR Part 904, the Regional Director will issue a permit at any time during the fishing year to the applicant.

(2) Upon receipt of an incomplete application, the Regional Director will notify the applicant of the deficiency. If the applicant fails to correct the deficiency within 30 days of the Regional Director's notification, the application will be considered abandoned.

(e) Duration. A permit remains valid for the remainder of the season for which it is issued unless revoked, suspended, or modified pursuant to Subpart D of 15 CFR Part 904.

(f) Transfer. A permit issued under this section is not transferable or assignable. A person purchasing a vessel with a seasonal vessel permit must apply for a new permit in accordance with the provisions of paragraph (b) of this section. The application must be accompanied by a copy of an executed (signed) bill of sale.

(g) Display. A permit issued under this section must be carried on board the permitted vessel at all times and such vessel must be identified as provided for in §640.6. The operator of a fishing vessel must present the permit for inspection upon request of an authorized officer.

(h) Sanctions. Procedures governing permit sanctions and denials are found at Subpart D of 15 CFR Part 904.

(i) Alteration. A permit that is altered, erased, or mutilated is invalid.

(j) Replacement. A replacement permit may be issued. An application for a replacement permit will not be considered a new application.

§640.5 Recordkeeping and reporting. (Reserved)

§640.6 Gear and vessel identification.

(a) Traps, buoys, and all vessels and boats engaged in the spiny lobster trap fishery must be identified by the number and color code issued by the Regional Director, or through Florida's identification system.

(b) An application for a Federal number and color code must be submitted and signed by the owner or operator of the vessel on an appropriate form obtained from the Regional Director. The application must be submitted to the Regional Director 45 days prior to the date on which the applicant desires receipt of the number and color code.

(c) Vessels and boats engaged in the spiny lobster trap fishery must permanently and conspicuously display such color code and number in a manner as to be readily identifiable from the air and water; such color representation must be in the form of a circle at least 20 inches in diameter and the identification number must be at least 10 inches high.

(d) Each trap, unless part of a string of traps, must be marked by a floating buoy or a buoy designed to be submerged and automatically released at a certain time. Each string of traps must be marked with a buoy at each end of the string.

(e) Buoys must be of such color as to be easily distinguished, seen, and located; the identification number must be legible and at least 3 inches high on each buoy.

(f) Each trap, can, drum, or similar device must have a legible identification number at least 3 inches high permanently attached as in the case of buoys.

(g) All spiny lobster traps fished in the EEZ will be presumed to be the property of the most recently documented owner.

(h) Upon the sale or transfer of all or part of an owners interest in spiny lobster traps which are fished in the EEZ, that owner must report the sale or transfer within 15 days to the Regional Director if the identification number and color code for those traps were issued by the Regional Director.

(i) An unmarked spiny lobster trap or buoy in the EEZ is illegal gear. Such trap, buoy, and connecting line may be disposed of in any manner considered appropriate by the Secretary or an authorized officer. An owner of such a trap or buoy remains subject to appropriate civil penalties.

§640.7 Prohibitions.

In addition to the general prohibitions specified in §620.7 of this Chapter, it is unlawful for any person to do any of the following:

(a) Fish for spiny lobster without a vessel number, or falsify or fail to affix and maintain vessel and gear markings, as required by §640.6.

(b) Place traps in the water or harvest spiny lobsters from traps before or after the dates specified in §640.20 (a).

(c) Harvest a spiny lobster with a trap except during the season specified in §640.20(a)(1).

(d) Possess spiny lobster or any parts thereof in the EEZ, except as specified in §640.20.

(e) Retain on board or possess on land a berried spiny or slipper lobster taken in the EEZ.

(f) Strip eggs from or otherwise molest a berried spiny or slipper lobster, as specified in §640.21(a).

(g) Pull or tend traps except during the hours specified in §640.21(b).

(h) Willfully tend, open, pull, or otherwise molest another person's traps, except as provided in §640.21(b).

(i) Exceed the recreational daily catch and possession limit, as specified in §640.21(c)(1).

(j) Retain a spiny lobster smaller than the minimum size, except as specified in §640.22; or purchase, barter, trade, or sell a spiny lobster smaller than the minimum size, as specified in §640.22 (a)(1) or (2).

(k) Use traps without degradable panels, or prohibited gear or methods, as specified in §640.23.

(l) Fail to return immediately to the water unharmed a berried (egg-bearing) spiny or slipper lobster, as specified in §640.21(a).

(m) Operate a vessel that fishes for spiny lobster in the EEZ with spiny lobster aboard in excess of the cumulative recreational catch limit, as specified in §640.21 (c) (3).

(n) Transfer at sea in the EEZ spiny lobster caught under the recreational catch limit specified in §640.21 (c) from a fishing vessel to any other vessel or to so transfer at sea any such spiny lobster taken from the EEZ.

(o) Fail to have on board or present for inspection an extension authorization, as required under §640.20 (a) (3).

(p) Interfere with, obstruct, delay, or prevent by any means a lawful investigation or search in the process of enforcing this part.

(q) Purchase, barter, trade, or sell a spiny lobster taken in the EEZ by a vessel that does not have a seasonal vessel permit, as specified in §640.4(a)(1).

(r) Purchase, barter, trade, or sell a separated spiny lobster tail taken in the EEZ by a vessel that does not have a tail-separation permit, as specified in §640.4(a)(2).

(s) Falsify information specified in §640.4(b)(2) on an application for a permit; or fail to report a change in such information, as specified in §640.4(b)(4).

(t) Fail to display a permit, as specified in §640.4 (f).

(u) Possess a separated spiny lobster tail, except as specified in §640.21(d).

§640.8 Facilitation of enforcement.

See §620.8 of this chapter.

§640.9 Penalties.

See §620.9 of this chapter.

Subpart B - Management Measures

§640.20 Seasons.

(a) Fishing season.

(1) The commercial and recreational fishing season for spiny lobster begins on August 6, one hour before official sunrise, and ends on March 31, one hour after official sunset.

(2) Prior to the season, spiny lobster traps may be placed in the water one hour before official sunrise on August 1 (soak period).

(3) After the season, traps must be removed from the water by one hour after official sunset on April 5 (removal period) unless an extension to the removal period is granted by Florida in accordance with Chapter 46-24, Spiny Lobster (Crawfish) and Slipper Lobster, Rules of the Department of Natural Resources, Florida Marine Fisheries Commission, Florida Administrative Code. The extension authorization must be carried aboard the boat retrieving the traps and must be presented for inspection upon request of an authorized officer.

(4) Except as provided in paragraphs (a)(2) and (a)(3) of this section, no trap may be transported on the waters of the EEZ during the period from one hour after official sunset on March 31 to one hour before sunrise on August 6.

(5) A spiny lobster trap, buoy, or rope in the management area at times not authorized in this paragraph will be considered unclaimed or abandoned property and may be disposed of in any manner considered appropriate by the Secretary of an authorized officer. An owner of such a trap remains subject to appropriate civil penalties.

(b) Special non-trap recreational fishery. There is a special non-trap recreational fishing season on the first full weekend preceding August 1 from 0001 hours, Saturday, until 2400 hours, Sunday.

(c) Possession. Spiny lobsters or any parts thereof may be possessed in the EEZ only during the seasons specified in paragraphs (a) (1) and (b) of this section, unless accompanied by a proper bill of landing or other proof indicating lawful harvest outside the EEZ. Holding a spiny lobster in a trap while in the water during the soak period or during the removal period, or an extension thereto, will not be deemed possession provided such spiny lobster is returned immediately to the water unharmed whenever a trap is removed from the water during these periods.

§640.21 Harvest limitations.

(a) Berried lobsters. A berried spiny lobster or slipper lobster must be returned immediately to the water unharmed. If found in a trap, a berried lobster may not be retained in the trap. A berried lobster may not be stripped of its eggs or otherwise molested.

(b) Pulling traps.

(1) Traps may be pulled or tended only during the period beginning one hour before official sunrise and ending one hour after official sunset.

(2) Traps may be pulled or tended only by the owner's vessel, unless the boat tending another person's trap has on board written consent of the trap owner.

(c) Recreational catch.

(1) The daily catch and possession of spiny lobsters in or from the EEZ is limited to six per person:

(i) During the fishing season described at §640.20 (a), except for spiny lobsters possessed aboard a vessel with the seasonal vessel permit specified in §640.4 (a) (1); and

(ii) During the special non-trap recreational season described at §640.20 (b).

(2) A person who fishes for spiny lobster in the EEZ may not combine the recreational catch and possession limit of paragraph (c) (1) of this section with any bag or possession limit applicable to State waters.

(3) The operator of a vessel that fishes for spiny lobster in the EEZ is responsible for the cumulative recreational catch, based on the number of persons aboard, applicable to that vessel.

(4) A person who fishes for or possesses spiny lobsters under the recreational catch and possession limit specified in paragraph (c) (l) of this section may not transfer spiny lobsters at sea from a fishing vessel to any other vessel.

(d) Tail separation. The possession of a separated spiny lobster tail is authorized only—

(1) Aboard a vessel having on board the tail-separation permit specified in §640.4 (a) (2); and

(2) When the possession is incidental to fishing in the EEZ on a trip of 48 hours or more.

§640.22 Size limitations.

(a) Length. Except as provided in paragraph (b) of this section, a spiny lobster —

(1) With a carapace length of 3.0 inches (7.62 centimeters) or less; or

(2) Aboard a vessel authorized under §640.21 (d) to possess a separated spiny lobster tail, with a tail length less than 5.5 inches (13.97 centimeters) — must be returned immediately to the water unharmed.

(b) Attractants. A live lobster under the minimum size may be retained for use as an attractant in a trap provided it is held in a live well aboard the vessel. No more than 100 undersized lobsters may be carried on board for use as attractants. The live well must provide a minimum of 3/4 gallons of seawater per spiny lobster.

§640.23 Gear limitations.

(a) Degradable Panel. Traps constructed of material other than wood must have a panel constructed of wood, cotton, or other degradable material located in the upper half of the sides or on top of the trap, that, when removed, will leave an opening in the trap no smaller than the diameter found at the throat or entrance of the trap.

(b) Prohibited gear and methods.

(1) Spiny lobster may not be taken with spears, hooks, or similar devices, or gear containing such devices. In the EEZ, the possession of speared, pierced, or punctured lobsters is prima facie evidence that prohibited gear was used to take such lobsters.

(2) Spiny lobsters may not be taken with poisons or explosives.

§640.24 Authorized activities.

The Secretary may authorize, for the acquisition of information and data, activities otherwise prohibited by these regulations.

Appendix C

Important phone numbers

National Diving Accident Network (DAN)
Duke University Medical Center
(919) 684-8111 (24 hour Emergency line)
(919) 684-2948 (office line)

Information on all decompression chambers in the US:
(512) 536-3278

Florida Decompression Facilities
Pensacola (904) 452-2141
Panama City (904) 234-2281 Extension 370
Gainesville (904) 392-3441
West Palm Beach (407) 844-3515
Miami (305) 350-7259 or 446-7071 or 445-8926

U.S. Coast Guard Marine and Air Emergency numbers
National Response Center (800) 424-8802
St. Petersburg, FL (813) 896-6187
Miami, FL (305) 350-4309
Key West, FL (305) 350-5328
Mayport (904) 246-7321
Charleston, SC (803) 724-4382
At sea: VHF 16 or HF 2182

Florida Marine Patrol Offices
General Headquarters, Tallahassee (904) 488-5757
District One, Panama City (904) 234-0211
District Two, Carrabelle (904) 697-3741
District Three, Homasassa Springs (904) 628-6196
District Four, Tampa (813) 272-2516
District Five, Ft. Myers (813) 334-8963
District Six, Miami (305) 325-3346
District Seven, Titusville, (407) 383-2740
District Eight, Jacksonville Beach (904) 359-6580
District Nine, Marathon (305) 743-6542
District Ten, Jupiter (407) 626-9995
District Eleven, Pensacola (904) 444-8978

Florida State Resource Alert Line
1-(800) 342-1821 (1-800-DIAL FMP)
Call to report fishery law violations in State waters

Bahamas Fisheries Information
1-800 327-7678

Index

About the Author

Martin A. Moe Jr. has been a marine biologist since 1960. He holds a masters degree from the University of South Florida and has worked as a fishery biologist, marine biologist, ichthyologist, and commercial marine fish culturist for over 30 years. His scientific and popular articles and books date back to 1962 when he began his career as a marine biologist for the State of Florida. He entered the private sector in 1969 and developed the basic technology for breeding Florida pompano in 1970. He accomplished the first commercial culture of marine tropical fish in a garage in 1972 and over the years, has reared over 30 species of marine tropical fish, incuding spawning, rearing, and even hybridizing French and grey Atlantic angelfish. He founded Aqualife Research Corporation in 1972 and Green Turtle Publications in 1982.

Books by Martin Moe

The Marine Aquarium Handbook
Beginner to Breeder

A practical handbook on the theory and methods of keeping and breeding marine tropical fish. Everything you need to know to set up and maintain a successful saltwater aquarium. 176 pages

ISBN 0-93996002-8
LC 87-30174 $12.95

The Marine Aquarium Reference
Systems and Invertebrates

A major reference for the modern aquarist. This book contains 512 pages of text, tables, figures, and drawings that clearly and simply explain the techniques and technology of modern marine aquarium systems, including reef systems. It also introduces the aquarist to the latest classification of invertebrates and other living organisms, with expanded discussions of the invertebrate groups most important to marine aquarists. This book is a companion volume to *The Marine Aquarium Handbook* and contains new (not duplicated) information. 512 pages

ISBN 0-939960-05-2
LC CIP 89-7554 $21.95

Lobsters: Florida • Bahamas • the Caribbean

The natural history and the science of the Caribbean spiny lobster. 512 pages.

ISBN 0-939960-06-0
LC CIP 91-23958 $22.95

You can borrow these books from your local library.

You can purchase them at your local book store, aquarium shop, and at many public aquariums. If you can not find them locally, send your order to the address below.

Green Turtle Publications, P.O. Box 17925, Plantation, FL 33318
Please include $2 for shipping. Florida residents also include the appropriate sales tax.